THE WAR OF
THE DOOMED

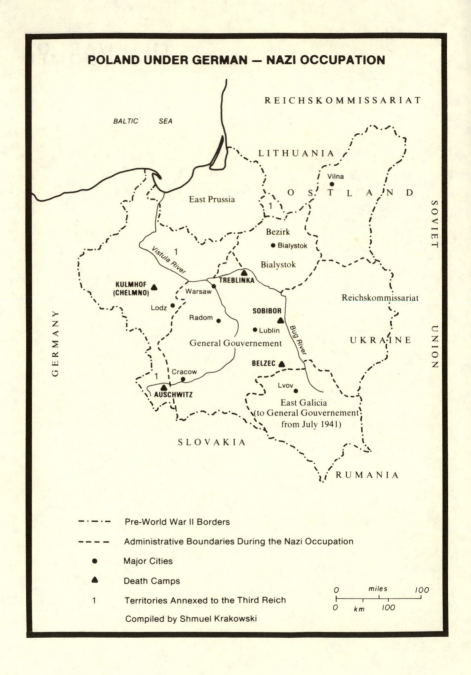

POLAND UNDER GERMAN — NAZI OCCUPATION

REICHSKOMMISSARIAT

BALTIC   SEA

LITHUANIA

East Prussia

O S T L A N D

• Vilna

Bezirk
• Bialystok

Bialystok

Vistula River

KULMHOF
(CHELMNO)

Warsaw

TREBLINKA

• Lodz

Radom

SOBIBOR

• Lublin

Reichskommissariat

Bug River

UKRAINE

General Gouvernement

BELZEC

Cracow

AUSCHWITZ

Lvov •

East Galicia
(to General Gouvernement
from July 1941)

GERMANY

SOVIET   UNION

SLOVAKIA

RUMANIA

- — · — · — Pre-World War II Borders
- — — — — Administrative Boundaries During the Nazi Occupation
- • Major Cities
- ▲ Death Camps
- 1 Territories Annexed to the Third Reich

Compiled by Shmuel Krakowski

0   miles   100
0   km   100

THE WAR OF THE DOOMED

JEWISH ARMED RESISTANCE IN POLAND, 1942–1944

SHMUEL KRAKOWSKI

FOREWORD BY
YEHUDA BAUER

TRANSLATED FROM THE HEBREW BY
ORAH BLAUSTEIN

HOLMES & MEIER PUBLISHERS, INC.
NEW YORK   LONDON

First published in the United States of America 1984 by
Holmes & Meier Publishers, Inc.
30 Irving Place
New York, N.Y. 10003

Great Britain:
Holmes & Meier Publishers, Ltd.
131 Trafalgar Road
Greenwich, London SE10 9TX

Book design by Stephanie Barton

Manufactured in the United States of America

Library of Congress Cataloging in Publication Data

Krakowski, Shmuel.
  The war of the doomed: Jewish armed resistance in Poland, 1942–1944

  Translation of: Leḥimah Yehudit be-Folin neged
ha-Natsim, 1942–1944.
  Bibliography: p.
  Includes index.
  1. Jews—Poland—History.   2. Poland—History—
Occupation—1939–1945.   3. Poland—Ethnic relations.
4. World War, 1939–1945—Jews.   I. Title.
  D810.J4K68413 1984   940.53'15'03924   83-18537
  ISBN 0-8419-0851-6
  ISBN 0-8419-0852-4 (pbk.)

CONTENTS

MAPS

FOREWORD

THE BOOK BEFORE US PRESENTS A DEEP AND INFORMA-
tive study of one of the turbulent problems in the history of the
Jewish people in our time: the reaction of the Jews to the murder of
their people on foreign soil. This book deals with only one of the
many forms in which this reaction manifested itself, that of armed
resistance. Other examples of active resistance, although without
arms, are many and their importance is vast. But they must be left for
another study. The issue of armed resistance has been treated in
previous surveys and narratives, usually varying between two ex-
tremes: that of deliberate or inadvertent oversight of Jewish fighting,
and that of exaggerated and fantastic apologetics. Legends have been
created, both negative and positive. The generation that has grown
up in Israel after the Holocaust has heard of nothing but the Warsaw
Ghetto uprising and has an image of the Jewish people watching
millions of its own being murdered without reacting, with the exception of Warsaw where a few hundred young men and women did
fight the Nazi murderers.

This book is meant to correct that distortion, and does so with
resounding success. A meticulous, scientific study, it first sets before
us the facts: the number of Jews who resisted the Germans with arms
in hand, where, and when; the results of their fighting from a military
viewpoint; what became of them and how many survived. The author also examines their relations with the Polish population, Jewish
communities and organizations, and the Polish underground movements and thus creates a reliable historical picture of the actions of the
Jews in light of the real circumstances of their existence.

This picture is both interesting and instructive. We are told here
of thousands of Jews who fought with arms in hand, and thousands
of others who did not, only because they were not given the practical

opportunity to do so. *The War of the Doomed* is a true act of historical rescue and teaches us about the fate of the Jews of Europe, and the fate of others.

Dr. Krakowski is a member of the Holocaust research staff at the Institute of Contemporary Jewry, and one of the senior employees of Yad Vashem. His research was made possible by the assistance of the Memorial Foundation for Jewish Culture. Additional valuable assistance was given by the Organization of the Survivors of Bergen-Belsen, and particularly by the late Joseph Rosensaft, who was chairman of that organization. Joseph Rosensaft was a proud and resolute Jew who did not yield the honor of his people and who defended any matter of Jewish interest that arose. Let this book stand as a memorial to his name.

YEHUDA BAUER

PREFACE

THIS BOOK ATTEMPTS TO DESCRIBE THE HISTORY AND basic aspects of the armed resistance movement within the Jewish population during the Second World War in central Poland, which under the Nazi occupation comprised an administrative district known as the *General Gouvernement* (GG). The main purpose of this book is to determine the basic facts and clarify the extent of the Jewish armed resistance movement in the *General Gouvernement* and to analyze its character, its uniqueness, and its results.

The armed struggle of the Jews under the Nazi occupation was waged in the midst of total annihilation. The Jewish people, destined for extermination, were confined to hundreds of ghettos and camps, isolated both from each other and from the outside world. Furthermore, the Jewish partisans operated under special circumstances in a foreign and often hostile environment, where they were outlawed not only because of the struggle they were waging, but primarily because of their very physical existence as Jews.

Jewish armed resistance was conducted in three totally different arenas—the ghettos, the camps, and the partisan movement. Each of these fronts had its own character, its own logic, and its own military consequences. The first two—the ghettos and the camps—were areas of struggle for Jews alone. Only Jews were confined to the ghettos, and it follows that they alone could establish organizations there for the purpose of armed resistance. The camps in the *General Gouvernement* also included non-Jewish prisoners, but because of their special circumstances, only the Jews took the risk of armed activity in these places.

Specific qualities also characterized the Jewish partisan movement. An immense difference marked the conditions under which the Jewish and non-Jewish partisan units operated. In addition, the status of the Jew in a nationally mixed partisan unit, and even the status of the individual Jew in a non-Jewish unit, was different from that of his non-Jewish comrade. Therefore, the Jewish partisan movement, although it operated in the same geographical area as did the Polish and the Soviet partisan forces (in the same forests), must be dealt with as a separate movement having its own development.

Because of these special circumstances, the Jewish armed movement was not unified, but remained divided and to a large extent spontaneous, with various operations organized and carried out, in most cases, in a totally independent manner. This movement, unlike the partisan movement of any other people in occupied Europe, lacked the support of overall national political organizations, or any government of the anti-Nazi alliance.

This study utilizes documents from Israeli, Polish, and German archives, supplemented by approximately 500 testimonies, largely those of surviving fighters of the armed underground. Also utilized were copies and microfilms, found in the Yad Vashem archive, of reports from German archives and from the archives of Polish historical institutes in Warsaw and London. To a marked extent, this reference material consists of published original sources, mostly collections of documents, diaries, memoirs, and, to a lesser extent, monographs and articles related to the subject.

This book is devoted to the lesser-known realm of Jewish armed resistance—the Jewish partisan movement. Until now, little attention has been given to this partisan movement in the *General Gouvernement* in historical literature, both scientific and popular. Most of the Jewish partisan units in the GG are not mentioned at all in published documents. From this rises the belief of the author that the chapters pertaining to the Jewish partisan movement will be the substantial contribution of this book to the historical study of the Jewish resistance movement in Poland.

A different approach was taken in the discussion of the resistance movement in the large ghettos, particularly the Warsaw Ghetto. A relatively large quantity of material has been written about the Jewish resistance movement in Warsaw, and only somewhat less about those in Czestochowa and Cracow. The literature pertaining to the Warsaw Ghetto uprising is particularly extensive. This literature, which has been published in Hebrew, Yiddish, English, German, French, Polish, Spanish, and Czech, already consisted, by 1953, of 100 books and 640 pamphlets and extended articles. It is, therefore, many times more extensive than work on all the other areas that, together, made up the GG district. The armed resistance movement in the Warsaw Ghetto has been written about by Friedman, Mark, Kermish, Gutman, Wulf, and others; the basic facts have already been established by them. But it appears that in spite of the achievements in the determination of facts, one must not always accept the evaluation of certain discoveries about the uprising without reservation, particularly the analysis of its military aspects. Therefore, the author has devoted more space, to the analysis of the military aspects of this uprising, with the hope of contributing his share to a better understanding of the uprising in the Warsaw Ghetto—a major pillar of the armed resistance movement.

A similar approach was taken for the description of the historical events in other large ghettos (Czestochowa and Cracow) and the well-known uprising in Treblinka and Sobibor. A slight emphasis was put on detailing generally known facts and on analyzing the circumstances and the phenomenon of armed activity in these places. In contrast with this, the discussion of the history of the armed underground in the prisoner-of-war camp in Lublin was expanded, as it hitherto has not been touched by historical literature.

Available information on armed resistance organizations in a number of small ghettos and camps is relatively brief. Precise detailing of facts pertaining to these smaller locations is more difficult, and archive material is almost completely lacking. The number of survivors from among the resistance fighters in smaller towns is few, and thus so are the number of personal testimonies. In addition, the effects of the armed struggle in these places were naturally slighter, which is reflected in the more meager German and Polish documentation. Nevertheless, the information that is available makes it possible, in the author's opinion, to investigate the extent, conditions, and possibilities of resistance in small ghettos and camps.

Finally, a special chapter is devoted to the participation of the Jews in the Polish uprising in Warsaw in the summer of 1944.

The limited framework of this book necessitated some restrictions on its scope from both a territorial and a thematic aspect. The author has, therefore, limited himself to the four districts that made up the area of the *General Gouvernement* until the outbreak of the German–Soviet war in the summer of 1941. The inclusion of the resistance in Eastern Galicia, which was annexed to the *General Gouvernement* in July 1941, would have necessitated not only the allotment of space to the history of additional Jewish partisan units and armed organizations in other ghettos and camps, but also the treatment of the Ukrainian question in those regions, or, let us say, examination of another complex problem.

The author also excluded from this work all discussion of the regions of Zaglebie and Silesia, which bordered the *General Gouvernement*. The Jewish resistance movement in these areas, largely connected to cities in the *General Gouvernement* and particularly to Warsaw and Czestochowa, operated, nevertheless, under slightly different conditions because these regions were annexed to the Third Reich.

The study's framework also excludes detailed discussions of a number of problems related to the subject of this study. For example, I dealt in only a very limited way with such problems as daily life in the partisan units, relations between the Jewish partisans and Jews in hiding, and the protection of family camps in the forests by the partisans. Nor does the author analyze the different manifestations of the armed resistance movement and the extent of its involvement with other kinds of underground activity, such as sabotage, underground education, escapes, and rescue operations. The full understanding of the armed resistance movement as one of the more substantial foundations of the Jewish population's general underground activity entails additional research into all of these forms of the Jewish resistance movement.

My gratitude is extended to my colleagues at Yad Vashem and the Institute of Contemporary Jewry who assisted me in the writing of this book, and especially to Professor Yehuda Bauer, who guided me all along the way.

The translation of this book into English was made possible by Mr. Bert Lewyn in memory of his parents, Yohanna and Leopold Lewyn.

THE WAR OF THE DOOMED

The publication of this book was made possible by the Alexander Silberman International Scholarship Foundation; the author is an Alexander Silberman International Fellow at the Institute of Contemporary Jewry of the Hebrew University of Jerusalem.

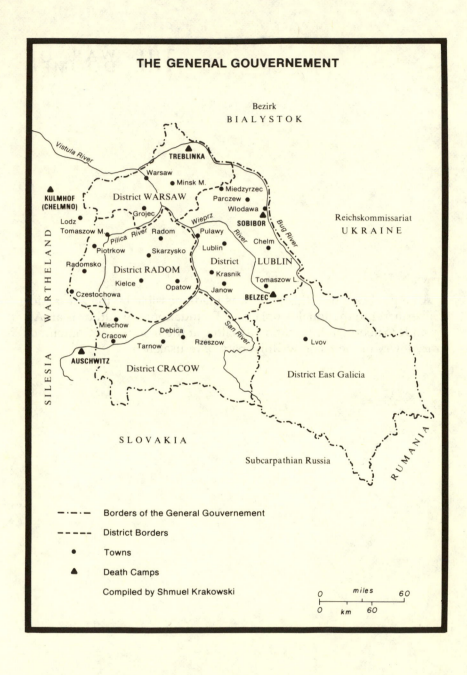

THE GENERAL GOUVERNEMENT

Bezirk
B I A L Y S T O K

Vistula River

▲ **TREBLINKA**

Warsaw
• Minsk M.
• Miedzyrzec
Parczew
Wlodawa

**KULMHOF
(CHELMNO)** ▲

District WARSAW

Reichskommissariat
U K R A I N E

Grojec

Wieprz

SOBIBOR ▲

Lodz •
Tomaszow M. •
Pilica River
Radom
Pulawy
Chelm

Piotrkow •
Skarzysko •
Lublin •

Radomsko •
District RADOM
District
LUBLIN

Kielce •
Opatow •
• Krasnik
Tomaszow L.

Czestochowa •
Janow •
BELZEC ▲

WARTHELAND

Miechow •
Cracow •
Debica •
San River
Lvov •

Tarnow •
Rzeszow •

▲ **AUSCHWITZ**

SILESIA

District CRACOW

District East Galicia

S L O V A K I A

Subcarpathian Russia

R U M A N I A

— · — · — Borders of the General Gouvernement

— — — — District Borders

• Towns

▲ Death Camps

Compiled by Shmuel Krakowski

miles
0 _____ 60
0 _____ 60
km

CHAPTER 1
SPECIFIC PROBLEMS OF THE JEWISH PARTISAN MOVEMENT

THE *GENERAL GOUVERNEMENT* WAS, FOR MORE THAN two years, a battlefield for a large number of Jewish partisan detachments. More than thirty Jewish partisan units (not including very small armed groups), whether independent or subordinated to the Polish People's Guard, were established between 1942 and 1943. Jews also fought in nationally mixed units of the People's Guard (units of Poles and Jews; Poles, Russians, and Jews; and Russians and Jews), of which they made up a considerable portion.

Hundreds of Jewish partisans belonged to Polish units of the People's Guard (GL), later called the People's Army (AL), and to the Home Army (AK), the Socialist Fighting Organization, the Peasant Battalions, and other less-known Polish armed organizations. The number of the Jews in commando units, which were transferred from liberated areas for combat operations in the rear of the German armies, was also considerable. Furthermore, the role of the Jews in the leadership of the Polish partisan movement must be indicated, because dozens of Jews acquired positions as capable commanders and organizers in the armed underground in Poland.

The partisan movement was not a realm of armed struggle for Jews alone; the vast forests served as natural bases of activity for non-Jewish partisans as well. On the contrary, Jews were only a minority in the armed underground struggle in the *General Gouvernement*. Is it possible, therefore, to speak of a separate Jewish partisan movement, or is it more valid to look at the Jewish partisan movement as only a part of the general (that is, Polish) underground in the *General Gouvernement?*

3

There are some basic reasons for treating the Jewish partisan movement as separate and distinct from the Polish partisan movement. This derives not only from the fact that scores of purely Jewish partisan units existed, most of which never came under the authority of the Polish underground leadership, but more from the fact that the conditions under which Jewish partisan groups were founded, organized, molded, and operated were totally different. The different roads that brought Jews and non-Jews to the underground movement, their basically different purposes, their sometimes unidentical enemy, and their totally different relations with the local population all make for the distinction. The Jewish partisans, both those who fought in Jewish units and those who fought in Polish units, faced difficult and unique problems, problems that the Polish partisans never experienced.

Before we discuss the special problems of the Jewish partisan movement in the *General Gouvernement* and the special situation of the Jewish partisan, it is necessary, for a better understanding of the subject at hand, to briefly survey the history of the Polish partisan movement.

THE POLISH PARTISAN MOVEMENT

The attempt made by Major Henryk Dobrzanski ("Hubala") to initiate partisan activities immediately after the defeat of the Polish army in September 1939 met with opposition from all Polish political elements. This attempt quickly ended in a decisive defeat, and for a long time there were no successors to Dobrzanski's partisans in the forests of Poland. The Home Army (AK), which came into being originally as the Union for Armed Struggle *(Zwiazek Walki Zbrojnej)* and which, in 1940, was already the strongest and best-organized force in the Polish underground, did not promote an armed struggle in the first years of the Nazi occupation. The main purpose of the Home Army was the preparation of a general armed rebellion, intended for the expected collapse of the German occupation in Poland. A secondary role was the development of an extensive espionage operation for the Allies and the execution of sabotage on the economic front. The goals of the Home Army were described by the Polish historian, Wladyslaw Pobog-Malinowski, as follows: "The main purpose of the underground army was not 'immediate warfare,' but the concentration and preparation of forces for an armed uprising against the Germans in the final stage of the war."[1]

Pobog-Malinowski writes further about this concept as it was explained in two articles in the AK's main organ, the *Biuletyn Informacyjny:*

> Rowecki's [General Stefan Rowecki, commander of the AK] basic stand on the struggle was expressed in two articles published in the *Biuletyn Informacyjny* in February and March of 1943. The headlines themselves are very revealing: "With Weapons in Hand" and "Armed Action? Yes, but with a Limit." In these articles, which complement each other, it is said that "if the barbaric enemy tries to exterminate the Polish people with the same methods he uses against the Jews," then, of course, orders will be given for an armed struggle. But at this time the order that stands is the one which expresses the position of the superior Polish authorities: "to wait with arms in hand, and not to get caught up in hasty deeds that would result in bloody defeats."[2]

In accordance with its strategy, the Home Army did not establish partisan units until the end of 1942. And even later (until the spring of 1944), the partisan movement was organized on a very limited basis.

The pioneers of the partisan struggle in the *General Gouvernement* were not, therefore, AK units and not the various groups belonging to the Polish underground, affiliated with the Home Army or not, but Red Army soldiers who had escaped from Nazi captivity. Beginning in July 1941, hundreds of thousands of prisoners-of-war from the defeated units of the Red Army were gathered in prison camps (actually extermination camps) in the *General Gouvernement.* Thousands managed to escape to the forests where they hoped to find shelter from German search patrols. Very small groups of escapees, who managed to acquire some arms, united and formed partisan units. Most of the escapees, however, were recaptured and killed shortly after their escape.[3]

In contrast to the Home Army, the Polish Workers Party (PPR), as soon as it was established in January of 1942, stressed the idea of immediate armed struggle, using all existing forces, in order to assist the Red Army. The main principles of the Polish Workers Party's program were expressed in a series of articles published in the underground party press. The first of these articles was published in the party's central bulletin, *Trybuna Wolnosci (The Platform of Freedom)*, on February 1, 1942. Entitled "The Nations' Front against the Invader," it reads:

> Sabotage, diversion, and partisan action are the weapons by which we must, already today, strike the enemy with full force. Sabotage,

diversion, and partisan action—this is the real basis from which the flame of national rebellion must burst forth. We are going toward the armed uprising . . . today, and not tomorrow. It is necessary to begin preparations for the outbreak of the uprising of all the people as a whole today, and not tomorrow. We must take on the load of supreme efforts.[4]

In May 1942, an article headed "We Will Not Let the Germans Spit in Our Faces," which called for Polish peasants to go out immediately to a partisan war, was published in the journal *Trybuna Chlopska (The Peasant's Platform)* destined for rural areas. One paragraph reads:

The war must end in an Allied victory, which is also our victory, already this year. The time has come, therefore, to begin acting . . . establish combat groups for the destruction of bridges, roads, railroads, trains, and all the war equipment of the enemy . . . . The next summer must bring defeat to the fascist army on the front and death to the wicked Germans and Hitlerian gendarmerie in Poland.[5]

A typical article headed "Passive Resistance is Not Enough," published in the *Trybuna Wolnosci* on July 1, 1942, was sharply critical of the position of the Home Army. Part of it reads:

The opposition is holding on by the nails to the slogan of passive resistance as the only possible form of struggle today in order to postpone indefinitely the armed struggle with the enemy. It thus makes the opening of an overall national war front difficult, threatens terror, and preaches patience, as if the war can be won by patience alone. However, the masses refuse to continue to wait and to watch passively the murderous deeds of the conqueror. The calls for passive resistance are meant to hide class distinctions—a fear of the new Poland, the fruit of the struggle of the people themselves. They cannot stop the rising tide of partisan struggles and sabotage and cannot stop the Polish people from going out to an immediate, active, and organized battle against the conqueror.[6]

Despite these appeals, the results of the efforts made to initiate partisan activities were, until the end of 1942, very meager. Only in May 1942 was the first partisan group of the People's Guard organized in Warsaw. This group's attempt to fight quickly ended in failure. Attempts in the fall of that year to set other armed groups of the People's Guard in action brought similar results. The Polish population was not yet ready for a partisan war. Because of this, by the end of 1942 the Polish Workers Party established partisan groups made up mostly of Soviet soldiers who had escaped from German captivity, and of Jews who had escaped from the ghettos.

A turning point in the Polish partisan movement came at the end of 1942 and the beginning of 1943, when the Germans began the deportation of the rural Polish population from the region of Zamosc in the southern part of the district of Lublin. It was then that a few groups of the Peasant Battalions who belonged to the Home Army were brought to the forests. On December 30, 1942, there was a clash near the village of Wojda between a seventy-three-man unit of the Peasant Battalions, a fifty-seven-man unit of Soviet partisans attached to it, and a German unit numbering a few hundred men. In the opinion of Józef Niecko, leader of the Peasant Party, "This was the first battle of the Polish partisan movement since the beginning of the Nazi occupation."[7]

In 1943, the Polish partisan units received additional manpower when hundreds of Poles oppressed by the enemy decided to go out to the forest. The Home Army then brought in a number of additional units in order to balance its forces against those of the People's Guard and to absorb the Poles who were hiding in the forests. Despite this, the presence of the Home Army units in the forest at that time was not at all proportionate to its potential. In the summer of 1943, the Home Army was already a large underground organization numbering 268,000 registered members.[8] This number is misleading, however, because the decisive majority did not participate in any underground activities during the entire span of the Nazi occupation. Yet it does reflect, to a certain extent, the potential of the Home Army.

It is surprising to note how meager the number of those registered and sent out to fight was. Partisan units under the command of the Home Army numbered only 2,000 men in the summer of 1943, and in the winter of 1943–1944 their number was only 3,160, of whom 70 percent were active east of the Bug River—that is, not in the *General Gouvernement*.[9] The political make-up of the Home Army is very significant. The largest group of registered members put under the command of the Home Army by various political groups was the National Armed Forces (NSZ)—extreme fascists and anti-Semites—who numbered 70,000. In second place were the Peasant Battalions, with 40,000 members.[10] The underground socialist organizations were much smaller than these. The People's Guard numbered only 1,500 partisans in 1943, in spite of its great efforts to involve as many people as possible in partisan activities.[11] The fascist units of the National Armed Forces, which were not under the command of the Home Army and which were active mainly in the forests since the end of 1942, were better organized and equipped. The largest of these, the *Swietokrzyska Brigade*, numbered 1,250 men in 1944.[12]

Until the spring of 1944, the Polish partisan movement was still far from being a mass movement. A drastic change took place at the end of spring 1944. AK units opened the *Burza* (Storm) campaigns in what were formerly the eastern border areas of Poland (the areas of Vilna, Polesie, and Volhynia). The purpose of these campaigns was to capture the important cities and towns while striking at the defeated German units and to establish in these places government institutions that would be subject to the government of Poland in exile before the advancing Soviet army could capture them. The *Burza* campaigns had, therefore, a political goal that was directed against both the Germans and the Soviet Union, and because of this it failed everywhere. A few of the AK units that were defeated by the Germans managed to cross to the west of the Bug River and brought the partisan war to the districts of Lublin and Radom.

The transfer of Soviet and Polish-Soviet commando units to areas west of the Bug began with the advance of the Red Army's offensive at the end of 1943. These units were made up partially of partisans and partially of regular army soldiers trained for operations behind the enemy's lines. The People's Army, which received large quantities of weapons from the Soviet Union and had developed into a serious partisan force, collaborated with these units as did a number of groups from the Peasant Battalions. Large partisan battles were taking place at this time. The largest of these occurred between June 9 and 25 in the forests south of the Lublin district with the participation of approximately 3,000 partisans. The partisan movement in the area of the *General Gouvernement* had reached its height.

At the end of 1944, the Red Army crossed the Bug River and captured the eastern areas of the *General Gouvernement*. The Vistula line soon became a fixed front, whose stability was maintained until January 1945 when the Soviet Army reopened its offensive. Some of the People's Army units and most of the Soviet raid units transferred their activities westward across the Vistula. The Home Army also tried to mobilize its forces for a *Burza* campaign in the Radom district, but the large concentration of German forces in the region, which had by then turned into a front, put an end to partisan activities there. The partisan and raid units had to either return to the liberated areas on the right bank of the Vistula, or be disbanded. Thus, the attempt to mobilize the AK forces failed. The Polish historian Zbigniew Zaluski writes about this as follows: "The concentration of *Burza* units was done slowly and not with full force. The 25th Regiment of the infantry was mobilized at the inspectorate of Piotrkow . . . . Of the 9,801 who appear on the list of underground members of the AK, 872 were to be found in the armed units. In the Iglarnia region in the district of Czestochowa only 13 percent of the registered members reported for duty. Only 35 percent of the available weapons were used."[13]

The Peasant Battalions, who succeeded in enlisting only 4 percent of those registered, whom they assigned to the partisan units, were much worse off.[14] During the month of September, almost all AK and Peasant Battalion units were disbanded. The report for October 1944 of the German "Mitte" Army Group states: "Most of the armed forces of the AK retreated from the area where our soldiers were found, or disbanded." In addition, a crisis of morale struck the Polish public following the failure of the Warsaw uprising. The same report of the "Mitte" Army Group states: "After the surrender of Warsaw the Polish population shows a greater perseverance at work."[15] Various underground documents confirm this. The following is part of the report of the Polish Government Delegacy on the situation in the Zyrardow area, dated November 3, 1944:

> The stand of the population on underground activity is negative. The matter has gone on for too long. The number of victims is too large, the results are poor, and there is a lack of faith in the political wisdom of the leadership. A feeling of powerlessness prevails. The appraisal of the Warsaw uprising and its results was negative. The attitude to the conquerer can be described as this: "If it weren't for the kidnapping and the deportations for labor in Prussia, it would be possible to live with this."[16]

After reaching the height of its development in the summer of 1944, the Polish partisan movement was almost dying out in the final stage of the Nazi occupation.

HOW THE JEWISH PARTISAN MOVEMENT AROSE

The special situation of the Jews, who were deliberately isolated by the Germans with a view toward their total destruction, made the development of a Jewish partisan movement completely different. The Jewish partisan movement did not develop by gradually accumulating power as the conditions ripened for the start of a partisan war. This movement came into being in a sudden and usually spontaneous manner during the summer of 1942, at a time of increased deportations to the death camps of Treblinka, Sobibor, Auschwitz, and Belzec. With the exception of a few rather weak groups of runaway Soviet prisoners, there was at that time no partisan movement in the *General Gouvernement*. The political conditions and the military situation were not yet ripe for partisan activities. The Jews especially were totally without objective conditions for the development of a partisan movement of their own, as a result of their isolation in ghettos and forced labor camps. But the Jews could not afford to wait. The deportation orders forced them to begin spontaneous, or at the very best, hastily organized escape actions to the forests, which alone could serve them as shelter.

The immediate hunts organized by the police prompted the establishment of armed groups whose purpose was to fight these hunts, and to secure the conditions needed for the illegal existence of refugees in the forests. The beginning of the Jewish partisan movement in the *General Gouvernement* is, therefore, linked to mass escapes at the time of the deportations. Unlike the Polish groups, which were organized, armed, and trained in cities and villages before they left for previously prepared bases, the Jewish groups were established only after those who hastily escaped arrived in the forest. Organizational frameworks were set up, arms were acquired, and the bases were established only in the forest, an area not yet familiar to most of the escapees.

Later (after the summer of 1942), more escapes from ghettos, forced labor camps, and even the concentration camps were organized. Groups of fighters from the Jewish Fighting Organization from the ghettos of Warsaw, Cracow, and Czestochowa turned to partisan activities. A certain number of those who took part in the uprisings at the Sobibor and Treblinka death camps also succeeded in joining the partisan ranks.

With only a few exceptions, all the Jewish partisans were in the forests as a result of their escapes from ghettos, transports, or camps. All Jewish partisans had, therefore, the status of escaped prisoners who were outlawed by virtue of their very physical existence as Jews.

Groups of Jewish partisans and Jews who were hiding under their protection in the forests were, in most cases, the only living remnant of whole communities that had been exterminated. The Jewish partisan was usually the only survivor of whole families that had been murdered. The lot of the Jewish partisan was, therefore, completely different from that of the Polish partisan, who did not come to the forest by way of an escape—where chances for success were so few—and who left behind home, family, friends, and acquaintances on whose help he could always rely.

Another book would be required to discuss in detail the problems and the lot of Jews who managed to escape at the time of the deportations from the ghettos, transports, and forced labor camps.

We are speaking of very large numbers. According to the assessment made for this study, more than 50,000 Jews fled to the forests in the four districts of the *General Gouvernement*. The majority of these were killed during the numerous hunts carried out against them by the Nazis. In this way 4,000 runaway Jews were murdered in the region of Parczew, 2,000 in the counties of Pulawy and Lubartow, 15,000 in the south of the Lublin district, a few thousand in other regions of the Lublin district, 14,000 in the district of Radom, 4,000 in Mazovia and Podlasie, and 8,500 in the district of Cracow.[17]

Escape itself was a difficult and dangerous undertaking, and its chances for success were very slim. The escapees had to pass through a network of police posts or to slip out of the hands of armed patrols. They were liable to suffer severe bodily injury in the event of a failed attempt to jump from a train, and liable to be tortured to death if they fell into the hands of the Nazi murderers again. At the very best, when they had reached their destination, the forest, they again faced great difficulties, mainly because of the necessity of immediately resisting the hunts. The runaways faced problems of preparing bases (underground bunkers) and acquiring food and water in an area which was very often inhabited by an unfriendly or openly hostile population. In spite of these difficulties, thousands of Jews made their way to the forests where they formed partisan groups in a swift and spontaneous fashion.

As a result of mass escapes to the forests, in the summer of 1942 the Jewish partisan movement began to rise and grow. This fact is mentioned by both Polish and German documents. As one of the organizers of the People's Guard in the region of Lublin, Kazimierz Sidor, states: "The Jewish population which fled to the forests served as an important basis for the establishment of the partisan movement."[18] Bogdan Hillebrandt, the Polish historian of the resistance movement, writes in a similar spirit:

> The number of those hiding in the villages and the forests in 1942 greatly increased as a result of escapes from the ghettos. This was due to the beginning of "Operation Reinhard" in the summer of that year, whose purpose was the transportation of hundreds of thousands of Jews from the ghettos to death in the extermination camps. Many Jews, mainly youths, who saw the fate awaiting them in the hands of Hitler's soldiers, fled from the ghetto in hope of finding refuge amongst the Polish population. *These people who were ready for all were an excellent manpower for the partisan movement.*"[19] (My emphasis)

Beginning in the autumn of 1942, the Jewish partisans were often mentioned in the reports and communiqués of the Nazi authorities and the German police in the *General Gouvernement*. The report by the governor of the Warsaw district for October and November 1942 stated:

> As to the banditry and the partisan movement, there has been no lull whatsoever. In the region of the Warsaw district there were 256 attacks in October, and 216 in November. This is not a matter of political gangs but of criminal gangs, established by fugitive Jews, and mainly by young Jewish women. The war against this banditry has been carried out in full force, but we have not succeeded in stamping it out altogether.[20]

THE ENEMY FORCES

The Jews who fled to the forests and began to organize partisan units were immediately forced to defend themselves against hunts carried out by powerful German police forces and units of Nazi collaborators. The Jewish units were also forced to protect themselves from attacks by certain organizations that were part of the Polish underground. All units of the Nazi police were given orders to persecute Jews in hiding and to fight against the Jewish partisan units. However, the main force used against the partisans in the GG forests was the *Ordnungspolizei*. The task groups which participated in hunts and large-scale operations against the partisans were made up mainly of battalions belonging to the 22nd, 24th, and 25th regiments of the *Ordnungspolizei* which were stationed in the GG. When the number of transports increased and escapes by Jews to the forests multiplied, the number of *Ordnungspolizei* in the *General Gouvernement* rose to 15,000. The second largest force used against the Jews in the forests was the Polish auxiliary police, known as the "Blue Police," which was subject to the *Schutzpolizei* command. This police force numbered 14,300 men in the GG district at the end of 1942.[21] As a report of the Polish Government Delegacy dated October 30, 1943 says: "The conquerer does not use the Polish police for political operations. However, this force's part in operations against the Jews is quite substantial."[22] In these operations, the Blue Police showed complete loyalty to their Nazi commanders. The Polish underground press openly stated that "the Blue Police showed great perserverance in the capturing of Jews."[23] A similar remark is included in the notes of a member of the Home Army, Dr. Zygmunt Klukowski, dated October 22, 1942. He writes: "The hunt after the Jews continues. Yesterday foreign gendarmerie soldiers and SS men. Today 'our' gendarmerie and Blue Police, who were ordered to kill immediately any Jew caught, are carrying this task out. They are following this order with great enthusiasm."[24]

Because of the strategic importance of the *General Gouvernement*, a large number of *Wehrmacht* forces were concentrated in its area. In October 1942, these forces numbered 600,000 soldiers; in 1943, their number reached 700,000. Although the *Wehrmacht* units were rarely used against the Jews between 1942 and 1943, their very presence limited and arrested the development of the partisan movement to a large extent.[25] *Ostlegion* units subject to the *Wehrmacht* were sent out more often to the operations against the partisans and the Jews. These units, primarily made up of captured Red Army soldiers who then worked for the Germans, were stationed in *General Gouvernement* in 1942. In March 1943 they numbered forty-two battalions, and in the summer of that year, sixty-five. These battalions, made up of three or four infantry companies (each numbering 150 to 180 men), heavy machine gun companies, artillery batteries, and a communications platoon, were much better suited for battles against the partisans than were the police. Beginning with the winter of 1942–1943, the *Ostlegion* units participated in every large-scale operation against the partisans.[26]

At the end of 1942, a new and more dangerous enemy to the Jewish partisans arrived in the forests of Poland—the units of the National Armed Forces (NSZ). The Jewish partisan units, which had organized against great odds, acquired certain quantities of arms, and developed some methods of fighting the German police hunts, now faced a well-armed aggressor who knew the area better than the Germans and who often enjoyed the help of the local population. A short while after the organizing process ended, NSZ commander Colonel Czeslaw Oziewicz issued an order to begin "Special Operation Number 1." This order included the following: "The partisan movement can and must act in earnestness at one and the same time to cleanse the area of the revolutionary and criminal gangs of the *minority units*, which are hostile to us, and to counterattack—in the framework of self-defense—against the penal authorities in cases of dreadful injustice during the conqueror's acts of repression." (My emphasis)

Polish historian Bogdan Hillebrandt explains what was to be understood by the words "minority units":

> The main goal of the National Armed Forces units was to wage a civil war against units of the People's Guard, which were referred to as "revolutionary and criminal gangs," and against "minority units,"

meaning, against *groups made up of Jews who fled from the ghettos to the forests*. Yet they intended to fight the Germans only if they perceived "dreadful injustice" on the part of Nazi penal authorities. In the opinion of the NSZ leadership it was even possible to justify the burning of villages and the murder of their own people, under certain circumstances, without arousing opposition. And on the other hand, it was necessary to eradicate any communist activity whatsoever."[27] (My emphasis)

Jewish partisans also were attacked often by some AK units. Order Number 116 by AK commander General Bor-Komorowski, dated September 15, 1943, served as official permission for these attacks:

> Well-armed gangs ramble endlessly in cities and villages, attack estates, banks, commercial and industrial companies, houses and large farms. The plunder is often accompanied by acts of murder, which are carried out by Soviet partisan units hiding in the forests or by ordinary gangs of robbers. Men and women, especially Jewish women, participate in the assaults. . . . I have issued an order to the region for area commanders to go out with arms, when necessary, against these plunderers or revolutionary robbers.[28]

One of the main targets of AK attacks carried out according to this order were the Jewish armed groups. This was admitted by historian Pobóg-Malinowski, an AK sympathizer who found it right to justify this order in the following words: "This order is due to the epidemic which is spreading madly, unpunished, in the country. [There are] groups of Jews hiding in the forests after their escape from the ghetto, bands of Soviet soldiers who managed to escape from captivity, Soviet partisans, and other do-nothings looking for an 'easy life,' criminals who escape from prison."[29]

It is not by chance that Pobóg-Malinowski mentions "groups of Jews hiding in the forest after their escape from the ghetto" first. The stress on the role of Jewish women in the AK commander's order was in the way of a hint that the subject on hand has to do with Jewish partisan groups. In contrast with all other partisan groups, the percentage of women in these units was considerable. The fact is that in many AK units, the order was interpreted as the outlawing of Jewish partisan groups. The AK commander's order placed the armed Jewish units, which fought against the Nazis and struggled for their own existence and for the lives of the Jews under their protection, on a par with the regular gangs of robbers whose number was very large in those days. The Polish underground press often wrote with alarm about the character of these gangs, who had nothing whatsoever in common with Jews who were hiding or fighting, and who joined the Polish underground organizations in substantial numbers. The following is a section of a typical article that widely and objectively discusses the real, and not the imaginary, problem of plunder. Entitled "The Source of Evil," this article was published in the bulletin of the Peasant Battalions, *Regionalna Agencja Prasowa Podlasie (The Agency of the Local Press of Podlasie)*, dated April 4, 1944:

> A wave of plunder is sweeping the whole country. The night terror of the bandits, which is no less dangerous, less cruel and disturbing than the day terror of the Gestapo and gendarmerie robbers, threatens the population. . . . At this hour we are witnessing a phenomenon a hundred times more threatening and dangerous to public life than ordinary thievery. This phenomenon can be defined in a few powerful words. *Corruption in the form of drunkenness, robbery, tyranny, cruelty, and savagery has spread through the lines of the organizations fighting for freedom* [emphasis in the original].

It continues:

> The assailants are usually from the neighboring village and mask their faces. The number of assaults of this kind is so large that, in most cases, they are not reported to the police. It is preferred to pass over them in silence in order to avoid acts of revenge. Membership in an organization protects the assailants. . . . The pacification and total destruction of the village of Osolinka is known in Podlasie. Responsibility for the tragedy that struck that village must be primarily placed on the AK command in the county of Bielsk Podlaski, which stationed a unit made up of known criminals from before the war in this area. They did not consider the safety of the population, or even the people themselves, whom they governed forcefully with terror and robbery. For the entire duration of their criminal activity (and to this very day), those people were registered as an organized group. No one kept track of their deeds, and no one restrained them in time.[30]

These elements had nothing whatsoever in common with the armed Jewish groups and nonfighting Jews who hid in the forest. Of course, there was a problem of food for those people, as there was for all partisan units in the forests. Jews hiding in the forest did not always have the necessary money or commodities with which to purchase food from farmers. Through little choice, these people became a burden on the villages. The Government Delegacy, which was, for all intents and purposes, the Polish underground government and whose authority was recognized by a substantial part of the Polish population, undoubtedly could have easily solved the problem of feeding the ten or twenty thousand Jews who were left in the forests after the first large-scale hunts. But the government representatives and the AK commanders chose a different path – the path of denying that the Jews were hiding in the forests. The fact is that the AK command (with the exception of the personal initiative of Colonel Henryk Wolinski) never suggested taking the armed Jewish groups into its ranks. Moreover, initiatives by Jews toward this kind of solution fell on deaf ears.

The attacks by the National Armed Forces and by some AK units seriously harmed the Jewish partisans in the forests and the villages, and also the Poles who helped the Jews. There were many cases when Poles were beaten and even murdered for the "crime" of helping Jews.

THE ATTITUDE OF THE LOCAL POPULATION

The relationship between the local rural population and the armed Jewish groups was crucial to the success of the escapees' activities. Without the support of this population, the food and clothing they supplied, the information they gave on the movements of the enemy's army and police force, and the shelter and care they gave to the wounded, it would not be possible to speak of the successful development of partisan fighting. The tragedy of the Jewish partisan movement lies in the fact that the Jews could not rely on this kind of help. It is also clear that the Jewish partisan movement could not rely on Jewish communities, because these no longer existed after the great deportations of 1942. The Jews who remained alive after 1942 were isolated from the outside world, locked up in forced labor camps, concentration camps, or minor ghettos, and had no means whatsoever of giving help to the Jews in the forests. The successes and failures of the Jewish partisan movement completely depended on the attitude of the local Polish population. Usually they were not sympathetic; real support or a show of sympathy was seen only in rare cases. There were four main reasons for this: Because of their completely different circumstances, the Jewish and Polish populations lacked common aims; a mood of apathy prevailed until the middle of 1943, which created a feeling of ill-will toward partisans in general; the nature of the Polish partisan movement in 1943 and 1944 was local; and anti-Semitism poisoned many minds in the Polish population.

Let us briefly survey these four reasons. The Jews and the Poles lacked common aims because their situations were completely different. Although the Poles suffered great terror from and severe exploitation by the Germans, their situation could in no way be compared to that of the Jews, who were condemned to total annihilation. In addition, the situation of the Polish rural population was much better than that of the Polish urban population, which was much more vulnerable to the horrors of the enemy. Most of the Germans' anti-Polish acts of terror were directed against the urban population, and especially against Polish intellectuals.

In 1942, while the Jews in the forests were trying to organize partisan groups, the Polish population, particularly the rural population, did not show an interest in an armed struggle against the conqueror, who was then at the height of his victory. Internal conditions and the military situations, which favored the Germans until the autumn of 1942, created a feeling of apathy in wide sections of the Polish population. According to a report of the Government Delegacy, sent to London on August 6, 1942:

> The common feelings now prevailing in the country are as follows: Until a short time ago, the Polish people were living under the influence of English promises that the course of the war would first be decided in Europe, that this would take place before the end of 1942, that afterwards a systematic destruction of the large cities in Germany would be carried out, that the bombing of Cologne on May 1 was only the beginning of the summer offensive, that the population on the coast of France is about to abandon its homes, fearing the danger of the battles about to take place between the English and the Germans, and that American landing forces were on alert, etc. But all these promises are fictitious. On the contrary, the German armies have the upper hand on the Russian front and are continuing to conquer territories. They are already near the Kuban River. In light of this situation, the Polish population is completely disappointed, and is sinking into total apathy.[31]

In a decision accepted at a convention held in Warsaw on October 19, and 22, 1942, in which forty representatives of Polish underground organizations participated, it was stated:

> The destruction of the Polish people, which was planned in detail even before the war, has been going on methodically since the first days of the war. Hundreds of thousands of Poles died in the raging terror of the enemy, among them very valuable and active people. Over a million are wasting away in prison and working in the service of the enemy in order to stay alive. Many millions deprived of places of work or means of

subsistence are condemned to hopelessness and to all the terrible impli-
cations arising from it. The enemy's acts of destruction strive not only
for the annihilation of the Polish population in the entire republic, but
also for the spiritual collapse of the Polish people. We determine that,
without the shadow of a doubt, in the latter respect, the conqueror's
actions bear fruit. . . . We are witness to the false propaganda propa-
gated abroad that Poland is on the verge of rebellion, but in reality the
public is deep in the passivity forced upon it.[32]

The stand taken by the underground organizations subordinated
the AK command to the Government Delegacy and influenced the
rural population's attitude toward partisans in general, and to Jewish
partisans in particular. These organizations, which formed the
greater majority of the Polish underground, viewed the armed activities of the partisans in the years 1942 and 1943 as premature and
destructive because they needlessly endangered the Polish population, and led to retaliations against it by the enemy. The propaganda
of these organizations called for the Polish population to wait and to
avoid clashes that would lead to acts of retaliation. These organizations also blamed the Soviet and Jewish partisans and the People's
Guard for causing meaningless sacrifices among the Polish population.

The partisans were blamed for causing unnecessary suffering to
the Polish population both in the reports and announcements sent to
London and in the articles and proclamations of the underground
press. Following is part of a typical proclamation, dated July 26, 1943,
published by the "A" agency, which was connected with the Government Delegacy:

> The partisan activities in the areas of Lublin, Kielce, and Warsaw teach
> us what use these acts are to the Polish population in the country and in
> the city. The Germans generally refrain from entering into battle with
> armed units, and take their Teutonic anger out on the quiet Polish popu-
> lation, by killing people and burning houses. Who has an interest in our
> people spilling their blood in a premature and purposeless war? Only
> our enemies. Therefore, in spite of the talk of "independence" and
> "nationalism" by the Polish Workers Party communists and the People's
> Army, we are facing a hostile force that we must destroy as we must
> destroy the greatest enemy of this time—the Germans.[33]

Words of this kind contributed substantially to the consolidation
of the hostile attitude of the rural population towards the partisans,
and characterized the reports of the Government Delegacy and the
underground press until the spring of 1944. Furthermore, statements
against the Jewish partisans were often replete with clearly anti-

Semitic expressions. So, for example, we read the following in a report sent by the Government Delegacy to London on March 27, 1944:

> Acts of sabotage and the dropping of paratroopers have increased substantially. The local bands, and especially Jews in hiding, who enthusiastically receive the Bolsheviks and serve as their main source of information for infiltrating the area, usually come into contact with Soviet pilots who parachute in. The warm attitude of the Jews towards the Bolsheviks dampens the sympathy of the Polish population to communism. The feelings that prevail in the population are those of hatred and mistrust of the Bolsheviks and fear of the Jews who remained alive. The opinion that is consolidating throughout the rural population is that the future Poland must be a nationalist Poland. They believe that it is impossible for the relations that existed before the war, granting the Jews, Germans, and the Ukrainians more rights and freedom of movement and more opportunities of acquiring wealth than the Poles, to be allowed to exist again.[34]

A decisive and complex influence on the determination of the attitude of the rural population towards the Jewish partisans was anti-Semitism, which was substantially strengthened by Nazi propaganda and a large portion of the underground press. The existence of anti-Semitism, which poisoned the minds of some of the Polish people, is confirmed by various documents from the Polish underground. Following are a few examples; the first, a report of the Government Delegacy sent to London on January 9, 1942, states: "It must be mentioned with great satisfaction that our people are not at all influenced by the process of Germanification. Traces of this influence are expressed only in a blind and cruel anti-Semitism. There is reason to suspect that the attitude of our public to the question of the Jews was such anyway—only in this case, the principles of Christian justice based on mercy have been totally cast out, and are definitely not applied to the Jews."[35] A similar statement is found in the diary of AK member, Dr. Zygmunt Klukowski, in a note dated October 26, 1942: "Because of their fear of German retaliation, the peasants capture Jews in the villages and bring them to the city, or kill them on the spot. They act with extraordinary cruelty toward the Jews. A kind of psychosis has taken hold of the people who, like the Nazis, see the Jews not as human beings, but as destructive animals that must be exterminated like mad dogs, mice, etc."[36]

The anti-Semitic propaganda in some of the Polish underground newspapers, which in their incitement against the Jews did not fall short of the Nazi *Stürmer*, substantially helped to worsen the attitude of the rural population towards the Jews and to increase anti-

Semitism during the war. It must be mentioned that the provocation carried out in the press, which referred to itself as an underground press, was a much more destructive influence than the German press, which was treated with reservation by the Polish population. To illustrate this propaganda, we shall quote sections from four underground journals that were popular in occupied Poland and published by anti-Semitic organizations:

From *Placowka (The Outpost)*, no. 44, October 21, 1942:

The time has come to tell ourselves that the Jews shall be no more in Poland. We will attain this by legislation which will forbid Jewish settlement. This prohibition will harm no one. It would only mean fully using the rights of the masters of the land, who only welcome pleasant guests to their home. Under this prohibition, the Jews who survive the pogroms will be forced to leave Poland, as will all those residents who, to this day, cannot hide their hatred of Poland, and who are foreign and useless to us.

From *Polska (Poland)*, January 2, 1943:

No matter how good the conditions for their development were, the Jews of Poland always worked against our homeland, and hated it and us. Because of this we shall be forced to take a clear stand on the Jews after the war, even if their number is greatly diminished. Jews will not be able to own land; the same would go for industry and communications media such as newspapers, cinemas, and publishing. We must establish the rule of *numerus clausus* in commerce and the professions, and if the Jews don't like it, the way to Palestine is open.

From *Warszawski Dziennik Narodowy (Warsaw National Daily)*, no. 14, April 3, 1943:

Jews are found everywhere, and want to rule everywhere. Their goal is to force their rule on the whole world. Political arguments and the tendency to waste energy on disputes and empty words have helped them in Poland. They incite quarrels, work against unity, and muddle minds so they can destroy the solidarity of the public with the help of people who lack a sense of criticism, but have a hunger for power. The Masonic and Jewish influence must not be allowed to come in the way of the love of the homeland and the deep patriotism of the Poles.

From *Narodowa Agencja Prasowa (National Press Agency)* no. 6, June 28, 1944:

We call out to all those who desire a free homeland and who refuse to become slaves of the Jews to unite against the assault of Judaism that is being supported by the left through the Free Masons, the Polish Socialist Party, and the small group which heads the Popular Party. The governing principle must of necessity be that the only masters of Poland can be only the Polish people.

This propaganda led to various reactions by representatives of the Jewish underground, but these came to nothing. One of the first responses was a letter by the central committee of the *Bund*, which was written on February 2, 1942, and handed to the delegate of the Polish government-in-exile. It read: "We know that His Honor cannot do anything against the destructive campaign being carried out by some of the underground press. But we are sorry to state that even in the press that represents the government, nothing whatsoever is being done against the anti-Semitic incitement."[37]

Later, particularly after the Warsaw Ghetto uprising, a number of articles attacking anti-Semitism and appealing for help for Jews in hiding appeared in the underground press that supported the government. However, during the entire course of the German occupation, not one article and not one proclamation appeared that called for the extension of help to Jewish partisans or to Jews fighting in the forests.

The attitude of the Catholic church in Poland had a great influence on the rural population's attitude toward the Jewish partisans (and Jews in general). Next to the Government Delegacy, the Catholic church was the most important institution in Poland and controlled the spirit of the Polish people during the German occupation. However, we do not know what position the church hierarchy took and what its actions were. The church's archives are closed, and the study of this question is, therefore, impossible.

It is a fact that some members of the Polish priesthood took part in helping Jews who escaped from the ghettos and the camps. But it is difficult to determine to what extent this was due to the private initiative of certain priests, and to what extent this was planned on a certain level of the church's hierarchy, if any planning existed at all.

ARMS SUPPLY

The problem of the supply of arms to the Jewish units demands special attention. In the following chapters, where we discuss the history of the various partisan units, we shall deal in greater detail with how the problem of arms and equipment was solved. It seems that minor purchases on the black market were the main source of supply for independent Jewish units. The Jewish units that, in time, were integrated into the People's Guard (GL) and the People's Army (AL) received arms as did the other units of these organizations. Yet it must be remembered that the People's Army units, including the Jewish units, received their main supply of arms only during the last stage of the partisan activities.

The situation of arms supply for the Jewish partisans was totally different from that of the armed Polish organizations. The main sources of supply for the Polish units were not within reach of the Jewish partisans. For an understanding of the special situation of the Jew in this area, a brief description of the arms supplies held by the Polish partisan movement is needed. This matter is of great importance because the vast apologetic literature on the partisans, which is very widespread, in Poland also, frequently speaks of the so-called success of the partisans in increasing the arms supply of their units with weapons captured in battle. These presumed successes are basically false, especially in the case of the Polish partisan movement.

Only a small quantity of arms was acquired as spoils of war. In addition, the number of arms that fell into the hands of the partisans was insignificant in comparison with the large number of partisan weapons that fell into the hands of the Germans. The Germans, for example, confiscated the following quantities of arms from the Polish partisan movement in the five months between December 1943 and April 1944: 1,216 rifles, 141 machine guns, 158 submachine guns, 875 pistols, 2 mortars, 50,258 grenades, and 216,000 rounds of ammunition.[38] Furthermore, numerous partisan arms fell into German hands in the period preceding the Warsaw uprising in the summer of 1944, and during the course of its battles.

At the very beginning, the Home Army had rifles, machine guns, and submachine guns sufficient for arming three regular infantry divisions. These arms came from supply depots of the Polish army that were concealed in safe places after the defeat of Poland in September 1939, for the future use of the Polish underground. From this source, the Home Army had the following quantities of arms in its warehouses scattered around the *General Gouvernement* and the nearby districts of Silesia and Lodz: 566 heavy machine guns, 1,097 light machine guns, 31,391 rifles, 6,492 pistols, 40,513 grenades, 25 antitank guns, 28 small pieces of artillery, and 5 million rounds of ammunition. During the course of the war, additional arms were parachuted in by England. Along with these, the Home Army managed to develop the secret production of submachine guns and grenades. Underground workshops produced over 200,000 grenades.[39]

The People's Army, which at first faced great hardships in the area of arms, later received substantial supplies of weapons parachuted in from the Soviet Union. The following supplies of arms were delivered for use by the People's Army between June and September 1944: 2,804 submachine guns, 1,257 rifles, 143 machine guns, 40 antitank guns, 81 mortars, 6,472 grenades, and close to a million rounds of ammunition.

The Polish partisan movement had large sums of money. Although nothing is known about the money the People's Army received from the Soviet Union, the sum received by the Home Army is known: the amount it received from abroad between 1939 and 1944 totaled more than 30 million dollars in gold and banknotes, 8 million German marks, and 90 million *zloties*, which were in circulation in the *General Gouvernement*.[40]

OTHER ELEMENTS

Some other areas where the Jewish and Polish partisan movements differed must be mentioned. These are the absence of an officers' corps, the impossibility of training fighters before battles, and the necessity of protecting and defending many hundreds of defenseless Jews who were hiding in the forests and the villages. These problems did not exist for the Polish partisan movement, nor for the units made up of escaped Soviet prisoners-of-war.

There was a sufficient number of professional officers from the prewar Polish army in the ranks of the Home Army and in the organizations under its command. At first the People's Army suffered a shortage of experienced commanders. But these difficulties were overcome quickly by bringing in Polish officers from France who had participated in the Spanish Civil War; by joining Soviet officers who had escaped imprisonment to the partisan units; and at a later stage, by the arrival of officers from regular Polish military units. All the Polish units had sufficient time to train and prepare before going out to bases in the forests and before military actions. The units that were made up of Soviet prisoners-of-war constituted a force which both had military training and a substantial number of officers. Only the Jewish units were outstanding in this way.

The Jewish partisan units lacked experienced officers altogether, and, moreover, the majority lacked political leadership. The Zionist youth organization, which took on the leadership of the resistance movement in the ghettos and established the Jewish Fighting Organization, was concentrated in large cities, whereas most of the fighters in the Jewish partisan units came from small towns, where escape to nearby forests was relatively easy. (The units formed by the Jewish Fighting Organization were an exception.) It must be mentioned that the dozens of Jews who were raised to the rank of officers and commanders during the partisan battles continued to fight in the regular Polish units, and with the exception of a few isolated cases, did not have any influence whatsoever on the fate of the Jewish units.

Another problem that was unique to the Jewish partisans was the need to protect Jews who had fled from the ghettos and the camps. Although a Jewish unit could be attached to the People's Guard, a non-Jewish unit never took on the weighty duty of protecting fugitives. This burden always rested with the Jewish unit.

Under these harsh conditions, in a situation that at times seemed hopeless, the Jewish partisans found allies without whom the struggle would have been impossible. Among these one must mention, first and foremost, the People's Guard. In contrast with other Polish underground organizations, the People's Guard strove to encourage partisan fighting in Poland to the best of its ability from the time it was established in the summer of 1942. This approach was not very popular with the Polish population and it met, as mentioned above, with sharp opposition from the other underground organizations. Under these conditions, the People's Guard saw the fugitive Jews, and also the escaped Soviet prisoners, as excellent manpower for the development of partisan operations until the time when the left-wing partisan movement would be accepted by the Polish population.

Among other allies of the Jewish partisan movement, one must count the scores of Home Army members, members of the Socialist Fighting Organization, and members of other armed organizations, who through their own initiative aided the Jewish partisans and the Jews who were searching for a way to join the Polish partisan movement. These people often gave their help against the will of their commanders. Special mention must be given to the fact that at the height of the raging terror of the Germans, the Jewish partisans found support and help in hundreds of peasant families, under conditions which forced total secrecy not only from the German authorities, but also from the people of the immediate vicinity—neighbors, friends, and relatives.

CHAPTER 2
THE FORESTS OF PARCZEW AND WLODAWA

THE AREA INCLUDING PARCZEW AND WLODAWA COUNTIES became one of the primary battlefields of the Jewish partisan movement. This is an area of forests and lakes, with forests covering approximately 30 percent of its 3,500 square kilometers. Although these are medium-sized forests, they continue in an almost unbroken line, forest after forest, along a belt that extends 70 kilometers from west to east, from Lubartow and Leczna on the Wieprz River to Wlodawa on the Bug River, and 50 kilometers from north to south. The largest of these forests extends from the town of Parczew in the north to Ostrow Lubelski in the south, covering an area of 200 square kilometers. Another line of smaller forests, only slightly separated, extends east of the forests of Parczew and up to the Bug River. Across the Bug River, the wide area of Polesie is also covered with forests and lakes.

In the southern part of Parczew and Wlodawa, many lakes make the approach to the forests in the north very difficult. The roads in these two regions are few and of poor quality, and no railroad track passes through. There are only two railway lines nearby, one going to Parczew, and the other to Wlodawa. The only real road is the one between these two towns. The others are dirt roads which do not suit the traffic of motor vehicles. This was an almost ideal area for partisan activities, especially those carried out by small units.

In this area, there were Jews living in fourteen towns and a number of rural settlements. The destruction of the Jewish communities began here on May 23, 1942, with the first deportation from Wlodawa to the extermination camp in Sobibor. In June of that year there were continuous deportations from Wlodawa, Slawatycze, and Podworna. On August 19, 1942, the Jews of Parczew were taken to the death camp of Treblinka. In October, the Jewish communities in Leczna, Ostrow Lubelski, Ryki, and Puchaczow were liquidated. On December 1, 1942, the Germans gathered all the Jews still alive, among them a substantial number who had been found hiding in forests or villages, and established a ghetto in Wlodawa. In addition to the few thousand Jews held in the Wlodawa Ghetto, there were, at the end of 1942, 330 Jews in a forced labor camp in Leczna and a few hundred Jews in a number of smaller camps in the two counties. On May 1, 1943, the Wlodawa Ghetto was liquidated, and two days later, the labor camp in Leczna. All the Jews from the Wlodawa Ghetto and the labor camps died in the gas chambers of Sobibor. The last of the small labor camps, the one in Adamow, was liquidated on August 13, 1943.[1]

During the liquidation of the ghettos and camps, Jews escaped en masse to the forests. Whole families, including women, old people, and children, ran away. And although these escapes reached their height in June, August, and October of 1942, Jews continued to flee to the forests in small groups until the end of that year, and individuals still fled to the forest throughout the next year.

It is difficult to determine the exact number of Jews who reached the forests and found some protection there from the Germans, even for a brief time. The large majority met death, sooner or later, during the frequent hunts. Many others died of hunger, cold, or disease in their hiding places in the forests.

Various groups of fugitive Jews tried to organize armed partisan units in different ways, in order to secure protection for families in hiding. These forests were not completely empty, as were most others in Poland. By the autumn of 1941, small groups of Soviet soldiers who had escaped from prisoner-of-war camps were already hiding here. In the forests of Parczew and Wlodawa, the fugitive Soviet soldiers received some help from the local Orthodox population. In contrast with the Polish Catholic majority, the Ukrainian Orthodox minority here showed a great degree of sympathy for the Red Army soldiers. They also gave them arms that they had hidden after the large battles between the armies of Poland and Germany, that took place during the second half of September 1939. This area was one of the last strongholds of the Polish army. The Poles in the regiments of the "Polesie" corps under the command of General Franciszek Kleeberg did not lay down their arms until the end of September 1939. After the surrender of these units, the peasants collected a sizable quantity of abandoned arms and hid them. Most of these arms later reached the hands of the partisans.

Most of the Russian fugitive prisoners-of-war did not remain for long in the forests of Parczew, which they viewed as a steppingstone eastward to the area of Polesie, where fairly large Soviet units were already operating. A few small groups, however, did establish a permanent base in the forests of Parczew. These were united in the spring of 1942 by a Soviet officer, Lieutenant Fiodor Kovalov, who had also escaped from captivity and whose partisan name was Teodor Albrecht. Other groups operated independently for a long time, and sometimes united with Jewish groups.[2] In July 1942, Jozef Balcerzak, a representative of the Polish Workers' Party, suggested to Kovalov that he join the People's Guard and continue the struggle against the Germans under its banner. Kovalov accepted this offer, and from then on his unit belonged, at least officially, to the People's Guard.[3]

Even before the deportations to the death camps, local Jews were in contact with Kovalov and helped the Soviet partisans. Haim Pszeplikier from Parczew, for example, bought arms from the local peasants for the Soviet partisans, and supplied them with various essential goods.

Jews who fled to the forests also eventually met up with Kovalov's partisans. The Russians, however, did not welcome Jewish refugees in the forests. These fugitives attracted hunts by the Germans, and these constituted the greatest fear for the partisans in the forest. But the Russians could not stand up to the stream of fugitives, and so, against his will, Kovalov was forced to deal with them.

Kovalov himself did not show any hatred for the Jews. He accepted a large group of Jewish youths into his unit, probably through the intervention of Pszeplikier, and a Jewish group called Pushkin's Group, was formed within the framework of the Russian's unit. A soldier known as Olek, who had participated in the war in September 1939, was made commander of the group. Olek had been taken prisoner after the defeat of the Polish army and had spent time in a Jewish POW camp on Lipowa Street in Lublin. At the end of 1939, the Germans took a few hundred Jews out of the camp and marched them along the Parczew-Miedzyrzec road. Most of the prisoners died on this march, either of the cold or by shooting. Parczew was a stopping point on this tragic march. When the prisoners were locked up at night there in the local synagogue, the Jews of Parczew managed secretly to smuggle a few dozen Jews out of the synagogue, and thus save them from death. Olek was among those saved. At the time of the deportation from Parczew in 1942, he organized a large group of escapees and reached the Parczew forests with them.[4]

As was mentioned above, the relationship between the Russians and the Jewish partisans in Kovalov's unit was generally fair. But this was not so for the unarmed fugitives hiding in the forests. Although Kovalov himself showed good will also toward these nonfighting Jews, the discipline in his unit was weak, and he did not always manage to impose his authority on his partisans. It can also be assumed that at this time, groups of runaway Soviet prisoners-of-war who did not join Kovalov's unit were wandering in the forests of Parczew. In any case, the Jewish refugees suffered greatly from the assaults and cruelty of various Russian groups.

The Jews who escaped to the forests brought with them small quantities of money and jewels, all that they had left after three years of systematic robbery by the Germans. They also brought with them the remainder of their goods—clothes, linens, and so forth—in hope of exchanging them for food from the local peasants in order to survive the coming winter. The younger ones hoped to acquire arms with the small sums of money they had. The Russians quickly learned to rob the unarmed Jews of their meager possessions. These assaults on the Jews, who had prepared bunkers for themselves in the forest, became more and more frequent. In addition, the Jews were subject frequently to acts of fraud. Knowing that what the Jews most wanted were arms, the Russians promised to supply them. Deceptively, they took money from the Jews and then disappeared.

Worse than savage assaults and malicious fraud was the plague of rape upon Jewish women. Former prisoners-of-war attacked Jewish bunkers in armed groups in order to take defenseless Jewish women. Zipora Koren, who survived in the forests of Parczew, tells how Russian partisans bound an old woman, tied her to a tree, and tortured her, because she refused to reveal the hiding place of her daughter whom they planned to rape. This was not an isolated incident but a widespread phenomenon in the forests of Parczew in the autumn of 1942 that sometimes led to tragic incidents between the Jewish partisans and the Russians.[5] Anshel Krechman, mentioned above, described the murder of a Jewish woman, Sarah from Parczew, by a Russian partisan, Alyosha Vasilevich, when she resisted his attempt to rape her. This murder was avenged by a Jewish partisan who killed Vasilevich.

There were also many incidents of arms theft from small Jewish groups who were just beginning to organize into armed units. In mixed Jewish-Russian groups, there were quite a few cases when, after a short period of joint fighting, the Russian partisans murdered their Jewish comrades-in-arms just to steal their weapons.

The Jews, who expected to find some peace in the forest, soon learned that, in addition to the tortures of hunger, cold, and the hunts of the German gendarmerie, other dangers awaited them at every turn there, also. This evoked hatred and fear of the forest, and many decided to leave and move to the Wlodawa Ghetto where, after a few months, deportations to the Sobibor death camp caught up with them.

Under these intensely difficult conditions, unknown by any other partisan movement, a few Jewish groups, in addition to the "Pushkin's Group," managed to acquire some arms and organize themselves into armed units. Most were destroyed during the first German hunts, but some held out for a longer period of time and even gained in strength. Among these were the groups of Lichtenberg and Knopfmacher.

Moshe Lichtenberg's group was established in Wlodawa, in October 1942, and soon numbered a few dozen people. The group established its base near the Adampol.[6]

Nachum Knopfmacher's group, which numbered fifteen people, organized and established its base (bunkers) at about the same time. This group was formed in the forced labor camp in Adampol. Members of the group managed to slip away at night from the camp and reach the forest. Their first weapon was a false gun, a homemade, wooden dummy. With this "weapon," they conducted a few confiscation raids for the purpose of acquiring money to buy arms from the local peasants. The first two weapons were bought from a peasant in the village of Kolacz. Their arms supply quickly grew to five rifles, a sizable quantity in the first stage of the partisan movement.

Despite this, and although bunkers were already prepared in the forest, Knopfmacher delayed the group's escape to the forest. They did not want to abandon the camp's other inmates, who included relatives of the group's members. However, a planned mass escape from the camp encountered difficulties, and having little choice, the group's members eventually had to escape to the forest alone. Yet, they did not give up their attempts to get other inmates out of the camp.

When these two Jewish groups—Knopfmacher's and Lichtenberg's—met in the forest, it was soon apparent that the two commanders had different opinions about the goal a Jewish partisan unit should strive for. Lichtenberg intended to begin immediate attacks against the Germans. Knopfmacher believed that one must worry, first of all, about getting Jewish inmates out of the work camps and out of the Wlodowa Ghetto. "It is more important to save our families than to kill Germans," Knopfmacher claimed. In contrast, Lichtenberg did not see any way whatsoever of freeing Jews who already were in the Wlodawa Ghetto or in the work camps. He, therefore, supported the beginning of retaliatory operations against the Germans. Being commander of the larger group, Lichtenberg wanted to impose his will on Knopfmacher's unit. The conflict between the two commanders grew larger and sharper.

According to Knopfmacher's testimony, Lichtenberg's men stole two rifles one night from the Knopfmacher group's bunker. This incident intensified the conflict and led to a tragic event. When the two commanders were meeting for a discussion in one of the Knopfmacher unit's bunkers, three partisans from Lichtenberg's group approached a second bunker where some arms were hidden. The guard, Baruch Schneidman, called out to them to stop. When one of the men, Haim Indel, did not hear the guard's call, Schneidman shot and killed him. This unprecedented tragic occurrence, of a Jew being killed at the hands of a Jewish partisan, left a general mood of depression behind. The two groups understood that the conflict must be eliminated. Knopfmacher agreed to join Lichtenberg's group but, nevertheless, did not give up additional attempts to get inmates out of Adampol.[7]

Shortly after this event, eighty Adampol inmates succeeded in escaping. But the runaways and the partisans who helped them encountered a strong German unit, and all of the fugitives and a few of the partisans were killed.

In November 1942, the Germans directed a series of large-scale hunts against the partisans and the refugees in the Parczew forests. Before, the Germans had made do with reconnaissance patrols or smaller *Ordnungspolizei* units. This time, German units the size of companies and battalions were sent to the Parczew forests. The first hunt took place in the middle of November. It is estimated that hundreds of Jews in hiding lost their lives. The German police units also succeeded in surrounding Kovalov's unit. The Russian partisans suffered grave losses, and the unit disintegrated. It was only two weeks after that, that Kovalov managed to gather the remnants of his unit and renew its operations. Somewhat better was the lot of Lichtenberg's unit, which continued to exist after the German hunt.[8]

The second hunt was held from December 6 to December 9, 1942. A German force numbering about 1,000 men—a company of *Wehr-*

macht infantry, *Ordnungspolizei* units, and a Ukrainian unit from the training camp in Trawniki—were used for this hunt. The Nazi forces were equipped with automatic weapons, machine guns, four small cannons, and armored vehicles.[9] Hundreds of hiding Jews died in this campaign, which Arieh Koren describes thus:

> We fled round and round in terror. We thought we had run twenty kilometers, but actually we circled an area of a half kilometer. There were many Jews in the forest then, maybe a thousand. Their behavior was not calm. They shouted, made fires, and when the hunt began, lost control and ran like a herd of rabbits from a hunter straight into the hands of the Germans. They died easily, and lost one another; afterwards children without parents, husband without wives, and vice versa wandered about the forest.[10]

Kovalov's unit was not seriously hit in this hunt. After the losses in the previous hunt, Kovalov had reorganized his unit. "Pushkin's Group" also survived. But the number of fighters in the Jewish unit had dropped from about one hundred to forty-five. Kovalov managed to surprise the Germans and to create confusion in the ranks of two of their units, which started to shoot at one another, each one believing it was shooting at the partisans. According to Polish sources, the German losses totaled thirteen dead and ten wounded. Of Kovalov's partisans, more than ten were dead. The losses of the Jewish group during this hunt are not known.

After the second hunt, Kovalov reached the conclusion that the hiding Jews greatly endangered his unit because it was they who brought about the German's attacks, so he tried to expel the Jews from the forests. But the Jews had nowhere to go, and Kovalov's attempt failed. The Jews who remained alive after the hunt continued to hold on to the forest.

The quiet that prevailed after December 9 was very short-lived. On December 24, the Germans opened a large-scale hunt, which came as a complete surprise to the Jews in hiding. None of them expected a renewal of the hunts at Christmas. The hunt went on for several days, during which the Germans slaughtered a few hundred more Jewish refugees.[11]

After the third hunt, Kovalov and his unit retreated to the forests near Wlodawa. The tie with the leadership of the Polish Workers Party (PPR) was cut off for a long time. Lichtenberg's unit (which had already been joined by Knopfmacher's group) also moved eastward to the forests near Wlodawa. Only the unarmed Jewish population, whose number dropped to 2,000 after the hunts, remained in the forests of Parczew. Most of these Jews managed to prepare bunkers for the coming winter, but could not acquire a sufficient supply of food. The mass of refugees still alive faced very difficult weeks. Any attempt to leave the bunkers for food involved the risk of revealing the hideout, and footprints left in the snow helped the Germans in their search. The Germans stationed powerful patrols all around the area surrounding the forest, and under these conditions, many refugees died of starvation and cold.

January passed without any large operation, but in February the Germans renewed their pursuit, employing a new method. The Germans had probably reached the conclusion that a hunt lasting only a few days did not bring the necessary results, even if large forces were used. Despite the large-scale hunts, they had not managed to destroy the partisans and find all the fugitives in their hideouts. They, therefore, used a different strategy based on a continuing operation of some 1,000 policemen in the forest. The Germans left the forest only at night, and returned at dawn in order to systematically clear additional areas. It is difficult to determine how many Jews died during the operations of February 1943.[12]

At the end of 1942, an organized Jewish group fled from the little town of Sosnowica. It was headed by Yechiel Greenshpan, a man who was destined to play a leading role in the partisan movement of this area. Greenshpan was then about 24 years old, a simple, uneducated man. After his arrival in the forest, he showed an unusual capacity for organization and earned the reputation of a talented and wise partisan commander. In its first days, his group's weapons consisted of two rifles and one pistol. One month later, the group found the remains of weapons hidden after the battles of September 1939. Although the hideout was near a German police post, the group managed to get hold of seven rifles, ammunition, and a small number of grenades.[13]

Yechiel Greenshpan came from a family of horse traders. This fact was not without importance for the continuation of his partisan activity. The members of the family, because of their trade, knew the area well and had ties with many of the local peasants. This helped them to a great extent in the acquisition of arms and in the establishment of a partisan base in the forest.[14]

In January 1943, Greenshpan's unit already numbered fifty persons. The unit saw its main duty as the protection of Jews in hiding. The presence of the unit and its continuing development decisively improved the situation of unarmed Jews hiding in the forest. Greenshpan's partisans helped them as much as they could by supplying food and by warning them of approaching German patrols. There was also an improvement in relations with various groups of runaway Soviet prisoners-of-war, who again appeared in the forests of Parczew. Assaults on Jewish family bunkers ceased, and there were no further incidents of rape of Jewish women. For the first time, the hiding Jews attained some measure of protection.[15]

Most of the Jews, who until March 1943 had hidden in different places in the forest, now gathered in the central part of the forest in an area called Altana. This concentration made additional improvement of the conditions of hiding Jews possible: it was now easier for Greenshpan's unit to protect the unarmed Jewish families and to supply them with food. It can be assumed that at that time nearly 1,000 Jews were gathered in Altana. They carried out various services for the partisans in Greenshpan's unit, such as tailoring and shoemaking, and in time, these services were extended to other partisan units who became active in this area. The situation of the Jews who had moved to Altana continued to be difficult, but it was certainly much better than that of families hiding on their own. Zipora Koren recalls her impressions upon her arrival in Altana:

> For a certain period of time we were alone in the forest. Our situation was very bad, and then a cousin of ours decided to join the other Jews. We looked for them for an entire day, and then, following a sound, we found a large camp. There were about a thousand Jews there. When we got there, our eyes opened wide with relief. Our Jews were leading an ordered life, kneading dough, cooking and baking just like at home. We had lived the whole time on bread and water, and so it seemed to us that we had arrived in Paradise.[16]

This description is somewhat exaggerated. Of course, there were relatively "good" days, when it was possible to secure a larger quantity of food for the refugee camp in Altana, so that all could eat their fill. But usually, there was not enough food, and the Jews of Altana went hungry. In spite of this, they felt they were safer here than in any other place in the forest.

Yechiel Greenshpan strove to enlarge his unit and planned the escape of Jews interned in forced labor camps. An operation on a farm in the village of Jablonia was such an attempt. There was a relatively small, forced labor camp for Jews near the farm. Aside from the German camp guard, there was a *Wehrmacht* squad stationed in the camp. These were not, therefore, very large forces. Greenshpan decided to destroy the camp and free the Jews held there. His entire unit took part in this operation; however, the unit did not succeed in

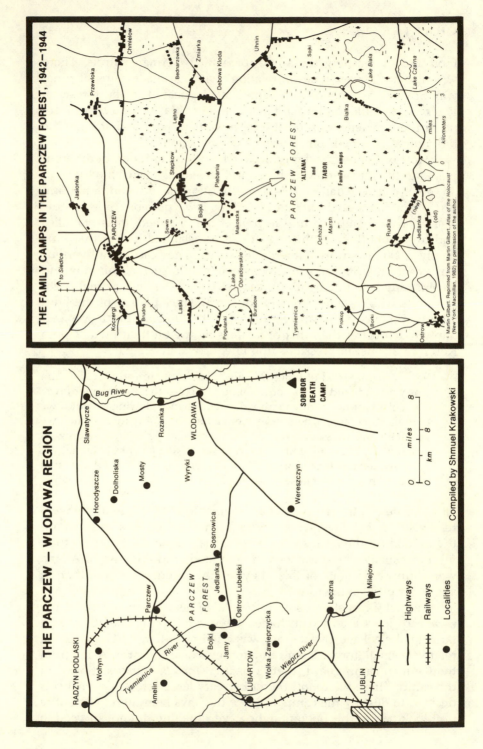

THE FAMILY CAMPS IN THE PARCZEW FOREST, 1942–1944

to Siedlce

Chmielow
Przewloka
Bednarzowka
Zmiarka
Debowa Kloda
Uhnin
Solki
Lake Biala
Lake Czarna
Jasionka
Letno
Stepkow
PARCZEW
Bialka
Plebania
Sowin
Bojki
PARCZEW FOREST
Koczergi
Brudno
Makoszka
'ALTANA'
and
TABOR
Family Camps
Laski
Lake
Obradowskie
Ochoza
Marsh
Rudka
Jedlanka (new)
(old)
Pogulanki
Buradow
Tysmienica
Prokop
Borki
Ostrow

miles
kilometers
0   1   2   3

© Martin Gilbert. Reprinted from Martin Gilbert, Atlas of the Holocaust
(New York: Macmillan, 1982) by permission of the author

THE PARCZEW — WLODAWA REGION

Bug River
Slawatycze
Rozanka
WLODAWA
SOBIBOR
DEATH
CAMP
Horodyszcze
Dolholiska
Mosty
Wyryki
Wereszczyn
RADZYN PODLASKI
Wohyn
Parczew
PARCZEW
FOREST
Sosnowica
Jedlanka
Ostrow Lubelski
Bojki
Jamy
Wolka Zawieprzycka
Leczna
Milejow
Tysmienica River
Amelin
LUBARTOW
Wieprz River
LUBLIN

miles
0   8
km
0   8

Compiled by Shmuel Krakowski

Highways
Railways
Localities

surprising the Germans who had reinforced their units around the camp and at the farm. After a battle that lasted several hours, the partisans took several Germans captive and killed a number of others. But the camp was not captured. In the meanwhile, a large German unit came to the aid of the besieged Germans on the farm. As a result, the partisans were forced to retreat to the forest before it was too late. It is almost certain that the Germans immediately liquidated the camp in Jablonia.[17]

Greenshpan's attempt to join with Lichtenberg's group was also unsuccessful. In spite of the recurring hunts, including the extended hunt in February, the number of men in the two units grew. Lichtenberg's unit was joined by a group of seventeen Jews who fled the Wlodawa ghetto under the command of Leon Lemberger-Lukowski. It is almost certain that Greenshpan and Lichtenberg met at the beginning of March 1943 in the vicinity of the village of Ochoza. Greenshpan suggested to Lichtenberg the unification of the two units, knowing that a joint unit could constitute a highly important partisan force. Lichtenberg and his men had to decide between Greenshpan's offer and a plan which they had formed beforehand to try to cross the *General Gouvernement* border in the beginning of spring, cross the Bug River, and reach Polesie, where large units of Soviet partisans were operating.

At about this time, Kovalov's unit returned to the forests of Parczew. New partisans had joined the unit—Russians, Poles, Jews, and Ossetians, which enabled Kovalov to reorganize his unit, dividing it into four groups according to nationality. The concentration of partisan forces in the Parczew forests was then, therefore, the largest in the GG at this time.

Meanwhile, because of unexpected circumstances, Lichtenberg's unit left the forests of Parczew. And similarly unexpectedly, a group of Russians fleeing from a prison camp reached Lichtenberg's new base. Their commander was an officer named Kolka whom Lichtenberg's partisans received with open arms. Kolka also had a plan for crossing the Bug River and reaching the forests of Polesie and suggested the establishment of a Russian-Jewish unit under his command. This plan suited Lichtenberg's aspirations.[18]

Kolka also contacted Greenshpan, but the latter refused to give up the independence of the Jewish unit. Lichtenberg thought differently. He did not believe that it was possible to continue activities in the Parczew forests, and was convinced that the conditions across the Bug were much better. It was true that the situation in the forests of Parczew was difficult. The pressure from the German *Ordnungspolizei* and the German army was growing greater and greater. In addition, armed groups belonging to the Home Army that were formed in several villages began to appear in this area. These groups assaulted both the Jews and the fugitive Soviet prisoners. In view of these circumstances, Lichtenberg gave up the plan to unite with Greenshpan's unit and joined Kolka. The number of people in the joint unit grew to several hundred, but only some were armed. According to Knopfmacher, this unit numbered 120 persons, Jews and Russians, only thirty of whom had weapons.[19]

The newly organized Jewish-Russian unit set out for the east and after three days of walking, reached the vicinity of the village of Kaplonosy near the Bug, where they had to find a place where the water was shallow and where there was no strong German watch. Kolka chose fifteen men, mainly Russians, to search the area and took the best arms with him. When the night passed and Kolka did not return, Lichtenberg sent out another search party to find out what had happened to the Russian commander and his own men who had accompanied Kolka. The party returned with the news that a German border guard patrol was approaching. When it became clear that the patrol numbered only four men, Lichtenberg ordered an attack. The German patrol was easily wiped out, but the sound of the shooting alerted a German company that was encamped near the village of Dubica. The partisans were forced to cross the river in haste, some in boats they had confiscated and others by swimming. In spite of their fears, the partisans were not attacked by the Germans, who probably did not want to enter a battle against an enemy whose strength they did not know. In this way, Lichtenberg's partisans quickly reached the east bank of the Bug River beyond the border of the *General Gouvernment*.[20]

The Jewish partisans soon met Soviet partisans from the Voroshilov unit near the village of Mesna in the vicinity of the town of Domachevo. The group's commander welcomed the Jews very heartily. The road to the zone of Soviet partisan activity was, therefore, open. Yet the Jewish unit's best weapons remained on the west bank of the Bug in the hands of Kolka's group. Lichtenberg did not know what had happened to Kolka and his men, but it was clear to him that the situation of the Jews would be much safer if they appeared at the Soviet partisan base with all of their men armed with better weapons.

Because of this, Lichtenberg decided not to continue eastward until he knew what had happened to Kolka and his group; instead, he returned to the west bank of the Bug River, taking seven men with him. Lichtenberg learned Kolka's whereabouts from local peasants.

However, he did not learn that Kolka had never intended to search for a place where the river's water was shallow, but had devised this plan only so that he could rob the Jewish partisans of their weapons. When they got far away from the main body of Lichtenberg's group, Kolka ordered his men to seize a barn for rest. Then, when the Jewish partisans in Kolka's search patrol fell asleep, the Russians stole their weapons and ran away to the nearby village of Lachowicze. After the Jews awoke and realized that they had been betrayed, they had no choice but to return to the Parczew forests, where they later joined Greenshpan's unit.

When Lichtenberg and his search party found Kolka in Lachowicze, Kolka and his men opened fire against them with machine guns. Moshe Lichtenberg, Mordechai Rosenberg, and Haim Fischman were killed. The five Jewish partisans who survived managed to escape. They crossed the Bug to the east and returned to their unit, where they reported Kolka's treacherous deed and Lichtenberg's death.

After Lichtenberg's death, Leon Nemtzer was made the new commander. He led the unit to the village of Wielkoryty, where they met with Soviet partisans from the Molotov brigade. The Soviet partisans demanded that the Jews return to their former zone of activity. They felt that each unit must operate in the area its people came from. Only after long negotiations and many efforts by Nemtzer did the brigade commander agree to accept the Jews into the Soviet partisan movement. He agreed to take them in not as a unit, but on the condition that the unit disperse and that the Jewish partisans be divided among the various Soviet units.[21]

After a year and a half of battling in the forest, most of the partisans from the former Lichtenberg unit joined the Red Army and continued their struggle against the Germans on different fronts. A few, such as Leon Lemberger-Lukowski and Joseph Shenenbaum, even fought on the faraway Finnish front. After the battles in Finland, Lemberger-Lukowski was attached to the sixth division of the Polish army, where he completed an officer's course, and as an officer participated in the battles of Warsaw, Kolobrzeg, and finally Dresden, where he was seriously wounded and had to have his leg amputated.[22]

In the spring of 1943, the partisans of Greenshpan's and Kovalov's units increased their operations in the forests of Parczew. The Germans retaliated with a new campaign against the partisans—"*Unternehmen Ostersegen*," which called for a special concentration of forces. Numbering 1,630 men, it was composed of four groups of the

Ordnungspolizei taken out of the 25th and 32nd regiments and the 3rd and 203rd battalions of this force and was commanded by Major Trapf.[23]

The operation began on Easter 1943, and again surprised the partisans and the refugees who did not think, as they had not thought four months previously, that the Germans would hold a campaign on a Christian holiday. Kovalov's unit suffered heavy losses and was disintegrated. The Jewish "Pushkin's Group" also suffered losses.[24]

The Germans also captured Altana, where the Jewish refugees were hiding. Several hundred Jews, who did not manage to escape from Altana and hide in other sections of the forest, were killed during this campaign. Others had to contend with a huge fire that broke out in the forest and lasted several days. Most tragic was the lot of the wounded. Those found by the Germans were slaughtered with great cruelty, others died in great pain with no help whatsoever at their side.[25]

In spite of the unexpectedness of this hunt, Greenshpan succeeded in pulling his unit out of the area of danger without suffering losses. In spite of the dangers, several hundred hiding Jews were also saved. After the end of the hunt and the retreat of the Germans from the forest, Greenshpan reorganized the refugee camp and renewed his partisan activities. Kovalov also reorganized his unit.[26]

After the massive Easter hunt, the lives of the surviving partisans and refugees returned to relative calm. It was then that representatives of the People's Guard command came to the forest. These were the local communist activist Jan Holod (known as Kirpiczny) and a representative from Warsaw, Kazimierz Sidor. They renewed the ties with Kovalov's unit and examined the possibility for increasing partisan activities in the area. This was in accordance with the basic policy of the Polish Workers Party (PPR), whose aim was to intensify underground actions as much as possible. Holod and Sidor contacted Greenshpan and suggested that his unit join the People's Guard and continue its activity as a Jewish unit in the framework of this fighting organization. Greenshpan and his partisans willingly accepted the offer. The Jewish unit was officially called "People's Guard Unit–Chil." The unit was so called after the name of its commander Yechiel (Chil) Greenshpan.

The PPR representatives saw additional possibilities for strengthening the People's Guard in the Parczew forests through the recruitment of refugees able to bear arms. As Kazimierz Sidor writes in his memoirs: "Although many young Jews had already fought in the ranks of the People's Guard, we did not have strong ties with the civilian refugees."[27] And yet, this contact eased Greenshpan's way in joining the People's Guard. When Holod and Sidor went to the refugee camp in Altana to speak for the partisan movement of the Polish Workers Party, representatives of Greenshpan's unit and of "Pushkin's Group" from Kovalov's unit went with them. A meeting was held at which Baruch Elbaum appeared as the main speaker for the People's Guard. In a short while, about 100 persons were recruited for Yechiel Greenshpan's unit. Sidor writes about this recruitment:

> The party gave Holod the task of dealing with the refugees. After several weeks of labor, Holod organized five platoons consisting solely of Jewish volunteers. At their head we placed experienced commanders from the People's Guard who had already distinguished themselves in partisan battles: Max, Katz and others. . . . Following this mission all the men able to fight were transferred to our battle units, and only old people, women and children remained in the camps under protection of their *Soltys* (village head). The *Soltys* had good connections in the surrounding area, and during the hunts would send the civilian population to hideouts determined by us. He performed his task well and never panicked.[28]

The role of *Soltys* was taken on by Hirsh Rubinstein, who had a group of twelve people appointed by Greenshpan to assist him. The tasks of this group were to ensure steady protection for the refugees from sudden attacks and to secure the supply of food.

A new base for the battle platoons was set up in the eastern part of the forest in the area of Bialka Jezioro near the village of Bialka. Until the fall of 1943 no other People's Guard unit was established in the forests of Parczew, and the Jewish unit remained the main partisan force of the Polish Workers Party in this area.

With the Jewish unit among the ranks of the People's Guard, the acquisition of additional arms became easier, and armed activities were increased. The unit's first operations after joining the People's Guard were an attack on the village of Widlanka and, later, a battle near Bialka. Attacking an agricultural farm in the village of Widlanka where a squad of *Wehrmacht* soldiers was encamped, Greenshpan's partisans confiscated enough cattle to supply meat to the battle units and the refugees, who by now had returned to Altana. The noise of this battle, however, alerted a large German unit stationed nearby, which succeeded in blocking the road back to Greenshpan's unit. Barely resisting the pressure put on them by the German unit, the partisans were forced to retreat in the direction of Ochoza. But that night the unit managed to break through the blockade, get to the forest, and shake off the enemy's chase. This was the unit's biggest clash with a German force thus far.[29]

The fact that the unit joined the People's Guard greatly strengthened and improved its operations, but it did not, as was expected, bring about an improvement in the lot of the nonfighting refugees. The partisans frequently operated in faraway areas, wandering across long distances and usually eating in villages they passed through or rested in. The problem of food for the refugees was much more complex. Very often, especially when the partisan unit was active outside the forest, the supply of food was stopped, and the refugees suffered greatly from hunger and from a lack of medical supplies. Kazimierz Sidor writes as follows of the refugees' situation:

> We did not succeed in organizing a steady food supply to the Jewish camps. These civilians received food, but not on a regular basis. The fourth year of the war weighed heavily on the village, and it could not feed a large number of outsiders. The fugitives suffered from hunger and a lack of medicines, soap, and clothing. Malignant itch [scabies] covered the bodies of most of those living in the camps. When we first noticed the signs of this disease on one of our inspections, we were convinced that some type of venereal disease was destroying the bodies of these poor people, and we ordered treatment by Salvarsan. A person who knew the itch from the time of the battles in Spain corrected my mistake.[30]

In the summer of 1943, the Germans increased the number of their forces in the area surrounding the Parczew forests. The partisans encountered greater and greater difficulties. Mikolaj Demko, GL commander in the district of Lublin known by his nickname of Mieczyslaw Moczar, described the state of the partisans at this time in a report sent to the GL headquarters in June 1943: "The Germans are moving about the area in so many groups that one cannot dream of defeating them. The same goes for their arms storehouses and other military installations, near which are garrisoned forces which dispose such great fire power, that we without ammunition supply cannot contest them."[31]

During that summer the Germans also held consecutive hunts that particularly hit the refugees, who were forced, again and again, to abandon Altana in a hurry and find new hideouts. And at the end of June a large-scale hunt called *Unternehmen Nachpfinsten* was directed against the partisans. As was the case in previous hunts, units from the 25th Regiment and 203rd Battalion of the *Ordnungspolizei* took part in this campaign. In July, several smaller hunts were held, but since these brought no substantial results to the Germans, another large-scale campaign, employing the same forces as the one in June, was directed against the partisans between August 29 and 31, 1943. This operation was not successful, either. The Jews hiding in the forests of Parczew were experienced by then and knew how to act during a hunt. The number of victims of these consecutive hunts was greatly diminished. Half a year previously hundreds of refugees had died in each German operation in the Parczew forests; that summer, the number of victims was down to a few dozen, if not less. The report of the Parczew police inspector on the August hunt mentions fifteen Jews killed.[32]

The Germans, however, were no longer the only foe of the Jews in hiding and fighting in the Parczew forests. In the middle of 1943, there was a substantial increase in the number of Home Army (AK) activities. The first assault by these AK groups, which were organized in many villages near Parczew and Wlodawa, was an attack on Jews and Soviet prisoners and took place as early as the end of 1942. During the winter of 1942–43, there had also been several clashes between groups belonging to the Home Army and Kovalov's unit. But after these clashes, talks were held between Kovalov and representatives of the AK and an agreement was reached to end the mutual attacks. In order not to anger the AK representatives, Kovalov denied, during these talks, that there was any contact whatsoever between his unit and the People's Guard or the Jews. According to the report of an AK officer who took part in the talks with Kovalov in January 1943, "The Russian unit's commander particularly denounced the Jews, of whom there are none in his unit, and whom he does not want. There are also no Poles in his unit. He spoke about the PPR with scorn. . . ."[33]

In June 1943, after a few calm months during which their agreement with Kovalov was upheld, the Home Army renewed its assault on groups of the People's Guard, particularly when these were outside the forest in the surrounding villages. The AK groups also began to penetrate the forest, harassed units of the People's Guard, and frequently murdered lone partisans. In his June 1943 report, Moczar (Mikolaj Demko) wrote: "Our units are now forced to fight on two fronts. The underground leadership [the AK command] is organizing units whose role it is to wipe out the 'communist gangs, prisoners of war, and the Jews.' They openly admit to having this role, which is the basis of their orders. They are fully armed and walk about almostly overtly. The Germans do not touch them, and they also do not attack the Germans."[34]

Among the sources from which we learn the seriousness of the clashes between the AK groups and the Jewish partisans during this time is the testimony of Eliahu Liberman, a partisan from Greenshpan's unit:

> In the Parczew forests, in Makoszka, there were also groups belonging to the AK. When they met a lone Jew they killed him. But when they met a Jewish group or unit in the forest, in a village during an operation, or during a food-confiscating raid, they refrained from entering into battle. They were afraid to provoke us. They knew that any time they tried to take away our weapons, we would fire. Yet more than one of our Jewish partisans was killed at the hands of the AK. It is hard to remember all the incidents of killing by the AK. I also don't recall the number of times and all the ways we encountered the AK units and entered into battle with them. One time three of our partisans went out on a patrol. These were Aharon Kot from Jezychow, Reuven Turbiner from Sosnowica, and Moshe (I don't recall his last name) from Kudeniec. A long time passed and they did not return. Chil (Yechiel) ordered a group of partisans to search for them. I was there with another twenty to twenty-five partisans. We wandered about for many days until we found their traces. We found the bodies of the three Jewish partisans behind a barn in the village of Glebokie. The Polish peasants told us about them. The three were captured in this village by the AK. They told us the AK killed them. We went to look for these AK men. If they killed the three Jewish partisans immediately or later—I cannot say. One time we met a large AK group. There were twenty or thirty of them, and they wanted to kill us. They opened with heavy fire on us. They were shooting our way for a long time. We lay down. Afterwards we surrounded them and captured them. . . . Such were the battles we were forced to enter into with the AK units because they provoked us. There were many killed on our side, especially when the AK succeeded in capturing Jews who were alone. But many of them also died because we did not give in."[35]

Kovalov's unit, during the summer of 1943, grew when a few dozen Poles from nearby villages joined it and changed leadership. In July 1943, Kovalov left the Parczew forests and headed eastward across the Bug to join the Soviet partisan movement. His place was taken by Jan Dadun, known as "Janusz," a Pole who was a local forest watchman and a sergeant in the Polish army. And once again, this unit became a target for AK attacks.

At the end of 1943, when Dadun was outside the base in the forest with a group of seven partisans, he was attacked by an AK unit under the command of Lieutenant Konstanty Witwicki, known as "Miller." The Home Army then did not have even one regular partisan unit in this area. But there were sabotage groups belonging to the Home Army whose members gathered for sporadic operations and later returned to their homes. These were the groups that were instructed to implement Order Number 116 to liquidate the Jews and members of the People's Army. It was one of these groups that attacked Dadun's group and killed all of the People's Guard's partisans. Only one Jewish partisan, known as Zelazny, (The Iron,) survived.[36]

During the crises that came with the increase in German forces and the intensification of AK operations in the Parczew forests, the partisans received valuable assistance from Soviet units operating in Polesie. Sent from the forests of Parczew to bring arms and equipment from the east, the first envoys from Greenshpan's units crossed the Bug in August 1943 and came into contact with a Soviet unit under the command of Zachar Filimonovich Poplavski. Here the Jewish partisans received arms, ammunition, explosives, and other equipment for the sabotage of trains. One of Greenshpan's men, Romkowski, stayed with the Soviet unit and took part in a course in sabotage. When he returned to the Parczew forests, he was made an instructor and trained other partisans in the sabotage of communication lines.[37]

At this time the GL command in the district of Lublin was organizing the reception of the first consignment of arms to be parachuted in from the Soviet Union. The exact quantities of arms that were obtained in this way are not known. It is only known that these were relatively large quantities. These arms, along with those brought in directly from Polesie, gave the partisans a firm stand against the pressure of the German police and the AK units in addition to the important sabotage actions against nearby railroads they were already capable of.

At the beginning of August 1943, Greenshpan's unit opened large-scale combat operations north of Wlodawa. They burned a tar factory outside this city that served the Germans and destroyed all its installations and stock. Afterwards, the unit destroyed two bridges on the Parczew-Wisznica road.[38]

The very meager documentation of the People's Guard that was preserved makes it possible to identify only some of the many train sabotage operations that were carried out by Yechiel Greenshpan's unit. Early on October 16, 1943, the unit operated on the Parczew-Milanow line, derailing an army train; on October 19, the unit carried out a major sabotage of the Parczew-Grodek line. According to various Polish sources, the Germans suffered heavy losses as a result of these operations. Early on October 22, the Jewish partisans ran a train on the Parczew-Milanow line off the track. This train carried the Waffen SS unit no. 99679. As a result of this operation, there was a forty-hour stop in train communication on the Lublin-Lukow line. We have no details on the actions of the Jewish unit during the following few months. It is only known that beginning in October 1943, the partisan operations against the German lines of communication in the area around Parczew forests continued at an accelerated rate.[39]

After the rebellion in the Sobibor death camp on October 14, 1943, many of the participants tried to reach the area of partisan operations. At least twelve of them succeeded in reaching Greenshpan's unit after great hardship. They had to escape pursuit by a German army unit (an air force ground service unit was the first to go after the rebels), pursuit by German police units, and pursuit by various nationalist groups belonging to the Polish underground.

In his testimony, Mordechai Goldfarb recounts the journey of a group of eight men and one woman. This group managed to reach a forest near the village of Hola after shaking the Germans. In the forest they met four Soviet Georgians who had escaped from the prison in Radom and joined them in their search for the partisans. In one village they met a group of sixteen Poles led by two brothers named Piatek, who introduced themselves as partisans. The Jews and the Georgians were convinced that they had found a partisan unit. But the Piatek brothers and their group had devised a plan. At night the Poles attacked their guests, killing six Jews (including the only woman in the group) and three of the Georgians. Only three Jews (Goldfarb, Lerner, and Boris) and one Georgian escaped. After wandering about for several days they found out from a peasant about the existence of a Jewish partisan unit. Following the peasant's instructions, they found Greenshpan's partisans and were accepted into the unit.[40]

Among others who made their way into the Jewish partisan unit was also Joseph Cynowiec, a former soldier who had fought in the war in September 1939, and who later escaped from the prisoner-of-war camp on Lipowa Street in Lublin. A short time after his arrival, Cynowiec was made chief of staff of Greenshpan's unit and put in charge of administrative affairs and the planning of combat operations.[41]

At the beginning of 1944, strong partisan units that had arrived from the eastern side of the Bug began to concentrate in the Parczew forests. The first of these was a rather small unit, commanded by Leon Kasman, a Jew known as Janowski, and was called the Janowski unit. This unit came to the Parczew forests in January 1944. It numbered about fifty people, mostly Poles from Polesie. In addition to the commander, other known Jews in the unit included Leon Bielski and Wanda (Ruth) Michalska.

Janowski's was a special unit, not under the command of the People's Army (which until the beginning of 1944, had appeared under the name of the People's Guard). The main role of the unit was the reception of arms dropped in from the Soviet Union. Greenshpan's unit also received some of these arms.[42]

Together with the Janowski unit, a second, smaller partisan unit came from across the Bug. Its commander was Lieutenant Aleksander Skotnicki, a Jew who was destined to play one of the most important roles in the partisan movement in the Parczew forests during the next months. Aleksander Skotnicki took part in the war in 1939 and was an officer in the 14th cavalry regiment (the Ulans). He then fled to the forests of Polesie, where he earned a reputation as a talented partisan commander. When the Soviet partisan command, striving for the increase of activities on Polish soil, decided to transfer a series of partisan units westward across the Bug, Skotnicki's group, along with the Janowski unit, was among the first units transferred. In addition to Skotnicki there were other Jews in this group, among them Sergeant-Major Abraham Miller, and sergeants Ignatz Farbstein and Abraham Winderman.[43]

In January 1944, the AL command decided to establish in the Parczew forests its first partisan battalion. Aleksander Skotnicki, seen by all as the man best suited for the role, was raised to the rank of captain and made its commander. Skotnicki, who had lost his wife and son in the ghetto, adopted the partisan name of Zemsta (meaning revenge in Polish).

It is interesting to read the written appraisal of Skotnicki that is included in a report sent to AL headquarters by Mieczyslaw Moczar, then the commander of the AL forces in the district of Lublin. Moczar writes:

> Zemsta, a lieutenant in the Polish army, a lecturer at the university and a very ambitious man, was a stranger to us from an ideological point of view. He is ready to fight against the Germans and is talented and energetic. With the proper cultivation he could become an outstanding commander. I have ordered that his work in the unit be examined and scrutinized. I will do my best so that he, for his part, will advance and grow to understand us. The first talks I held with him brought positive results. He declared before me that he would try to strengthen our army.[44]

The battalion that was organized under Aleksander Skotnicki's command was named the Holod Battalion in memory of the communist activist Jan Holod, mentioned above. One of the organizers of the Polish partisan movement in the Parczew forests, Holod had fallen in battle on January 6, 1944, during a clash between the partisans and the Germans near Ostrow Lubelski. The Holod Battalion, numbering about 400 partisans, was composed of a command staff, a patrol unit, and four fighting companies.

The role of second-in-command of the battalion was given to Gustaw Alef-Bolkowiak. He was a communist activist who fled the Warsaw Ghetto before the deportation in the summer of 1942 and one of the first partisans in the People's Army. The relationship between Skotnicki and his seconds-in-command, two Jewish officers having different ideological beliefs, as not very friendly. Alef-Bolkowiak mentions this himself:

> The man appointed commander of the battalion was Captain Zemsta, formerly an officer in the cavalry and a lecturer in the faculty of veterinary medicine in the University of Lvov, who came across the Bug not long ago with a group of partisans. Captain Zemsta quickly succeeded in earning the respect of the partisans for his courage, which bordered on daring, for his organizing ability, his knowledge of the military profession, and his warm and open relationship with his subordinates. He was not a member of the PPR, but as a believer in democracy he understood that the only way to independence was the way of the Polish Workers Party. 'Mietek' [Moczar's nickname] offered me the role of second-in-command to the battalion's commander, Skotnicki, in charge of political-educational affairs. I agreed without hesitating. As far as I could see, Zemsta received the news without enthusiasm. "So, you want to be a commissar, just like the Soviet Union? If so, why be called an education officer?" Zemsta asked sharply. According to Bolkowiak, Skotnicki added: "Pardon me, comrade, I am not against this institution of political commissars. I am just afraid of evil commissars. I had a bad experience with them across the Bug."[45]

Another Jewish partisan transferred to the Holod Battalion headquarters was Lieutenant Stanislaw Jerzy Lec, a well-known poet and satirist from Poland and member of the underground in the Tarnow ghetto, who fled to the partisan movement. In the Parczew forests he received the nickname of "Lukasz." The role of commander of the headquarters guard was given to one of the veteran Jewish partisans, Jan Rak, known as Zbik. Also attached to the headquarters guard was Natalia Szuc, a Jewish woman who, until the fall of 1943 hid in a village near Ostrow-Lubelski. When her hiding place was found and her life was in danger, she was saved by Greenshpan's partisans. And in the patrol unit that was under the direct command of headquarters there were, among others, four Jews, one of whom had escaped from Treblinka.[46]

Greenshpan's unit joined the Holod Battalion as its fourth and largest company. There were also Jews in the first company, mostly veteran partisans who had been in Kovalov's unit. The second and third companies were new units, composed mostly of Poles.

After this reorganization, the AL partisans in the forests of Parczew carried out military actions on a scale previously unknown. Among the various operations of that period, two carried out by the Jewish company in February 1944 are particularly famous. The first took place on February 6, 1944, when the Jewish partisans destroyed six kilometers of telephone wire on the Lublin-Wlodawa line. Ten days later, on February 16, the Jewish company took over the large village of Kaplonosy, and during the battle, seized the local police building and razed it to its foundations.[47]

One time when the Jewish company was operating in a fairly remote area, a harsh blow fell upon the residents of the family camp. A large unit of collaborators, mostly Uzbeks from the Ostlegion number 790 stationed in Wlodawa, broke through the thicket of the forest by surprise. Wearing white camouflage coats, they succeeded in evading the partisan guard. After burning the forest watchmen's huts near the village of Bialka, they turned on the Jewish family camp. Most of the camp's residents, who had been warned in time, managed to flee. Those who remained behind were killed. Uzbeks also destroyed the underground hideouts and the bunkers that served as shelter for the camp's residents in the winter. Afterwards they retreated from the forest.[48]

With the additional arms brought in by the Janowski unit and the experience acquired during endless partisan battles, the Jewish company was well off. It was a disciplined unit much valued in battle, and similar in character to a regular army company. A description of the Jewish company at the end of the winter of 1944 is found in the testimony of the Polish partisan Mikolaj Koczmiela, who witnessed the entrance of the Jewish partisans into the village of Olchowa while he was there for medical treatment. He writes:

> One evening the Jewish unit of Lieutenant "Chil" [Greenshpan] arrived in Olchowa. The unit was equipped with a machine gun, explosives to sabotage roads with, and light weapons. The patrol showed great initiative because it was not only a matter of the units' security, but also of the security of the families that were under the protection of Lieutenant "Chil." He himself, as a sergeant from before the war, succeeded in transforming people who before the occupation had no contact whatsoever with weapons into disciplined soldiers.[49]

The position of the partisans in the Parczew forests greatly improved with the arrival of large Soviet partisan units. As of February 1944 these forests served as a junction for Soviet partisan units crossing the Bug on their way to the forests in the southern area of the district of Lublin and the Carpathians. The first of these units to arrive was the first Ukrainian partisan division named after Kovpak under the command of Colonel Vershihora, which crossed the Bug in the area of the Parczew forests early on February 9, 1944.[50]

In March, two new partisan units arrived—The Wanda Wasilewska brigade and a Jewish group under the command of Shmuel (Mieczyslaw) Gruber.

The Wanda Wasilewska brigade was established in the forests of Polesie as a partisan unit within the framework of the Soviet forces under the command of Alex Fiodorov. There were about twenty Jews in the brigade, among them paratroopers, soldiers, and officers in the regular Polish army who had been transferred to Polesie to organize partisan activities. In January 1944, when a Jewish group numbering thirty people joined this unit, the number of Jews in the brigade rose to about fifty. When the brigade came to the Parczew forests, it opened with a major attack against the railroads. After a short while, the unit was joined by Polish partisans from the vicinity of Parczew and Ostrow Lubelski, and soon numbered 500 persons.[51]

The thirty-member partisan group commanded by Gruber came from the west of the Wieprz River. Its members were the remnants of two Jewish partisan units that had fought from the fall of 1942 in the forests of Pulawy and Lubartow on the west bank of the Wieprz.

Gruber's partisans had worked before with the Janowski unit that had come west a few weeks earlier to organize the supply of arms coming in by air for the partisans in the Kozlow forests. They now moved to the forests of Parczew. On their way east, the two units faced many clashes with the Germans. The first clash took place during an attempt to cross the Wieprz when, on March 15, the partisans were surrounded by a large German unit. Only with the coming of night did Gruber and his group manage to break through. Later, Commander Leon Kasman also had to extricate his unit from German encirclement. However, one of his men was killed, and several others injured, including Leon Kasman, seriously wounded in the leg.

The last clash took place on March 26. The Jewish group ran into a small German unit in the village of Kolacze. Although three partisans fell in this clash, the German unit was wiped out. Two Germans were taken prisoners, and five guns with ammunition were seized.

Two days later Gruber's group entered the forests of Parczew and on March 29 met Greenshpan's company then encamped in the village of Skorodnica. The impression the Jewish partisans from the Parczew forest made on Gruber's group is described by Shmuel Gruber in his testimony: "Our group was amazed at the ways the partisans across the Wieprz operated. Until now we operated only at night, because during the day we were forced to hide in the forests or with the peasants. While here, across the Wieprz, all the activities took place in daylight. They had supply wagons and rode on horses."[52]

The next day the Jewish partisans left the village. On the way they encountered a small German unit, which, after a short battle, retreated to Sosnowica. When Gruber's group reached the partisan base in the depths of the Parczew forests, it was incorporated in the first company of the Holod Battalion. There were now two Jewish units in the battalion—the fourth company and the Jewish platoon in the first company. There were also a few Jews in other units so that in all, 150 Jewish partisans made up about one-third of the battalion.

With the coming of spring, the drops of Soviet arms increased. The partisans received large quantities of automatic weapons, machine guns, ammunition, explosives, radios, medicine, uniforms, and food. Conditions for the partisans and for the refugees in Altana were greatly improved. Skotnicki's battalion intensified its activities, and the first and fourth companies of the battalion often performed joint actions under the command of Yechiel Greenshpan.

The intensification of partisan activity in the Parczew forests naturally disturbed the Germans. A new campaign against the partisans known as *Unternehmen Immergruen*, was planned. It lasted from April 9 through April 27, 1944. The course of the campaign went according to the usual German plan, using about the same number of forces used against the partisans in most of the campaigns in 1943 and again centering on the police units of the 25th Regiment and 203rd Battalion of the *Ordnungspolizei*.[53]

The position of the partisans, however, was completely different from what it had been in 1943. The tactics and forces employed against the partisans in 1943 were no longer effective in 1944. The Germans could no longer think of gaining control of the forest areas with *Ordnungspolizei* forces. On the contrary, at the height of the campaign, the partisans managed not only to defend their bases but also simultaneously to carry out a series of military actions beyond the borders of the forest. Some of these important operations were carried out by the Jewish company. Along with other companies of Skotnicki's battalion, the Jewish company participated in an attack against Parczew on April 16. This was the first time that partisans entered a county town in the *General Gouvernement*. During this operation the building housing the regional offices and a police post were destroyed. The next day the police commander in Parczew, Captain Greiner, sent out a report on the past day's events. It included the following: "On 16.4.44, at about 8 P.M. the building housing the county offices in Parczew was attacked by an armed band. . . . The partisans took documents with them and then burnt the building. The policemen at the district post were bound up. The firemen were not allowed to extinguish the fire. They took the judge with them. Among the partisans (who numbered about fifty men) were Poles, Russians, and Jews."[54]

The description of these events is accurate except for the number of partisans who took part in the attack, which actually was much higher. Three large units of Soviet partisans came to the Parczew forests in April. These were the units of Major Chepiga, Lieutenant Colonel Prokopiuk, and Lieutenant Colonel Kunicki. In this way a concentration of about 2,000 partisans, mostly Soviets, was created. This was a very large number of forces in terms of the topographical conditions of this forest, which is not among the largest. Moreover, following the Soviet army offensive in the direction of Byelo-Russia, the partisans who, until then had operated in Polesie and Volhynia, planned to cross the Bug westward in order to shift the partisan war to the area of Lublin. Because of this, the partisan units from the Parczew forests were transferred to the forests of Janow and the Puszcza Solska in the south of the district of Lublin, thus vacating the Parczew forests for the new units that were to come from the east.

Accordingly, the AL command prepared a plan to transfer the Holod Battalion and the Wanda Wasilewska Brigade to the forests of Janow. The Janowski unit was also ordered to move to the Janow forests. Before departing from the Parczew forests, however, the Holod Battalion assembled in the village of Bojki on the edge of the forest near Ostrow-Lubelski. It was decided to hold celebrations here for the battalions' departure which would also serve to publicize the partisan cause. Marking both the First of May celebrations, which is the traditional worker's holiday for the left wing, and the Third of May holiday, the anniversary of the declaration of the Polish constitution in 1791 traditional to the right wing, the partisans' celebration was designed to symbolize the unity of the Polish people in its war against the German conquest. The celebration was also meant to demonstrate the partisans' power. The Holod Battalion appeared in the village in Polish army uniforms (dropped in by air) in full military order and style, and the residents of Bojki and the surrounding small villages took part. The main speakers were Mieczyslaw Moczar (Demko) and two Jewish officers: Aleksander Skotnicki and Gustaw Alef-Bolkowiak.[55]

In addition, the commander of the People's Army, General Michal Rola-Zymierski came from Warsaw to make an appearance, and showed great interest in the Jewish partisans. He spoke at length with the partisans of the Jewish fourth company and asked them in detail about their struggle and their lives. The presence of women in the battle units, including the twenty women in the Jewish company who fought side by side with the men, received special attention.

At the end of the celebrations, an order by the AL commander on promotions concerning a large number of Jewish partisans, was read aloud. The commander of the Jewish company, Yechiel Greenshpan was promoted to the rank of first lieutenant. The rank of second lieutenant was awarded to the Jewish partisans Joseph Cynowiec, Shmuel Gruber, Mark Dworecki, Stefan Finkel, Marcin Pelc, and Joseph Rolnik. About forty Jewish partisans were made corporals and sergeants. There was an atmosphere of excitement filled with hope and confidence among the Jewish partisans.

On May 5, after the partisan celebration, the Holod Battalion was instructed to depart. By this time the Soviet units, the Wanda Wasilewska Brigade and the Janowski unit already had left the Parczew forests for the forests of Janow. But at the last minute the order concerning the Jewish fourth company was rescinded; it was instructed to return to the Parczew forests. The official explanation for this was the need to hold a few more partisan operations before the final evacuation of the forest. The real reason was different and no less serious. It was known that the Jewish company would not leave the Parczew forests before the problem of the protection of the refugees in Altana was solved. But headquarters had not succeeded in securing the needed protection, and this, most likely, was the reason for leaving the Jewish company at its Parczew base.

While the partisan celebrations were going on in Bojki, the Germans opened a major new campaign against the partisans, called "Unternehmen Maigewitter." This was the first campaign to be planned and organized by the army, and not by the Ordnungspolizei as in former campaigns. The implementation of the plans was delegated to the fifth division of the Waffen SS–"Viking." Air force units also took part in this campaign. Police units (regiments number 4 and 25 of the Ordnungspolizei) performed a secondary role only. These were the largest forces ever employed against the partisans in the General Gouvernement.[56]

On May 6, news of a large concentration of Waffen SS units

reached the partisans' headquarters. The Jewish company, which was planning to return to its base in the Parczew forests, was ordered to check the advance of the *Waffen SS* spearhead units, in order to enable the Holod battalion forces that remained behind to leave the Parczew forests. Greenshpan's company took its position by the Tysmienica River not far from Ostrow-Lubelski. The following day, on May 7, the Germans attacked the partisan positions. The battle lasted until the evening. With nightfall, the Jewish company retreated to the center of the forests of Parczew. The Germans gave up the idea of entering the depths of the forest and headed west, where battles that were already in progress with partisan units had succeeded (as it happened, to their disadvantage) in getting far away from the Parczew forests. The Jewish company, therefore, remained alone in these forests.

After the first clashes with the Germans, the AL command and the Soviet units' command decided to change the route to the Janow forests in order to bypass the central line of advance of the main column of the *Waffen SS* fifth division. The partisans, therefore, headed not south but west with the aim of reaching the Tarnow forests and from there, of turning south to the Janow forests. This route was chosen by the Holod Battalion (now without the fourth company), the Soviet units, the Wanda Wasilewska Brigade, and the Janowski unit.

Small German forces twice tried to block the partisans' way. On two occasions, on May 11 near Dabrowka, and on May 12 near Amelin, battles broke out during which Aleksander Skotnicki, the battalion's commander, managed to ward off the German attack and continue the march. On May 14 most of the partisans were to be found in a small forest near the town of Rablow. The Germans succeeded in surrounding the partisans here. A serious battle broke out, lasting two days. Skotnicki's battalion defended their position on the northern edge of the forest. The courage shown by the Jewish partisans from the first company who fought with them in this battle was emphasized in many reports of Polish partisans, who especially mentioned the military proficiency and abilities of Captain Skotnicki.[57]

The AL partisans suffered heavy losses in the battle near Rablow. According to Polish sources, the AL partisan losses totaled forty dead and about fifty wounded. But it cannot be doubted that the losses were much greater. The number given by Gruber also appear inaccurate. According to him, the Jewish company had four dead.[58] However, the Soviet partisans managed, although not without losses, to break through the German ring and reach the Janow forests.

Following this unsuccessful battle, the Polish partisan units dis-integrated. Many of the partisans who came from nearby areas re-turned to their homes. Only a few of the survivors found their way to the Janow forests, where the People's Army forces were reorganized. The Jews who took part in the battle as part of the Wanda Wasilewska Brigade and the Janowski unit reached the Janow forests with the survivors of their units. Lieutenant Alef-Bolkowiak along with a small group of Polish and Jewish partisans broke through to the area of Pulawy, and there organized a new partisan unit. Captain Aleksander Skotnicki, who decided to make his way to the Parczew forests, took most of the partisans of the Jewish platoon and small groups of Polish partisans with him. Three days later, on May 18, 1944, Skotnicki's group was surprised by the Germans near the village of Wolka Zawieprzanska and a battle ensued. Although the partisans suc-ceeded in getting away from the Germans and making their way to the Parczew forests, they suffered some losses, among them their commander, Captain Aleksander Skotnicki. After his death, he was awarded the rank of major and the highest military honor—the Grun-wald Cross. After the war, his remains were brought to the military cemetery in Warsaw and buried among the Polish national war heroes.[59]

The Jewish partisans under the command of Gruber reached the Parczew forests and were annexed to Greenshpan's company, which was reorganized. Gruber was made Greenshpan's second-in-command, and the Jewish company was divided into two platoons, commanded by Ephraim (Frank) Bleichman and Mark Dworecki.[60]

After the Rablow battle, various groups of defeated Polish fighters also began flocking into the Parczew forests. The AL com-mand decided to reorganize the Holod Battalion, which had been defeated near Rablow. Mikolaj Meluch, known as Kolka, was made commander of the battalion in place of Skotnicki. Meluch's venomous anti-Semitism made any cooperation whatsoever with the Jews im-possible. Meluch began his command by giving the Jewish company orders that needlessly and seriously endangered the lives of the parti-sans. He wanted to remove the Jewish women from the partisan unit at any price. Yet worse than this was his attitude toward the subject of the refugee camp. He refused to recognize the right of the fugitives to exist in the forest, and caused great difficulties in supplying food to the camp. In view of this situation relations between Meluch and Greenshpan, whose company was now the focus of AL partisan forces in the Parczew forests, were quickly broken off. Yechiel Green-shpan reached a fateful decision. He informed Meluch that he,

Greenshpan, no longer recognized him as his superior. The Jewish company left the ranks of the AL, remaining alone in the forest and depending only on itself.

This state of affairs became known to the local AK groups, whose forces in the Parczew forests at this time were substantially strengthened. On June 9, the defeated units of the 27th Division of the Home Army, after suffering very heavy losses during the Polish attempt to carry out the "Storm" plan in the Volhynia, crossed the Bug and now concentrated one of the largest units of the AK in the Parczew forests.

The Home Army and the People's Army had an agreement at this time to stop their attacks on one another. Because of this agreement, the AK groups did not attack Jewish partisans who belonged to the People's Army. Now that the Jewish company had withdrawn from the AL, however, the local AK commanders determined that nothing would stand in the way of their renewed attacks on the Jews. An AK group assaulted the refugee camp in Altana and demanded that the camp's guard give up its weapons. This attack is described in the testimony of Lewenbaum, member of the Altana guard:

> We were surrounded by AK men. They rode horses, wore Polish army uniforms, and were armed from head to toe. They said they would disarm us because we were not fighters but robbers. Our commander was Sheftel from Wlodawa. He refused to give them the arms, and I saw our men secretly slipping away with their weapons. I thought we should hand over some old rifles; if not, they were ready to kill us.
>
> Night came and we were besieged. My wife stood by me with her gun. I knew she would not hand it over. She was whispering nonstop, "They will kill us." But I saw that we were not yet lost because one side remained open, that is to say there was a way out. The AK men took our horses, our clothes, our weapons and left.[61]

The Jewish partisans found a way out of the new danger. At the beginning of June, two large partisan units arrived in the Parczew forests from the east. These were the units of Colonel Banov and General Baranovski. Rumors spread among the Jewish partisans that General Baranovski was a Hungarian Jew. While the AK was carrying out its assault on Altana, Greenshpan and his company, on their way to Baranovski's base, were told of the situation in Altana. General Baranovski showed a great understanding of the situation of the Jewish partisans and refugees. His reaction was immediate. After he went for an inspection of the refugees' camp and saw what the situation was, the AK command was notified that General Baranovski took the protection of the refugees in Altana onto himself. The notice also warned against a recurrence of the attacks. The Jewish company was annexed to Baranovski's unit.[62]

The Jewish partisans in Baranovski's unit took part in a battle near Wola Wereszczynska on June 18, 1944. The battle was caused by a new German campaign, known as *Unternehmen Vagabund*, that the Germans had opened, again employing police forces. Apparently, the Germans did not have a clear idea of the new concentration of Soviet partisan forces in the Parczew forests. They probably assumed that after the *"Maigewitter"* campaign, police units would be sufficient for the defeat of the "remnant" of the partisans in this area. This campaign against the partisans, in which the 4th and 25th regiments of the *Ordnungspolizei* took part, ended in total failure. Shmuel Gruber tells of the downing of a German plane by the Jewish partisans in the Wola Wereszczynska battle, but this story is not confirmed by other sources. The Jewish partisans lost six men in this battle.[63]

It was only after the Jewish company was annexed to General Baranovski's unit that Meluch dispatched a communiqué on this matter to the AL commander in the district of Lublin, Mieczyslaw Moczar, who was then in the Janow forests. Moczar, meanwhile, had gone to Warsaw, so the head of intelligence in the district headquarters, Lieutenant Waclaw Czyzewski, issued the following information to the main command of the AL: "Following the departure of Lieutenant-Colonel Mietek, a messenger arrived here from Lieutenant Kolka in the Parczew forests. Lieutenant Kolka writes to the district command that the Jewish unit broke off from the Polish command and, in an arbitrary fashion, moved into the framework of a Soviet unit. Later the lieutenant writes that after the departure of Lieutenant-Colonel Mietek, there was an undermining of discipline. In short he is lost for advice."[64]

The withdrawal of the Jewish company from the People's Army was interpreted by General Rola-Zymierski as an act that undermined the prestige of the People's Army. He, therefore, decided to respond without delay. A letter was sent to Greenshpan in which the general ordered an absolute return to the ranks of the People's Army. The letter included the promise that the outbreaks of anti-Semitism for which Meluch was responsible would not recur. Meluch was dismissed from the battalion's command, and in his place Zbigniew Stempka was appointed. Known as Mora, Stempka was an AK officer who had recently withdrawn from the Home Army and joined the AL camp. This former AK officer was very sympathetic to the Jewish company which returned to the People's Army.[65]

There was also a change in the Lublin district command. Moczar was transferred to the Radom district, and in his place came Ignacy Robb-Narbut (a Jewish officer whom we shall encounter later in this book). At the same time the Klim unit came to the Parczew forests. This unit included several Jews and, among them, the well-known parachutist, Lucyna Herz. The situation of the Jews in the Parczew forests again improved, and as a result, the activities of the Jewish unit were again intensified. This intensification characterized the company's actions during the first half of July 1944. In the beginning of the month, a platoon of this company, under the command of Second Lieutenant Dworecki, carried out three successful missions against army trains on the Lukow-Radzyn line. Another platoon, under the personal command of Greenshpan, defeated a motorized group of the SS and killed several Germans. On July 13, an army train on the Parczew-Lukow line was destroyed by a platoon led by Dworecki. The Germans suffered heavy losses and train communications stopped for thirty hours. Another platoon under the command of Second Lieutenant Gruber, successfully organized an ambush on the Radzyn-Wisznica road. A German vehicle was attacked, and many arms needed by the partisans were taken.[66]

Suddenly there was a deterioration of the situation in the Parczew forests. The AL central command returned Robb-Narbut to Warsaw. In his place, Lieutenant Colonel Stefan Kilianowicz, known as Grzegorz Korczynski, was made commander of the district of Lublin. He served as the AL commander in the south of the district of Lublin, where he had frequently sent Jewish partisans on extremely dangerous operations and had needlessly endangered their lives. As will be seen, Korczynski was largely responsible for the tragedy that later befell the Jewish partisans in the Janow forests. The Jewish partisan company and the Jewish refugee camp were not subordinated to this man.

Korczynski received the command of the district in mid-July 1944. At this time the Germans began the last antipartisan campaign in the district of Lublin—"*Unternehmen Wirbelsturm.*" A force including eight infantry battalions, a large number of police units, and air force units was thrown against the partisans in the Parczew forests. Because of the new Red Army offensive, the Germans wanted to clear the region of partisans at any price, since this area was soon to be almost on the front line. The partisans were thus confronted with their greatest challenge on the very eve of the liberation.[67]

Because of the situation at hand, Korczynski went to General Baranovski's headquarters. Their meeting was held on July 18, 1944.

It was agreed that because of the shortage of partisan forces, and in order to resist German pressure on the forest area, the partisans should try to break out of the Parczew forests in different directions. The Soviet units would break through to the east in the direction of Wlodawa; the Polish units would turn south.

The Soviet units' attempts to break through were successful, and by the following day the Soviet partisans were already outside the encircled area. But the AL units' position was much more complicated. The 27th Division of the Home Army was gathered in the southwestern section of the forest. Korczynski turned to the division's commander, Tadeusz Stumberk-Rychter, and suggested a joint program of action. Stumberk rejected the offer and took his unit out of the forest before the Germans completely surrounded it. With the departure of the Home Army's 27th Division, the left wing of the People's Army forces was laid open, and this allowed the Germans to break through the forest into the area of Korczynski's base. This breach had to be closed in order to delay the Germans' further entrance into the forest and to allow for preparations to be made for breaking out of the German encirclement. The most vital mission was blocking the road to the forest from Ostrow Lubelski. Only a week before, Ostrow had been taken over by AK units. On July 18, these units departed, leaving the way to the forest open to the Germans. Korczynski transferred the Jewish company to this very dangerous and sensitive area to stop the advancing German column. Korczynski's order stated: "Capture a position at the edge of the town of Ostrow in order to attack the German advance force, and afterwards retreat to the Parczew forests."[68]

When the Jewish company arrived in Ostrow according to Korczynski's command, a great panic broke out in the town. Many residents left their homes hastily and ran to the forest. Town representatives turned to Greenshpan requesting that he give up the defense preparations. According to them, a battle in the town would needlessly endanger the residents. The Germans would burn Ostrow down in retaliation for the partisan activities. Furthermore, the people of Ostrow Lubelski blamed the Jews for inviting catastrophe to the town. Greenshpan sent a request to Korczynski to change the order and allow him to prepare defense positions outside the town. Korczynski replied in the negative and demanded that his order be followed under any conditions.

The Germans attacked the town on July 19. Leon Doroszewski, a Pole, testified that the Germans captured the town on that same day after a short clash with Greenshpan's company, emphasizing that the

Jews retreated without losses. In contrast, Shmuel Gruber tells in his testimony of a long battle. But he also stresses that, in the battle of Ostrow, the Jewish company suffered no losses.[69]

It is certain that Greenshpan decided not to enter into a long and hopeless battle with the Germans, but to retreat after a short exchange of fire. This was, undoubtedly, the right decision, and it was only because of it that the company was not wiped out on the eve of liberation. The unit's retreat had no negative effect whatsoever on the fate of the other partisan units under Korczynski's command, because even before their retreat from Ostrow Lubelski, Korczynski having failed to break through the German lines in the vicinity of Jedlanka, had already retreated to the depths of the forest.

After this failure, Korczynski decided to try again to break through the German lines, this time not to the south but to the west. Meanwhile, they discovered that the Germans were advancing to the Makoszka area on the northern end of the forest. Korczynski transferred the Jewish company that arrived from Ostrow to this area. The next day the Jewish partisans took a new position on the northern edge of the forest. This was vital to them because it bordered the nearest road leading to Altana. The Jewish company, therefore, had special reason to defend this position with the utmost effort. At midnight on July 20, after great delay, a messenger from Korczynski arrived, bringing with him permission to leave the defense position and an order to join the central forces, which had already managed to cross the German lines and were beyond the area of the siege. Yet it turned out that the messenger was very late in coming, and that it was no longer possible to join the forces under Korczynski's command.

At this danger-filled hour, the Jewish company and the refugee camp remained alone in the forest, surrounded by large German forces and having to rely solely on their own strength.

Because of this, Greenshpan decided to leave the positions in the area of Makoszka and try to open on his own a way out in the area of Jedlanka. There were two considerations for deciding on this particular area. First of all, it was necessary to pass through Altana in order to prepare the refugees for the departure. Their staying in the forest meant certain death. And secondly, Greenshpan estimated that after Korczynski's failed attempt, the Germans would not expect the partisans to try to break through in the same place.

Greenshpan's plan was completely successful. In Altana the civilian refugees joined the partisans. And, indeed, the German defense of the road to Jedlanka was weak. Escape was possible.

But even after breaking out of this trap, the situation of the Jews was very grave. As it turned out, all the roads and all the paths in the surrounding area were crowded with retreating German army units. Along the road to Ostrow, a German armored column was retreating. It was evident that any clash with the retreating German army would lead to the total destruction of the Jewish partisan company and to the murder of all the surviving refugees.

Greenshpan ordered all the partisans and refugees to hide in the tall wheat in the fields and ordered them, in the strongest terms possible, not to make any sign that would indicate their presence and betray them. The situation was desperate. The partisans and the refugees had not eaten in two days. They had no water, and in the heat of the summer, this was especially oppressive. Moreover, any careless movement could bring on destruction.[70]

With nightfall, Greenshpan decided to go back to the forest in hope that it would be easier to hide his people there. This attempt was not successful. Even the secondary paths in ths area were crowded with German army units retreating westward. Coming out of the fields was too dangerous.

That night, the last German units completed their retreat westward. Units of the Soviet Eighth Army entered the Parczew forests on the morning of July 23, 1944. The partisan Avraham Lewenbaum describes this meeting with the Soviets: "I was sick and weak. I fell asleep exhausted under a tree. Someone from our group, Yankel Holender, woke me up saying that the Russians were already there. Soon Russian soldiers and artillery began streaming in nonstop day and night. One major, a Jew, burst out crying when he met us. He said that he had been marching from Kiev and we were the first Jews he had met."[71]

The next day, Korczynski supervised the concentration of the surviving partisans. The Jewish company presented itself in Ostrow Lubelski, and from there the Jewish partisans of Korczynski's unit marched to Lublin where they took part in a partisan parade held immediately after the liberation of the city. On the whole, 120 Jewish partisans entered Lublin under Greenshpan's command.[72]

The civilian refugees who survived the German occupation in the refugee camp of Altana moved to Parczew where they lived until 1946, at which time most of the Jewish survivors decided to leave Poland. About 200 civilian refugees survived in the Parczew forests. These were the remnant of 4,000 Jews who had escaped to the Parczew forests during the liquidation of the area's ghettos.[73]

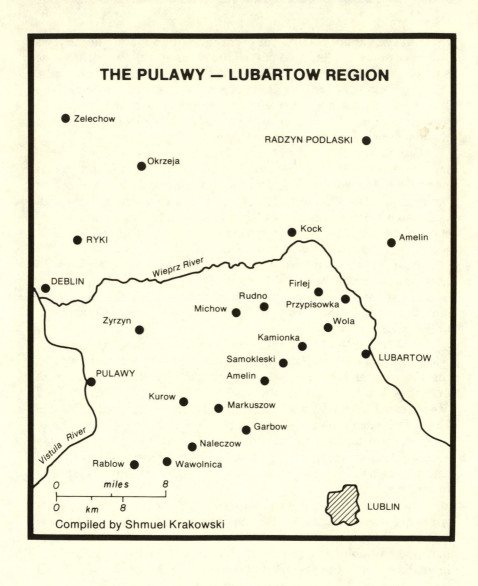

THE PULAWY — LUBARTOW REGION

Zelechow

RADZYN PODLASKI

Okrzeja

Kock

Amelin

RYKI

Wieprz River

DEBLIN

Firlej

Rudno

Przypisowka

Michow

Wola

Zyrzyn

Kamionka

LUBARTOW

Samokleski

PULAWY

Amelin

Kurow

Markuszow

Vistula River

Garbow

Naleczow

Rablow

Wawolnica

0   miles   8

0   km   8

LUBLIN

Compiled by Shmuel Krakowski

CHAPTER 3
BETWEEN PULAWY AND LUBARTOW

UNLIKE THE SURROUNDINGS OF PARCZEW AND WLOD-
AWA, the topography of the area north of Lublin, between Pulawy
and Lubartow, did not favor partisan activities. It is a flat, densely
populated area, and its small forests—the forests of Kozlow, Wola,
and Garbow—were suitable as bases for small partisan units only.
Furthermore, because two main roads and railway lines going from
Warsaw through Lublin to Lvov, and from Brest through Lublin to
Cracow, passed through this strategic region, a significant number of
German army and police forces were concentrated there.[1]

Despite the lack of proper conditions, this area became, from the
fall of 1942, a zone of intensive battle for the Jewish partisan movement. Moreover, until the end of 1943 the Jewish partisan units were
the only forces fighting in the forests of this region. It was only at the
end of 1943 that the Polish underground organizations brought their
own armed groups to these forests for the purpose of developing
partisan activities.[2]

The Jewish partisan movement in the forests north of Lublin was
composed mainly of two groups of fugitives—Jews who had fled
from small towns in the surrounding area and Jewish prisoners-of-
war who had escaped from the camp in Lublin.

Among the first to come to the forests were fugitives from Markuszow, Michow, and Kurow who had escaped in May 1942, when
the first deportations from these towns to the Sobibor extermination
camp began. Almost the entire Jewish population of Markuszow escaped to the forests of Wola. The signal for the mass escape was given
by Shlomo Goldwasser, chairman of the local *Judenrat*, who after

receiving information that the deportation was expected on May 9, informed all the Jews in the town of it and advised them to flee. Similarly, in October 1942, many other Jews fled from the small community of Kamionka.[3] Jewish youth groups in Markuszow and Kamionka had succeeded in organizing and equipping themselves with modest quantities of arms before the deportations. Immediately upon their arrival in the forest, these groups organized themselves into separate partisan units, numbering about fifty people altogether, including a fifteen-member youth group organized by Ephraim Bleichman in Kamionka.[4]

An important role in the consolidation of the Jewish partisan movement in this area at the beginning of its activity was played by a Soviet officer, known as Tolka, who had escaped from German captivity. It has not been possible to find out his last name; it is only known that he came from Kharkov. Tolka quickly earned the complete trust of the Jewish partisans and their unreserved recognition of his authority. Tolka coordinated activities and consolidated the forces of the armed Jewish groups, who, because of the unsuitable conditions, at first had not joined into one unit. Although the groups still operated independently in various parts of the forest, they met Tolka at least once a week to receive directions and orders. Their basic strategy was continual movement and constant shifting from forest to forest, since any extended stay in one place brought danger of discovery and destruction.

Hundreds of Jews in hiding were killed during a large hunt held in mid-October 1942, in the forests of Wola. Among them were the Markuszow refugees and most of the escapees from Michow. But because the Jewish armed groups were then in the forests of Kozlow, a distance of ten kilometers to the south, they were able to avoid losses and possibly even total annihilation.[5]

The first group of prisoners-of-war to escape from the camp in Lublin came under the command of Kaganowicz to the forests of Kozlow at the end of October. (The details of their organization and escape are described in chapter 12.) They found themselves unarmed in an unfamiliar forest. The PPR liaison men, whose arrival was announced by the Polish communist activist Pawel Dabek, did not come. At the same time the Germans started a hunt in the forest. It was only with grave difficulty that the group succeeded in eluding the Germans who were combing the forests. Kaganowicz's men soon realized that without contacts and without arms a quick death awaited them in the strange and unfamiliar territory. Kaganowicz introduced a plan to cross the Wieprz and break through to the Bug

River on the east, the region from which the inmates of the Lublin prisoner-of-war camp came. They hoped that in an area familiar to them it would be easier for them to initiate partisan activities. They also hoped to form ties with the Soviet partisans, whom they expected to meet farther east. But their attempts to reach the eastern bank of the Wieprz did not succeed. It was evident that it was impossible for an unarmed group, which could not defend itself against German patrols, to reach the river. There was no doubt that if the group did not acquire arms, in a short time it would be destroyed.

The only way out of this situation was the acquisition of arms hidden in Lublin by prisoners-of-war. Stefan Finkel was sent back to Lublin to get them, while the rest of Kaganowicz's group found a hideout in the forest near the village of Kawki, 15 kilometers north of Lublin, where they awaited his return.

On the morning of November 12, two armed groups of prisoners who had escaped their workplaces in Lublin reached the forests as a result of Stefan Finkel's efforts. They arrived near the forests of Kozlow, north of Lublin, in vehicles confiscated from the Germans, and after unloading the trucks set out to meet Kaganowicz. However, because a large hunt was being conducted in the forest at the time, there was no one at the appointed meeting place. After wandering in the forest for some time, they found Kaganowicz's body. The next day they found the rest of the group waiting for help to break out of the encirclement, at odds over the loss of their commander. One was seriously wounded and others were lost in the forest during the hasty flight from the advancing German hunt. It was imperative to leave the forests of Kozlow as soon as possible. The group decided to move, that very night, to the nearby Garbow forests.

The move to the Garbow forests delayed a meeting with a third group of prisoners who had escaped from another workplace in Lublin. This group was unarmed, and the Germans' hunt forced them into hasty, nonstop flight from place to place, during which some were lost. Only later did this third prisoner group meet with their friends and receive some of their weapons.[6]

Even so, the fugitive prisoners were in peril. In a strange and unfamiliar area, with no contacts among the local residents, the escaped prisoners were at a lost for advice and did not know what to do in terms of partisan activity. A rescue came by way of a meeting with the Jewish partisans operating under the command of Tolka. Most of the prisoners, under the command of Jegier, immediately accepted the offer to join the Jewish partisans and recognize the authority of Tolka. However, a number of prisoners, with Shmuel Gruber at their

head, decided to carry on with Kaganowicz's plan to go east. Gruber
and the members of his group again tried to cross the Wieprz, hoping
that this time they would succeed in reaching the east bank of the
Bug. The mission did not succeed. The prisoners were unexpectedly
cut off by the Germans, and in the battle that ensued, three Jews were
killed and three were wounded, among them Gruber himself.[7]

After the fugitive prisoners joined them, the number of partisans
in the groups under Tolka's command reached eighty. Later, when
more fugitives from the forced labor camp in Jastkow joined them,
Tolka reorganized his unit, dividing it into groups that operated in
different parts of the Wola, Garbow, and Kozlow forests. The groups
were still in close contact with each other and their activities were
coordinated according to Tolka's instructions. And still their most
important objective was the acquisition of arms.

Ephraim Bleichman contributed greatly to the success of the partisans' actions, particularly in the beginning. He was familiar with all
of the surrounding area, knew a large number of the local peasants,
had proved to be an exceptionally experienced guide for the partisans. Afterwards, he also showed himself to be a capable commander. It was Bleichman who helped to get information concerning
arms hidden in September 1939 by the local population, which enabled Tolka to take his partisans to such places to buy or confiscate
arms. In this way the partisans had by the end of 1942 already acquired about twenty pistols and rifles.

Arms were also acquired by assaults on small German patrols.
The first successful ambush apparently was held at the end of
November 1942 on the Kurow-Markuszow road, during a surprise
attack on a German motor patrol. Several Germans were killed and
some wounded during this action. This encounter, the first time the
partisans had captured arms from the Germans, ended in complete
success and contributed greatly to raising the partisans' morale.[8]

At the end of November, Stefan Kaminski, known as "Geniek,"
was sent by Pawel Dabek to make contact with the representative of
the Polish Workers Party in Lublin. Kaminski bound the Jewish partisans to the PPR cell established then in the village of Przybyslawice.
This cell extended a great deal of help to the partisans, particularly by
flying in food and sometimes by providing places for fighters to stay
during combat operations. Later, similar aid was given to the Jewish
partisans by the PPR cells that were established in the villages of
Przypisowka and Wola. In contrast, the population of other surrounding villages were hostile toward the partisans. When the Jewish
partisans appeared in the vicinity of their villages, the peasants im-

mediately made a lot of commotion, rang the church bells, called in the Germans, and sometimes even went out with arms against the partisans. The hostility of these peasants was a major factor in the murder of many of the civilian Jewish refugees hiding in the forests.[9]

On December 19, 1942, the Germans opened another large-scale hunt, aimed simultaneously against the partisans in the forests of Kozlow, Wola, and Garbow. According to Mark Dworecki, more than half of the refugees from Markuszow, Kamionka, Michow, and Kurow who had succeeded in hiding until then, died in this hunt. More than 400 Jews were killed. There were also some clashes between the Germans and the partisans. One such clash occurred when the Germans discovered a bunker where a group of former prisoners-of-war from Lublin were hiding. Armed with a machine gun, the Jews managed to defend their bunker. One of these men, Stengel, was fatally wounded and later died. The five remaining fugitives joined the other partisans. On the whole, the partisan groups emerged unharmed from this hunt, undoubtedly because of the additional arms they acquired and the capable command of Tolka.[10]

By the end of December, the partisans' activities ceased because of the heavy snows. They had to discontinue the continual movement from one point to another because tracks left in the snow would have led the Germans to the partisans; they decided to build bunkers for the duration of the winter. The Jews in hiding, who survived the previous hunt, also prepared bunkers. Embrasures were made in the bunkers to ready their defense; sleeping boards were prepared, and supplies of food and water were brought in. The partisans went out to combat action very rarely, and this only after a thorough check of the area. Despite this, several successful combat actions were carried out in January 1943, among them the seizure and destruction of a German patrol by Bleichman's group, during which the group took its first submachine gun.[11]

On February 19, the Jewish partisans received a heavy blow; their central bunker was uncovered, probably by local peasants. A large German hunt unexpectedly followed. The bunker was destroyed, and the partisans inside with Tolka at their head, were killed. Several dozen families of hiding Jews were killed. Among the partisans who survived was a group of ten fighters commanded by Jegier, which had gone to one of the nearby villages at the time of the hunt in order to get food. Bleichman's group, numbering close to twenty people, and Helfgot's group of eight, whose bunkers were in a different part of the forest, also survived.

After the calamity that struck the partisans' main force, the survivors chose Jegier as commander in place of Tolka. Israel Rosenberg was elected second-in-command. A few days later Jegier's partisans met Gruber's group in the forests of Garbow, where the latter group had been hiding for a month. After some unsuccessful attempts and the loss of some of its men, this group had finally given up its plan to make its way east. Gruber's men settled down in hideouts they had prepared and did not take part in any actions. Some, including Gruber, were still recovering from wounds they had suffered during their various unsuccessful clashes with the Germans.

The situation for the partisans and the remainder of the hiding Jews deteriorated considerably. For the first time in the region of Pulawy, a peasant family was executed by the Germans for giving help to Jews. This incident further hardened the peasants' attitude against the partisans and against the hiding Jews.[12]

The renewal of ties with the Polish Workers Party at the end of February, however, brought a certain amount of relief to the partisans. The PPR organizations in the area overcame the crisis that had befallen them with the arrest of the PPR leader, Pawel Dabek, and again strengthened their forces. In place of Dabek, Michal Wojtowicz was appointed PPR leader and was assigned the task of organizing armed groups in the area. Wojtowicz contacted the Jewish unit under Jegier's command, which at the time was the only armed unit active there. A plan was drawn up for the intensification of activities for the Jewish partisans, who had agreed to operate under the auspices of the People's Guard leadership. The unit under Jegier's command (which included Bleichman's, Helfgot's, and Gruber's groups) numbered about forty people. Because this was much too large a unit for the relatively small forests in the area north of Lublin, they were ordered to form two separate operating units. One, named the Emilia Plater unit was to remain under the direct command of Jegier; the second, named the Jan Kozietulski unit, was to be Gruber's command. Jegier was entrusted with the upper command and was to coordinate the activities of the two Jewish units. The Polish Workers Party gave these units the task of carrying out combat actions in the area north of Lublin up to the Wieprz River, and from Pulawy on the Vistula on the west, to Lubartow on the Wieprz to the east.[13]

The renewal of ties with the Polish Workers Party and the partisans' acceptance of GL command significantly improved the conditions under which the Jewish partisans operated. The first problem solved was that of supplying food to the partisans. This was achieved mainly with the help of the PPR cells that were active in a number of villages. A detailed system for providing supplies to the partisans was developed, which not only eased the burden on the village, but also provided certain benefits to the peasant population. The partisans would confiscate farm products from the peasants (with their silent agreement) and give them receipts for much larger quantities. This worked in the peasants' favor, because at that time they were released by the Germans from mandatory food-supply quotas if they could prove that they fell prey to confiscations by the partisans. Peasants who were under the influence of the Polish Workers Party provided food and informed the Germans of confiscations by the partisans only after the partisans were already reasonably far away. Sympathetic peasants also took wounded partisans into their homes until they recovered, and in certain cases, also gave shelter to the partisans' families who had, until then, hidden in the forest. At times the peasants also sheltered Jews whose hideouts had been discovered.

The Jewish units also established close ties with a number of the local Peasant Battalions' cells. Jegier, who displayed great personal initiative in gaining the sympathy of local underground commanders, was largely responsible for this. His habit of distributing, among the peasant population, certain products that were taken from the Germans, such as wine (after the capture of the wine factories in Samoklenski), fish, and sugar was especially successful. Particularly close cooperation was established with a Peasant Battalions group in the village of Tomaszowice. It was here that the partisan Hershel Fishbein recovered from the wounds he had suffered in one of the earlier battles.

On the other hand, relations with the AK groups that had been established in various villages in the area were strained. The first serious clash with the regional AK unit took place at the end of February 1943. The Jewish partisans came to the village of Lugow to survey the area and stayed with a local Polish resident, who was thought of as a friend. They were surprised by local AK men and murdered. A patrol sent by Jegier discovered the killers and found the bodies of the victims. The person responsible for the killing was shot, and two houses belonging to AK members were burned. A Polish patrol that was called in was met by the partisans' fire. This successful retaliatory operation served as a warning, and for a certain time AK attacks on Jewish partisans ceased.

In the summer of 1943, there was a recurrence of confrontations with the Home Army. At the center of the conflict this time was the confiscation of food from a few aristocratic estates that served as the main encampments for the Home Army. Out of the desire not to overburden the peasants in the friendly villages (it was impossible to "confiscate" continually from the same peasants without arousing the suspicion of the Germans), the partisans decided to acquire supplies for themselves and for the Jews under their protection from the local estates. The estate owners were given the choice of voluntarily providing certain quantities of food to the partisans. They refused and secured protection for themselves by enlisting members of the local AK organizations, or even by inviting German soldiers to their estates. An agreement, however, was reached with some estate owners in Boguczyn, Tomaszowice, and Milocin, after a series of clashes with local AK cells, and they promised the partisans small quantities of food.

The two Jewish units stepped up their activities in the spring of 1943. In principle the two units operated in different areas, with the exception of important actions carried out jointly under Jegier's command. The first in a series of important combat operations was the clash with the Germans in Garbow at the close of March 1943. The partisans under Gruber's command unexpectedly encountered a German police unit that had come to confiscate meat from local peasants. A battle ensued in which a German policeman was killed. The partisans suffered no losses. Another clash occurred on April 2, near the village of Siedliska. The unit entered a battle with the German gendarmerie, in which one gendarme was killed. The partisans had one wounded, and captured some rifles.[14]

On April 12 there was a serious skirmish near the village of Pryszczowa Gora. While the partisans under Gruber's command were in this village, a peasant managed to slip away and inform the gendarmes of the situation. The exchange of fire between the partisans and the Germans lasted several hours, and in the end the gendarmes were forced to abandon the village. The Jewish partisans suffered no losses. After the Germans retreated, the informer was executed. This incident highly intimidated the peasant population, but it also raised their respect for the fighting partisans.

On April 14, during the evening, the unit under Jegier's command entered Garbow and destroyed a dairy that was serving the Germans, despite the fact that there was a police post nearby. Along with the building that housed the dairy, the partisans destroyed the lists of quotas the peasant population in the region was required to supply to the Germans. This caused extreme satisfaction among the peasants. On April 17, in the town of Plotyczka, the joint units under Jegier's command fought for a few hours with a German gendarmerie and police unit numbering sixty men. This battle also ended with the

Germans' retreat. The Jewish partisans did not suffer any losses. On April 19, Gruber's partisans carried out a long-range raid during which they took over the village of Gadowo in the county of Opole Lubelskie, thirty kilometers from the unit's main base. Here, also, the partisans destroyed a dairy that was serving the Germans.[15]

In April, another group of fifteen fugitives from the prisoner-of-war camp in Lublin reached the Jewish partisans. In this way the partisan units grew and, despite the losses they suffered, their number reached about fifty fighters. They continued to be the only partisan force active in the area.[16]

On May 10, Jegier's unit broke into Markuszow, the birthplace of many of the Jewish partisans. They took over and destroyed the building that housed the administration offices and, at the same time, burned documents pertaining to supply quotas. The next day the same unit entered Garbow, five kilometers from Markuszow, where they destroyed another administration office. The same day an attack group belonging to the unit took over the village of Wolka and destroyed more documents concerning the supply quotas.[17]

The Germans decided to put an end to the partisans in the forests north of Lublin. On May 17 and 18, the largest hunt to date in this area was held. Taking part in the hunt were 2,000 army troops, 200 men from auxiliary air-force units, and units of the *Ordnungspolizei* and the gendarmerie.[18]

Despite the large number of forces used and the favorable topographical conditions, the Germans did not manage to force the partisans into an unwanted battle. The partisans, who had received prior notice, succeeded in getting away from the German pursuit and came out of the hunt unharmed. However, many of the noncombatant Jewish refugees still hiding in the forest were killed. After this hunt, most of the survivors left their forest hideouts and found shelter in the villages, in bunkers and lands belonging to a few peasants. In most cases this was in return for a fee, paid by the Jewish partisans who paid for the protection and support of at least one hundred Jews in hiding through means acquired during combat. Among the various measures of protection used by the partisans were the death sentences they handed down and carried out on peasants who handed Jews over to the Germans.[19]

After the German forces that had taken part in the hunt dispersed and the army returned to its barracks, the partisans renewed their activity. On June 4 the two Jewish units attempted an unsuccessful operation against the Lesce estate. Because one of the partisans fired prematurely, they lost the element of surprise. A

Wehrmacht platoon, which was encamped in the estate, was called in. The Germans took defensive positions and, despite the numerical superiority of the partisans, after a two-hour battle they managed to retreat, taking one wounded man with them.[20]

A battle with a German unit on the road near Naleczow, however, ended in a marked success. The two Jewish units under Jegier's command ambushed a German company that was confiscating agricultural products in one of the villages. The surprised Germans fled in haste, taking their wounded with them, and leaving behind wagons loaded with confiscated wheat. The partisans distributed the wheat to the village population, an act that had wide positive ramifications. Later that month, Jegier's unit attacked Markuszow and Garbow for a second time, again destroying the offices of the municipal authorities.

Another operation carried out in June was the attempt to free the prisoners of the forced labor camp in Jastkow. The attempt to take over the camp failed, but the prisoners succeeded in organizing some escapes and in freeing a few prisoners during their deportation to the Poniatowa camp. Some of these fugitives joined the partisans; others, who were not able to fight, were placed in a bunker in the vicinity of the village of Wola Przybyslawska.[21]

Until June 1943, the Jewish units operated independently, in principle, and had no close contact with the People's Guard command although they were annexed to this organization and enjoyed the support of the PPR members in the villages of Przypisowka, Wola, and Wola Przybyslawska. At the end of May, the headquarters of the People's Guard appointed Mieczyslaw Moczar commander of the region of Lublin. Moczar was given the task of overseeing the GL units, organizing a better coordination of their activities, and intensifying combat actions, particularly the sabotage of trains.

Moczar went to the Jewish units' zone of operation in the company of the Jewish partisan Gustaw Alef-Bolkowiak. The news brought by Bolkowiak of the existence of a large Jewish partisan unit in the nearby Parczew forests, made a strong impression on the Jewish partisans from Lubartow. Moczar's visit to Jegier's unit is described by Bolkowiak as follows: "Moczar stayed with the Jewish partisans for a few days and talked with them mainly about the problem of railway sabotage. The partisans were not materially prepared for this sort of action. They did not have explosives. Because of this they broke into the machine workshops in Garbow where they equipped themselves with tools for dismantling tracks. They carried out the first operation near Motycz."[22]

This first operation is described in the testimony of Natan Westschneider, a partisan from Jegier's unit. The partisans managed to dismantle the railway track, but the effects of this action were minor. A few cars went off the track and communications ceased for a few hours, but the damage caused to the enemy was of no value. The lesson learned from this action was that effective train sabotage necessitates the use of explosives. Yet these were supplied to the unit only at the end of 1943. Meanwhile, railway sabotage was held back, and the unit continued its attacks on economic targets.

A new hunt against the partisans and Jews in hiding opened on June 30. On the first day of the hunt the partisans succeeded in slipping away from the enemy. But the Germans did manage to capture four Polish members of the Polish Workers Party who had been in touch with the Jewish unit and had supplied it with information on the Germans' movements. The next day in the village of Kolda, the partisans were surprised by the Germans, who had been guided by the village head *(soltys)*. In the battle that followed, fifteen Jewish partisans were killed, the greatest loss suffered by the partisans in this area since February 1943. On the following day, July 2, there was a confrontation near the village of Irena, and one Jewish partisan was killed. During another clash with a unit of the *Ordnungspolizei* and the German gendarmerie near the village of Wawolnica on July 6, three more Jewish partisans were killed.[23]

The unit's losses during the first days of July curbed its actions for a month. But in August the combat activities were again intensified. One of the better-known operations, organized in cooperation with a group from the Peasant Battalions, was performed on August 14, 1943. It is described in the underground journal *Agencja Informacyjna-Wies (The Village News Agency)*, in the September 7, 1943, issue:

> On August 14, four men from the Peasant Battalions in the region of Pulawy attacked the estate in Garbow with the aim of destroying the threshing machine. During the course of the operation a battle was held with the estate's German guard. The GL's "Emilia Plater" unit came to the aid of the fighting Peasant Battalions' partisans. The battle ended with the retreat of the Germans who left their bicycles behind. According to the German announcement, a gang of "bandits" numbering about thirty men appeared at 10 A.M. It surrounded the Wehrmacht's post in Laskow and called on it to surrender. The battle continued until reinforcements of Trupenpolizei arrived from Pulawy.

According to Polish sources, one German was killed in this operation, and one was wounded. One of the partisans, Eisenberg, was also wounded.

In the summer of 1943 a local People's Guard unit numbering fifteen people was organized in the village of Przypisowka. These people were local peasants, members of the PPR underground cell, who from then on reinforced the Jewish partisan force during important combat operations.

Furthermore, in the summer and early fall of 1943, the Jewish units were reinforced with new partisans—Jews who had escaped from the POW camp in Lublin and the surrounding area, and even from as far away as Warsaw. There are no definite statistics regarding the number of people in the Jewish unit at that time. A report from the Government Delegacy on the situation in Poland in October 1943, however, estimated that the Jewish unit in the region of Pulawy and Lubartow consisted of one hundred fighters.[24] Nor is there detailed information on the Jewish unit's activities in October. We know only that according to the report of the German gendarmerie, the Jewish partisans were very active at this time in the area of Kloczew.[25]

Although it is also difficult to assess the number of Jews still in hiding that fall, we do know that the protection of the Jews in hiding continued to be the Jewish partisans' main concern. With money taken from the Germans in battle, the partisans paid peasants who hid Jews or supplied them with food. Quite often it was necessary to punish people who handed Jews over to the Germans, or who killed them. Pinchas Zyskind tells, for example, of how the Jewish partisans burned down the house of a peasant who turned in hiding Jews, and Dov Berezin tells of a death sentence handed down for the murder of hiding Jews. Bronislawa Garbacz, who escaped from the ghetto in Kurowka Podlaska and joined Jegier's unit, tells of the execution of a woman from the village of Kolenbrody in the region of Lublin, who turned hiding Jews over to the Germans for twenty kilograms of sugar.[26]

After a period of little combat during September and October, the partisans' armed activities increased. The largest in a series of clashes took place on November 23, when Jegier's unit captured Markuszow after overcoming a unit of German gendarmerie. Many products were again confiscated, most of which were distributed to the local Polish population. During the same month, the Jewish partisan group under the command of Ephraim Bleichman set out for the forests of Parczew, where they obtained explosives, submachine guns, ammunition, and instructions for mining railways.

After the return of Bleichman's group, train sabotage became the main task of the Jewish partisans in the area of Lubartow. A series of successful actions during which trains were attacked or forced off the tracks were carried out, particularly in the area of Motycz on the Warsaw-Lublin line. Mark Dworecki, one of the most experienced partisans in the mining of railways, particularly stood out during these actions. In addition to sabotaging trains, the Jewish partisans carried out a successful series of food confiscations from the estates of Tomaszowice, Lesce, and Garbow.[27]

Then in December 1943, the AL command organized a new partisan unit, called the Maciek unit, under the command of Jan Wojtowicz. The Jewish unit was now no longer alone in the forests of Pulawy and Lubartow. Wojtowicz's unit was made up mostly of local peasants, members of the Polish Workers Party, but from ten to twenty Jews from the Emilia Plater unit were also attached to it at various times.

Shortly after, from January 4 to 19, 1944, the Germans held a fifteen-day hunt in the area of Lubartow. This hunt, called *Unternehmen Wintersport*, was undertaken by *Wehrmacht* units and forces from the 25th battalion of the *Ordnungspolizei*. But this time, the German hunt produced no results whatsoever. On the contrary, the partisans soon became stronger.

The group led by Ephraim Bleichman again went to the Parczew forests and returned in February with the Janowski communications unit that had organized the parachuting of Soviet arms consignments for the partisans in the area. The next time Bleichman's group went east it brought back the paratrooper unit of Major Klim.[28]

Thanks to the drops organized by the Janowski and Klim units, the Jewish partisans received new submachine guns, machine guns, and explosives. Wojtowicz's unit also received a large number of arms. This supply contributed to the renewed intensification of combat actions. In addition, the Jewish partisans assisted the frequent movements east to the forests of Parczew, guiding Polish underground leaders on their way out of occupied Poland to Moscow through the Parczew forests to the eastern bank of the Bug. These leaders were Osobka-Morawski, Spychalski, Haneman, and Sidor.[29]

On March 15, sixteen Jewish partisans under the command of Gruber and Bleichman completed another successful mission. Returning from the Parczew forests after acting as liaisons, they received notice near the village of Jama that there was an SS and Ukrainian punishment expedition in this village, and that they were to attack. The action came as a complete surprise to the Germans and was crowned with success. Eight Germans were killed, and ten were taken prisoner and later executed. The partisans also captured many arms including three machine guns, ten submachine guns, and a few rifles. One partisan was killed, but the rest safely retreated after learning of the advance of the German armored column. After this operation the Germans burnt the village.[30]

In contrast, the joint operation against Samokleski, held at the same time, ended in total defeat. The partisan forces, which included Wojtowicz's unit and some members of the Jewish unit under Jegier's command, were surrounded by the Germans. In the attempt to break out of the siege, thirteen partisans were killed.

In the middle of March 1944, the AL command decided to transfer most of the partisan forces from the region of Lubartow to the forests of Parczew. Only Wojtowicz's unit was to remain behind. The partisans of the Janowski, Klim, and Jewish unit were to move to the Parczew forests. Before going, however, a group of Jewish partisans was ordered to transfer to the west bank of the Vistula two Soviet radio technicians, who had parachuted into Poland to carry out espionage for the staff of the First Byelo-Russian Front. The group was under Jegier's personal command. When the group passed near the village of Mesna it encountered a German unit. In the battle that ensued, the commander of the Jewish unit, Shmuel Jegier, was killed, the partisan Shmuel Rubinstein was seriously wounded in both legs, and according to Rubinstein's testimony, six Germans were killed. Jegier's death was a serious blow to the Jewish partisan movement in this region. The command now passed into the hands of Gruber, and he moved with the remainder of the joint Jewish unit (not including the partisans who were transferred to Wojtowicz's unit) to the forests of Parczew.[31]

On the whole, more than 150 Jewish partisans fought in the area north of Lublin, between Pulawy and Lubartow. Of these only forty survived until the liberation of Lublin. About 110 partisans died in battle. It is difficult to assess the number of Jews who hid and were killed in the forests, but it is likely that about two thousand Jews died in the forests of Garbow, Wola, and Kozlow. Only a few dozen of the Jews who hid in the forest survived to the end of the German occupation.

CHAPTER 4
SOUTH OF LUBLIN

THE BEST CONDITIONS FOR PARTISAN ACTIVITIES IN THE
area of the *General Gouvernement* were found in the southern part of
the district of Lublin. This area, which includes the counties of Janow,
Bilgoraj, Krasnystaw, Zamosc, and Hrubieszow, is largely covered
with forests. It is hilly and has a substantial number of small lakes.
There are three groups of average-sized forests in the western part of
this area. These are the forests of Janow and the somewhat smaller
forests of Lipsk and Goscieradow. The great forest of Puszcza Solska,
whose area is about 1,400 square kilometers, lies in the eastern part of
this region. Most of this area, and especially its eastern part, is hilly
because the Roztocze mountains range passes through here. The
lakes, found mostly in the northern and less-wooded part of this area,
block the approach to the forests of Janow and Puszcza Solska.

The southern part of the region of Lublin was only of minor
strategic importance to the Germans, because the main roads leading
from Poland to the east passed farther to the north (the Warsaw-
Brest-Moscow line) or farther to the south (the Cracow-Lvov line). As
a result, relatively few German army and police forces were stationed
here, and this had positive ramifications for the development of partisan activities.

Until 1939, more than 80,000 Jews lived, in the five southern
counties of Lublin mentioned above, in about forty towns and twenty
villages. A small number worked in agriculture, a very rare phenomenon in the *General Gouvernement*. In September 1939, a certain number
of these farmers and their non-Jewish colleagues hid a small quantity
of arms left behind by the defeated Polish units. These people later
became the pioneers of the local partisan movement. In accordance
with the February 15, 1941, order from Zoerner, governor of the

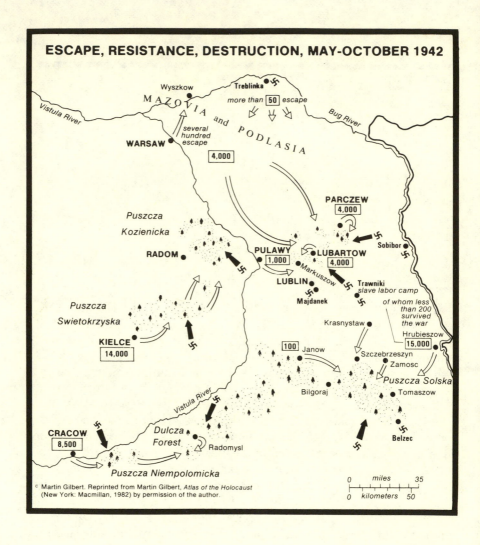

ESCAPE, RESISTANCE, DESTRUCTION, MAY–OCTOBER 1942

district of Lublin, limiting the areas in which Jews were allowed to reside, special neighborhoods for Jews were established in all of the towns. But with the exception of Krasnystaw and Izbica, in practice no towns established closed ghettos. It was therefore easier for Jews to establish ties with groups in the forest and to organize mass escapes.[1]

The beginning of the partisan movement in southern Lublin, and the beginning of the Jewish partisan movement, were almost identical to those in the Parczew forests. The partisan movement here was established by Red Army soldiers who had escaped from German captivity. Many of these soldiers benefited from the active support of Jews in the villages and the small towns, who treated the Russians with great friendliness and placed their trust in them. For example, two brothers, Yaakov and Yeheskel Met, organized a group of Jews in the village of Gorajec, between Frampol and Szczebrzeszyn, for the extension of wide-scale aid to the Russians. They equipped them with arms hidden in September 1939 and supplied them regularly with food. The main beneficiary of their aid was the largest Soviet partisan group in the area, under the command of Captain Rayevski.[2]

As in the area of the Parczew forests, the Jewish partisan movement in the south of the Lublin district got its start during the deportations carried out by the Germans and immediately acquired the nature of a mass movement. The transports to the extermination camps from this area began as early as April 1942. On April 8, a large number of Jews from Izbica were sent to the extermination camp in Belzec, and on April 11 and 12, the Jews of Zamosc and Krasnik were sent. The month of June saw the height of the transports to Sobibor: on June 2, the Jews of Hrubieszow were taken away, and on June 10, the Jews were driven away from Uchanie. Other Jewish communities in the region of Hrubieszow were liquidated in June. The transports were speeded up in August 1942. On a single day, August 9, the Germans carried out deportations from Bilgoraj, Szczebrzeszyn, and Tarnogrod. The expelled Jews met their death in the gas chambers of Belzec.[3]

During the deportations, the Jews in the small towns of southern Lublin showed persistent resistance, both active and passive, perhaps greater resistance than in most other areas of Poland. The younger ones escaped in large numbers to the forests in order to form armed units. Older people, women, and children resisted passively by hiding in the ghettoes, in nearby buildings, or in the villages. The diary of Dr. Klukowski contains a faithful description of the continuous deportations and of Jewish resistance in the town of Szczebrzeszyn. The first deportation there began on August 8, 1942, the day Dr. Klukowski wrote the following:

> As of the morning, no Jew was seen in the city. I went out to see what was actually going on. All the Jews, without exception, were ordered to appear before eight o'clock in the morning at the market near the Judenrat. They were allowed to take with them a 15-kilogram pack, food for five days, and 1,500 zlotys. The mayor told me that 2,000 Jews from Szczebrzeszyn must be brought to the Ukraine, and the railroad people told me that a fifty-five-car train was ready and waiting at the station. Not one Jew appeared on his own free will. They, therefore, started to seize them and bring them to the market square. I asked a gendarme from the local station who spoke perfect Polish what would be done if the Jews did not come. He answered curtly: "Then we will shoot them to death."
>
> It is seven o'clock in the evening. The whole afternoon, gendarmes, Gestapo men, Sonderdienst soldiers, Blue policemen, city guards, Judenrat members, and Jewish policemen were wandering about the street and looking for the Jews in their homes . . . but most of the Jews hid in such a way that they could not be found. Many Poles, particularly youths, are enthusiastically assisting in the search after the Jews. The excitement in the entire city is growing.[4]

The second deportation from Szczebrzeszyn was held on October 21. The course of this action is also described in the diary of Dr. Klukowski:

> The "deportation" of the Jews began at six o'clock. What this really meant was their end in Szczebrzeszyn. The whole day, until sunset, unforgettable things were going on. Armed gendarmes, SS men, and Blue policemen wandered about the city, chasing after the Jews and following their tracks. They drove them into the market and organized them into groups in front of the municipality building. They drove them out of various hideouts, broke down gates and doors, broke shutters, and threw hand grenades into a few cellars and apartments. They were shooting with pistols, submachine guns, and machine guns that were positioned in various places. They beat them, kicked them, and were generally cruel in an inhuman way. At three o'clock they took 900 Jews—men, women, and children—out of the town, forcing them to run by hitting them with sticks and rifle butts, and shooting the whole time. Only members of the Judenrat and the Jewish police rode in wagons. The action did not stop with their departure. They continued to look for those still hiding. They announced that death awaits anyone hiding Jews or their belongings. Those who discovered Jewish hideouts were promised a prize. The Jews who were caught were shot on the spot

without mercy. The Poles had to bury the dead. How many, it is hard to say. Their number is estimated at 400 to 500. I will try to get the exact number from the Municipality. From the number mentioned, it is possible to estimate that about 2,000 are still hiding. Those who were captured were brought to the station. Where they took them—I do not know.[5]

On the second day of the deportation Klukowski wrote:

The search for the Jews is continuing. The foreign gendarmes and the SS men left yesterday. Today our gendarmes and Blue policemen, who received instructions to kill any Jew captured on the spot, are at work. They are following their orders with great enthusiasm. Since the morning they have been bringing corpses of Jews in wagons from all parts of the city, and especially from the Jewish quarter known as Zatyty. They are digging large pits in the cemetery and burning them there. They have been taking Jews out of all kinds of hideouts all day long. They were shot on the spot, or brought to the cemetery and killed there. Over thirty Jews were gathered in the municipal jail. With my own eyes I saw how they took them out of the jail and ran them through the market to the cemetery.[6]

On the third day of the deportation Klukowski wrote the following:

In Szczebrzeszyn, the Gestapo operated with the aid of the local gendarmes and the Blue police, and with the help of some of the city's residents. Especially outstanding was a young policeman from Sulow, Matysiak. The gatekeeper, Skoczak, cracked the skulls of Jews, who had been taken out of their hideouts, without the use of a gun or a pistol. Other civilians for their own pleasure helped enthusiastically. They took the Jews out of hiding places, beat them, kicked them, etc. There were those who abused these poor people all day long. Others transported the corpses and dug pits in the cemeteries. The noise of shooting was heard from time to time.[7]

The action ended on October 24. It, too, is described by Dr. Klukowski:

Everything is continuing. The Gestapo men from Bilgoraj are wild. With the aid of the civilian population, gendarmes, and policemen, they are taking Jews out of all sorts of places, shooting them on the spot or bringing them to the cemetery and killing them there. They gather some of them in the municipal jail, and later on take them in larger groups to the cemetery. I saw how they moved these groups. The gendarmes, policemen, and unarmed Poles enlisted to help out, wearing black German uniforms, walked on the side. They beat the Jews nonstop on the back, the head, and every other place. . . .

They were continually bringing Jews to the cemetery. The whole day they were transporting corpses. The Jews' possessions were taken out of their apartments to the market square. Quite a number of the city's residents shamelessly took anything that came into their hands. Images of beaten Jews, groups being brought to be killed, Jewish corpses thrown carelessly on wagons dripping blood are always before my eyes. Most of the victims are women, children, and old people. You see relatively few young men. They are either better able to hide or have already managed to escape to the forest. It is said that they are threatening revenge and will burn the city for the behavior of its civilian population.[8]

Szczebrzeszyn was not outstanding. This was the usual course of deportation, resistance by the Jews, and reaction from the Polish population in all of the cities and towns in the southern part of the Lublin district. In some cases, as for example in Tarnogrod, there were incidents of active resistance. In all places, without exception, Jews escaped to the forests. The total number of those who fled from the five counties in southern Lublin reached 20,000, where, largely because of conducive geographical conditions, the rate of escape was greater than in any other part of occupied Poland. All of the towns in this region were relatively close to large areas of forests that could provide shelter from the pursuit of the Germans.

Yet, as was the case in the area of the Parczew forests, the majority of fugitives were killed in the first German hunts. This is evident from the 200 or so grave sites strewn over the forests and fields of southern Lublin, uncovered after the war.

And yet, even in spite of these extensive hunts, hundreds of Jews succeeded in organizing partisan units and carrying out the struggle. A row of family camps, similar to the camp of Altana in the Parczew forests, was established under the protection of the partisans. But the fate that awaited the partisan units and the family camps there was completely different from that of the Jews in the Parczew forests. In the latter, a Jewish partisan company succeeded in surviving as a whole until the liberation, along with about 200 people from the family camp. But in the forests of Janow and Puszcza Solska, whole partisan units were destroyed, and not a living soul survived from the many family camps. A great tragedy befell both the Jewish partisan movement and the family camps that were under the partisans' protection.

The almost complete annihilation of the Jewish partisan units has left us with only fragmentary information about their existence, which in no way enables us to determine the important details of the establishment and actions of these units. We have found only slight references to the existence of a few Jewish units in German police documents that have come to us. The following are a few examples only. For instance, the communiqué of the commander of the *Ordnungspolizei* in the district of Lublin to the *Ordnungspolizei* commander of the *General Gouvernement*, dated July 6, 1943, tells of a clash between a cavalry unit and a Jewish group near Kowalina, five kilometers southwest of Krasnik. In this battle the Germans killed ten Jews and captured arms and ammunition.[9] The communiqué of the gendarmerie commander in the district of Lublin of August 17, 1943, speaks of a battle in the village of Podgranicznik (in the Rybczewice community, 30 kilometers northwest of Krasnystaw). In this clash two Jews were killed.[10] The communiqué of the *Ordnunsgpolizei* commander in the district of Lublin, dated August 26, 1943, describes a clash between the German *Truppenpolizei* and a large partisan unit on August 21 in the vicinity of the village of Poreba (in the Zwierzyniec community, 26 kilometers east of Bilgoraj), and tells of the presence of Jews in the partisan unit. The communiqué of the commander of the Lublin gendarmerie, dated August 29, states that *Wehrmacht* soldiers discovered three bunkers and killed eleven Jews on August 27 in the area of Sawin in the county of Chelm Lubelski (in the forest of Malinowka, 20 kilometers from Chelm Lubelski). And finally, at a meeting of the GG government on March 29, 1943, the governor, Hans Frank, reported that 800 Jews had fled to the forests in the area of Chelm, and that this increased the numbers of "gangs," (meaning the partisans).[11]

We find similarly fragmented pieces of information about the existence of Jewish units in a few Polish sources. For instance, the extremely right-wing underground paper, *Wielka Polska (The Great Poland)* reported on October 27, 1943, that in the period between June 3 and July 12, Polish units wiped out two armed Jewish units (called "gangs of robbers" by the paper).

Without additional sources, little can be learned from this kind of information and, therefore, it is impossible to identify the Jewish units and armed groups that are mentioned. It is also impossible to make any numerical assessment of the size of these groups.

More substantial information, however, has survived on the partisan group commanded by Mendel Heler, which operated in the area of Tomaszow Lubelski. In this town, an underground Jewish youth organization was established with the aim of acquiring weapons in order to move into the forest for partisan activities.

The organization encountered great hardship in the acquisition of arms. The first agents who promised to help, Poles, betrayed the group, and caused the deaths of a few members of the organization. After some time the group succeeded in acquiring a rifle and a pistol. With these arms, the youth group went out to the forest. The first clash with the Germans took place in the middle of December 1942, when the Jewish group attacked a German patrol in the area of Rogizna forest, hoping to acquire additional arms. A few Germans were killed.[12] At the same time, the Germans were carrying out suppressive actions against the village population in the area. The rightwing underground journal *Polska (Poland)* put the blame for the enemy's actions against the Polish population on the Jewish partisans, and opened a campaign denouncing the armed Jewish group. The December 17, 1942, issue of this journal reads: "Our people are made responsible for everything. As for example the fact that in Tomaszow Lubelski, the Jews organized into a gang and killed two German gendarmes."

After a short period of combat activity, the group from Tomaszow was defeated, under circumstances that remain unknown.

We have somewhat better information on the Jewish units that were connected, at least for a short time, with the People's Guard. Among the first Jewish partisans were those who were part of the unit headed by the Soviet officer Rayevski. This first group, who had begun to escape to partisan units as early as May 1942 with the first deportations, had been living in the villages of Reczyca, Goraj, and Gorajec, where they had managed to hide a few arms left behind in September 1939 by the retreating Polish army units. When they fled to the forest, these people made up the nucleus of a Jewish group that joined Rayevski's unit. Hundreds of other Jews hid in the forest or in the surrounding villages under the protection of the partisans. Having no alternative, the partisans were forced to concentrate on the acquisition of food for the people hiding in the forests, and to concern themselves with payments to peasants who agreed to hide Jews in the villages.[13]

In June, or the beginning of July, 1942, a few Poles, headed by the Spuzak brothers, from a village in the Szczebrzeszyn area, joined Rayevski's unit. This unit, therefore, now had mixed nationalities, but there is no doubt that the Jewish partisans made up the majority of the unit. And in the summer of 1942 Rayevski's unit was the largest and best equipped in the south of the district of Lublin. It had three submachine guns and a few rifles, and each fighter had a pistol and grenades. When the Germans discovered the existence of this unit, they made great efforts to destroy it. However, Rayevski's partisans succeeded again and again in evading the pursuit of the much stronger German police and army units.

Defeat came only by chance. At the end of July, the partisans stopped for a night in the village of Deszkowice. A few of the Russians got drunk and went to sleep in a barn. Having been called in by local people, the Germans arrived very soon thereafter and surrounded the village. Despite this, most of the unit's people managed to escape. Only those sleeping in the barn remained behind, to be burned alive when the Germans set fire to the barn.

After this incident, Rayevski decided to leave the district of Lublin and turn east. The partisans had already received news that the movement in Polesie was substantially strengthening. Because the district's local population was so hostile toward the partisans, Rayevski was determined to face the danger of crossing the Bug. However, the Jewish partisans, who could not abandon the hiding families to their fate, refused to go with the Russians. Rayevski and his group of eighteen people decided to leave without them. They promised the Met brothers, who headed the Jewish partisans, that after forming ties with the Soviet partisans operating in Polesie they would make sure that a liaison was sent to the Jewish partisans and would make efforts to transfer them and the hiding families across the Bug. So a few Poles, together with the Jewish partisans, remained at the unit's main base in the vicinity of Kosznia, between Frampol and Turobin.

Kosznia's residents, however, were extremely antagonistic toward the Jewish unit established in their area. The local forest watchman collaborated with both the AK group established in the village and the Germans. It was he who supplied the Germans with detailed information on the whereabouts of the Jewish partisans and led the Germans to a surprise attack on the partisans in which two partisans were killed. Yet, despite the superiority of the German forces, the unit succeeded in holding onto its positions until nightfall, when the Jewish partisans retreated and escaped.

With definite evidence of the forest watchman's collaboration with the Germans, the partisans decided to kill the betrayer—a sentence they carried out when the Germans were far away. But the Home Army exploited this killing for the purpose of spreading anti-Jewish propaganda. Claiming that the Jews killed innocent Poles, they managed to enlist a few hundred local peasants for a campaign to expel the mostly Jewish partisan unit from the forest.[14]

Stefan Kilanowicz, the Polish communist activist known as Grzegorz Korczynski, who had taken part in the Spanish Civil War, came to southern Lublin in August 1942. He was given the task of establishing a People's Guard partisan unit in this area and wanted to establish ties with the partisans of the former Rayevski unit or with other partisan groups, particularly Soviet and Jewish ones that were not connected to the Home Army or the Peasant Battalions operating in the area. Soon he did contact a few groups, among them the Jewish partisans of the former Rayevski unit. And although in the beginning the ties were somewhat weak, in time the Jewish group was annexed to the new People's Guard Tadeusz Kosciuszko unit that Korczynski formed.

A second group that Korczynski incorporated into his unit was a group of forty Jewish prisoners-of-war from the Polish-German war of 1939 who had been imprisoned in the POW camp on Lipowa Street in Lublin. (Their organization and the circumstances of their escape will be discussed in greater detail in chapter 12, with the armed underground in this camp.)

The Jewish group operated in the area of Krasnik for a short time only. It was suddenly attacked by Poles with whom it had been in contact and from whom it had expected assistance. With the exception of two, Jan Szelubski and Bleicher, who survived miraculously, all the Jewish partisans were killed. We do not have enough information on the identity of the killers. It can be assumed that the killing was carried out by members of the POW organization with whom Korczynski had connections. After the war, this killing served as the basis for legal proceedings against Korczynski, who was held fully responsible for the action. Yet, because of the political circumstances of Poland after the war, the matter was covered up and the trial was postponed. Its details were never made public.[15]

Another group that joined Korczynski's unit was made up of Jews who had fled under the command of Yaakov Freitag from the village of Reczyca. A few Jews who managed to escape from Majdanek concentration camp also joined this unit. Their commander was known as Robert.[16]

On October 2, 1942, about 300 Jews fled the town of Frampol during the deportation. Some of them had acquired guns earlier and hid them in the forest. A new Jewish unit was thus established and soon joined Korczynski's unit. A group of five escaped Soviet prisoners-of-war under the command of Ciencow also joined Korczynski's unit. Among them was a Jewish officer from Kiev called Grisha.[17]

Korczynski's unit and its first actions were not well received by the local AK organizations, however. Korczynski himself wrote about this:

When our unit opened combat action, they saw it not only as harmful but as unpatriotic. In different talks I held with the heads of the organization [the regional commanders of the AK], they made me swear by God that I would not carry out armed actions, because every action held now only helped Moscow and provided the Germans with an alibi for killing people. It was difficult to explain to them that smoke was rising from the ovens in Auschwitz as early as 1940, when there were no People's Guard units around to provide an alibi.[18]

Because of his commitment to the PPR's stand, Korczynski could not deviate from the plans calling for anti-German actions. This met with a very sharp reaction on the part of the Home Army, which went out against Korczynski's unit.

Before its reinforcement, Korczynski's unit underwent a serious internal crisis. In the beginning of October, a group of twelve Soviet partisans came from across the Bug. Most likely, they were Rayevski's emissaries. They contacted the Jewish partisans who had formerly belonged to Rayevski's unit and suggested that they cross the Bug and go east. A dispute broke out in Korczynski's unit. Korczynski spoke out strongly against any attempt to leave the district of Lublin, an act that was against the principles of the Polish Workers Party, which was trying to develop partisan activity on Polish soil. On the other hand, the Russians from Ciencow's group and some of the Jews favored the idea of crossing the Bug, despite Korczynski's protests. In the end, the Russians and a few of the Jews, among the Majdanek camp fugitives with Robert at their head, withdrew from Korczynski's unit and joined the Russian group returning east. The attempt to cross the Bug, however, did not succeed. The long-distance march was an impossible undertaking for a large and under-equipped group. Only a few of the partisans succeeded in crossing the Bug, and later, in joining the Soviet partisans. Most returned to their former places and rejoined Korczynski's unit.[19]

After their return, the unit was reorganized and divided into several squads. Robert, one of the Jews who had escaped from Majdanek, headed one of these squads. On October 15, this squad carried out a successful ambush on the road near Bychawa, attacking two trucks carrying gendarmes. They threw a grenade at one of the trucks and opened fire on both, killing four Germans. One partisan was killed. This action and the ones that followed it took place far from the unit's base, which was then in the forests of Lipsk.

On October 21 certain events took place which led to the death of Robert. The partisans were on their way toward Ludmilowka in the region of Anopole. When they reached a hut in the forest of Brzoza, it turned out that Ott, the forest watchman who was supposed to wait for them, had disappeared. The Polish historian Rosinski describes what followed:

> The forest watchman—a member of the ZWZ [*Zwiazek Walki Zbrojnej*, the earlier name for the Home Army]—was supposed to inform the People's Guard of the disposal of German units and the situation in the area. This was suspicious because the ZWZ commanders had threatened the partisans that they would "teach them a lesson" in retalitation for their combat actions. Unfortunately, these threats were not taken seriously.

> The forest watchman brought the gendarmes along a hidden path to the unit's headquarters. At one o'clock in the afternoon, the gendarmes opened an attack which was preceded by a clash with some partisans who were on a patrol. The unexpected German action made organized defense impossible. Despite heavy firing by the enemy, the partisans managed to get away from the mountain through a narrow crevice, leaving one dead and one seriously wounded behind. One of the very bravest, the squad commander Robert, was fatally wounded in the stomach by a bullet.[20]

In this way, the fugitive from Majdanek, Robert, was killed.

After this clash, Korczynski decided to divide his unit into small groups that would operate from different bases. Because of the hostility of the members of the underground connected with the Home Army, which enjoyed the support of most of the local population, actions by a large GL unit operating out of one base seemed impossible. Most of the partisans were sent in small groups to the forests of Lipsk or Puszcza Solska, and the majority of the Jews went with them. There is no information on their fate or their actions during the winter of 1942–1943.

Korczynski, himself, along with a group of twenty partisans including several Jews, moved to the area of Zaklikow. There they established a partisan base in Ludmilowka, the only village in the area that was under the influence of the Polish Workers Party. In this village, Korczynski organized a group of fifteen local peasants. There were, therefore, altogether thirty-five men under Korczynski's command, among whom were two Jewish groups under the command of Yaakov Freitag and Reuven Pintel.[21]

A short while later, events took place which hastened the death of the Jews interned in the Janiszow forced labor camp. Rosinski describes this also:

In November the GL men brought two people, Yankel and Shlomo, who had escaped from the camp in Janiszow, to the commander in Ludmilowka. They came to ask for immediate help in the name of all of the prisoners in the camp, because the camp's commander, Peter Ignor, had boasted that within the shortest time possible the Germans would liquidate the camp and transport the survivors to Majdanek "for soap." The fugitives described the situation at the camp in detail. After gathering the information, Korczynski decided to carry out an operation at the Janiszow camp with the aid of the local underground cells in order to save the 600 prisoners who were still alive. . . . On November 6, after dark, and taking all precautions, the unit moved from Ludmilowka. Yankel and Shlomo served as guides.[22]

The attack on the camp and the capture and execution of the guards were a complete success. After a detailed description of the attack on the camp Rosinski continues:

The camp was dispersed. *The prisoners who volunteered for the unit were not accepted because of their weak physical condition and because of the lack of arms and quarters.* Only those prisoners who had served in the army and had military training were accepted. The rest were shown the way to the forests of Lipsk, Janow, and Goscieradow, where they were to hide and gradually join the ranks of the People's Guard. . . .[23] [Italics mine.]

During the last stage of the operation, vehicles bearing gendarmes came in from the direction of Zaklikow. Because they were afraid to come close to the camp itself, the gendarmes opened fire from the distance of one kilometer, hoping to force the partisans into an exchange of fire so they could determine their number.

The partisans were faster: they shot the guards and, after helping the prisoners escape, retreated in the direction of the forest of Gizowka. Ignor alone was killed in the morning.

During the operation in the camp, the partisans took the camp's safe (containing some tens of thousands of *zlotys* and a substantial quantity of jewels and money stolen from the prisoners), a few rifles, three pistols, a submachine gun, grenades, and many bullets. Also taken were food, clothing, eighty pairs of shoes, and a radio. All these things were taken to Ludmilowka on wagons and hidden in the base. These things were a valuable addition to the unit's supplies. Additional arms and better clothing and shoes for the winter were thus made available to the partisans.[24]

Rosinski ignores the fact that the forest was inaccessible to crowd of several hundred former prisoners, both because of the lar distance that had to be covered during a difficult time of year (the of fall) and because of the lack of prepared bases and connections. After the first wave of joy swept through the prisoners, they realized that what they were actually facing was inescapable, immediate destruction. Only sixty prisoners succeeded in evading the German police unit and hiding in the depths of the forest. Hundreds of others, who did not see any way of hiding from the German police forces that followed them, decided to return to the camp, assuming that this would save them from certain death. A few dozen of them were killed immediately by the Germans, and the majority was transferred to the forced labor camp in Budzyn.

The sixty people who had managed to avoid the German pursuit tried to organize in the forest, hoping to establish a partisan unit. They were quickly attacked and killed by various armed Polish groups.[25]

During the winter of 1942–1943, Korczynski's partisans in Ludmilowka and the Jewish groups in the forests of Lipsk and Puszcza Solska were not very active. Then, in the beginning of February 1943, Joseph Shapiro, a Jewish communist activist and a former officer in the Spanish Civil War arrived in Ludmilowka. He came as a representative of the People's Guard command, which had made him the political commissar of Korczynski's unit. Shapiro brought along instructions for intensifying the partisan action in the south of the district of Lublin.

Korczynski's unit went to the forests in the middle of February to meet the partisans living in bunkers, taking organizational steps necessary for the intensification of activity in southern Lublin. Korczynski and Shapiro joined the Jewish and Russian partisans who, until then, had been operating on their own, and following talks with the commanders of these groups, established the so-called Tadeusz Kosciuszko operational group in 1943. Korczynski was its commander and Shapiro its political commissar. It had two Jewish units, ʌamed after Berek Joselewicz and Staszic; two Polish units, under the ⁻nand of Felis and Choina; two Russian units, under the com-
ᶠ Atamanov and Ciencow; and a mixed Russian-Polish-Jewish
⁻ the command of Jastrzab. In addition, a few Jews fought
ʻʌnit.[26]

ʻk of the new operational group was railroad sabo-
ⁿ-Lwow line. But before the unit could begin its
blow befell it. On April 4, the operational
ʻas surrounded by a strong German unit, after
ᵊd Garbacz betrayed it. In the battle that took
ʌrters staff was killed, among them the polit-

ical commissar, Shapiro. Under circumstances that were not explained, only the commander, Grzegorz Korczynski, survived. This had a negative effect on his control of the units, and from then on the various groups operated independently. In August 1943, the Kosciuszko operational group was officially dismantled.

The Berek Joselewicz unit had a base in Puszcza Solska, and was led by Edward Forst. Little information survives about its activities. From a few Polish documents, it is possible to gather only a few details on the battles it carried out in April and May of 1943. It is known, for example, that on April 24 this unit, together with the unit under the command of Atamanov, warded off the attacks of a very large German force that was holding a hunt in Puszcza Solska. On May 1, the Jewish unit, the Polish Mickiewicz unit, and Atamanov's Soviet unit were again attacked.

On June 27 the Germans launched a hunt called *Unternehmen Wehrwolf* against the partisans in southern Lublin. The hunt lasted until July 11 and was carried out by very large forces—two *Wehrmacht* infantry regiments (one from the 154th and one from the 174th divisions), a few *Ostlegion* units, battalions from five SS *Ordnungspolizei* regiments (the 4th, 13th, 25th, 26th, and 32nd regiments), two *Schutzpolizei* companies (the 203rd and 252nd), one motorized gendarmerie company, a police cavalry unit, the Lublin cavalry battalion, and air support—all led by the *Ordnungspolizei* commander in the *General Gouvernement*, General Becker.[27]

The partisans suffered heavy losses in this hunt, and the Jews in the family camps in the forests were also seriously hit. As a result of the hunt, there was a certain slackness in the partisan movement, particularly in the regions of Bilgoraj and Zamosc, the focus of Becker's units. The Soviet units, seeing that it was no longer possible to continue the struggle in this area, crossed the Bug to the east. These were Ciencow's unit, Atamanov's unit, Wolodin's unit, and all the Russians from the unit under the command of Palen. The Jews who had fought in these units left with the Russians. The Polish unit under the command of Choina disintegrated, and the partisans of the second Polish unit (Mickiewicz's unit) returned home, only to reorganize later as a raiding group in the village of Karpiowka, the birthplace of most of the partisans. The losses suffered by the Jewish Berek Joselewicz unit are not known, but they were probably quite serious. In August 1943, the unit ceased to exist. Most of the surviving partisans transferred to the Soviet unit under the command of General Fiodorov. It can be assumed that all of these partisans died in the course of the unit's continuous battles. This is evident from the lack of even one testimony of a Jewish partisan who had belonged to this unit.[28]

The second Jewish unit, called the Staszic unit by the People's Guard, to which it was very loosely tied, was active in the area between Frampol and Szczebrzeszyn until the spring of 1944. One of this unit's important operations was an attack on a train in the area of Stalowa Wola in the beginning of 1943. For this operation, the unit moved a great distance away from its main base in the forests of Jozefow. But when, at the end of the operation, the unit returned to the base, it became a target for German attacks during the antipartisan *Unternehmen Wehrwolf* campaign.

Surrounded by strong German forces in the area of Ruda Sokolowska, the unit divided into small groups of two or three men, in order to break out of the German encirclement. In their desperate attempts to break out of the siege that week, many partisans died and many Jews hiding under the protection of the partisans were killed. Afterward, it took about a week for the survivors to find each other.

This hunt completely cut off the ties between the unit and the People's Guard, and thus the Jewish groups, now greatly weakened, operated alone. After some time the unit was joined by a group of Russians from the defeated Soviet unit, who suggested crossing the Bug to the east. Most of the Jewish partisans agreed to this suggestion, but there were those who opposed it. In the end only a small group of a few score partisans remained in the region.[29]

For most of the partisans who decided to leave the area, the journey was not successful. They reached the Bug but could not cross it. After some unrewarding attempts during the course of two weeks, the partisans returned to their former base, where they again united the groups and began preparing bunkers for the winter.

During the winter of 1943–1944, the unit limited its actions to the acquisition of food, particularly attacks on warehouses or stores that were under the enemy's supervision. During this period, the peasants' attitude toward the Jewish partisans improved, undoubtedly due to the expectation of a quick end to the war. A few Jews who previously had hidden in bunkers in the forest were sheltered now in nearby villages, and the peasants provided the partisans with information on the positions of German units. Aside from those concealed in the villages, there were still some Jews hiding in bunkers under the protection of the Jewish partisans.

On New Year's Eve, 1944, the Jewish unit attacked the Ryczyn estate, where some Volksdeutsche had settled. The attackers terrified the Germans, who were in the midst of a Sylvester night celebration.

The partisans confiscated large quantities of food and clothing for themselves and for the hiding population.

At the end of the winter the tie with the PPR representatives was renewed. It was suggested to the Jewish partisans that they again come under the command of the People's Army. Meanwhile, the Jews learned that the strong Soviet Kovpak unit under the command of Vershihora had reached the nearby region of Tarnogrod, and the majority decided to join it. The Jewish partisans were accepted into the "Kovpak" unit on March 1, 1944, and, thereafter, fought in its ranks. Only a small portion of the unit stayed behind to annex itself later to units of the People's Army. In the heavy battles that took place in the spring, most of the partisans, both those who stayed behind and those who joined the Soviet units, were killed. Only a few members of the Jewish unit lived to see the end of the war.

The forests east of Krasnik, between Janow and Turobin, were an important center of the partisan movement. At the end of October and the beginning of November 1942, thousands of Jews fled to these forests, after the rise in deportations from the surrounding area. As in other areas in the district of Lublin, most of the fugitives were killed during the first German hunts. Yet about 1,000 Jews succeeded in surviving in the forests until the winter, and scores of them began organizing armed units in hope of carrying out partisan actions. However, they soon encountered a new and dangerous enemy, which benefited from the support of the local population. This was the armed Polish gang, which, headed by Andrzej Kielbasa, nick-named *Dziadek* (Grandfather), took upon itself the job of killing Jews. Later on, Kielbasa became affiliated with the Home Army unit, which was headed by Maly and then moved to an NSZ unit under the command of Znicz. These units were often engaged in the treacherous murder of Jews.[30]

No less dangerous was Sobotnik's gang, which was composed of peasants from the village of Godziszow. After a mass murder carried out by Kielbasa, the surviving Jews were forced to leave the forest of Pilacki. In a nearby forest, some joined a partisan unit organized by Avraham Braun, who had taken on the task of securing protection for the Jews in hiding. According to Zysmilch (one of the unit's few survivors), Braun's unit numbered close to forty people at the end of 1942. Very little is known of the actions of this unit at the end of 1942 and the beginning of 1943.

Known by his partisan name of Adolf, Avraham Braun organized a camp for the Jewish fugitives, as Yechiel Greenshpan had done in the forests of Parczew, and near the family camp, he built bunkers for the partisan unit. At the beginning, Braun's partisans were primarily concerned with acquiring food for themselves and the Jews hiding under its protection. At the same time, the unit carried out attacks on small Polish police and German gendarmerie posts in order to acquire arms. Some time later, they established ties with a loose group of thirty people operating in the surrounding area, which was made up of Soviet prisoners-of-war who had escaped from P.O.W. camps.

Together the two groups attempted a series of attacks on trains which, however, usually failed. The unit still lacked the means and experience needed for this sort of action. Zysmilch describes one of these operations, an attempt to dismantle railway tracks: "Although a few cars went off the track and the train was fired at, the Germans succeeded in organizing their defense and opened intensive fire against the partisans. The partisans were forced to retreat. In this operation the partisan Yehoshua Kleiman was killed."[31] After these attempts, the train sabotage operations ceased, and the unit concentrated on attacks against small enemy posts.

In the spring of 1943, the unit made contact with the People's Guard, which wanted to subordinate to its command the Polish, Jewish, and Soviet units that were operating independently. Braun's unit was annexed to the People's Guard and given the name Adolf, after its commander. It can be assumed that the unit grew at this time to number seventy or eighty people.

In the summer of 1943, when the number of People's Guard units in the region of Krasnik rapidly increased, headquarters decided to reorganize the existing small units into partisan battalions. Following this reorganization, two People's Guard partisan battalions were established in the forests of Knieja, east of Krasnik: they were Battalion No. 3 under the command of Wladyslaw Skrzypek, who was known as Orzel, and Battalion No. 4 under the command of Karol Lemichow-Herzenberger, who was called Lemiszewski. Battalion No. 3 was made up mostly of Poles; Battalion No. 4 was made up of two companies—the Jewish Adolf unit and a Russian company. Thus, the Jewish and the Russian units that had worked side by side during the winter of 1942–1943 were joined together into one battalion.[32]

This reorganization, carried out in September 1943, was supposed to improve and strengthen the combat actions. Yet the opposite occurred; the reorganization of the partisans in the forests of Knieja unexpectedly brought a tragedy upon the Jewish unit. The man mainly responsible for this tragedy was the battalion's commander, Herzenberger.

Karol Lemichow-Herzenberger, a German from the banks of the Volga, had been a lieutenant in the Red Army. After he fell prisoner at the beginning of the German-Soviet war, he volunteered for the German police and quickly rose to the rank of police commander in Bychawa. He served there at the time of the liquidation of the Jewish community. At the end of Spring, 1943, Herzenberger contacted the then-commander of the People's Guard in southern Lublin, Kilianowicz Korczynski. As was agreed between the two, Herzenberger fled to the partisans and Korczynski made him battalion commander.[33] At about the same time, the People's Guard representatives made contact with Kielbasa's gang. Hoping to increase the Guard's influence among the local peasants, they suggested that Kielbasa join this left-wing organization. In a talk he held with the battalion commanders and other officers of the People's Guard, Kielbasa did not, at first, show any enthusiasm for this offer.[34] But after talking with the commanders of the two battalions stationed in Knieja, Kielbasa expressed his willingness to join the People's Guard, under the condition that the Jews be expelled. The events that took place after the first talks between Herzenberger, Skrzypek, and Kielbasa clearly indicate that Kielbasa's terms were accepted. A plan was drawn up for the sudden and total destruction of the Jewish company.

Three documents, containing different versions of the events leading to the killing, have come down to us. Without mentioning the liquidation, the partisan Stanislaw Bieniek briefly writes about this in his book of memoirs, published as *I am a Son of the Polish People:* "In Knieja we were in contact with Romek, a representative of Kielbasa's band of robbers. He came to us for talks. When he entered the camp, he began talking with a Jewish guard who gave him his rifle. Shooting broke out, after which we were forced to hastily retreat."[35] The Polish historian Zbigniew Jerzy Hirsz, Bieniek's editor, adds the following comment to this short statement: "The guard did not hand his gun over. It was taken away from him in a treacherous manner. Romek asked only to look at the rifle, promising to then give it back. But he did a different thing: he brought the rifle to the commander Karol Herzenberger (known as Lemiszewski) and accused the guard of handing the weapon over of his own free will."[36]

There is no doubt that Zysmilch's testimony has more truth to it. It appears from his testimony that the guard, who had previously been told that a representative of a "friendly" unit would be coming for talks, welcomed Romek warmly, let him pass through, and showed him the way to the battalion commander. Herzenberger viewed this behavior as a breach of orders regarding guard duty. The guard was supposed to stop anyone coming in and to call in a superior officer to check out the newcomer's identity. A hastily arranged court handed down a death sentence on the guard. The next day the Jewish company was told to assemble to hear the verdict and the reason behind it. The Jewish partisans, who did not at all suspect that this was a plot against them drawn up by Herzenberger and Kielbasa, could not understand the severity of the guard's sentence. Two brothers of the accused in the unit were especially bitter. Despite this, the Jewish unit reported in. It was quickly surrounded by people who, until, then had been its comrades-in-arms, and by Kielbasa's men who promptly opened fire with machine guns on the Jewish partisans. Nineteen were killed immediately, but the Jewish partisans managed to return fire and wound Herzenberger. Then the majority of the Jewish unit managed to escape the attackers' line of fire and to flee the GL base in Knieja.[37]

After these events, the GL district commander, Mieczyslaw Moczar, sent GL general headquarters a report describing the incident in a false and misleading way. In this report sent sometime during the second half of October 1943 (the exact date is not given), Moczar writes:

> A tragic event took place in Battalions No. 3 and 4 under the command of Orzel and Lemiszewski. When one man disarmed two Jews who were standing guard, he took away their guns and brought them to the headquarters staff saying, "If all your soldiers were like these, you would have all been killed." The two guards were immediately shot by commander Lemiszewski. The Jews then grabbed their weapons, shooting began, and more than ten Jews were killed. The rest fled. Lemiszewski was wounded in the kidneys. He is one of our best and ablest commanders, unbending when it comes to the needs of the organization. The loss of this man is a heavy blow to our partisan movement in this area.[38]

It must be indicated that GL general headquarters did not react to this report and that no investigation was conducted to clarify the circumstances of this tragic event. What is also typical is that in the above-mentioned report, there is not one word expressing sorrow for the murder, whose victims were, as was dryly stated, "more than ten Jewish partisans." Sorrow was expressed only for the wounding of Herzenberger. As it turned out, Herzenberger's wounds were not very serious. He was operated on and treated by a partisan Jewish doctor from Warsaw known as Dziadek (not to be confused with Dziadek Kielbasa) who was over sixty years old. The doctor's real name cannot be found. After a short time, Herzenberger returned to command the battalion which now, of course, did not include the Jewish company.

A Russian officer known as Prohors (or Prochor) who could not reconcile himself to the murders left Herzenberger's battalion with the Jews. After the Jewish unit left the People's Guard, Prohors served, for all intents and purposes, as second commander to Avraham Braun and personally led many of the unit's combat operations.[39]

Despite Herzenberger's efforts and the massacre of the Jewish partisans, Kielbasa did not enter the People's Army. Instead, he joined the Znicz unit of the National Armed Forces, a unit that less than a month earlier, on August 9, 1943, had besieged the GL Kilinski group in the village of Borow and killed twenty-six of its fighters. Among those killed was Yaakov Freitag, the commander of the Jewish group that was made up of fugitives from Reczyca. This was not the only killing of People's Guard partisans by the Znicz unit. The wave of killings increased, particularly in May 1944. These attacks by the Znicz unit and other NSZ units working with it, such as the Cichy and Zab units, killed many Jewish partisans and Jews hiding in the forests or the villages.[40]

On December 26, 1943, Herzenberger died in a clash between the partisans and the Germans. After his death, GL headquarters attempted to renew its ties with the independent Jewish Adolf unit, telling the Jews that the events leading to the murder of some of their partisans took place against the directions and instructions issued by headquarters. The Jewish partisans accepted the offer. During the winter of 1943–1944 the Jews made up a substantial part of the GL forces operating out of bases in the forests of Lipsk. According to the testimony of the Polish partisan Jan Krol, these People's Guard units included the unit under the command of Lenek, made up of Russians and a few Jews who together numbered forty-three people; Grzybowski's unit; Jastrzab's unit; Bohdan's unit; and Prohors's unit, which was made up entirely of Jews.

At the beginning of January 1944, a group of seventy partisans who until then were active in Polesie moved to the forests of Lipsk, together with paratroopers from the regular Polish army who had been dropped in for operations at the enemy's rear. Some of these paratroopers were Jews. The commander of this unit was Ignacy Borkowski (known as Wicek), a veteran of the Spanish Civil War.

Receiving the command of all GL units in the forests of Lipsk, Borkowski formed what was known as the First Battalion of the Lublin Brigade. One of the units in this battalion was made up of the Jewish Adolf platoon, which according to the testimony of Hirsh Brones numbered twenty-four partisans at the time. The number of Jews in other units in the battalion under Borkowski's command is not known.

Captain Borkowski was sympathetic to the Jews and showed a lot of understanding for the Adolf unit, which was heavily burdened with the task of protecting the Jewish refugee camp. His friendly support lifted the morale of the Jewish partisans.[41]

A short time before Captain Borkowski arrived, a Jewish partisan, Major Michal Temczyn, came to the forests of Lipsk. A doctor, Temczyn was appointed head of the People's Army medical service in the district of Lublin and, therefore, also belonged to the district headquarters staff. Temczyn gained the complete respect of the AL partisans and was described in the memoirs of Tadeusz Szymanski as follows: "He was modest, not tall, and in addition a very courageous man. He worked with great diligence, and spared no efforts or energy."[42]

During the first months of 1944, fugitives from the surrounding forced labor camps reached the partisan movement and expanded the ranks of the Jewish unit. On January 22, twenty-six Jewish prisoners escaped from the forced labor camp near the airport in Klemensow, and in April, sixty more prisoners escaped from the labor camp in Krasnik. Only eight of them reached the partisans and joined Adolf's unit, but later, thirteen Jewish prisoners among those who escaped from the camp in Budzyn succeeded in reaching the partisan movement. In the spring of 1944 the partisan forces in the whole district of Lublin were strengthened, when the well-armed Soviet partisan units of Jakovlow, Karasiov, Sankov, and Vasilenko streamed into the forests of Janow, Lipsk, and Puszcza-Solska. After the battle of Rablow (described in chapter 2) the Janowski and Wanda Wasilewska units, which included a few dozen Jews in their ranks, moved into this area. With them came the Soviet units that took part in the battle of Rablow. A short time later the Soviet unit under the command of Lieutenant-Colonel Prokopiuk also went there.[43]

From March to May 1944, the forests of southern Lublin were under the complete control of the partisans. However, the situation for the Jews suddenly began to deteriorate in March. With the growth of AL forces came a reorganization and the formation of a number of new battalions. Jan Fiol ("Rys") was appointed commander of the second battalion, to which the Jewish Adolf unit was annexed. Fiol was an anti-Semite and, like Meluch in the forests of Parczew, he began to create difficulties for the Jews. Fiol ordered the dismantling of the Jewish unit and their transfer to various Polish units, which would have meant the loss of the protection and help for the Jews in the family camp and for those hiding in nearby villages. The Jews refused to obey. When they gained the support of Captain Borkowski, who after some time was appointed commander of the brigade, and that of other officers on the command staff in southern Lublin, Fiol's instructions were rescinded. Lublin district headquarters issued another order, dated April 9 and signed by Major Jan Wyderkowski, who became deputy commander of the district of Lublin: "I order the commander of the first brigade to form a field unit of Jews alone and under their command."[44]

When it reorganized the dispersed Jewish unit and transferred the brigade's command to Borkowski, AL headquarters began to regain the trust of the Jewish partisans. Yet, just as it seemed that the situation was improved and expectations for a quick and liberating offensive by the Red Army were running high, a hard and unexpected blow befell the partisans.

On June 9, 1944, the Germans opened their largest antipartisan campaign in Poland, aiming to liquidate the partisan forces in the forests in southern Lublin. This campaign, called *Sturmwind*, (*Sturmwind 1* in the forests of Lipsk and Janow; *Sturmwind 2* in Puszcza-Solska) was carried out by the forces of three *Wehrmacht* divisions (Divisions No. 154, 174, and part of No. 213), along with the Karpaty Kalmuc Cavalry Regiment, a certain number of *Ordnungspolizei* units, and an air force bomber squadron. The overall number of German forces was 25,000. At the head of this concentration was the commander of the German forces in the *General Gouvernement*, General Haeneke; General Bork was chief-of-staff.[45]

The partisan forces numbered close to 5,000 people. Of these, 3,000 were in the Soviet units, 560 were in the Polish units of the PPR, 570 were in the Home Army, and 700 were in the Peasant Battalions. There were at least 100 Jewish partisans in the People's Guard units, half of whom were from the Jewish Adolf unit. There were also a number of Jewish partisans in the Soviet units.

The Soviet and AL units comprised a joint defense force under the command of Lieutenant-Colonel Nikolai Prokopiuk; the Soviet Jewish officer, Lieutenant Andrei Gorovich, was made the chief-of-staff. Because of their mutual hate and their subsequent confrontations, no understanding or coordination was reached with the units of the Home Army and the Peasant Battalions. So these two forces warded off the Germans' attacks separately. Only at the end of the

campaign, just before the defeat of the partisans, was some under-
standing reached, and the surviving members of the Home Army and
Peasant Battalions units accepted the command of Lieutenant-
Colonel Prokopiuk.[46]

In the battles against the German's superior forces, which continued nonstop until June 26, the partisans suffered heavy losses.
Many Polish partisan units were totally wiped out.[47]

When the staff of the second battalion, under the command of
Fiol, panicked after the losing battle of June 16 and fled, the units
under the command of Fiol ceased to exist for all practical purposes.
The Wanda Wasilewska brigade and the Janowski unit retained only
20 percent of their members, and most were killed. The few who
survived dispersed and returned to their homes. Almost all the Polish
units, with more than 50 percent of their men dead, also disintegrated. Over the two-day period of July 25 and 26, in a battle between
the Tanew and Sopot rivers, 700 Polish partisans were killed, and a
few score were taken prisoner only to be shot a few days later. According to the Polish historian Waldemar Tuszynski, this was "one of
the most tragic episodes in the history of the Polish partisan movement." The well-armed and thoroughly trained Soviet units suffered
relatively few losses. Some even succeeded in breaking out of the
German encirclement and reaching the Carpathian mountains.[48]

The Jewish Adolf unit carried out one of their most difficult battles in the area of Mamuty Gorne, where units of *Wehrmacht* Division
No. 154 had attacked. The partisans suffered heavy losses, and the
German units broke into Knieja, the family camp area. Almost all of
the Jews who were hiding there were killed. According to Zysmilch's
testimony, only fifteen Jewish partisans survived. Together with
other defeated groups, they reached Zapleczkow, where they remained until the latter half of July, 1944, when the Red Army
liberated the area.[49]

A few other Jewish units were active south of the city of Lublin in
relatively small forests, which were considered unsuitable for partisan activity. The first Jewish partisan force in this area was the group
headed by Zadok from Lublin. This unit was established in the fall of
1942 and numbered twenty partisans, all of whom were killed.

Another unit, which operated nearby, existed for a longer time.
Commanded by Heniek Zimmerman, this unit was established at the
end of 1942 and at various times numbered between twelve and
twenty people, with about seventy Jews hidden under their protection. Only twelve survived to the end of the war.

At the beginning of 1943, Zimmerman's group attacked a Polish police station in Piotrowice and disarmed the seven policemen there. The station's documents were destroyed, and the policemen were warned against turning over hiding Jews to the Germans. Later attacks were carried out against nearby German gendarmerie posts. In April 1943, a clash took place with a German patrol numbering seven men in a forest, near the village of Kreznica. Four Germans were killed, the others fled, and the unit took its first machine gun.

The unit was defeated at the end of the summer of 1943. The unit was in the village of Majdan Debinski, when a German penal unit suddenly appeared and in the battle that ensued, killed most of the partisans. Zimmerman and a few of his men managed to flee to the forest, but at the edge of the forest, Zimmerman was fatally wounded. The surviving partisans remained in the forest until the liberation.

Another small group of Jews, together with some escaped Soviet prisoners-of-war, was active in the area of Gluska, 5 kilometers from Lublin. The commander of this group was a Soviet lieutenant, a Jew whose partisan name was Iwanek. We know that this group was active until the end of 1944 when it was destroyed, and from a German police report, we know that it took part in a battle on July 17, 1943, in which three partisans were killed. There is no information on this group in other sources.[50]

A small group of seven or eight people who operated in the area of Bychawa, 25 kilometers south of Lublin, is mentioned in the testimony of Mordechai Sternblitz.[51] This group existed until spring, 1944, when it joined the Soviet partisans who came into this area.

Moshe Braun reported in his testimony on two other Jewish groups active in the area of Bychawa. One was active in a forest near the village of Bystrzyca; the other, made up of fugitives from the POW camp on Lipowa Street in Lublin and of some Jews who had fled from nearby places, operated close by. It can be assumed that the two groups united into a small partisan unit after suffering some losses. The last month before the liberation, this unit was the target of attacks by armed Polish groups. Only one man, Moshe Erlich, survived.[52]

The participation of Jewish partisans in a clash in Bychawa during the last month before the liberation is mentioned by the German gendarmerie, in a report dated July 17, 1944. According to this report, a partisan unit made up of Jews, Russians, and Poles from Krzczonowa, east of Bychawa, attacked a police post in Bychawa on July 16, 1944. The circumstances and results of this attack, however, are not mentioned.[53]

In all, more than 500 Jewish partisans fought in the south of the Lublin district. Almost 400 of them were organized within the framework of specifically Jewish partisan units, and more than 100 additional Jewish partisans came to Lublin from the east with the units of Kasman (Janowski), Klim, and as part of the Wanda Wasilewska brigade.

There is a great deal of similarity between the Jewish partisans in southern Lublin and those in the forests of Parczew. In both areas, most of the Jewish partisans came from towns that were close to large forests and organized fighting groups immediately upon their escape to those forests. And both areas gave rise to leaders who tried to unite the various armed units. Avraham Braun (Adolf), for instance, tried to fill a role similar to that of Yechiel Greenshpan in the forests of Parczew. Yet unlike the Jews in the Parczew forests, few from the fighting Jewish units, and no one from the family camp survived to the day of liberation.

CHAPTER 5
THE DISTRICT OF RADOM

A FTER THE DISTRICT OF LUBLIN, THE DISTRICT OF RADOM was the second largest center of partisan activity in the *General Gouvernement*. The geographical conditions here were very suitable for partisan activity, because forests cover about 25 percent of the district. The density of the forests is particularly great in the counties of Kielce (46 percent of the total area), Konskie (40 percent), Ilza (38 percent), Kozienice (35 percent), Opoczno (33 percent), Wloszczowa (30 percent), Staszow (29 percent), and Przysucha (27 percent), and two of the largest forests in Poland can be found here—Puszcza Swietokrzyska (covering an area of 70,000 ha) and Puszcza Kozieniecka (29,000 ha).

As in the district of Lublin, the beginning of the partisan movement in Radom was directly linked to mass escapes during deportations to extermination camps. The deportations from the district of Radom began on August 5, 1942, in the city of Radom, and continued nonstop until the deportation from Konskie on November 7, 1942. During this time, 300,000 Jews from the district were taken to the Treblinka death camp and exterminated. Many others fled to the nearby forests.

Of the 3,200 Jewish residents of Zarki, 1,600 escaped; of the 4,000 Jewish residents of Wodzislaw, 1,000 fled. In Gomulice, 500 of the 1,000 Jews ran away; about 2,000 Jews fled from Ostrowiec; several hundred ran away from Jedrzejow; and about half of the 8,000 Jews in the ghetto of Opatow escaped. About 300 Jews, mostly youths, escaped from the nearby town of Iwaniska, and on September 5, 1942, more than 1000 of the 2,500 Jews of Pilica fled during the deportation from that town.[1] Hundreds of Jews also managed to escape the ghetto of Czestochowa, and during 1943 and 1944, after the liquidation of the ghettos, there were escapes from the many forced labor camps which had been established in the district of Radom.

As in the district of Lublin, the refugees in Radom formed independent partisan units to ensure the possibility of armed resistance for themselves and their families. In certain cases, such units arose spontaneously, immediately after escape. In other cases, the organizational foundations were laid in the ghettos or camps before the escape.

In contrast with the Jews of Lublin, the Jews in the district of Radom were the pioneers of the partisan movement, because almost no partisan groups had been established there by fleeing Soviet war prisoners. Only later, during the second half of 1943, did a few hundred Soviet prisoners join the partisan movement there. Unlike the Soviets in the district of Lublin, they had not run away directly from POW camps but had previously, before reaching the partisan movement, served in units established by the Germans, particularly the "Ostlegion" units.

Until the end of 1942, the Jews were undoubtedly the decisive majority among the partisans in the district of Radom, that is, the majority of those fighting out of bases in the forest. In 1943 they still were, from a numerical viewpoint, a very substantial factor in the partisan forces in this area. Only in the spring of 1944 was there a drastic decrease in the percentage of Jews in the partisan movement. This was mainly for two reasons. First, the Jewish units suffered many losses and, because of the extermination of the Jews, there was no flow of new forces into the Jewish partisan movement. Secondly, thousands of members of the Polish underground were drafted into the partisan movement, when the expectation arose for a quick liberation of the area. In addition, when hundreds of Soviet partisans were transferred from the east for combat operations at the rear of the German army in the region of Radom, hundreds of Russians, former Red Army soldiers, deserted the Nazi units and turned to the partisans.

In October 1944, with the fixing of the front along the Vistula and the concentration of large *Wehrmacht* forces in this area, the Polish partisan movement in the district of Radom ceased to exist. Almost all of the Polish units were dismantled, and the Soviet units moved east to the liberated areas. The Polish historian Bogdan Hillebrandt writes the following on this:

> After the AL brigade moved to the liberated areas and the AK regiments were dismantled, the partisan activities in the region of Kielce stopped. The small units left in this area tried to sustain themselves until the

liberation and did not carry out actions against the enemy, while the three AL units that were established in the county of Konskie in the middle of October carried out intelligence rather than sabotage activities.[2]

Despite the very difficult circumstances, three Jewish partisan groups did survive to the day of liberation. Aside from these, there were also Jews in the three People's Army units mentioned above that remained in the area of Kielce until the end of 1944. The commander of one of these units was the Jewish partisan Julian Eisenman-Kaniewski.

In the fall of 1942, at least eight Jewish partisan units were formed and carried out combat action. At that time, according to the data of Polish historians, the entire Polish underground had six partisan units, among them four People's Guard units, one Peasant Battalions unit, and one unit that was called *Jedrusie*. Of the four GL units, three had a high percentage of Jews and one, the "Lions" unit, was made up entirely of Jews. There were also a few Jews in the Jedrusie unit.

In 1943 there were eleven Jewish partisan units that we know of, in the district of Radom, and, particularly during the second half of that year, there was a substantial increase in the Polish partisan movement's activity. On the whole, twenty-five Polish underground units were active then; among them were fourteen GL units, eight AK units, and five Peasant Battalions units. Of the GL units, five were mixed Polish-Jewish units, and three were made up only of Jews.[3]

The units that were active in the years 1943–1944, both the Jewish and the Polish, averaged twenty to thirty fighters each.

In the spring of 1944, the Polish partisan movement in Radom evolved into a mass movement which lasted for several months and reached its height in August. According to Hillebrandt, there were about 10,000 people in the ranks of the Polish partisan units, which included 6,400 in AK units, 2,900 in AL units (among them a very substantial number of Soviet soldiers who had escaped from service in German units), and 700 in independent Peasant Battalions that were not under the command of the Home Army or the People's Army. At this time, most of the Jewish units had already been destroyed. By 1944, only five small Jewish partisan units were active, and the percentage of Jews in Polish partisan units also had diminished. These numbers changed at the end of 1944 when, in certain areas, the Jewish partisan groups were again the only armed units operating in the forests.[4]

On the whole, thirteen Jewish partisan units, on which we have some accurate information, were active in the district of Radom. Besides these, there were eight other units which had a substantial percentage of Jews. We shall briefly describe their history.

THE REGION OF PINCZOW

In the area of Pinczow the Jewish partisan unit *Zygmunt* operated, carrying out combat actions for more than two and a half years. This unit was made up of two armed Jewish groups, established at the beginning of the fall of 1942.

The first Jewish group was made up of fugitives from the ghettos of Dzialoszyce and Pinczow, where deportations were carried out in August 1942. This group at first numbered twenty-seven people, but during the first month of its activity it was joined by fugitives from nearby ghettos.[5]

In the fall of 1942, the Polish Workers Party began to organize the partisan movement in the area of Pinczow and the neighboring area of Miechow and, for this purpose, established a command staff for the region. It was headed by the PPR activists Wladyslaw Jaworski and Franciszek Szwaja. Moshe Skoczylas, himself a communist activist, made contact with these PPR men while he was still in the ghetto of Dzialoszyce and renewed this tie after the deportation from the ghettos in the region of Pinczow and the establishment of separate Jewish units. The Jewish partisans agreed to the local People's Guard command and thus constituted the first GL unit in the forests of Pinczow.

Aside from Skoczylas's unit, there was a second relatively well-armed unit in the same forests. This unit was also formed by fugitives from the ghettos in the region of Pinczow and was headed by Michael Majtek. When Wladyslaw Jaworski heard of the combat activity of Majtek's unit, he gave Skoczylas the task of contacting Majtek. Majtek quickly consented to join the People's Guard and unite with Skoczylas's group, and together they formed a fairly large Jewish partisan unit in the forests of Chrober.

At the beginning, the unit's actions were limited to economic sabotage. This led later to armed clashes of different proportions with the Germans. The unit initiated battles with the aim of acquiring arms and also attempted, in a few dozen missions, to destroy targets that had economic value for the enemy. The first large-scale battle took place at the end of October 1942, when the German gendarmerie held a hunt against the Jewish unit in the forests of Chrober. The hunt failed. The Germans encountered tough resistance and retreated from the forest, taking with them several dead and more than ten wounded. The losses of the Jewish unit totaled two dead and five wounded.[6]

Skoczylas, who was wounded in the battle, was taken to Dzialoszyce by the Pole Zachariasz, a PPR man who had been in contact with the Jewish unit. Here Skoczylas received medical aid, but later he was captured by the Germans under circumstances that remain unclear and sent to the Plaszow concentration camp and then to Auschwitz. The command of the unit passed into the hands of Zalman Feinstat, known as "Zygmunt," and from then on the unit was called the Zygmunt unit.

Two Polish partisan units were formed in the Pinczow region in the spring of 1943—the first Siekiera unit and then the Stefan Kola unit. Another unit, by the name of Mnich, (also known as Mlot) was organized in the region of Miechow and was also active in this district. The Jewish Zygmunt unit was no longer alone in the forest; it usually operated in collaboration with these two units.

After suffering heavy losses in the summer and fall of 1943, the Siekiera and Stefan Kola units, both of which contained a number of Jews, merged and continued fighting under the name of Stefan Kola. According to Polish sources, in December 1943 this joint unit numbered forty-eight fighters, among them six Jews. Two of the Jewish fighters, the brothers Adam and Yitzhak Bornstein from Wislica, were killed by National Armed Forces in January 1944. The others fell in battle with the Germans. There were no Jewish survivors from the Siekiera and Stefan Kola units.[7]

The Zygmunt unit took part in its largest battle on October 12, when a large German force attacked the People's Guard forces made up of the Bartosz Glowacki unit (not to be confused with a unit by the same name headed by Yechiel Brawerman), the Stefan Kola unit, and the Zygmunt unit. According to Wladyslaw Jaworski, then regional secretary of the Polish Workers Party, the German force numbered 3,000 men and included artillery and lightly armored trucks.[8]

The German attack began with a crushing surprise strike against the Glowacki unit, which forced the unit to retreat to the area of Kolkow, where the Stefan Kola and Zygmunt units were stationed. The joint partisan units succeeded in holding their own until nightfall. Then, at 10 P.M., they managed to break through the German siege and escape in the direction of Gora, and from there, to the Sancygniow forests. According to Polish sources, the German losses totaled twenty dead and thirty wounded, and the joint partisan forces suffered three dead and nine wounded.[9] The losses suffered by the Zygmunt unit in this battle are not known.

The partisans, however, suffered a serious defeat, in a battle that took place in the middle of February 1944. The Zygmunt unit, which numbered 100 people, was then in the village of Pawlowice, where they planned to stay for about a week before transferring their activities to the district of Jedrzejow. The day before the unit was to leave, a strong German gendarmerie force, including the first battalion of the 17th regiment of the *Ordnungspolizei* stationed in Busk, entered the area and surrounded the partisans. When the unit's commander, Zalman Feinstat, tried to make a getaway on the frozen Nida River, the Germans opened artillery fire. Thirty-nine partisans were killed, Zalman Feinstat among them. Four Jewish partisans were captured after their ammunition ran out and later hanged in Busk. More than thirty members of the unit succeeded in evading the Germans, but only a few survived until the second half of January 1945 when the region of Kielce was liberated.[10]

Another unit, known as Jozek's unit, was also active for a short while in the district of Pinczow, but it had no ties with the Zygmunt unit. In September 1942, this unit came under the command of the People's Guard. It then numbered nineteen people—seventeen Jews and two Poles. According to the plans of GL headquarters, this unit was to move east from the region of Pinczow, cross the Vistula, and reach the forests in the area of Mielec, where it was to begin combat and sabotage actions in what was a center of war industry. The attempt to cross over to Mielec did not succeed. The unit was destroyed under unknown circumstances, and all of its members were apparently killed.[11]

THE *LWY* (LIONS) AND *WILK* (WOLF) UNITS

The Jewish Lions unit was highly active between the end of 1942 and the beginning of 1943. It was established through the unification of various groups of partially armed fugitives from the ghettos of Drzewica, Opoczno, and Przysucha in the northwestern part of the Radom district. These groups were in the forests of Opoczno, Konskie, and Przysucha during the wave of deportations of the Jewish communities to the Treblinka extermination camp. At the same time, the Polish-Jewish Wolf unit of the People's Guard, which had come from the county of Grojec, was carrying out armed actions in the county of Opoczno. This unit, which at first included eighteen people, grew to thirty fighters when it was transferred to the region of Opoczno. Its commander was Jozef Rogulski; the second-in-command was Julian Eisenman-Kaniewski, a Jew. The Jews made up about half of the Wolf unit. Among them were Gustaw Alef-Bolkowiak and Zosia Jamajka, both of whom had fled the Warsaw ghetto. A group of Jewish fugitives from the ghettos in the region of Opoczno also joined this unit.[12]

At the end of December, the local Jewish groups that had collaborated with the Wolf unit agreed to join the People's Guard and were added to the newly formed Lions unit of the People's Guard. Furthermore, Julian Eisenman-Kaniewski and a number of other Jews from the Wolf unit of the People's Guard were transferred to this unit to reinforce it, so that, by January 1943, the Lions unit was the most active partisan unit in the region to Kielce. According to a detailed list of the combat and sabotage activities of the resistance movement in the Radom district, drawn up by the historian Hillebrandt, seventeen partisan actions took place in January 1943. Nine of these were carried out by the Lions unit, three by the Wolf unit, three by the "Land of Kielce" unit, one by the Jedrusie unit, and one by a unit that remains unidentified. This indicates that 50 percent of the combat actions in the month of January were carried out by the Jewish unit. Furthermore, the facts that there was a substantial percentage of Jews in the Wolf and Land of Kielce units and that the Jedrusie unit was the only purely Polish unit testify to the intensity of the Jewish partisan movement during the first stage in the development of the partisan movement in the district of Radom.

The Wolf and Lions units continued to fight all spring. On February 9, a hunt was begun in the forests of Gilnow by a motorized battalion of the gendarmerie, *Ordnungspolizei* units, and a *Wehrmacht* force numbering 300 men. This large-scale anti-partisan campaign, called *Attyla*, led to a serious battle between the Germans and the Wolf unit which was then in the forest. Because of the superiority of the German forces the unit's commander, Rogulski, ordered a retreat to the depths of the forest. Hillebrandt comments on how this happened: "Due to the courage of three GL fighters, Slowik, Zosia, and Mietek who warded off the enemy's pursuit by firing at the Germans (and paying for their dediction with their lives), the remaining partisans were able to retreat to the inner parts of the forest." Two of the people mentioned above were Jews: Zosia Jamajka was a Jewish woman who had fled the Warsaw ghetto, and Mietek had also escaped from there.

Some time later there was a clash in the inner part of the forest between the Germans and the Wolf unit. The unit suffered heavy losses and its commander was seriously wounded. Following this battle the unit ceased to exist. Most of the surviving partisans moved to the region of Grojec where Rogulski, after recovering from his wounds, renewed the partisan activity. The Lions unit remained alone in the area of Opoczno and carried out a series of combat actions during February and March.

In the spring of 1943, the Lions unit underwent a serious crisis. After the Wolf unit left the area of Opoczno the local peasants' attitude toward the partisans deteriorated. The peasants who had helped the Wolf unit refused to aid the Lions unit. The former had been under the command of a Pole and had a Polish majority; its Jewish members tried to look like Poles. But matters were different for the Lions unit, which was known to be a Jewish unit. Anti-Semitic feelings that had been particularly strong among the local peasants before the outbreak of the war (the well-known pogrom in Przytyk occurred there) were not weakened in the course of the German occupation. The hostile attitude of the local Polish population paralyzed the activity of the Lions unit to a marked degree.

During the spring of 1943 the Lions unit was frequently persecuted by the NSZ units that were established in the region of Opoczno. In May 1943 the name of the Lions unit was changed to Ludwik Warynski, and the unit was joined by a few Russians who had escaped from captivity. Yet the unit, which was operating under very unfavorable conditions, began to disintegrate. Almost all of its fighters were killed, and at the end of July 1943 the People's Guard command decided to dismantle the unit. Its six surviving fighters were transferred to the newly established Wiktorowicz unit.[13]

THE GARBATY AND BARTOSZ GLOWACKI UNITS

In September 1942, Stanislaw Olczyk, a Pole, organized a People's Guard partisan unit in the area of Wierzbica, 15 kilometers south of Radom. This unit was made up partly of local peasants, partly of Jews who had escaped from nearby ghettos, and partly of escaped Soviet prisoners-of-war. Olczyk, the commander, adopted the name "Garbaty" and the unit was also given this name. The second-in-command was Yechiel Brawerman, known as Baca, a fugitive from the Opatow ghetto. Brawerman is described in the memoirs of the Polish partisan officer Jozef Jarosz as "one of the bravest partisans in the Kielce region."[14]

In October 1942, the Garbaty unit moved to the forests between Ilza and Starachowice, where it was reinforced by partially armed Jewish groups that had escaped from the ghettos of Ilza, Starachowice, and Radom. The Garbaty unit, together with the groups of fugitives from the three ghettos, numbered 130 people.

While it was in the vicinity of Ilza and the forests of Starachowice, the unit carried out a series of important armed actions. On October 12, for example, it intercepted a train in the Kunow station, 10 kilometers northwest of Ostrowiec Swietokrzyski. Later on, it destroyed a Polish auxiliary police post in the village of Mirzec, 13 kilometers west of Ilza, taking guns and ammunition.

At the beginning of December 1942, a group of seventy-six Jews, who were in contact with the GL headquarters in the district of Radom, escaped from the Radom ghetto. The fugitives, including women and children, were to come to the place where the Garbaty unit was stationed. Those able to fight were to be annexed to the unit, and bunkers were to be built so the rest could hide under the partisans' protection in the forests of Ilza. On December 6 (or 16), the fugitives, led by Jozef Zietala, reached the Garbaty unit. When they left the ghetto, the fugitives were physically weak. Then, they had to make an exhausting, walking journey about 50 kilometers from Radom in harsh winter conditions and under circumstances that forced them to take the worst roads, usually at night.

On the morning of December 6 (or 16) the fugitives, led by Jozef Zietala, reached the partisan unit, which was waiting near the shack of the forest watchman, Kutery. The journey of such a large group, however, did not pass unnoticed by the German gendarmerie, and before it was possible to prepare hideouts for the newcomers, the partisans' scouts reported the approach of a German hunt. Strong gendarmerie units, which had received notice of the fugitives' march, suddenly arrived from the west and the northeast. It was too late to retreat. The Garbaty unit and the fugitives were surrounded. The German attack began at 9 o'clock aided by mortar fire. According to the Polish historian Garas, the Germans also used lightly armored trucks.

The Garbaty unit numbered 120 fighters and was divided into eight squads. The two strongest were equipped with a heavy machine gun, two light machine guns, and ordinary rifles. These two squads were commanded by Olczyk and given the assignment of breaking through the German lines. The remaining forces were to stop the Germans until a breach could be made which would allow the surrounded partisans to escape.

After a few hours of strenuous fighting, the partisans succeeded in breaching the eastern section of the encirclement and moving the Radom refugees and three partisan squads. The remaining forces of the Garbaty unit encountered unexpected fire and were destroyed. Olczyk and Brawerman were seriously wounded, and, after this battle, the Garbaty unit ceased to exist. According to the statistics drawn up by the People's Guard command (unconfirmed and probably exaggerated), about forty Germans were killed in this battle.

The fate of the members of the three squads that escaped the siege and that of the refugees is not known. They were probably killed in the pursuit of the German gendarmerie immediately after the battle of Kutery, although it appears that a few fighters hid in the surrounding area for some time, and maybe even tried to renew their partisan activities. It can be assumed that only a small number of these fighters joined the unit that was reorganized by Brawerman.

In February 1943, after a short period of inactivity Yechiel Brawerman began organizing a new People's Guard unit—the Bartosz Glowacki unit, which moved to the southeastern part of the Radom district. It was a combined Jewish-Polish unit and included a few of the survivors of the defeated Garbaty unit.

The first battle of the unit under Brawerman's command took place on March 5, 1943, near Katy Denkowskie about 2 kilometers east of Ostrowiec, after the partisans were surprised by a German hunt. Following a three-hour battle, the partisans managed to break out of the siege, but lost five men; two were wounded. According to Polish sources, the German losses totaled three dead and two wounded.

On March 27, the unit was surrounded for a second time. Following a serious battle, the partisans escaped at night out of the encirclement. They lost five men and had one wounded. For his successful leadership in these battles, Brawerman received a second-class commendation by order of the People's Guard general headquarters dated April 12, 1943. In May 1943, the "Bartosz Glowacki" unit carried out a series of combat actions together with the Polish Langiewicz unit. Then at the end of May 1943, it appears that Brawerman's unit merged with a unit made up of Soviet war prisoners who had escaped from the camp in Swiety Krzyz. The commander of the Soviet unit, Captain Andreyev, was appointed commander of the joint unit whose partisan name was also Bartosz Glowacki. Brawerman was second-in-command.

At the end of June, Captain Andreyev and a group of Soviet ex-prisoners left the unit and crossed the Vistula to the east. Then most of the Poles in the unit were sent to their homes, and the unit was made up largely of Jews. But, under circumstances that have not been properly explained, the unit disintegrated a short while later, and few of the fighters joined the new GL Zawisza Czarny unit that was organized in June 1943.[15]

THE *ZIEMI KIELECKIEJ* (LAND OF KIELCE) UNIT

One of the People's Guard first units was the Land of Kielce unit. As in all other GL units established in 1942, the Jews played an important role there also. Established in Warsaw as early as June 1942, and numbering fourteen people, half of its fighters, it appears, were Jews. Its commander was August Langer (erroneously mentioned as Lange in GL documents). At the end of July, the unit reached the southeastern part of the region of Kielce (around Staszow, Sandomierz, and Opatow), where it began its combat activity. Its first action, carried out on the eve of July 28, 1942, in Janowiec on the Vistula, was an attempt to destroy a Polish police post. The mission failed and the unit's commander, Langer, was seriously wounded. A short time later, however, the unit was reinforced by a group of Jews who had escaped from nearby ghettos.[16]

In the beginning of October 1942, the People's Guard main headquarters sent a new commander to the unit. He was the Jewish partisan Ignacy Rosenfarb ("Robb-Narbut"), soon to be known as one of the People's Guard's most talented commanders. (He was mentioned earlier, in the chapter on the partisan movement in the Parczew forests.) Like Aleksander Skotnicki, Rosenfarb was one of the few Jews who attained an officer's rank in select cavalry units before the war. And like Skotnicki, Rosenfarb was kept out of the officers' academy. He earned his commission in the 4th cavalry regiment because of his extraordinary military abilities. An interesting description of Rosenfarb was written by the Polish partisan Jerzy Piwowarek:

> The first meeting with the new commander took place not far from Chotcza. It must be said that from the first moment he made a very positive impression on us. We were impressed by his military stance and his very attractive outward appearance. Later we came to know the commander's other qualities from his organizational and combat actions.

> It must be admitted that, at the time of First Lieutenant Narbut's arrival, things were not managed properly in the unit. Discipline was a little

slack, and the training was not as good as it should have been. No wonder that at first the new commander gave special attention to these two matters.

Narbut trained us himself. We had physical exercise and studied fencing and topography. We had shooting practice and field training. We studied from an infantry instruction book. The commander also taught us the basics of first aid, how to fight the enemy's planes and defend ourselves from them, anticavalry warfare, etc. The intensive exercises displayed their effect in a conspicuous way. Our hands were weak from the fencing exercises, and the rifle butts that had been buried in the ground for too long cracked. But all of it benefited us in later combat actions. The good training, the establishment of strict yet sensible discipline, the personal charisma of the commander, and his ability to win people over quickly turned our Land of Kielce unit of thirty-five people into an excellent team of soldiers able to carry out serious combat missions.[17]

During the five months of combat action under the command of Rosenfarb (November 1942 to April 1943), the Land of Kielce unit carried out about forty operations. The most important of these was on December 15, 1942, when the unit took over a mine in Rudki, near Nowa Slupia. Several German guards (*Werkschutz*) and one gendarme from the nearby post were killed. The entrance to the mine was blocked with small carts and later flooded with water. The unit lost only one man, the Jewish partisan known as Felek, who had escaped from the area of Chotcza.[18] Hillebrandt says the following about the operation: "Of all the actions of the partisan units which had some effect on German war production in the GG, the destruction of the equipment in the mines of Rudki was the most effective. This sabotage action, carried out in December by the Land of Kielce unit, led to a work stoppage in the mine for more than ten days. [19]

In April 1943, the unit underwent a serious crisis that almost completely paralyzed its combat activity and in the end brought about its disintegration. There were several reasons for this crisis. Jerzy Piwowarek names two principal ones: first, Commander Rosenfarb was called to Warsaw by central headquarters, accompanied by a few other experienced fighters, among them Rozlubirski, a Jew; second, the Germans initiated a cruel penal campaign against villages that were sympathetic to the partisans. On April 11, for example, German gendarmes killed twenty-two residents of the village of Wzdol Rzadowy for collaborating with Narbut's unit. Among those killed were many members of the Home Army, who, despite their affiliation with that organization, had helped the fighters of the Land of

Kielce unit.[20] After this incident the Home Army opened an intensive propaganda campaign against the People's Guard, accusing it of giving the Germans unnecessary excuses to repress the Polish population. This propaganda had distinct anti-Semitic overtones. It is interesting that in the Home Army's May 1943, report sent to London, the Land of Kielce unit is described as a "Communist-Jewish gang operating in the vicinity of Bodzentyn and Nowa Slupia under the pretense of being a Polish partisan unit, and that the commander of this band, a Jew, displays animal-like cruelty."[21]

This propaganda was undoubtedly an important factor in the deterioration of the support of the local peasants for the partisans. As a result, the unit could no longer continue its activities. In the middle of May, the Germans held several hunts using sizable forces, which caused heavy losses to the partisans. The Land of Kielce unit ceased to exist. It appears that with the exception of Rosenfarb-Narbut and Rozlubirski, who had returned to Warsaw, all of the unit's Jewish fighters were killed in battle.[22]

THE PARTISANS OF THE JEWISH FIGHTING ORGANIZATION (ZOB) FROM CZESTOCHOWA

According to the Jewish Fighting Organization's policy on the continuation of the armed struggle outside the ghetto (see chapter 11), the preparation of partisan bases in forests began early in Czestochowa. They decided to establish these bases in the forests near Koniecpol and Zloty Potok, about 50 kilometers east of Czestochowa.[23]

In January 1943, Berel Gewircman (Bolek) and Chaim Rosenthat (Maciek) were sent from the ghetto to organize the base near Koniecpol. Their first foothold was the house of the Pole, Roman Pindelak, which stood alone near the village of Michalow, 8 kilometers from Koniecpol.

After some time, additional shelters were found with the peasants Hajdas and Czapla, who were sympathetic to the Jews. But it became clear that without the support of the Polish partisan movement, the Jewish partisans would have few opportunities to act.

In March 1943, representatives of the Jewish Fighting Organization came into contact with two Jews (known only by their first names, Shmuel and Chaim) hiding nearby, who knew the surrounding area well and were acquainted with many of the local people. After some time, it was possible to make contacts through them with representatives of the Polish underground, probably members of a local cell of the Peasant Battalions. However, during the meeting between the ZOB representatives (Gewircman and Shmuel) and the representatives of the Polish organization, the Poles suddenly opened fire. Shmuel was killed on the spot, and Gewircman miraculously succeeded in escaping. This first tragic meeting with representatives of the Polish underground left a sorry impression on the Jewish fighters, but also served as a warning to them to remember to take the greatest precaution.

After the liquidation of the ghetto in Czestochowa and the failure of an attempted uprising on June 25, 1943, five fighters reached Pindelak's house. Some time later, a GL representative called Krzaczek, with whom Mordechai Silberberg, the ZOB commander in Czestochowa, had had contacts before the liquidation of the ghetto, arrived. Krzaczek was told of the plans for organizing a Jewish partisan unit in the surrounding area. The main factor in carrying out these plans was equipping the fighters with arms. Money which had been brought by the group that had escaped from the ghetto in June 1943 was given to Yitzhak Winderman, who went with Krzaczek to Radom to acquire arms through the connections that Krzaczek supposedly had. On the way, Krzaczek murdered Winderman and stole the money. The PPR put out a death sentence on Krzaczek for this murder, yet this was another heavy blow to the ZOB partisan groups that were anxious to start fighting.

It was only after some time and because of the efforts of Chaim, mentioned above, that Gewircman's group was able to make contact with Stanislaw Hanyz, a local Polish communist activist. Hanyz, who assumed that a Jewish partisan unit would not have many chances to act because of the local peasant population's negative stand, strove to establish a nationally mixed unit that could be disguised as a Polish unit. For this, he annexed two Poles, Morawski and Kulawiak, who had been in hiding (for reasons unknown) to the ZOB and later on, a few Russians.

The preparation of bases for the winter became the most important task. Intensive actions against the enemy were planned by Hanyz for the beginning of the spring, when it was hoped there would also be an intensification of the activities of other People's Guard units. A bunker was built near the village of Stazyna in the area of Wloszczowa, and the partisans began to equip it with food and supplies needed for the winter.

Along with these preparations the partisans also held a series of armed actions from the new base. These actions were carried out under Gewircman's command, while Hanyz was the unit's overall commander. He often visited the partisans, organized the supply of arms and food, and delegated tasks to the unit.

In the beginning of September Hanyz came to the base and ordered the unit to send a group of fighters to scatter cattle that had been confiscated by the Germans from local farmers and were to be taken to Germany. Aside from its clear propaganda value, this operation was also meant to supply the unit with meat for the winter. While carrying out the mission, the partisans were suddenly attacked by an AK unit under the command of Szymbierski (Orzel). At first, the stunned fighters did not notice the hostile intentions of the unit's members, who were wearing Polish uniforms. The AK men captured four Jews, a Russian, and two Poles. One of the Jewish fighters escaped; the remaining Jews and the Russian were shot on the spot. The two Poles, Morawski and Kulawiak, were killed after the Home Army, with threats and beatings, forced them to reveal information about the partisan unit and its base in Stazyna.

On the dawn of September 12, Orzel's unit set out for the ZOB base, following the directions it forced out of Morawski and Kulawiak. The Jewish partisans, however, had left the base in time. The ZOB men were saved, but the bunker that had been prepared with such great effort was pillaged. The situation was grave. The only hope was to return to Pindelak's house, and his attitude, because he feared retaliation by the Home Army, was already less sympathetic. AK members had already broken into the house of Hanyz's aged parents, destroying the building and beating up the young communist activist's parents. Fortunately, Hanyz was not at home at the time.

In the midst of this new and dire situation, the Jewish partisans received a great deal of help from Tolka, the daughter of the farmer Hajdas, mentioned above. She willingly became a liaison for the Jewish partisan movement, and it was largely thanks to her that the partisans succeeded in maintaining their ties with the ZOB members in the Hasag camp in Czestochowa, and later with the leadership of the Jews underground in Warsaw.

As a result of these contacts, representatives of the Jewish underground in Warsaw came to Gewircman's group. They were Faiga Peltel (who came on two occasions), Shalom Grajek, Inka Sweigert, and the Polish woman, Maria Sawicka. With money received from them, they were able to buy some guns and food. In addition, contact was also made with Stanislaw Olczyk, who had just organized the Garbaty unit. In view of worsening conditions for partisan activity, the ZOB men raised the possibility of joining the Garbaty unit itself. Olczyk, however, refrained from absorbing such a large group of Jews into his unit. A group of General Vlasov's men who had escaped the German service had joined him, and they contributed to the anti-Semitic sentiment in the unit. The People's Army headquarters wanted Vlasov's men to remain in the unit, because when they had deserted from German service, they had brought with them substantial quantities of arms. One of the victims of the anti-Semitism which prevailed in the Garbaty unit was the communist activist Rachel (Rosa) Sapszewska, nicknamed Zosia, who was among the founders of the unit. In May 1943, while recovering in the house of the farmer Laskowski, a Garbaty unit collaborator, she was murdered treacherously by Laskowski and Czeslaw Stolarczyk. However, in time Olczyk did agree to absorb some of the ZOB fighters into his unit, on condition that they conceal their Jewish origins.

The rest of the ZOB members continued to hide in the homes of Pindelak, Hajdas, and Jaksznik and to go out on missions according to instructions given by Olczyk or Hanyz.

At the end of 1943 another tragedy befell Gewircman's group, when some of the fighters who were in Jaksznik's yard were suddenly surprised by an AK unit. These men beat the Jewish fighters and then turned them over to the Germans.[24]

After this incident, Faiga Peltel again went to the Jewish Fighting Organization and brought news of the AK's murder of the Jews back to Warsaw. In response, Colonel Wolinski in the Home Army's main headquarters ineffectually intervened. Among other points in the "Survey of the Activities of the Department for Jewish Affairs," which he sent to AK headquarters in December 1943, Colonel Wolinski said the following:

> The collaboration of the Army with Jewish organizations was not confined to Warsaw, but was to encompass all of Poland. This aspiration was expressed in the order of central headquarters of February 1943, pertaining to the issue of aid to closed ghettos that wish to fight with arms in hand. According to this, the Polish military commands were to extend all possible aid to Jewish groups that are under the command of the ZOB or the ZZW. The actions of our units towards the Czestochowa ZOB unit, which is hiding in the vicinity of Koniecpol and trying to come under our command, are most unpleasant and negate the spirit of the order mentioned above. In spite of the instructions of the local headquarters to give this unit concessions and help, massacres were carried out against this unit on two occasions by Orzel's group (apparently an NSZ group).[25]

Gewircman's group remained in the area of Koniecpol throughout 1944, and occasionally carried out combat operations delegated by Hanyz. The last fight of the ZOB fighters, in collaboration with the Garbaty unit, against the Germans took place on January 17, 1945, about two days before the liberation. On the day of liberation, only seven of the fighters of this unit were alive.

Foundations were to be laid for partisan activity in the forests of Zloty Potok, not far from Koniecpol. Lieutenant Langiewicz, an AK man, promised to help organize a base in this area. The first three groups destined for operations in Zloty Potok left the Czestochowa ghetto at the end of May 1943. These groups were made up largely of former Polish army soldiers who had taken part in the war in September 1939 and together numbered about thirty-two people. Their entire equipment consisted of six pistols and grenades which had been made in the ghetto.

The groups came to their appointed place without a hitch. However, once there, they found that the Polish liaisons that Langiewicz had promised did not appear. The fighters, who did not know the area, soon became a target for hunts carried out by the police in cooperation with the local population. Those who remained in the ghetto, surprised by the misunderstanding that occurred in Zloty Potok, decided to send another group of fighters under the command of Potaszewicz. This group was to leave in a car belonging to the Hasag plants, with a German driver who was to be bribed. But the driver betrayed the ZOB men; he called in a German police unit, which stopped the car and opened fire on the Jewish fighters. Only Lolek Blank succeeded in escaping. Potaszewicz, who was seriously wounded, was captured and tortured to death during his interrogation. The remainder of the fighters were killed on the spot.

When it became apparent that there was no chance for partisan activity without the help of the local population, and particularly without intelligence reports, the group in Zloty Potok sent messengers to Lieutenant Langiewicz to clarify the situation. They returned with the news that Langiewicz had been arrested by the Gestapo. A very short time later came the news of the liquidation of the ghetto and the failure of the attempted uprising.

Lacking means of communication and equipped with only few arms, the repeatedly betrayed ZOB men nevertheless decided to try to find their friends in the forests of Koniecpol. They sent emissaries from Chrzastkow to find Pindelak's house, which they knew to be a meeting point for Gewircman's group. While crossing a bridge on the Pilica River, the emissaries were attacked by a German police patrol.

One was killed and the other (Jacobson) managed to escape and return to Zloty Potok.

Finally, they made contact with some people who introduced themselves as representatives of the Home Army's *Grom* (Thunder) unit. They suggested that the Jewish partisans go to the Zeleslawice estate where, supposedly according to the instructions of a superior AK officer, they would get food. Later they were told they would be moved to Czarna Kepa to join a Polish partisan unit said to be operating there. When the Jews reached Zeleslawice, they found they had been betrayed: A treacherous trap was set for them, with German police units stationed all around. Two members of the Jewish unit who had entered the yard for talks with AK representatives who were supposed to be waiting for them were captured and executed. The Germans also opened heavy fire against the members of the group who were waiting for the results of these "talks." Almost all of the fighters were killed. Only three survived. Having no alternative whatsoever, they went to the Hasag camp, where a group of former ZOB members from Czestochowa were carrying out underground activities.[26]

THE OSTROWIEC GROUPS

A Jewish forced labor camp had existed in Ostrowiec Swietokrzyski since the end of 1942. Almost from the very beginning, an underground group was active there, under the direction of the brothers Kopel and Moshe Stein. After some time, they succeeded in acquiring and smuggling in twelve pistols. These arms were used to equip the first group of seventeen people who escaped from the camp through ties with the local *Zwiazek Odwetu* (Revenge Union), under the command of the Home Army. At first the collaboration of the two groups went smoothly. A bunker was built in the nearby forests with the aid of the Polish organization, and the Poles organized combat training for the Jews and equipped them with arms. Yet a tragic betrayal occurred soon after. On February 9, 1943, following an order from above, the commanders of the local Revenge Union group, Jozef Mularski, Edward Perzynski, and Leon Nowak, prepared a swearing-in ceremony for the fugitives, which was supposed to precede the beginning of combat actions. During the ceremony, the Poles opened fire on the Jews. Only two succeeded in escaping. The rest were killed. This tragedy delayed all other attempts to escape from the camp for a long time.

Only in the spring of 1944 was contact made with Mieczyslaw Rybkowski, commander of the People's Army in the district of Radom. Contact was also made with the Jewish Fighting Organization leaders in Warsaw. An emissary from Warsaw, Frania Beatus, was sent to Ostrowiec in accordance with an order from the ZOB commander Yitzhak Zuckerman. She brought the camp's underground organization 25,000 *zloties* for the acquisition of arms and "Aryan" documents. For her contacts with the camp, Frania Beatus paid with her life.

Following the betrayal of one of the camp's inmates, the underground activities of the Stein brothers were discovered. The two brothers were taken to the Gestapo for interrogation. Despite the tortures they suffered, they did not reveal any information concerning the underground to the Germans. As a consequence, they were shot in the camp's courtyard. The command of the camp's underground then passed into the hands of David Kepinski.

On June 23, 1944, thirty members of the organization escaped from the camp equipped with fourteen pistols, two rifles, and three grenades. The fugitives reached a forest in the vicinity of Wolka Bodzychowska, 5 kilometers from the camp, where they were to wait for Rybkowski's emissaries. However, because of the arrest of Rybkowski a few days before, communications with AL headquarters were entangled. After a short while, the fugitives succeeded in making contact for a very short time with regional AL headquarters by means of Sternik, a PPR activist.

Finally, the fugitives established a base in the forests of Krzemionek, where they met with a group of nine well-equipped Soviet partisans. The two groups united and worked as one. After a few operations against the police, designed to increase the unit's supply of arms, the group's equipment soon numbered three submachine guns, three rifles, a few pistols, and a few score of grenades. On July 29, 1944, the unit sabotaged an army train carrying a load of ammunition and explosives headed for the front.

In August 1944, the German army concentrated forces on the west bank of the Vistula. This force prepared defense positions, after the Red Army's offensive was stopped on the Vistula's right bank. Because of this, conditions under which the partisans operated grew very harsh. When ties with the AL regional headquarters were again cut off, the Jewish partisans decided to break through the front line on their own. On August 20, the first attempt to cross the front was made. It failed. The partisans came across a strong SS unit near the village of Brzeziny, 10 kilometers from the Vistula. There was no escape from a battle. In the lopsided fight clash with superior enemy forces, half the partisans were killed and half of their arms were lost. The survivors retreated to the vicinity of Ruda Koscielna, giving up for then the plan to break through to the east. Only after two months did they try to cross the Vistula again. But this attempt failed also. The Germans saw the partisans and attacked them right on the edge of the river. Two partisans were killed, but the others succeeded in escaping from the Germans.

Some time later, in one of the clashes with a German patrol, four partisans were killed and two were wounded. The Germans lost two men and the partisans took their weapons. In another clash they attacked a German vehicle carrying cigarettes and canned meat. Two Germans were killed and the vehicle was destroyed. On October 4, the unit attacked the village of Sadogora and burned the building where the local commander of the German unit, a captain, was quartered. The German officer was killed.

The unit was finally attacked by Germans on November 3. In the battle that ensued, eight of the unit's fighters were killed, and the survivors had to retreat to Czarna Glina near Ostrowiec, where they established a new base and built three bunkers. There they were attacked by a Hungarian army unit that was stationed nearby. The partisans again suffered some losses.

When the Red Army liberated the Ostrowiec area, only six Jewish fighters of this unit were still alive.[27]

OTHER FIGHTING GROUPS

Ber Ackerman commanded a large and very active partisan unit in the forests of Ciepielow and Zwolen during the last months of 1942 and the beginning of 1943. This unit included a group of youths who had escaped from the Radom ghetto with a few guns and a group of Jews who fled the towns of Ciepielow, Kaznow, Lipsko, and Zwolen. In February 1943, they made contact with an AL unit that had organized in this area under the command of Jan Kowalik, and the two groups sometimes carried out joint actions. A group of noncombatant Jews hid under the protection of Ackerman's unit.

When Jan Kowalik was killed in April 1943, and the command of his unit passed into the hands of Lieutenant Tumanian, a Soviet officer, Ackerman's unit still continued to collaborate closely with this unit. The two units were attacked on several occasions by the Germans and also by AK units.[28]

Another Jewish unit, under the command of Avraham Haberman, was active in the same area, but it had no connection with Ackerman's unit. Hundreds of Jewish refugees hid all around this area. On November 23, 1943, the partisans suffered heavy losses after they were surrounded by a far stronger force of German gendarmerie and Polish police in the area of Lyse Wody. According to the testimony of Israel Glatt, sixty-four Jewish fighters died in that attack, including the unit's commander, Haberman.[29]

The Soviet officer Vasil Voichenko commanded a unit active in the district of Opatow in 1943. It was made up of Jewish refugees from nearby ghettos and escaped Soviet prisoners-of-war. In September 1943, the unit became affiliated with the local GL headquarters and, from then on, was called the Sokol unit. On November 23, 1943, the unit was surprised by the Germans. According to Polish sources, twenty-one partisans died in this battle, and nine Jews (among them two women), were captured. After a short interrogation, they were all shot.

A group of Jewish fighters held on for a longer time, until 1944, in the region of Sandomierz. The group numbered between ten and twenty people and was, at first, armed only with pistols and grenades. Its main task was the protection of Jews hiding in the area. This protection was based, among other things, on the punishment of informers and blackmailers. The Jewish partisans were forced to face a series of clashes not only with the Germans, but also with a local AK group under the command of Antoni Jarosz. During the last stage of its activity, the unit gained more arms—a submachine gun and three rifles. Even so, this group and the Jews who were hiding under its protection were killed apparently when German army forces were concentrated in this area in the summer of 1944, and the front on the Vistula River was stabilized.

A Jewish unit existed for a longer time, until the liberation in January 1945, in the forests of Szydlowiec, between Radom and Przysucha. It was made up mainly of Jews who had managed to jump off a train that was on its way from Szydlowiec to Treblinka at the end of 1942. Under the command of Avraham Finkler, this unit initially numbered thirty-nine people. During the two years of its activity, it lost sixteen people. Twenty-three fighters survived until the Red Army arrived and, with the first units of the 9th Army Corps, entered Szydlowiec, the birthplace of the partisans. This was on January 16, 1945.[30]

In the town of Iwaniska, in the county of Opatow in the Swietokrzyskie mountains, several armed groups were organized through the initiative of a young rabbi named Chaim Yechezkel (Haskel) Rabinowicz. Before the deportation to Treblinka on October 15, 1943, three hundred Jews escaped from Iwaniska and reached bunkers that had been prepared in the nearby forests. Some of the fugitives had arms and organized small fighting groups. According to the testimony of one of the few surviving Iwaniska refugees, Ignacy Goldstein, they did not choose a leader, preferring instead to operate in small separate groups, whose chances they believed were better than those of a whole unit, whose actions would encounter much greater obstacles and hardships, as well as dangers to its very existence. Yet these small groups, equipped with few arms, became an easy target for hunts held by the German police with the support of the local peasants. During one of the first hunts, Rabbi Rabinowicz was killed. Most of the other fugitives and members of the fighting groups were killed during the first month. Because it was impossible to continue to exist in the bunkers, some of the fugitives, who survived until the end of 1942, moved to the ghetto in Sandomierz. Most of them died during the next deportations to Treblinka. A few survived after being deported to the forced labor camp in Skarzysko-Kamienna.[31]

An attempt to organize a fighting unit was also made by the fugitives from the town of Staszow. Over one thousand Jews escaped from this town to the forests. Most of them died shortly after, during the hunts held by the German police; others died at the hands of the local AK units. Only in the village of Czajkow did the fugitives receive support from a local cell of the Peasant Batallions. With their help, a group under the command of Nataniel Ehrlich was organized to protect the refugees. This group, however, did not succeed in acquiring arms, and only a few of the refugees survived to the day of liberation.[32]

CHAPTER 6
MAZOVIA AND PODLASIE

MAZOVIA AND PODLASIE, WHICH WERE PART OF THE district of Warsaw during the Nazi occupation, stretch along a monotonous plain, containing only a few small forests in the east, in the vicinity of Wyszkow, Sokolow Podlaski, and Wegrow. From a topographical point of view, then, this area was highly unsuitable for partisan activity. Furthermore, the entire area was densely populated, with a well-developed network of roads and railway lines. Another factor which limited the development of the partisan movement there was its large concentration of German army and police forces. The strategic importance of Warsaw as a political, administrative, and industrial center was also prominent. The city was a central road junction, and the strategic railway lines that crossed this area—the Warsaw-Brest line, leading to Moscow, and the Warsaw-Bialystok line, leading to Leningrad—were particularly important.

The Jewish population was expelled from the western part of this area—the counties of Grojec, Lowicz, Skierniewice, and Sochaczew—as early as February 1941. The Jews from the eastern part of Mazovia—from Wyszkow, Ostrow Mazowiecka, and their surroundings—had been "driven out as early as November 1939. By the summer of 1942, there were Jews only in the Warsaw Ghetto and in several towns in the east of Mazovia and Podlasie. Then the deportation to the Treblinka extermination camp began. On July 21, the deportation from Minsk Mazowiecki was held, and on July 22, the deportations from the Warsaw Ghetto were started. On August 22, the Jews were taken from Siedlce, Sokolow Podlaski, and Wegrow. On August 25, the deportation from Kaluszyn was held. And on August 30, the Jews were driven out of Zelechow.[1]

As in other parts of Poland, the deportations from this area were accompanied by mass escapes and by attempts to organize partisan groups for the purpose of armed resistance. However, the conditions for fighting were much more difficult here than in the regions of Lublin or Kielce, and the fugitives' chances for success were much fewer. Most of the fugitives fell into the hands of the Germans soon after their escape. And this area, apparently more than any other, witnessed the most tragic phenomenon of all—that of fugitives willingly reporting to German police stations for lack of hideouts in the villages or in the forests and because there were such limited prospects of survival. An article titled "The Greatest of Tragedies," appearing in the October 1942 issue of the Polish underground journal *Prawda*, among other sources, describes this phenomenon:

> Jews from Wolomin, Otwock, and other settlements in the vicinity of Warsaw, who had been wandering in the forests like wild animals, came, tortured by hunger and cold, to the greatest despair and reported of their own will to the gendarmerie stations to be "sentenced to be shot." A few of these incidents are well known. In one such case, a whole group came forth saying, "Kill us, death is better than this kind of life." There was no ammunition in the gendarmerie station, so one gendarme took a bicycle and went to get some. The "condemned" waited. The gendarme returned. The Jews were shot. In another case an old Jew appeared with his daughter, a young and beautiful girl. They were once rich and still carried a quantity of jewels with them. They apathetically gave them to the gendarme who, according to procedure, ordered them to strip. In an honorable and calm manner the girl placed parts of her clothing on the ground one after the other. Wearing only an undergarment, barefoot, tall and proud she faced the killers. "Is this good?" she asked. "You have to kneel," they said. They both kneeled. There was a blast of shots and the end came. "She is always before my eyes," confessed our informer, a German sergeant who was a platoon commander. "I get completely drunk and cannot forget."[2]

The fugitives often returned to the walled ghetto, which still existed in some places and was the only refuge left for a Jewish fugitive. Yet a few were lucky in spite of all this, and even in this area without suitable conditions, managed to hide in the forests and form Jewish fighting units. A number of units arose spontaneously in the vicinity of Zelechow, Radzyn Podlaski, and Minsk Mazowiecki, and a Jewish partisan unit, established by the survivors of the Jewish Fighting Organization in Warsaw, was active for a short time in the forests of Wyszkow.

PARTISAN GROUPS IN THE AREA OF ZELECHOW

From the fall of 1942 to the arrival of the Red Army in the summer of 1944, the area of Garwolin and Zelechow was the backdrop for the intensive actions of small Jewish partisan units. As in other areas of the *General Gouvernment*, the partisan activity here was initiated by Soviet soldiers who had escaped from German captivity. Groups of Russians, headed by such men as "Fat Ivan," "Bulanow," "Victor," and others, were established as early as spring, 1942. The one who became most prominent in the course of time was Serafin Alekseyev, a private from the 55th Division of the Red Army. An exceptionally energetic man, Alekseyev had escaped during a prisoners' march in March 1942 and soon became a central figure in the Soviet partisan movement in the area. In the southern part of this region, other fairly intensive actions were led by Nikolai Paramonov, a Soviet officer who had escaped German captivity. Yet topographical conditions made the existence of large partisan units impossible. Because of this, the Russians operated in very small groups, which would unite temporarily for important combat actions under the leadership of Alekseyev or Paramonov.

The Jewish underground in Zelechow formed ties with Alekseyev quite early by extending help to the Soviet partisans. A few Jews and Soviets joined this group, even before the liquidation of the Jews in Zelechow. However, mass escapes to the forests and the planning of partisan activities on a larger scale began only with the deportations to the extermination camps. On September 30, 1942, the Jews were deported from Zelechow. At the exact same time, Jews were also taken away from other towns in this area. One week later, the Jews were deported from the nearby town of Lukow. Among other things, the number of murders that accompanied the deportations testifies to the wide-spread phenomena of mass escapes and passive resistance. About 800 Jews who were caught hiding in the forest or the villages or trying to escape, were shot in Zelechow and its immediate surroundings. In the nearby town of Irena, more than 1,600 of the 5,000 Jewish residents were shot. The number of those shot in the whole Lukow region is estimated at over 2,000.[3]

Among the fugitives who escaped during the deportations were the members of the organization that was in contact with Alekseyev. This group, which numbered a few dozen people and was headed by Joseph Mlynowski, joined his unit. The Jews, who at that time had only one rifle and two pistols, made up about half of Alekseyev's unit.[4]

Apart from Mlynowski's group, a few other independent Jewish groups concentrated in the sparse forests of this area. The largest of these was under the command of Shmuel Oszlak. Others were under the leadership of Antek Zelechowicz, Hirsh Rochman, and Ephraim Abigo.

Most of the partisans fled the ghettos during the deportations. With them were also Jews from Zelechow who had escaped from the train on the way to Treblinka. In the beginning, immediately after their escape, they were aided by Protestant ministers in the village of Jagoda. In the course of time they came into contact with Jewish partisan groups, already active in the area, and were accepted into their ranks. Later, Jews who had escaped from forced labor camps in Adamow and Deblin also joined these groups. Scores of civilians, among them many relatives of the fighters, hid in the forests with the partisans and enjoyed their protection.

Because the harsh geographical conditions made it impossible to form a large partisan body and the limited size of the woods could contain only very small groups, large family camps of hiding Jews, like the ones in the forests of Parczew and Janow, could not be established. Women, children, and older people had to hide in bunkers that were scattered throughout the area, or in the villages.

Groups of Jews operated independently, as did Russian units in this area, and joined together for specific objectives, such as warding off large-scale hunts or carrying out attacks on police stations. The membership of these groups was not consistent. Partisans usually wandered from one group to another, generally because their units disintegrated after the frequent hunts held by the Germans. After large-scale hunts, the surviving fighters generally avoided returning to the same group and formed new combinations. Often they joined the first armed Jewish group they met up with, without trying to find their original unit. There were also cases of arbitrary moves from one group to another as a result of a personal conflict with the unit's commander or with its members, and for other reasons. These incidents, which were very common particularly at the beginning of the partisan activity, were a logical result of slack discipline in the independent groups.

The head of one group, Shmuel Oszlak, became a central figure among the Jewish fighters here, just as Alekseyev had become for the local Soviet partisan movement, and his group had a special place in the Jewish partisan movement in Zelechow. Almost immediately after his arrival in the forests, Oszlak made contact with Alekseyev. Other groups also formed ties with Alekseyev or Paramonov, and the relations between the Jewish partisans and the Soviet partisans in this area were orderly. Joint combat actions under the command of Alekseyev or Paramonov were held at frequent intervals.

At the end of 1942, Alekseyev and Paramonov established ties with the People's Guard command. From then on, Alekseyev's unit and the Jewish and Russian groups that were affiliated with it appeared under the banner of the People's Guard as the Jan Kilinski unit. Paramonov adopted the name Dabrowski, and his unit adopted the same name. In the course of time these units were joined by a small number of Polish PPR members; the Jews, however, still made up the largest national group among all those who operated in the area of Zelechow between the fall of 1942 and the end of 1943.

The history of Levinson's group is characteristic of the instability of the units in this area. Meir Shalom Levinson fled with a group of Jews to the Dabrowiec forest in October 1942. After one of the hunts, they moved to the forest of Gilow. Here they met Antek Zelechowicz's unit and operated for some time as a part of it. Soon it became apparent that this area was too narrow to serve as a base for a partisan group numbering more than fifty people. Zelechowicz, therefore, divided his unit into smaller groups, which continued to coordinate their activities under his command. After another hunt, these groups scattered. Levinson, together with eighteen fighters, moved back to the forests of Dabrowiec and established a new unit. After some time, the group returned to the forest of Gilow, where they came in contact with Alekseyev's unit and agreed to come under Alekseyev's command. For several months, they carried out combat missions according to Alekseyev's planning and instructions, at times with his company. But after still another hunt, in which the group suffered heavy losses and completely disintegrated, Levinson gathered together Jewish groups and formed a new unit. The tie with Alekseyev's unit was renewed, and Levinson's group sabotaged railway lines, destroyed bridges, and cut off telegraph lines. Certain circumstances brought about a break between the group and Alekseyev, and after a period of independent activity, they established ties with Paramonov. Together with his unit, the Jewish partisans carried out a series of combat actions in which Levinson's men suffered heavy losses. Then during the last months of German occupation, the survivors of this unit hid in a concealed bunker in the forest, with no contact with other partisan groups and no practical opportunities for carrying out combat actions of any importance.

Harsh topographical conditions were also the reason the partisans were often very poorly equipped. The limited forest area made it impossible to drop in arms as had been done, for example, in the forests of Parczew since the end of 1943. The equipment of this area's partisans came mostly from small acquisitions and from what was taken in attacks on small police stations.

The most frequent actions were of necessity those which had the aim of obtaining supplies for fighters and for Jews hiding in the area. A series of successful attacks were carried out against police stations in the villages of Zloczew, Jarczew, Myslawa, and Czechocin, and a number of important operations freed prisoners from forced labor camps. The first of these was the attack on the Jewish forced labor camp in Adamow, carried out in collaboration with a Russian group under the general command of Alekseyev and Mlynowski on the night of November 20, 1942. The partisans surprised the German guard, freed about 200 prisoners, and helped them reach the forest, although only a few were accepted into the fighting unit. The partisans did not have enough arms and bunkers to absorb or even hide the liberated prisoners. And so the fugitives were easy prey for the German hunts in the forests immediately after the operation.

Oszlak's men came into contact and aided the underground organization in the Jewish forced labor camp near the military airport in Deblin. The Jewish partisans also took part, together with Paramonov's unit, in a successful attack on a forced labor camp of Polish youths, called the Yunak's camp, near the Golab railway station on June 4, 1943. The German guard was completely wiped out, the camp was burned down, and all of the prisoners were freed.

In the summer of 1943, the Jewish groups affiliated with Alekseyev and Paramonov began sabotage actions whose main objective was the destruction of railway lines and bridges. Having only primitive means, the groups dismantled railway lines usually by opening the tracks' connections and setting bridges on fire to whatever degree possible. Unlike the partisans in the district of Lublin, who had explosives as early as the end of 1943, the groups here had none.

The first important operation against railway lines was held on September 26, 1943. A train was intercepted in the Leopoldow-Okrzeja section, and railway movement was stopped for twelve hours. Groups of Jews and Russians carried out a second operation on this section a few weeks later on November 10 and destroyed an engine and three cars. At about the same time the partisans attacked a train that was carrying Polish prisoners to Auschwitz near the Leopoldow railway station. The engine was hit by bullets, and the train was forced to stop. The freed prisoners fled in every direction, and a few joined the partisans.

The partisans played an important role in extending help to Jews in hiding. They organized payments, the source of which was mainly money taken during attacks, for the peasants who provided the hide-outs and provided the necessary protection by punishing betrayers who turned in hiding Jews and endangered those hiding them. Mendel Gerecht describes one such incident. While passing through a certain village, his group found Jews bound in one of the houses. The peasant, who had until then hidden them in return for payment, had decided, when their money ran out, to turn them in to the Germans. The partisans killed the peasant, and the two rescued Jews joined Waldman's partisan group. Both were killed in battle soon before the liberation of the area of Zelechow.

The Jewish partisan movement in the area of Zelechow was eventually crushed in the constant battles that took place between 1942 and 1944, and all the fighters were killed. One of the first defeats was in a clash with the Germans in the village of Jarczew at the end of April 1943. Joseph Mlynowski, the commander of the Jewish group, fell in this battle, and all but one of the partisans of his group were killed. Most of the fighters of the Jewish unit that was under the command of the brothers Max and Sergiey (last name unknown) were killed in an unsuccessful skirmish with the Germans near Ciechocin. Among the few survivors was Melech Rosenberg. Oszlak's unit suffered heavy losses during a clash in Huta Zelechowska at the end of the summer of 1943. The Germans, who had received information from the local residents, called in gendarmerie companies from Zelechow, Garwolin, and Deblin. A two-hour battle between the partisans and superior German forces followed. The partisans managed to break out of the siege, but suffered many losses.

On October 20, 1943, the Germans began an antipartisan campaign aimed mainly at Oszlak's unit, which was then in the forests of Gilow. In this campaign, which lasted two days, the besieged partisans managed to escape only with great difficulty. When they finally breached the Germans' lines, many Jewish fighters were killed and the unit's commander, Shmuel Oszlak, was seriously wounded. He then shot himself to death so he would not fall into the hands of the Germans.

At the end of 1944, as a result of information received from a local peasant, the German gendarmerie succeeded in surprising the unit under the command of Hirsch Rochman. Eight fighters fell in this battle, among them the unit's commander. In May 1944, shortly before the liberation of the area, fifteen more Jewish fighters were killed in a skirmish near Okrzeja.

The Jews suffered as many losses in clashes with local AK groups as they did in those with Germans. The Home Army's main purpose in the forest was to interfere with "quota collections" from local residents, which were carried out by the Jewish partisans, that is, the partisans' confiscation of food from large agricultural estates. The first major clash took place on July 26, 1943, when the Jews were suddenly attacked by an AK group after a successful confiscation campaign in the village of Felikszyn. Five Jews died. A second serious battle with the Home Army broke out around September when the Jewish partisans were on the Teodorow estate. Suddenly, they were surrounded and attacked by large AK groups and, in the two-hour battle, three Jewish partisans were killed. Three AK members also died. The Jewish unit finally succeeded in warding off the attack and broke through the siege. In retaliation, a Jewish group under the command of Mendel Gerecht broke into the Zalesie estate near Ryki and executed two AK commanders.

Home Army attacks on Jews increased in the beginning of 1944, and AK members brought Germans to the bunkers of Jewish fighters in the forests at more frequent intervals. The partisans tried to find and capture those responsible and pay them their due. This, in turn, met with increasingly angrier responses from the Home Army, which had been protecting informers and those who turned Jews over to the Germans to be killed. There were many bloody clashes. An early April penal mission taken on by a seventeen-man partisan group, led by Yakov Rochman, aimed at retaliating against an informer who had brought the Germans to Hirsch Rochman's partisan base, ended in a great tragedy. As mentioned above, a local informer called in the Germans, who prepared devious ambushes for the Jews. Eight partisans, among them the group's commander, Hirsch Rochman, were killed. Later, when the penal mission neared the village of Krystyna, it encountered a much larger and better equipped AK company. In the ensuing battle between the unmatched forces, all seventeen Jewish fighters were killed.

The AK units attacked not only Jews, but also Soviet partisans, who were under the direct command of Alekseyev. Because of the intensification of the Home Army's activities, an obstacle to the Soviet partisan movement, Alekseyev decided to move his forces east and unite with the Soviet units commanded by Colonel Ivan Banov ("The Black"), which was in the nearby region of Bialystok at this time. Alekseyev's departure weakened the Jewish partisan movement to a marked extent. After Oszlak's death, they did not succeed in finding among themselves a commander who was able, at least temporarily, to coordinate the actions of the various Jewish partisan groups. Because Alekseyev had earned the trust and respect of the Jewish partisans, the lack of a Jewish commander comparable to Oszlak was not felt very strongly, until his departure. But when he left, the Jewish groups, which had suffered many losses, were no longer able to carry out any important actions. The Jewish partisans spent the months of May and June of 1944 in their bunkers; they took action only to defend themselves when their bunker was found or when they felt it was in danger of discovery.

This situation lasted until the end of June 1944, when a group of twenty AL members sent from Warsaw came to get arms that had been dropped in from the Soviet Union and transfer them to Warsaw. The commander of this People's Army group was Captain Miroslaw Krajewski, known as Piotr. When they met these AL fighters, the Jewish partisans willingly agreed to join Krajewski's company. However, as a result of the quick advance of the Soviet offensive, the plan to drop in arms did not materialize, and on July 27, Krajewski's partisans joined the attacking Red Army units.

Of the more than one hundred Jewish partisans who fought in the area of Zelechow, only eighteen survived.[5]

GROUPS IN THE AREA OF MINSK MAZOWIECKI

The conditions in the area of Minsk Mazowiecki were similar to those in the area of Zelechow. Jewish fighters also gathered there, and began to form groups from among the fugitives of the ghettos of Otwock, Radzymin, Falenica, and Kaluszyn as early as the end of 1942. These groups were joined by a few Warsaw ghetto fugitives and Josef Czarny, a fugitive from Treblinka. Because their circumstances, methods of operation, and fate were not basically different from those of the groups in Zelechow, we will limit ourselves to a brief discussion of these groups in Minsk Mazowiecki.

A relatively large unit, numbering over twenty people, was active from September 1942 to August 1943 in the forests near Kaluszyn. This unit was forced to fight not only against the Germans but also against the well-armed NSZ members who came into this area in the beginning of 1943. On August 17, a five-man patrol was surprised by a strong NSZ force, and all five were killed. Soon after this, the unit was attacked by the German gendarmerie and, after suffering heavy losses, ceased to exist. The partisans who survived hid nearby until the area was liberated.[6]

The force that was established from the fugitives in the forest of Stazew near Parysow was also substantial in number. This unit operated independently until the end of 1943, when its survivors joined a Soviet unit that had been transferred to the area. During the entire time of their activity, the Jewish partisans extended their protection to Jews hiding in the forest and supplied them with food and clothing. From the testimony of Tuvia Miller, one of the surviving fighters, it appears that the relatively long existence of this group under such very harsh topographical conditions was made possible, to a large extent, by the friendly attitude of the local AK commander, Wozniak. Miller writes the following on this:

> One time someone came to us and said: "Boys, this week, I don't know if tomorrow or the day after, a large hunt may be held against you. You must get out of here." This stranger was the AK commander, Wozniak, from Studzew. Every once in a while, when he would receive an order to liquidate us, he would come to us and tell us about it so we could get away. He would come, check out the area, so to say, but not look very closely. With this he would carry out the order as it was stated and go out on the mission. In this way, he always coordinated his action with us, and we were safe in these forests.[7]

Aside from these relatively larger units, we have information on two smaller groups of Jewish partisans that collaborated closely with groups of escaped Russian prisoners, who operated under the leadership of Piotr Finansov and an officer called Semion. These groups were active for a short time only, and were probably totally destroyed in the spring of 1943.[8]

PARTISAN GROUPS IN PODLASIE

The area of Podlasie, in the eastern part of the district of Warsaw, had more suitable conditions for partisan activity. The forests in this area served as temporary shelter for several hundred fleeing Jews, most of whom came from Lukow, Kock, and Radzyn Podlaski. From various German and Polish sources, it is clear that during the winter of 1942–43 at least a dozen groups of armed Jews were established by these fugitives and that most of them were destroyed during the first months of their activity. A relatively large unit, which existed for a longer time, was organized by a former Polish army sergeant, Baruch Libefrajnd. This unit numbered forty fighters, mostly refugees from Kock who were hiding in the forest.

This force was able to carry out action largely because of the aid given it by Stanislaw Guz, a Pole, who also helped the group to acquire its first arms. Stanislaw Guz, whose entire family was killed by the Germans because of the help he gave to runaway Soviet prisoners-of-war, aided the Jewish unit for the entire time that it was active.

The operating conditions of Libefrajnd's group worsened to a marked extent when armed AK groups appeared in the vicinity of the villages of Wola, Targowica, and Piasek, southeast of Kock, and began to use these villages as bases for attacks against Jewish partisans. This danger forced the Jewish partisans to leave the area of Podlasie. The Jewish unit succeeded in reaching the east bank of the Bug River, where it formed ties with the Soviet Dzierzynski partisan unit. The Russians were interested in concentrating the partisan activity west of the Bug, on lands populated by Poles, and because of this they ordered the Jews to return to their former area of operation. Equipped with automatic weapons and explosives, the Jews warded off attacks by the German police and AK groups. Most of the partisans, however, were killed in the frequent clashes with the enemy, and only a few survived until the liberation of Podlasie in June 1944.

We have fragmentary information on two other Jewish partisan groups that operated in Podlasie. The first was a force numbering about thirty people, which was organized from the refugees of Radzyn and commanded by Yitzhak Kleinman. It established its base in Stara Wies, halfway between Radzyn and Kock. During the months of February and March 1943, Kleinman's group carried out a series of successful combat actions—attacks on small German patrols on the Radzyn-Kock road and the destruction of a dairy in Stara Wies. Apparently, this group was wiped out in the beginning of spring, 1943. The few surviving partisans, among them Yitzhak Kleinman who was ill with typhus, managed to reach the only ghetto still existing in this area—the ghetto in Miedzyrzec Podlaski. They met their death during the liquidation of the ghetto on May 2, 1943.

The second group, which was also made up of refugees from Radzyn, was organized by the four Paczek brothers—Gershon, Leizer, Avraham, and Berl. Despite the heavy losses it suffered in the summer of 1943, this group held on until November, when it was finally wiped out by local AK groups.[9]

THE MORDECHAI ANIELEWICZ UNIT

The Mordechai Anielewicz partisan unit, established by the survivors of the Jewish Fighting Organization in the Warsaw Ghetto, was active for a short time in the forests of Wyszkow. The circumstances under which this unit was formed were totally different from those of other Jewish units in the areas of Zelechow, Minsk Mazowiecki, and Podlasie. Most Jewish partisan groups were formed spontaneously by fugitives from the deportations in the ghetto, or by fugitives from the camps. Only after the escape to the forests were the organizational frameworks of these groups created and arms and experience acquired. The Anielewicz unit was different. It reached the forest as an armed unit and was made up of people who, for more than half a year, had belonged to a fighting underground organization. They brought with them the vast experience from their underground activity and their participation in the Warsaw Ghetto uprising. From the viewpoint of the nature of the organization, its discipline and combat experience, and its arms, the situation of the Anielewicz unit was much better than that of most other Jewish units just beginning combat activity. All of these factors pointed to strong possibilities for continuing the struggle against the Nazis from forest bases. Yet, as shall be seen, other conditions, and most of all the negative position of the Polish underground, made all hopes evaporate.

The Anielewicz unit was made up of two groups of the Jewish Fighting Organization that had left the ruins of the Warsaw Ghetto after its liquidation. The first group, numbering forty people and led by David Nowodworski, was taken out of the ghetto through the sewer network by two liaisons of the Jewish Fighting Organization, Regina Fuden and Shlomo Barczynski. On May 10, the organization's emissary *Simcha* liaison took the second group, numbering thirty-four fighters, out of the ghetto. The two groups were taken to the small forest of Lomianki near Warsaw by a GL member, Wladyslaw Gajek.

Until May 20, this large group, numbering close to eighty people, was apparently in the forest, where they could be discovered easily by the Germans and had almost no possibility for armed action. The fighters also had no drinking water or food. The People's Guard, which helped members of the Jewish Fighting Organization to get out of Warsaw, had no plans ready to employ the Jewish fighters for partisan activities. The fighters in the Lomianki forest were, therefore, in a very bad state. They sent emissaries to various branches of the Polish underground, but the Home Army command showed no interest in the fate of the members of the Jewish Fighting Organization, who had taken part in the ghetto uprising and were now looking for ways to join the partisan movement. And although a representative of the Polish People's Army (PAL), Boleslaw Nosowski, did try to find ways to transfer the Jewish fighters to the city of Ryki near

Lublin, where they were to operate as a part of that organization, it seemed that this solution was in no way possible.

It was only on about May 20 that the People's Guard command agreed to transfer the Jewish fighters to the forests in the area of Wyszkow, about 60 kilometers from Warsaw. This place was chosen because it was close to Warsaw and because the People's Guard wanted to create a new force in an area where, until then, it had no affiliates or units of its own. Yet this was a very bad choice. The Jewish fighters had to operate in an area that was completely unknown to them, without support from the local population, and without even the slightest possibility of collaboration with other partisan forces. Worse, the very fact that the Jewish fighters were transferred to the forests of Wyszkow by the People's Guard and asked to act as a partisan force under the command of the PPR quickly led to conflicts with the local cells of the Home Army.

When they arrived in Wyszkow, the fighters were organized into three separate squads: one under the command of Adam Schwarzfus, called the White Janek, the second under the command of Mordechai Growas, and the third under the command of Ignacy Podolski. These squads usually operated independently and did not choose a common leader from among their fighters.

In the beginning, the attitude of the local peasants to the partisans was fairly tolerant and they supplied the partisans with food and clothing. But a drastic change for the worse came about as early as July 1943, when the local AK organizations began provoking the Jewish partisans and inciting the village population against them. This attitude can most likely be viewed as a result of the Home Army's decision not to tolerate a new partisan force connected to the People's Guard in an area that, until then, had been under its influence. It is also likely that anti-Semitic tendencies were also at work. Hence, the Jewish partisans were forced to operate equally on two fronts—against the Germans and against the Home Army, with a generally hostile local village population.

A major clash took place, apparently as early as July 1943, between Growas's squad and the far superior AK forces. All of the members of the squad fell in the battle. In view of this tragic situation, Zygmunt Igla was sent to Warsaw to protest to AK headquarters. Igla contacted the commander of the Jewish Fighting Organization, Yitzhak Zuckerman, and the Bund leader, Feiner. But protests to the AK command brought no results. Igla returned to his unit bringing some material help (money and clothing that he had received from Zuckerman), but no promises to curb the repeated AK attacks. The

Anielewicz unit was also visited by the emissary of the Jewish resistance movement in Warsaw, Faiga Peltel.

Despite the very grave situation, the Anielewicz unit decided to begin sabotaging railway tracks. An important operation, headed by Schwarzfus and Rosenfeld was carried out early in September 1943 on the Malkinia-Tluszcz line, between Orle and the Debe railway station, where the partisans forced a train carrying Germans off the track. The German police retaliated with a large-scale hunt. Schwarzfus's squad was surrounded and almost totally wiped out in a battle near the village of Krawcowizna. Sixteen Jewish fighters died, among them Schwarzfus. According to Polish sources, the Germans had only two dead and three wounded. After this battle only three members of Schwarzfus's group survived, and they joined Ignacy Podolski's squad, which was still in existence.

After the defeat near Krawcowizna, and in face of the continuous attacks of the AK and NSZ forces, the remainder of the Anielewicz unit disintegrated completely. According to a report by Bronislaw Jaworski, a Polish PPR activist, most of the partisans of Ignacy Podolski's group fell in battles with the National Armed Forces. The few survivors, who saw that there was no possibility of continuing the war in the forests of Wyszkow, returned to Warsaw. They joined the underground activity there and later took part in the Polish Warsaw uprising in 1944. The few that remained joined the Soviet partisans who came to the area later. The majority of these Russians had collaborated with the Germans, under the command of General Vlasov, and now wished to make up for their crime of serving in Nazi units by joining the pro-Soviet partisan movement. The commander of one of these units, in which a few of the partisans of Anielewicz's unit continued their combat activity, was Ignacy Podolski, who headed the unit until his death in battle in April 1944. After his death, the partisans, who were under heavy pressure from the Germans and from the AK, moved to the area of Bialystok, where they joined a large Russian partisan unit headed by General Kapusta.[10]

OTHER ARMED GROUPS

Apart from the units listed above, small fighting groups were active for almost the entire period of the deportations to extermination camps, that is, from the summer of 1942 to the summer of 1943. Apparently all of these groups were totally wiped out in clashes with the enemy.

We know of the existence of these groups only from the German and Polish documents that have come down to us. Unfortunately, these fragments of information enable us neither to identify these groups, nor to reconstruct their actions. It is, therefore, difficult to determine their makeup, character, and history. Yet the information that we do have is worth mentioning.

The collaboration of Jews with the first partisan groups in Mazovia, which were established by escaped Soviet prisoners, can be deduced from the *Wehrmacht* field-command report for the period May 16–June 15, 1942. Among other things, it says the following: "The bands are made up of escaped Russian prisoners-of-war. . . . The communists and Jews supply them with information, arms, and food. The collaboration of the Jews has been proven by the reports of the gendarmerie. A number of times Jewish men and women were seen together with the members of the bands, and were shot to death while fleeing."[11]

The report of the Polish Government Delegacy on the situation at the end of 1942 also gives information on the existence of armed Jewish groups. One of these reports was sent to London on January 6, 1943. According to the terminology used in these reports, the armed Jewish groups are called gangs. Following is a part of that report:

> It is most typical that the stories of people from the counties of Lukow, Radzyn, Sokolow, and other places contain insistent information on the participation of Jews in assaults, whose objective is the confiscation of supplies. These have been carried out recently in the villages, on the roads, and in various settlements. The gangs, which take money and clothing (particularly furs, shoes, sweaters, etc.) and food, undoubtedly, as the testimonies verify, include Russian-speaking people and also Jews. This testifies to the fact that—as was foreseen—the persecution of the Jewish population really pushed some of the survivors of the terror to search for a refuge by relying on Bolshevik terrorists, or simply on bands of robbers who wander around the field towns between the Vistula and Bug rivers.[12]

A number of communiqués from the German gendarmerie in the district of Warsaw mention the confiscation raids that were being carried out by armed Jewish groups in May 1943 in places near Warsaw—Marki, Ursinek, and Falenica. The report of the *Ordnungspolizei* from Miedzyrzec Podlaski, dated July 17, 1943, speaks of a skirmish with an armed Jewish-Polish group, as a result of which one German was killed and three others were wounded.[13]

In the report of the Government Delegacy for the month of August, information is given out on the situation in the district of Warsaw. Among other things, the report states:

> In the period surveyed in this report, the police captured more than ten Jews, most of them were armed, in hunts it carried out. All of them were shot. . . .
>   The county of Sokolow-Podlaski: Young Jews, who are forming small groups, are hiding in the forests in the region. About 90 percent of them constitute a communist element. They assault the villages in the area and steal food. In rare cases the local population brings them food and takes fairly high prices for it. . . .
>   The forestry department of the district of Warsaw issued an order that all guards in the forest areas must report on Jewish hideouts, bands and on others wandering about. . . .
>   The county of Minsk: The police continued to shoot Jews caught in the region. . . .
>   The county of Radzyn: A large number of young Jews have been wandering in the forests lately. They are armed with short-range weapons, made in Germany and Russia. A few of these groups also have automatic weapons. The Jews carry out assaults of robbery on wayfarers and also on settlements.[14]

Similarly fragmented bits of information on armed Jewish groups are included in the communiqués of the German *Ordnungspolizei*. In the communiqué of the *Ordnungspolizei* command in the town of Uhnin, in the county of Radzyn, dated August 28, 1943, we read: "On August 27, 1943, a unit numbering thirty-five Jewish partisans disconnected the telegraph lines on the Uhnin-Debowa-Kloda section, 34 kilometers southeast of the city of Radzyn. The partisans retreated after a clash with a *Wehrmacht* battalion."[15] The communiqué of the *Ordnungspolizei* command in the city of Miedzyrzec, dated September 10, 1943, says: "On September 9, the police and the gendarmerie attached a building in the city of Miedzyrzec that held Jewish robbers. The head of the patrol, Johan Renischek, was wounded. Five Jews, three men and two women, were captured and shot."[16] And in the communiqué of the *Ordnungspolizei* in the town of Uhnin, dated September 11, 1943, we read: "On September 8, at 8 P.M., twenty carts carrying a Jewish gang numbering 100–150 people arrived here. They set fire to grain storehouses in the Uhnin estate in the region of Debowa-Kloda, 35 kilometers southeast of Radzyn. They burned 140 carts of rye, 20 carts of wheat, 15 carts of barley, and 10 carts of oats. The damages are estimated at 10,000 *zloties*."[17]
We find similar reports on unidentified armed Jewish groups in

the communiqués of the German police and also in reports of the Government Delegacy written throughout 1943 and in the first months of 1944. In one of the last of these documents, a communiqué from the commander of the military police in the town of Tluszcz, dated May 6, 1944, we read:

> On May 5, 1944, a hunt was held in the vicinity of the city of Tluszcz by a force which included the following: one gendarmerie officer and four privates; one *Wehrmacht* officer and twenty-seven soldiers; seven Kozaks. At 8:30 A.M. in the area of Rynia Nowa, in the county of Strachowka, the hunt encountered an armed gang. Seven of the robbers (three men and four women) were killed in the exchange of fire. We captured three guns, a hand grenade, one mine, and fifty gun bullets. One man from the gang, who was captured, admitted before dying that the group had numbered ten people. These were Jews who had operated in this area for the past half year. The commander of the hunt was Schlicht, a gendarmerie officer.[18]

CHAPTER 7
THE DISTRICT OF CRACOW

CRACOW, A HIGHLY MOUNTAINOUS DISTRICT COVERED with forests, had suitable conditions for the development of a partisan movement. Yet the Polish partisan movement was weaker there than in other areas of the *General Gouvernement*. In fact, it was almost nonexistent. The first attempts in 1943 to organize People's Guard units almost always ended in immediate disaster. Only in the spring and summer of 1944 did some important Polish units carry out actions. The Polish historian Józef Garas lists the following factors that held back the development of the partisan movement in the district of Cracow, despite its favorable conditions:

> More army and police forces were stationed in the district of Cracow than in other areas. This was for the protection of the GG governmental offices and the Nazi military, police, and administrative commands that were placed in Cracow. . . . The area of the Puszcza Sandomierska was turned by the enemy into a huge military camp for army and SS units with training fields, instruction, convalescence, and supplies centers which served the eastern front. In the area of Blizne-Pustkow, there were experimental centers for the 'V-2' weapon, which was produced here. The military areas and the properties of the SS spread at the expense of settlements and villages in the surrounding area, whose residents were condemned to dispossession and extermination. . . . In the southeastern part of the district of Cracow, that is, in the southern and eastern areas of the region Rzeszow, the activity of the extreme Ukrainian nationalist fascist organization, which had strong ties with German imperialism, was influential in curbing the Polish liberation movement. What were also certainly influential were the tactics of the German conqueror, who strove to stir up artificial nationalistic problems among, for example, the matter of the 'Gorals' (mountain people), or other ethnic groups.[1]

Garas suggests that still another factor held back the development of the partisan movement. This was the fact that one of the main lines of the Silesia-Cracow-Lvov railway, one of whose branches led to Kiev and the other to Rumania, passed through the district of Cracow.

The same factors that held back the Polish partisan movement held back to an even greater extent the many attempts of Jews to establish partisan units. In the district of Cracow, more than in any other area of the *General Government,* Jews (mainly those who came from the small towns) tried to find ways to survive by establishing armed units in the forest. A few factors caused the flights in this area to be more massive. The large number of forests made it easier to escape from the small towns to nearby woods or to the mountains. Yet, although it was easier to escape, it was very difficult to survive in view of the large number of enemy forces and the lack of support of the local village population.

The extermination of the Jews in the district of Cracow began in the last days of May 1942 with the deportation from the Cracow ghetto. During the three summer months of that year, most of the Jews of this district were taken to the extermination camp in Belzec and murdered.[2] The deportations were accompanied by mass shootings of the sick, the aged, and the children, and also of the Jews who passively resisted, hid, or attempted to run away. According to Polish data, about 60,000 Jews were shot to death during the deportations and buried in seventy-three mass graves, most of which are found in Jewish cemeteries. In certain cases, as in the towns of Nowy Targ, Jaslo, Zmigrod, Tarnow, Lubaczow, and Zaslaw, the majority of the Jewish population was shot to death. Often the deportations were delayed because of the resistance shown by the population. But even then, in all cases, most of the resisters were captured and immediately killed.

The issue of passive resistance displayed by the Jewish population during the deportations and the high rate of escapes by Jews in the district of Cracow are issues demanding another study. Most of the fugitives were captured and shot immediately. According to Polish statistics, about 400 mass graves of Jewish refugees who were shot and buried in the forests and fields, along the roads, and so forth, containing no fewer than 8,500 bodies, were found after the war. It seems, therefore, that during the deportations and the escapes approximately 70,000 Jews were shot; in other words, every fourth Jew was shot to death.[3]

Attempts to organize partisan units were made by large groups, made up mainly of youths, from the thousands of fugitives who fled to the forests and the mountains. The objective conditions, as mentioned above, undermined these attempts from the start. Despite this, some Jewish units did survive for an extended time and managed armed struggles against the German forces. In many regions of the district of Cracow, these groups were the only partisan forces active at the end of 1942 and the beginning of 1943. However, here more than in other areas, the destruction of the Jewish units was complete. Fighters from only two units (the ZOB partisan unit in Cracow and Amsterdam's unit) outlived the war. We know of fifteen other units only from very fragmented bits of information in German and Polish sources.

In this chapter we will briefly describe the history of the unit that was under the command of Amsterdam and Singer, and give some limited information on other Jewish units (not including the Jewish Fighting Organization unit in Cracow, which will be discussed in Chapter 11), whose existence is known to us only from Polish and German sources. The lack of Jewish testimonies possibly proves the supposition that no one from these units survived; it can be assumed that more Jewish partisan units than those mentioned by the Polish and German sources were also active here.

THE PARTISAN UNIT OF AMSTERDAM AND SINGER

During the deportation from Radomysl and its surroundings, the Jews made a mass escape to nearby forests. An attempt to organize a partisan unit from among these fugitives was made by the Amsterdam family (the father Yehuda with his sons Avraham, Mendel, and Yohanan). They were Jewish farmers from the village of Malec in the county of Mielec, near the Dolcza forests. The Amsterdam family organized an armed unit here which at first numbered sixty people, which resembles the activity of Yechiel Greenshpan in the forests of Parczew. A small number of women and children hid under the protection of this unit.

In the middle of 1943, the unit grew to number about seventy-five fighters. A camp of unarmed Jewish refugees, who were searching for shelter in the Dolcza forests, in the part known as Wzgorze Orzechowe, was established but had no connection with the unit. Almost all of its people were killed during the first hunts held by the German gendarmerie at the end of 1942.

At first, the equipment of the Amsterdam unit consisted of a few pistols bought from Polish farmers living in the surrounding area.

The consolidation of the unit and its hold on the area for an extended time were aided by a fortunate incident—the discovery in the forest of a few crates of hand-grenades left behind by one of the defeated units of the Polish army in September 1939. Although training the people in the handling of grenades was a serious problem, (only a few of them had undergone training in the Polish army), these grenades served as the unit's principal arms almost until the end of its activity in the Dolcza forests.

In April, 1943, another fortunate incident occurred. A stricken Soviet plane, probably transporting arms for a Soviet sabotage unit that was to begin operations in the south of Poland, made an emergency landing on the plateau of the Dolcza forests. The pilot and doctor from the crew survived and joined the Jewish unit, and a quantity of arms and ammunition was taken out of the burning plane.

The Amsterdam unit was divided into six or seven squads, consisting of ten fighters each. At the head of each squad was a commander, who was directly subordinated to the unit's top commander. Strict army discipline was enforced. Each group had a separate, well-camouflaged bunker, at an appropriate distance from all the others.

In the course of time, it became apparent that the operating possibilities of a large unit were limited, and so it was divided into two independent units. One remained under the direct command of Avraham Amsterdam; the other was headed by Yeshayahu Singer from Radomysl. In April 1943, on Passover, the unit commander, Avraham Amsterdam, was accidentally killed while cleaning grenades. The command of the consolidated unit was delegated to Yeshayahu Singer. Second-in-command was Yohanan Amsterdam, brother of the deceased founder and commander of the unit.

The Jewish unit was forced to face endless battles during the hunts held by the German gendarmerie and the Polish police and suffered heavy losses. The first serious clash with the enemy took place in the summer of 1943, when one of the unit's groups was besieged by surprise in its bunker by a German force. Seven fighters fell in the clash. In another serious skirmish at the end of 1943, this time with a local AK unit in one of the surrounding villages, the second of the Amsterdam brothers, Mendel, was killed. A hunt by large German forces was conducted against the Jewish unit in the beginning of the spring of 1944. Yet this time, the well-concealed bunkers, along with the partisans' experience and the discipline that prevailed in the unit, paid off. Not even one of the bunkers was found, and despite the large number of German forces that penetrated the depths of the forest, there was no battle with the Jewish unit which, because of the disproportion of forces, would have ended in the unit's defeat.

In September 1944, the Soviet army reached the rear of the Dolcza forests and stopped at a distance of a few kilometers from the Jewish unit's base, which suddenly became the front. The Germans concentrated large forces in the Dolcza forests, now their front line of defense, and the situation for the Jewish partisans markedly deteriorated. On November 11, the Germans held a large-scale hunt to "clean up" the partisans in the area near the front line. The unit lost seventeen people, and had two wounded, and this at a time when medicines and medical aid were in seriously short supply. It became impossible for the partisans to remain in the forest; however, leaving the Dolcza forests for other areas was equally impossible, because of the concentration of the German forces in the surrounding area. In the midst of this grave situation, Yeshayahu Singer reached the danger-filled decision to breach the front line.

On the night preceding the planned escape, scouts were sent out to determine the most suitable place for breaching the German front line. At dawn on November 26, the forty-seven-man unit advanced, crawling toward the front. A front post was attacked with grenades. Taking the Germans by surprise, the partisans were able to reach an antitank ditch. However, the German soldiers who recovered from the short-lived confusion opened with machine-gun fire, and Yehuda Amsterdam (father of the Amsterdam family), Feiwel Meiz, and Israel Feigenbaum were killed. After coming out of the antitank ditch, the partisans stumbled on a Soviet army mine field. Thinking the partisans were a German patrol, the alerted Soviet soldiers opened fire on them. Nine partisans were killed and fifteen were wounded, some seriously, in the mine explosions and the Soviet fire.[4]

Helena Ausenberg gave the following testimony on the passage through the mine field:

> I stepped on a mine and my leg was cut off. My sister, who was also wounded by mine shrapnel, was at my side. My brother-in-law wanted to carry her on his back and leave me, but my sister would not agree. She held one of my hands, and my brother-in-law the other, and we continued in this fashion for 1.5 kilometers to the Soviet lines. I suffered inhuman pains. The bone was broken, and the leg was held on by a strip of skin. All night we lay in the field. At night the Russians did not want to come to our help. They were forced to wait until the morning because the area was mined. At dawn they pulled out the mines and took us. However, one Soviet soldier, a Jew, stepped on a mine which cut off his leg. I lay unconscious all day without medical care. Only the next day

did they take me to a military hospital and amputate my leg. One week later, they moved me to the military hospital in Pustkow. My sister, who was slightly wounded, was taken to Rzeszow. Six months later they moved me to Mielec, where I met with my sister.[5]

About thirty partisans managed to reach the Soviet line, fifteen of them wounded. Five of the wounded died in the Soviet hospital in Pustkow. Ten survived.[6]

OTHER PARTISAN UNITS

In November 1942, a Jewish unit, made up mostly of fugitives from the Rzeszow, assembled outside the town. The principal organizer and commander of this unit was Leib Birman, who had succeeded in forming ties with the local Polish Workers Party while still in the Rzeszow Ghetto. It is not known what kind of help Birman received for the organization of the partisan unit. But from the documents of the People's Guard, it appears that this unit was under the command of the People's Army in the region of Rzeszow and that it was called the Iskra unit.

The Polish historian Garas gives the following details regarding the combat activity of this unit during December, 1942: In the beginning of the month, the unit took over a watermill in Pogwizdow, northeast of Rzeszow, confiscated tens of thousands of *zloties* for the unit, and by destroying the gears, completely paralyzed the mill for several days. After this, the unit moved to the surroundings of Stykow. On the way, it was discovered by the Polish police, which began to pursue it. The partisans set up an ambush for their pursuers in the village of Stykow. The ambush succeeded, the policemen were disarmed, and their weapons were taken for the unit. At the end of December, the unit was surprised by the Germans in the vicinity of Rzeszow. When most of the fighters were killed in this clash, the unit ceased to exist.[7]

We also know of the existence of a small Jewish group in the surroundings of Dabrow from some Polish documents. One of them is a report by the Information and Press Department of the Government Delegacy, which speaks of the situation in the district of Cracow in October 1942, in tones hostile to the Jews:

A band, made up mostly of Jews, was seen in the county of Dabrow. This gang numbers ten people, and is mainly occupied with robbery. It surveys the general feelings of the people towards the Jews, and threatens that things "will get worse" as long as they treat the Jews badly and do not condemn the barbaric methods used by the Germans against them. The opinion prevailing among the Jews is that the Poles are guilty of cruelty towards the Jews. One day they will take revenge against the Poles.[8]

The Polish partisan Jozef Lysek writes about the existence of Jewish units in the eastern part of the district of Cracow: "Three Jewish groups, numbering about fifty people, carried out armed partisan actions while hiding in the forests of Jawor and Siedlisk. The German attacks crushed the two groups, but one group, headed by Leon Galczynski, survived until the liberation after suffering great hardships."[9]

As in the case of many other partisan units, it is impossible to determine additional facts about the groups mentioned here. We also have no information on the fate of Galczynski's fighters after the war.

Garas also writes about a Jewish group which escaped the Warsaw Ghetto and was active for some time in the region of Tarnobrzeg. According to him, this group collaborated in the spring of 1943 with the People's Guard partisan unit that was under the command of Stanislaw Jaskier.[10]

The existence of nine armed Jewish groups is known to us from German archive documents. Three telegrams, which were sent by the police and the SS commander in the *General Gouvernment* to the chief of the antipartisan war staff, *Waffen* SS Generale Kurt Knoblauch, speaks of the destruction of three Jewish partisan units in the district of Cracow. The first telegram, dated January 3, 1943, tells of the destruction in the vicinity of Cracow of a Jewish partisan group numbering twenty-five people by a special *Einsatzkommando* under the command of police officer Baum. The second telegram, dated January 7, reports the liquidation of a fourteen-man Jewish partisan group in the area of Brudziewice. And the third telegram speaks of the destruction of a Jewish partisan group numbering eleven people on January 9 in the area of Wola Sakowa, by a special unit commanded by Oberwachtman Water.[11]

In the daily report of December 25, sent by the German army commander in the *General Gouvernement* to Army headquarters in Berlin, it is said that the first battalion of the Storm-Troop Regiment of the 154th Division, reinforced by a local gendarmerie unit, liquidated a Jewish partisan group on December 21 in a forest east of Padykow, 8 kilometers southwest of Dolina. According to this report, seventeen Jews were killed and one German soldier fell in the clash.[12]

We find information on other Jewish groups in recommendations for the awarding of decorations for the gendarmerie in the area of Cracow. From these documents we know that during the systematic hunts held in April and May 1943, a gendarmerie unit under the command of Franz Huetter liquidated a Jewish partisan group numbering forty-four people and destroyed the nine bunkers that served as its base.[13]

In a clash on June 6, 1943, near Jastrzebniki in the county of Miechow, the 63rd Motored Platoon of the gendarmerie, under the command of Gerhard Strauss, liquidated a Jewish partisan group that was under the command of Nisenbaum. On September 11, a company of the 7th Battalion of the *Ordnungspolizei* in the 23rd Regiment liquidated a Jewish partisan group that was active in the forests near Jadlowka, 22 kilometers southeast of Tarnow. Another recommendation for a decoration speaks of the devoted service of the gendarmes Josef Bauer and Franz Wohl, who in an exchange of fire fatally wounded the Jewish partisan Rauch, who was well known in the vicinity of Sanok.[14]

The recommendation of *Schutzpolizei* Major Adalbert Quasbarth is most interesting. In it we read:

> As of June 23, 1942, Major Adalbert Quasbarth of the *Schutzpolizei* command of the city of Cracow was appointed commander of a special group for the war against armed gangs. While serving in this capacity, he personally commanded all of the large operations against the armed bands, and particularly the large-scale campaigns against them held on July 27, September 13, and September 28, 1943.
>
> In these operations, during exchanges of fire with the gangs, he succeeded in achieving positive results due to his experienced management and excellent command of the operations. On the whole, ninety-two Jewish bandits, forty-eight Polish bandits, and two escaped prisoners were liquidated in these operations. A large quantity of arms, pamphlets, and a radio transmitter were also taken.[15]

Many attempts to cross the border to Slovakia and Hungary were made from the district of Cracow. Among those searching for ways to cross the border were a number of Jews who established armed units. Particularly deserving of mention is the Jewish Fighting Organization group from Bedzin, which, after a period of activity in Podkarpacie, reached Budapest by way of Slovakia and continued its underground activity there in the framework of the Zionist Youth Organization.[16]

CHAPTER 8
JEWS IN POLISH PARTISAN UNITS

UNTIL NOW, JEWISH UNITS AND NATIONALLY MIXED units in which Jews made up a substantial part of the fighters have been the subject of this book. This chapter examines the situation of Jews as individuals in units that were composed primarily of Poles.

Individual Jews came to Polish units both because they had previous ties with members of the Polish underground, and completely by chance, after escaping from camps and after long searches in the forests. There were Jews in almost all of the fighting organizations of the Polish underground, but their situations were different from one to another and from place to place, depending on the political affiliation of their organizations or the outlook and tendencies of the commanders of given units. Their situations also depended on the circumstances under which the Jewish partisan joined the Polish unit.

The largest number of Jews in this category were found in the ranks of the People's Guard (People's Army). We know relatively more about them than about Jews in other units of the Polish underground, and can distinguish several types of individual Jewish fighters in the ranks of the People's Guard:

1. Activists of the Polish Communist Party who were among the principal founders and organizers of the People's Guard.
2. Jews who escaped the ghettos (particularly the Warsaw ghetto) because of their ties with PPR members, usually people who had previous contact with the communist movement in Poland.
3. Professionals and experts (doctors, engineers, chemists, and radio technicians) who were called on to enlist by the People's Guard command.

4. Partisans from Jewish units of the People's Guard who, following the destruction of their units, were transferred to Polish units being organized at the time.
5. A small number of partisans who survived the continuous fighting in an independent Jewish framework and fugitives from camps who after many hardships and great suffering succeeded in reaching a Polish partisan unit.

The following Jewish fighters were among the principal organizers of the People's Guard:

Pawel Finder was dropped into Poland from the USSR at the end of 1941 with the first group of paratroopers and was one of the founders of the Polish Workers Party—the new Polish communist party. From December 1942 until November 1943, Finder was the first secretary of the PPR's central committee, meaning that he was the political leader of the People's Guard when it was on the rise. It is worth mentioning that this was the period of the Warsaw Ghetto uprising, as well as of rebellions in a number of other ghettos and camps, and also the time that most Jewish partisan units were organizing. Arrested on November 14, 1943, and imprisoned in the "Pawiak" prison in Warsaw, Finder was executed on July 26, 1944, during the evacuation of the prisoners, on the eve of the Red Army offensive in the direction of Warsaw.[1]

Hanka Szapiro-Sawicka was the principal organizer and first head of the *Zwiazek Walki Mlodych* (Youth Struggle Organization). This was a youth organization affiliated with the Polish Workers Party, whose ranks provided most of the partisans for the People's Guard. On March 18, Hanka Szapiro-Sawicka was seriously wounded after a short skirmish with the police and the Gestapo in the streets of Warsaw. She died of her wounds the following day in Pawiak.[2]

Janina Bir was the representative of the central committee of the Polish Workers Party in the districts of Lvov and Lodz. She was later given the task of organizing the department of women's fighting units in the People's Army and was appointed commander of these units. She was captured by the Gestapo on June 17, 1944, and tortured to death during her interrogation.[3]

Sabina Goldszlak (Jadwiga Ludwinska) was the representative of the central committee of the Polish Workers Party in the district of Cracow and the principal organizer of the People's Army.[4]

While we emphasize the presence of Jews in the PPR leadership, which was actually the political leadership of the People's Guard, it is important to point out that the number of Jews in this organization was not large. For example, of the twenty members of the central committee of the Polish Workers Party in 1942 and 1944, only two (Pawel Finder and Izolda Lerner-Kowalska) were Jews. Of the twenty-one secretaries of the regional committees, only Janina Bir was Jewish. It is also worth noting, by the way, that the situation in the PPR leadership was completely different from the pre–World War II situation of the Polish Communist party, whose leadership included a substantial number of Jews. For our subject it is more important to emphasize the lack of initiative on the Jewish question on the part of any of the Jews in the PPR leadership. We know of no information that can testify to their special interest in the fate of the Jewish people during the Holocaust. These people presented themselves as Poles and did their best to hide their Jewish origins even from those closest to them.

It is difficult to assess the number of Jews in the second category listed above. At least a few dozen Jews escaped from Warsaw during the big deportation in the summer of 1942 because of their ties with the Polish Workers Party. Most of them joined groups from which the GL command tried to organize the first partisan units. A number of Jews also escaped the Czestochowa ghetto because of their ties with the Polish communist activists Józef Sowinski and Jan Swistak. These people were to join the Stefan Czarnecki unit of the People's Guard which was organizing at that time in the area of Piotrkow.[5]

Because of the hasty preparations, the lack of experience, and the lack of support of the local village population, all these first attempts on part of the People's Guard ended in failure. The majority of those involved were killed in their first large clash with police forces, before being able to carry out any important actions in the field. We have only fragmentary information on the fate of these people and are not even able to determine the names of most of them. The few who survived these attempts, however, eventually became commanders in the People's Guard. Among the Jews in this group, the following must be given special mention: Ignacy Rosenfarb (Robb-Narbut), commander of the "Land of Kielce" unit and afterwards commander of Warsaw's western suburbs (Warszawa-Lewa Podmiejska), operations officer in the main headquarters, commander of the area of Czestochowa, commander of the district of Lublin, and finally again an officer in the People's Army main headquarters; Gustaw Alef-Bolkowiak, second-in-command of the Holod Battalion and later commander of a partisan unit in the district of Lublin; Ryszard Nazarewicz, head of intelligence in the 3rd Regiment of the People's Army; Josef Schapiro, second-in-command of the Kosciuszko partisan unit; Lena Wolinska, head of the bureau of the People's Army main headquarters; Gustaw Sternhel, commander of the People's Guard forces in the city of Warsaw; Barbara (Stanislawa) Sowinska, head of the department of intelligence in the main headquarters of the People's Guard; Gustaw Rozlubirski and Hirsh (Ryszard) Zelwianski, both company commanders in the Czwartaki partisan battalion.

In the third category (professionals), the part of the Jewish doctors must be mentioned. Almost all of the doctors in the People's Guard units were Jews. The contribution of the following Jewish doctors was of primary importance: Henryk Ber-Mlodzianowski, Edward Klaffen-Dabrowski, Stanislaw Sierpinski (Victor Margulis), Michal Temczyn, and Anka Wolf.

Among the chemists whose work was of great importance for the organization of sabotage operations, top roles were filled by the following Jews: Ignacy Sandler-Romanowicz, Michal Jaworski, and Mieczyslaw Weinkiper-Wiatraszek. Sandler-Romanowicz laid the foundations for the development of this branch in the People's Guard and was the head of the chemical service until his arrest in September 1942; after his death, Michal Jaworski became the head of this branch.

Finally, the role of the Jewish radio technicians must be emphasized. Radio contact between the PPR leadership, the AL command, and Moscow was entrusted to two Jews, the paratrooper Maria Kamieniecka-Rutkiewicz and Mieczyslaw Hejman. The latter organized a line of radio stations for broadcasting and receiving and ran a course of instruction for radio-telegraphists. He fell in battle on the streets of Warsaw on February 9, 1943. Maria Kamieniecka-Rutkiewicz was arrested by the Gestapo, imprisoned in Pawiak in Warsaw, and only by miracle was rescued from death.[6]

The Jewish partisans from the People's Guard, the largest of the groups listed above, were discussed many times in the previous chapters. We saw that of the nine Jewish units that operated in the framework of the People's Guard, only one unit, the one under the command of Yechiel Greenshpan, survived until the end of the Nazi occupation. The fighters in the two units commanded by Shmuel Jegier and Shmuel Gruber joined Yechiel Greenshpan's unit in the last stage of the occupation. The remaining six Jewish units that belonged to the People's Guard were completely wiped out. The survivors of these destroyed Jewish units joined various new organized units of the People's Army.

In most cases, the Polish partisans supported the Jewish partisans in the beginning, often because these Jews were more experienced in partisan fighting, and in the partisan life, than their Polish comrades. Later, however, beginning in 1944, the attitude towards the Jews in many of the AL units deteriorated, mainly because many groups that joined the People's Guard detested the units of the *Ostlegionen* when the Germans' impending defeat became apparent. The People's Army was also joined by members of the nationalist organization—the National Armed forces. For example, an NSZ unit under the command of "Zab" was accepted into the People's Army in the area of Lublin. Many members of the *Ostlegionen* joined the AL in the area of Kielce in the summer of 1944.[7]

A few dozen Jewish partisans who survived the continuous battles in independent Jewish units also reached the Polish units of the People's Army. The same was true of a number of Jews who escaped from forced labor camps. For example, thirteen Jews who escaped from the forced labor camp in Budzyn reached the AL unit under the command of Tadeusz Szymanski, which was active in the vicinity of the town of Krasnik.[8] The situation of the Jewish partisans who had fled from the camps was very similar to that of partisans from Jewish AL units, as was the situation of the scores of Jewish partisans who fought in the ranks of the *Socjalistyczna Organizacja Bojowa* (SOB Fighting Socialist Organization). Some Jews had senior positions in this organization. Mieczyslaw First and Illa Genachow, who were among the founders of the organization, must be mentioned first and foremost. There were also Jews among the commanders of the partisan units in this organization. Shimon Yoffe (Mieczyslaw Maslak) was the commander of a combat unit in the area of Warsaw; Maksymilian Boruchowicz (Borwicz) was the commander of the SOB partisan units in the region of Miechow; Dr. Julian Aleksandrowicz was second-in-command of the SOB partisan unit in the area of Kielce; and Jan Truszkowski played an important role in the sabotage operations carried out by the SOB partisan unit active in the area of Czestochowa. A similar role was played by Arthur Spindler (Szczesny) in the SOB unit commanded by Klos-Warecki, which was active in the region of Kielce.[9]

About twenty Jews who escaped from the forced labor camps in Pionki, Szebnia, Ostrowiec, and Starachowice reached the partisan units of the Fighting Socialist Organization. The testimonies of the surviving partisans of this group tell of a generally positive attitude on the part of the Poles in the SOB units towards the Jewish camp fugitives accepted into this organization. For example, Adolf Wolfgang, who escaped from the camp in Szebnia in order to join the Karpaty SOB partisan unit, which was under the command of Konrad, writes the following on the atmosphere that prevailed in the unit regarding the Jews: "During our free moments, we would debate about many issues, and at times we touched on the question of the Jews. Many of our friends expressed sorrow in view of the tragedy of the Jewish people. Some of us asked why the Home Army liquidates the Jews who are hiding in the forests and striving for revenge against the savage fascist beast in the form of man."[10]

There were, at the very least, a few hundred Jews in the cells of the AK underground, in spite of the general anti-Jewish policy dictated from above. They were generally Jews who hid on the "Aryan" side and were accepted into the Polish underground as Poles. In addition, more than 1,000 Jews fought in the ranks of the Home Army during the Polish Warsaw uprising in the summer of 1944. (See chapter 13.)

A small number of Jews reached the Home Army's partisan units. Many Jews, both those who escaped from the Nazi camps and those who experienced long battles in independent Jewish units tried to find Polish partisan units. Some of them, whose number is not known, paid with their lives for these efforts, as quite a number of the Home Army's partisan units would kill any Jew they met in the forests.

A few Jews, however, were accepted into AK partisan units, thanks mostly to the positive attitude of the local commander, although after joining the Home Army, they often had to hide their Jewishness from all their comrades-in-arms. Some, disguised as Poles, even rose in rank in certain cases and were appointed commanders in partisan units of the Home Army. A Jewish woman named Julia Celinska, who escaped from the Majdanek concentration camp and later fought in an AK partisan unit in the area of Lublin, testifies that her commander, who was called "Slawek," told her in confidence that he was a Jew and that his name was Michael Hoffman. No one in his unit knew of his Jewish origins.[11] Emmanuel Singer, a member of the special group whose task was to receive equipment dropped in from England, also played an important role in the partisan movement of the Home Army. Singer was accepted to the Home Army thanks to the generosity of the Polish captain, Stanislaw Lubczynski.[12]

The situation of the Jews who encountered partisan units of the Peasant Battalions was the same. Here also a Jew could reveal his identity only in rare cases. And despite everything, Jews rose to important positions in this organization also. For example, the commander of the partisan units of the Peasant Battalions in the area of

Miechow was the Jew Zygmunt Nebrzydowski ("Henryk").[13] Josef Birger ("Wacek"), who had escaped from the forced labor camp in Kurow in the district of Lublin and joined a local unit of the Peasant Battalions, was also appointed commander of his unit after a time.[14]

There were also cases where Jewish fugitives from ghettos and camps, who were not familiar with the political situation in the Polish underground, met units of the National Armed Forces and tried to join them. These attempts cost the Jews their lives unless they managed to appear as non-Jews. Such was the case of Yakov Kleinman, who hid for some time as an agricultural worker in the village of Stawki in the county of Krasnystaw. In March 1944, he escaped to the forest because his life was in danger and was stopped by a patrol of the NSZ unit under the command of Lieutenant Cichy. He said he was a Pole who had run away from the area of Poznan. Lieutenant Cichy's unit belonged to that part of the National Armed Forces that later joined the Home Army. Kleinman's report on the speech that Lieutenant Cichy made when his unit was dissolved after the liberation of Krasnystaw by the Red Army is very interesting. In his farewell to the partisans Cichy said:

> In the last months after years of labor and war, our unit, like other NSZ units, accomplished great things. Before us was the task of destroying both communism in Poland and the Jews, who spread communism under the guise of the PPR organizations, the People's Army, the Peasant Battalions, and other groups which did not obey orders sent from London [meaning the Polish government-in-exile in London]. We filled this role most energetically.[15]

CHAPTER 9
JEWS IN COMMANDO UNITS

A SIZABLE PORTION OF THE FORCES THAT FOUGHT IN THE rear of the German army in the *General Gouvernement* as of 1944 were sabotage and patrol units called commando units. These units were dropped in by air, or came from Volhynia and Polesie, crossing the Bug westward. Sent by and under the command of either the general staff of the Red Army, or the staffs of the First Byelo-Russian Front, the First Ukranian Front, and sometimes also the Internal Defense Forces (NKVD), these were made up partially of specially trained Red Army soldiers and partially of partisans formerly active in Byelo-Russia and the Ukraine.[1]

Between March and June 1944, fifteen of these units, numbering 4,400 men, were transferred to the *General Gouvernement*.[2] These were well-armed and well-equipped units, trained for combat duties at the enemy's rear, and there is no doubt that their activity was more effective than that of the local Polish partisan units. There is also no doubt that these units can be credited with the majority of the losses suffered by the German forces occupying the *General Gouvernement* in the first half of 1944.[3]

The Soviet commando units' main area of operations was the district of Lublin. As the front advanced in June 1944, units were moved forward to the district of Radom. In September 1944, with the stabilization of the front along the Vistula and the growth of concentrated forces of the German army, these units could no longer operate on the west bank of the Vistula, and returned to the district of Lublin, which had already been liberated.

During the time that these groups were in the *General Gouvernement*, they were joined by local Soviet partisan units made up of Red

Army soldiers who had escaped from German imprisonment. In many cases, these units were also joined by individuals or groups of Soviet citizens who had served in various armed regiments of collaborators (such as the Vlasovs, the *Ostlegionen* units, and auxiliary guard or police units), who, in view of the certain defeat of the Nazis, tried to go over to the partisan camp. Only in exceptional cases were members of the local population, Jews and Poles, accepted into the Soviet commando units.[4]

Many Jews, both Red Army soldiers and former partisans in the Ukraine, however, did fight in the Soviet commando units. Because we have no access to Soviet sources (the archives are closed), we cannot attempt to assess the number of Jews or their part in these units. But a few Jews are mentioned in Polish sources. They describe, for example, the activities of Andrey Gurevich (chief-of-staff of Galiguzov's unit), Raisa Zavyerodnaya, Nosim Hosfogel, Aharon Yeruchomowich, and others. It is worthwhile to mention the interesting things written by the Soviet colonel, Nikolai Prokopiuk, about the Jew, Genadi Eichner, who was among the few local people accepted into a Soviet commando unit: "Only one man, Genadi Eichner, who experienced the hardships of partisan life, and was talented, brave and full of resourceful ideas, was accepted into Lieutenant Neshchimenko's group during the time that it was active in Poland."[5]

Prokopiuk also quotes from the testimony of the Soviet partisan G. Sushcheva and paraphrases Lieutenant Neshchimenko, who provided these details about Eichner's life:

> Genadi Eichner was born in Warsaw in 1923 to a Jewish family. His parents and relatives were killed in the Warsaw Ghetto. He was in a concentration camp in France, from which he succeeded in escaping. After walking all over Europe, he wandered about for a long time in Poland until he reached Lieutenant A. Neshchimenko's group. When we met him, he looked like a skeleton covered in skin and dressed in rags. We decided to accept him into the group and have never regretted that step. He was unusually brave and knew German and some other European languages fluently. He was officially accepted into our group after he parachuted into Czechoslovakia.

Lieutenant Neshchimenko also gives a highly positive evaluation of Eichner. He said that while the patrol group was in Czechoslovakia it got hold of the German plan for the protection of the Beskids with the help of the underground organization from Morawska-Ostrawa. Eichner and two Czechs, Karol Karas and Tonda Kubala, were sent through the front line with this plan (of which several copies were made). They safely reached the First Ukrainian Front command which was east of Cracow. Here the traces of G. Eichner were lost, and his fate remains unknown.[6]

Mordechai Kalmanowicz was accepted into the Vasilenko Soviet commando unit. Until his acceptance into the unit, Kalmanowicz hid in the village of Eliszow in the area of Lublin. Kalmanowicz reports on the vast participation of Jews in the Soviet Kirowski and Stalingrad commando units and the Vasilenko unit. This is reaffirmed by Yaakov Garbow, a former partisan in the district of Lublin, who belonged to one of the Soviet commando units that were transferred to Lublin.[7]

Along with the Soviet commando units, raid and sabotage units, made up partially of Polish army soldiers who had been in the Soviet Union and partially of partisans, were transferred to the *General Gouvernement*. The first of these was the Janowski unit, which was under the command of the Jewish officer Leon Kasman. The second-in-command was also a Jew, Leon Bielski, as were several other people in this unit, among them a woman, Ruth (Wanda) Michalska.[8]

The second Polish commando unit was the Wanda Wasilewska brigade, which was transferred to the west bank of the Bug in February 1944. This brigade has been organized in the western Ukraine, where groups of soldiers from the Polish army had been sent, among them some Jews. While the brigade was organizing, it was joined by a group of thirty local Jewish partisans.[9] So, after its organization, there were more than fifty Jews in this brigade, or about 10 percent. These two units have already been mentioned in chapters 2 and 4.

The third Polish commando unit was made up of a group of fifty-six soldiers who had been transferred to the south of Podlasie, joined by local Polish partisans, mainly members of the local Peasant Battalions. This was also the way a unit called "Poland is Not Yet Lost" (*Jeszcze Polska nie Zginela*) was formed. Its commander was a Jewish officer, Colonel Moshe (Robert) Satanowski. The second-in-command, Captain Josef Kratko, was also Jewish. Neither the number of the other Jews in this unit nor their names can be determined.[10]

In May 1944, the so-called Polish Partisan Command organized in Rowne in the Volhynia. Its main tasks were equipping the existing partisan units of the People's Army and establishing and organizing new units. Along with the Polish Partisan Command, a select paratroopers' unit, called the "Special Storm Battalion" was formed, from paratroopers who were dropped into the *General Gouvernement* to organize sabotage and patrol operations. In the summer of 1944, when a quick liberation of the country was expected, thousands of Polish youths joined the partisan movement, and paratroopers from the

Special Storm Battalion became the principal organizers and the commanders of the large Polish partisan units that were established at
this time.

The Jewish officer Lieutenant Colonel (and later, Colonel) Henryk Torunczyk, a former officer in the Republican army during the
Spanish Civil War, was appointed commander of the Special Storm
Battalion.[11] The Pole Jan Mietki, an officer in this unit, writes the
following about Torunczyk: "The command of the Storm Battalion
was then given to Lieutenant-Colonel Henryk Torunczyk, an excellent officer who had vast military and political experience both in the
revolutionary movement and in the battles of the Spanish Civil War.
Several other officers, Polish communists who had taken part in the
battles in Spain, were on the battalion's staff. These were Leon
Rubinstein, Jan Perkowski, Antoni Szpakowski, and David Krauze."[12]

Three hundred and sixty-three paratroopers were dropped in for
operations in the General Gouvernement; at least 10 percent of them
were Jews.[13]

During the period of the organization of large Polish partisan
units in the region of Kielce and Cracow, the following Jewish paratroopers held positions of importance: Josef Greenberg was appointed chief-of-staff of the Land of Kielce brigade, and Boris Zagner
was a company commander in this same brigade. Yitzhak Gutman
was appointed commander of the Liberation of the Homeland partisan battalion, active in Podhale. Adam Kornhendler (Kornecki) was
appointed chief-of-staff of the Land of Kielce brigade. Jozef Schwarz
was second-in-command of a battalion in this brigade.[14]

It is worthwhile to mention that the only woman in the Special
Storm Battalion, Lieutenant Lucyna Herz, was also a Jew. She was
dropped in for sabotage operations in the area of Lublin and after its
liberation was appointed commander of a Storm company. Seriously
wounded in the battle of Warsaw, Lieutenant Herz died in October
1944 at the age of 25. After her death she was promoted to the rank of
captain and awarded the highest military honors: the Grunwald
Cross and the Virtuti Military Cross.

CHAPTER 10
THE WARSAW GHETTO UPRISING

WARSAW WAS THE MAIN CENTER OF THE RESISTANCE movement in Poland, both for the Jews in the ghetto and for the Poles. The first attempts at armed resistance in the Warsaw Ghetto were made as early as 1941. In the spring of 1942, the Anti-Fascist Bloc, whose objective was the preparation of an armed resistance, was established. Unfortunately, the Anti-Fascist Bloc did not succeed in properly organizing for action by the time of the big deportation to the Treblinka death camp, which began on July 22 and lasted until September 13, 1942. The Jewish Fighting Organization, which was established during the first days of the deportation (on July 28, 1942), did succeed in carrying out some armed actions, however only minor ones.

Since there is extensive literature covering the Warsaw Ghetto underground before the big deportation and the first actions of the Jewish Fighting Organization, our discussion will not cover the actions of the underground at that time. This chapter is dedicated only to the military problems of the uprising and the direct preparations for it. We will begin, therefore, with a description of the events that took place after the big deportation, that is, after September 13, 1942.

THE IDEA OF THE UPRISING

When the Germans discontinued deportations from the Warsaw Ghetto on September 13, 1942, the following was already clear to the population that survived the slaughter: first, the deportation was not to work camps but for extermination, the fate of those deported and

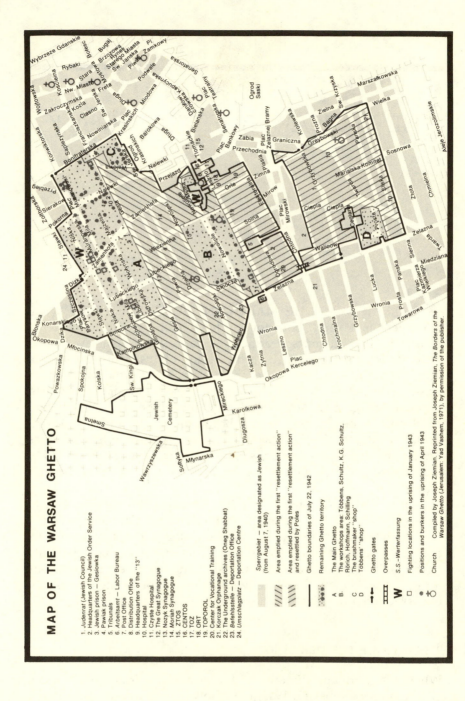

the place and method of extermination were known. Second, the discontinuation of the deportation was only temporary.

However, in the meantime, life returned to a form of relative stability, gloomy as it was. Although the situation was worse than before the deportation, certain conditions enhanced the renewal of the underground activity.

The majority of the underground activists had no doubt that an armed uprising must be prepared in case the deportations were renewed, and this was expected at any moment. Although no one explicitly defined what the nature of the armed uprising should be, all of the leadership's actions show that they had reached an unequivocal consensus as early as the first weeks following the action of September 1942. It was obvious to the initiators and activists planning the resistance that the conditions of the Warsaw Ghetto made it impossible to consider systematic development of the struggle against the enemy, gradual intensification of the armed resistance, or preparation for the revolt which might break out upon the collapse of the Third Reich. It was clear that the only possibility was preparation for a final armed uprising, while strengthening all forces available to the Jews for the time when the Germans would renew the deportations. It was understood that this would be a special kind of revolt with no precedent in the past and that its strategic objective would also be exceptional. It was necessary to prepare for an uprising that was doomed to defeat from its onset, an uprising in which it would be impossible to surrender, and which all knew must end with the destruction of the entire ghetto. It was an uprising that would be carried out in total isolation; an uprising in which all "the cards"—including the choice of place and time for the beginning of the struggle—were from the start in the hands of the enemy; an uprising where the "trump card" of almost all other rebellions—the surprise—was missing.

An Uprising Doomed to Defeat

Even the most superficial estimate of the forces the Germans could employ in the following few months against the ghetto, and on the other hand, the estimate of the forces which could be prepared by the Jews of Warsaw, even in the best of situations, would necessarily lead to a conclusion no one could refute—there was no chance whatsoever for a long-term struggle. The activists in the ghetto had no illusions in this respect. As early as October 1942, in a talk held with representative of the Polish Government Delegacy Jan Kozielewski ("Karski"), on the eve of his illegal departure to London, and attended by Bund leader Dr. Leon Feiner and Zionist representative Dr. Adolf Berman, the following was said:

> We want you to tell the Polish government, the governments of the Allies, and the principal leaders of Allies that we here are defenseless against the Germans. We cannot defend ourselves and no one in Poland can defend us. The leaders of the Polish underground can save a few of us, but they cannot rescue a large number of people. The Germans are not trying to enslave us, as they are other nations. We are being liquidated in a systematic way.[1]

The only possibility which existed was that of organizing and planning an armed uprising, in order to cause trouble and losses to the Germans. These could be made greater if the preparations for the uprising could last longer, if the pause in the deportations would continue, and if help from the outside were to increase.

An Uprising under Conditions of Isolation

It was evident that the uprising in the Warsaw Ghetto would be completely isolated in place and time. It was impossible to depend on simultaneous armed uprisings by Jewish communities that still existed in other ghettos or Jewish camps, because the organization of such an operation was impossible and futile. No one could coordinate actions in centers that were completely cut off from one another and isolated from the outside world by barbed-wire fences and guarded walls, especially when the conditions for planning a revolt were different from place to place. The organization of such a rebellion was also futile. The Germans then had forces many times larger than those needed for the repression of the most serious rebellion, even one held simultaneously in various places. This sort of revolt could not have had any influence whatsoever on the fate of the Warsaw Ghetto.

Nor could serious action on the part of the Polish organizations be depended on, let alone practically considered. As said before, the Polish partisan movement was still weak, and even if its attitude to the Jews had been very sympathetic, it was in no way prepared for a large-scale operation to support them. In addition, the Polish population, whose situation was totally different from that of the Jews, did not want this kind of action. The Jewish people were forced into immediate and desperate measures under the worst possible conditions, while the Polish public had time to unite its forces for the planning of an armed rebellion, which was to be held only in the case of the military defeat of Germany. A more serious move by the Polish organizations was not considered, and no Jewish political activist ever requested it.

The Initiative in the Choice of the Place and Time for the First Blow

The most strategic element in almost any revolt is the initiative in choosing the place and time of the initial blow, that is, planning to surprise the much stronger enemy. A rebellion usually starts with a strike by the rebels against one of the enemy's important targets that happens to be weakly protected at the time. The first victory must be the rebels', otherwise the revolt usually comes to a quick end.

The Jews in the Warsaw Ghetto did not have this choice. They would have to act the moment the Germans entered the ghetto to renew the deportation, and the decision in this matter lay in the hands of the Germans alone. The organizers of the uprising were forced to subordinate their decisions to those of the enemy from the very beginning. It was necessary to plan the battle not from the initial blow, but from the least hopeful aspect—defense.

Many of the documents that have come down to us clearly testify to the fact that the leaders of the resistance movement in the Warsaw Ghetto had no illusions whatsoever. They gave themselves a full account of the seriousness of the situation, foresaw the tangible results of the uprising, and understood its weak points well. In spite of this, they made the greatest attempts to raise and realize this rebellion. Despite their full awareness of the results that were to come, they began the preparations with the maximum effort.

The objective of the uprising has been emphasized by both the underground leaders of the ghetto and by the Polish resistance movement activists. Among these, Colonel Henryk Wolinski, head of the department of Jewish affairs in the AK command, in his survey of the department's activities, states: "The stand of the Jewish Fighting Organization was that the fate of the Warsaw Ghetto, as well as that of other Jewish communities, had been decided. Extermination awaits them sooner or later, and because of that they want to die with honor, that is, with arms in hand."[2] Similarly, Zivia Lubetkin wrote in her memoirs: "It was obvious to us that the Germans would liquidate us. We said to ourselves that in this situation, we must at least kill as many Germans as possible and stay alive as long as possible."[3]

Following are the remarks of Dr. Emanuel Ringelblum, who kept a record of the ghetto:

"Our fate had been decided," the Jews said. Every Jew carries with him a death sentence, handed down by the greatest murderer of all times. We must think, therefore, not so much of the saving of lives—a matter which appears most difficult—but of death with honor, death with arms in hand. The oath we swore to the memory of our dead has been fulfilled. The ghetto has begun to arm itself and to prepare to receive new blows, which are awaited at any moment.

Later, he wrote:

It was evident that no one expected the ghetto to defend itself for an extended period of time. It was clear that this would be a struggle between a fly and an elephant. But the national honor of the Jewish people committed the Jews to resist, and not let themselves be taken away to be slaughtered without reprisal. . . . I remember a talk I held with the commander of the Jewish Fighting Organization and member of the General Council of Hashomer Hatzair, Mordechai Anielewicz, who fell in the battles of April. He correctly estimated the chances of the unequal struggle, foresaw the destruction of the ghetto and its residents, and was certain that neither he nor any of his fighters would outlive the liquidation of the ghetto. He saw that they would be lost like homeless dogs, and that no one would even know their final resting place.[4]

THE PREPARATIONS FOR THE UPRISING

Any revolt must be preceded by suitable preparations. In any case, an uprising is preceded by certain political and propagandist preparations, organizational work, and the arming and training of the rebels' army, or at least the core of this army. It was not possible to act differently in the Warsaw Ghetto. Since the argument for an armed rebellion triumphed within the underground organizations, the necessary preparations had to follow. And this had to be done at an intensive rate.

After the discontinuation of the deportation, almost the very next day, preparations began in the Warsaw Ghetto in all vital directions: political, propagandistic, organizational, and also in the areas of armament, supply, and training. Very intensive work also began in ground preparations for the battles that were to take place.

The preparation for the uprising can be divided into two periods: from September 1942 to January 18, 1943, and from January 21 to the outbreak of the uprising on April 19, 1943.

On January 18, the Germans renewed the deportations. However, this time they encountered resistance by the armed groups of the ghetto. Battles went on for four days. In spite of their awareness and readiness, the Jewish groups were again surprised by the Germans. These groups, whose arms were few and defective and whose organizational framework was loosely knit, resisted in a disorganized and unprepared way. However, in spite of its chaotic nature, this attempt at resistance came as a surprise to the Germans, who were not used to holding deportations in the midst of a battle with those being deported. Although the Jewish groups suffered very heavy losses, they gained very valuable experience. From this time on, the ghetto turned into an arena of constant resistance, and this had its influence on future preparations.

One must, therefore, speak separately of the preparations for the uprising in the period that preceded the battles of January, and the preparations of February–April 1943. For the sake of continuity, however, I shall describe first the overall preparations for the uprising, and later, the battles, although within the description of certain preparations, I will, of course, refer to the influence that the battles of January had on later preparations.

The Political Preparations

The political preparations began in three main areas. First, the unification of the various political groups in the ghetto was brought about for the purpose of intensifying the effort. Second, political and military ties were formed with the Polish resistance movement, whose support was requested for the preparation of the uprising. Third, the leadership of the resistance movement in the Warsaw Ghetto continued in its attempts to influence other Jewish communities still in existence in Poland to put up armed resistance.

Ringelblum writes the following on the efforts that were made to unify the underground organizations in the ghetto:

> The war made the Jewish public face problems of a special nature. The political relationships that existed before the war were now obsolete. It was imperative to establish one front ranging from left to right. The war of the Germans against the Jews was a war of extermination. It was directed against all levels and classes of the Jewish population as a whole. The Germans did not distinguish between the Zionists and the Bundists. They hated the former and the latter as one, and wanted to annihilate them both. Because of this, it was necessary to establish one national front against the German fascist forces of annihilation. The Jewish public was faced with the grave problem of life and death, and no one person could take upon himself the responsibility for such serious issues. Only with joint forces was it possible to deal with the problems that life brought.[5]

In spite of the clearly common aims, the unification of the ghetto was not an easy matter. The political differences which grew out of the prewar reality played far too large a role out of force of habit. In spite of the fact that the situation had completely changed, and although the awareness of the killing being carried out by the Germans had already increased, the habits, opinions, and feeling that grew in a totally different world, completely unlike the world of the ghetto, still had a powerful influence. Too often, political blindness and ideas that were unrealistic under the existing conditions predominated.

Slowly, too slowly in relation to the needs of the ghetto, the leaders of the various groups that supported an armed struggle against the enemy found a common ground. The political unification of the Zionist and communist organizations came first. The Jewish National Committee was established in which the following groups were represented: the left-wing Poalei Zion, the right-wing Poalei Zion, Hashomer Hatzair, Dror, Hechalutz, the General Zionists, Akiva, Gordonia, and the communists. In a meeting of these organizations, held in October 1942 in the secret apartment of Hashomer Hatzair on Mila Street, No. 16, it was decided to form one military organization. Its name was the *Zydowska Organizacja Bojowa* (Jewish Fighting Organization), after the fighting organization established in July 1942 by the Zionist left in the beginning of the deportation.

The Bund refused to join the Jewish National Committee. But after long negotiations it did agree to collaborate in the development of the fighting organization, on the basis of the coordination of efforts with the Jewish National Committee. Thus was established the coordinating committee, which included the National Jewish Committee on the one hand and the Bund on the other. This committee had its beginning on October 20, 1942, and it officially confirmed the Jewish Fighting Organization as the only militant organization in the ghetto. The committee's leadership, and the departments of information, finances, and supplies were founded. The coordinating committee chose Mordechai Anielewicz as commander of the Jewish Fighting Organization.[6]

The groups that remained outside the Jewish National Committee included the religious organizations, which continued to reject the purposefulness of the armed struggle against the Nazi occupiers, and the Zionist Revisionist movement, which, although it took a stand for an armed struggle, did not politically unify with the other organizations. The Revisionists established a separate military organization called *Zydowski Zwiazek Wojskowy* (Jewish Military Union). Only on the day before the outbreak of the uprising was the coordination of the military operation of the Jewish Fighting Organization and the Jewish Military Union finally achieved.

This split had a bad effect on the course of preparations for the uprising. The reasons for this separation are not well known, and it is difficult to determine them on the basis of existing documents. Although the Revisionists' leader in the Warsaw Ghetto, Dr. David Wdowinski, did state that he supported this unification, he did not explain why he did not achieve it. Professor Ber Mark suggests that the negotiations between the two military organizations did not succeed because the Jewish Fighting Organization was prepared to accept the fighters of the Jewish Military Union only on an individual basis, and not as a separate block.[7]

The Propaganda for the Uprising

Propaganda is a vital part of the general preparation for any armed uprising. Its aims are to get active support, to encourage the effort the revolt demands, and to gain sympathy for the objectives of the struggle. Without the proper propaganda, without the creation of an atmosphere of struggle, the rebels are doomed to isolation and to decisive failure. The leaders of the underground movement in the Warsaw Ghetto, of course, understood this. Extensive propaganda was carried out in order to gain the support of the public in the ghetto, in word and in deed, for the armed uprising and for the efforts being made to train capable fighters.

Even from the viewpoint of the propaganda, however, the resistance movement in the ghetto was a special case, unprecedented in the history of armed uprisings. The most important element in the propaganda campaign of any revolt is the vision of the better future after the victory with the emphasis on what can be expected in case of success. This was the case in all of the revolts in the countries of occupied Europe (Yugoslavia, Slovakia, France), and also in the Polish Warsaw uprising in the summer of 1944 (see chapter 13), where the collapse of the enemy in the Polish capital seemed imminent. Yet it could not be like this in the Warsaw Ghetto of September 1942.

We have already spoken of the aims of the uprising. It was known beforehand that, at the very least, the majority of the fighters would not outlive the rebellion, that neither the fighters nor their families would taste the fruit of the struggle. The response of Mordechai Anielewicz, commander of the Jewish Fighting Organization, is known: "We will die like homeless dogs." And this was neither an unrealistic nor a pessimistic estimate. Was it possible to enlist the entire public merely with the slogan, "death with honor"?

There was also another very important element in the propaganda: the need to consider the propaganda of the enemy, which tried in every way to convince the ghetto's Jews that the Germans were interested in Jewish labor, and therefore were not intending to liquidate the ghetto completely. Marek Edelman writes the following on this: "The German propaganda is working meanwhile. It is again trying to confuse the Jews by creating a myth of a Jewish reservation in Trawniki and Poniatowa, where, supposedly, they are planning to transfer the factories of Toebbens and Schultz. They are saying that there 'productive' Jews who would work diligently for the Germans will be able to pass the time of the war quietly."[8]

It was necessary to disperse the doubts that still lingered in the hearts of some of the ghetto's people, who were considering whether it was not better to give up the hopeless struggle on the chance that maybe this time the Germans were interested in a work force, and that their purpose, for the benefit of the economy, was not to kill the Jewish workers but to transfer them to labor camps.

In the period preceding the uprising, the fact that the Germans were really planning to employ part of the ghetto's population in the forced labor camps in Poniatowa and Trawniki for a certain time weighed heavily on the propaganda for the revolt. The leaders of the underground movement knew this. They were faced with the dilemma of whether to carry out the uprising, whose meaning was certain liquidation, even if part of the ghetto's surviving population was to be transferred not to the extermination camp in Treblinka but to Trawniki and Poniatowa, or whether to give up the struggle. And although the leadership of the resistance movement never displayed any hesitation as to their decision on this matter, doubts like these lingered in the minds of some factions in the ghetto's population. The military organizations, therefore, were forced to take a definite stand in the propaganda that was carried out for the uprising. Kozlowska explains this problem well:

> The situation which forced the decision was created in the ghetto before the April uprising: The Germans, who expected resistance by Jews in the event of further deportations, decided to liquidate the ghetto in a "quiet" way. That meant that they decided on small quotas of people who were to be sent to the labor camps in Trawniki and Poniatowa, or organized voluntary call-ups. In this way, they wanted both to get free labor for a certain time and to create conflicts among the Jews, by promising the alternative of passing war only in the camps. The Jewish Fighting Organization opposed all these offers, so that instead of thousands, only a few individuals turned up for the transport.
>
> The Jewish Fighting Organization, which protected the Jews from

the deportations, first with words and then with arms, took into account that people's lives in the ghetto might be shortened by a few months, months which could be gained in Trawniki and Poniatowa. However, one could not speak of a purposeful struggle and hopes for survival in terms of these camps.[9]

The militant organizations of the ghetto, however, did not limit themselves to a verbal struggle with the German propaganda. They also took action against it. In the memoirs of Marek Edelman we read: "The Jewish Fighting Organization is carrying out an extensive propaganda campaign. It puts out a number of posters which it hangs on houses and on the walls of the ghetto. In reply, Toebbens is preparing a declaration to the Jewish population. But its two editions were confiscated by the Jewish Fighting Organization while still at the printers."[10] And this was not the only case of active intervention against the German propaganda.

The Organization of the Armed Units

As a result of the inability to completely unify the political organizations, the Jewish Fighting Organization and the Jewish Military Union were founded. In addition, because of the specific conditions of the Warsaw Ghetto, many small armed groups were established which were known by all as the "wild groups."

The largest and most representative organization was the Jewish Fighting Organization, which enjoyed the greater support of the Jewish public in the ghetto, although it may have had fewer arms. Two factors had a decisive influence on the structure of this organization: the partition of the ghetto into separate areas and the political makeup of the Jewish National Committee and the Coordinating Committee.

The partition of the ghetto led to the formation of four tactical units, each affiliated with one of these areas. The military preparations had to take into account the parts of the ghetto that were isolated from one another, which were: 1) the largest area, between Nalewki, Gesia, and Dzika streets, known as the "big ghetto" or the "central ghetto"; 2) the area between Nalewki and Bonifraterska, known as the "brushmakers' quarters," because it contained workshops for the production of brushes; 3) the area between Karmelicka, Leszno, Zelazna, and Nowolipki, known as the "Toebbens' area," which held the factories of the Toebbens and Schultz firms; and 4) the area around Prosta Street, known as the "little ghetto."

The influence of the political makeup of the Coordinating Committee and the Jewish National Committee on the structure of the

Jewish Fighting Organization was as follows: Representatives of the Bund and of the various political organizations making up the Jewish National Committee belonged to the ZOB command staff. The basic organizational unit of the Jewish Fighting Organization was the combat group (parallel to a platoon), which was made up of members of a specific political organization who were under the command of a member of that organization.

The determining factor in this choice of staff was not the person's organizational affiliation, but his ability. The makeup of the staff of the Jewish Fighting Organization was as follows: Mordechai Anielewicz, commander; Yitzhak Zuckerman, second-in-command in charge of armament; Marek Edelman, intelligence; Hirsch Berlinski, planning; Yochanan Morgenstern, finances; Tuvia Borzykowski, supplies; Michael Rosenfeld, staff member.[11]

During the initial preparations, the various groups were housed in different factories. Turkow describes the organization as follows:

> The members of the Jewish Fighting Organization lived in various shop area (factories and workshops), and because of this the groups were organized according to the shops they belonged to. Because the fighting organization built its units according to party affiliation, there was a Hashomer Hatzair group in one shop, a Dror group in another shop, the left-wing Poalei Zion in a third shop, and in others—communist, Bund, Akiva, right-wing Poalei Zion, and the Zionist Youth groups—that is, groups of all of the organizations that belonged to the Jewish Fighting Organization. Although each group was under the command of the general staff, its direct commanders were members of the same party that the fighters of the group belonged to. Members of another organization were not accepted into the group.[12]

As a result of the experience acquired in the battles of January 18–21, 1943, the ranks of the ZOB were reorganized. The structure of the ghetto was given greater consideration. Command staffs were set up according to the areas of the ghetto, and the groups operating in each area were subordinated to its staff. Thus, Israel Kanal commanded the central ghetto; Marek Edelman commanded the brushmakers' quarter; and Eliezer Geler commanded the Toebbens's area.

After the battles of January 1943, the concentration of the combat units in special apartments was found more effective. The ZOB groups were moved out of the factories and transferred to the underground's apartments, where they were on constant military alert for the uprising. Edelman writes: "This concentration in special apartments had as its aims preventing a repeat of the surprise in the

Germans' actions, instilling military spirit and discipline in the people, and bringing them into constant contact with arms. Guard patrols, whose task it was to warn of any danger coming close, were on alert day and night near the walls of the ghetto."[13]

A description of a secret apartment of the Jewish Fighting Organization is found in the writings of the ghetto's historian, Dr. Ringelblum:

> A few days before the April uprising, I saw one of the Jewish Fighting Organization's positions. This was an apartment containing two rooms and a kitchen on Swietojerska Street, No. 32. The *wacha* of the German *workschutz* (factory guard) was about three floors below. Day and night there were ten people on alert in the apartment. The arms were there also. The fighters were not permitted to leave the apartment. They received their food there. The entrance into the apartment was through the attics of nearby houses. They knocked on the door in a specific way. Three women fighters who were in the apartment were busy preparing food. They also carried out various dangerous tasks according to the orders of the fighting organization. The discipline and the order were exemplary. This group, affiliated with the left-wing Poalei Zion, had already carried out successful confiscation raids (known as "Exes") for the armament of the ghetto, etc.[14]

In the period preceding the outbreak of the uprising, the Jewish Fighting Organization had twenty-two combat groups. These groups were divided according to their affiliation with the political organizations, thus:

—Dror, five combat groups; commanders—Zacharia Artstein, Ber Brauda, Hanoch Gutman, Itzhak Blaustein, Benjamin Wald.

—Hashomer Hatzair, four combat groups; commanders—Jozef Farber, David Nowodworski, Yehoshua Winogron, Mordechai Growas.

—Communists, four combat groups; commanders—Henryk Silberberg, Yurek Greenshpan, Hirsh Kawa, Aharon Bryskin.

—Bund, four combat groups; commanders—Jerzy Blones, Wolf Rozowski, Leib Gruzalc, David Hochberg.

—Akiva, one combat group; commander—Leib Rotblat.

—Gordonia, one combat group; commander—Yaakov Feigenblat.

—Poalei Zion, left wing, one combat group; commander—Hirsch Berlinski.

—Poalei Zion, right wing, one combat group; commander—Meir Majerowicz.

—Hanoar Hazioni, one combat group; commander—Yaakov Praszkier.

Much less is known about the structure of the Jewish Military Union. The existing sources, testimonies that were written many years after the events took place, contradict one another. However, in spite of this, these testimonies help to determine some undeniable facts. The Jewish Military Union, as we have already emphasized, was under the influence of only one party in the ghetto—the Zionist Revisionists. The political guidance of the union was in the hands of a political committee whose members were Dr. Wdowinski, Leib Rodal, and Dr. Michael Stryjkowski. Pawel Frenkiel was appointed commander of the Jewish Military Union.

The Union included more than ten combat groups, or squads, which were scattered among different combat positions in the central ghetto, the brushmakers' quarter, and the Toebbens's shops. The main forces of the Jewish Military Union, however, were concentrated in a block of houses on Muranowska Street, Nos. 1–9. Here were positioned the combat groups that were under the command of Eliyahu Halberstein, Mayer Tublus, Josef Goldshaber, and Leib Rodal. These forces were subordinated to the union's command staff, which had its headquarters in a house on Muranowska Street, No. 7–9. In the area of the central ghetto, there were five other combat groups commanded by David Mordechai Applebaum, Henryk Federbush, Jan Pika, Leizer Staniewicz, and Binsztok, and in the brushmakers' quarter there were three groups, commanded by Haim Lopata, Yitzhak Bilewski, and David Shulman. The actions of these groups were coordinated by Shmuel Luft. In the area of the Toebbens's factories there were groups under the command of Pinchas Tauba, Simcha Korngold, and Natan Schultz.[15]

On the eve of the uprising, the Jewish Military Union groups were concentrated and on combat alert, as were the groups of the Jewish Fighting Organization. The condition for being accepted into the Jewish Military Union was cutting off all ties with one's family and remaining in underground positions, where full military alert was enforced, and from which the groups went out to many combat actions that were already being carried out before the outbreak of the uprising. Following is a description in Ringelblum's history of the underground apartment which housed the headquarters of the Jewish Military Union:

The apartment was in an empty house, one of those known as "wild houses" on Muranowska Street, No. 7. The apartment contained six rooms and was on the first floor. In the leadership's room there was a high-quality radio, which received news from the entire world. Near it was a typewriter. The members of the leadership of the Jewish Military Union, with whom I spoke for many hours, were armed with guns inserted in their belts. Hanging on hooks in the large rooms were different kinds of arms: machine guns, rifles, different kinds of pistols, grenades, ammunition pouches, and German uniforms. These were of good use during the battles in April.

There was a lot of movement in the leadership's room, like the room of a real army command staff. Orders were given out to the various positions, where arms were accumulated and where the future fighters were trained. Reports were brought in on confiscation raids carried out by certain groups against wealthy people for the benefit of the Jewish Military Union. In my presence, arms were bought from a former Polish army officer for the total of a quarter of a million *zloties*; an advance payment of 50,000 *zloties* was given him. Two submachine guns for 40,000 *zloties* and a large quantity of hand grenades and bombs were also bought. I asked why the apartment was not camouflaged, and they answered me that betrayal on the part of the members themselves was out of the question, and that if an unwanted person came here, a gendarme for example, he would not come out alive.[16]

Alongside the Jewish Fighting Organization and the Jewish Military Union, a number of independent groups arose which took care of their own armament. These small groups of fighters were known as "wild groups." Turkow writes:

The January resistance of the Jewish Fighting Organization created great sympathy for this organization even on the part of those groups that previously had opposed the idea of an armed struggle. Even Orthodox circles, which, with the exception of a few individuals, did not take a positive stand towards the Jewish Fighting Organization and openly expressed their opposition to the attempt at resistance, now changed their position. Yesterday's "irresponsible adventurers," as the underground fighters were called, now grew into heroes in their eyes. The Orthodox youth, whose number in the ghetto was already very small, now showed a great desire to join the "party," as they called the fighting organization. However, the ZOB did not accept into its ranks all those who turned to it mainly because of the lack of arms. Because of this, the "wild units" were formed.[17]

The sources that have come down to us do not provide enough of a basis to determine precisely the number of armed Jewish groups that took part in the uprising. It is known that on the eve of the uprising, there was a sizable increase in the ranks of the Jewish Fighting Organization. It is also known that in the course of the uprising, many members of the "wild groups" joined the ZOB or ZZW fighting groups.

Arming the Combat Groups

The means by which the military organizations tried to acquire arms were varied. Intensive demands for help were made to the Polish underground organizations. For this purpose, the Jewish Fighting Organization maintained ties with both the Home Army and the People's Guard. The Jewish Military Union received substantial aid in the acquisition of arms from the Polish People's Independence Action (PLAN) and the Security Corps (KB). Arms production was developed in the ghetto. Both the military organizations and the independent groups organized the acquisition of arms and their transferral into the ghetto, using their own means.[18]

There is fairly precise data regarding the arms that the Home Army supplied to the Jewish Fighting Organization. Relying on archival material, the authors of *The Polish Armed Forces in World War II, Part 3: Home Army* state that the following quantities of arms were supplied to the Jewish Fighting Organization: 90 pistols with two magazines and ammunition, 500 defense hand grenades, 100 attack hand grenades, 15 kilograms of plastic and fuses and detonators, 1 light machine gun, 1 submachine gun, explosives such as clock bombs, and time bombs. This list matches the information given by Colonel Henryk Wolinski, Marek Edelman, and Zivia Lubetkin.[19]

There are no documents by which we can determine, even approximately, the amounts of arms supplied by the People's Guard to the Jewish Fighting Organization. Undoubtedly, these quantities were quite modest. In the period of preparation for the ghetto uprising, during winter 1942 and spring 1943, the People's Guard still did not have substantial amounts of arms.

There are no documents whatsoever to enable us to determine the amount of arms delivered to the ghetto by the Polish People's Independence Action or the Security Corps. Ber Mark writes about sixty grenades that a PLAN group smuggled in for the Jewish Military Union through a tunnel near Karmelicka Street and of three crates of grenades that were brought in by the KB group headed by Captain Henryk Iwanski through the underground's tunnel that led from the Aryan side of the ZZW bunker near Karmelicka Street.[20]

A substantial part of the ghetto's weapons came from secret arms workshops, where Molotov cocktails were produced and arms brought in from the Aryan side were fixed and reinforced. Jonas Turkow and Dvorah Goldkorn write extensively on these workshops. According to Edelman, they were able to make four or five Molotov cocktails per fighter.[21]

Another source of arms supplies for the ghetto's military organizations was the purchase of weapons on the Aryan side and later smuggled into the ghetto. This was achieved partly by connections made through the Home Army and the People's Guard, and partly through independent ties. Jonas Turkow writes about contacts with a Polish group that supplied the ghetto with some rifles, guns, hand grenades, and ammunition and with an arms workshop in Radom, which resulted in the successful smuggling of guns and ammunition into the ghetto.

It must be remembered that the prices paid by the ghetto for these arms were many times higher than those paid by Polish underground organizations. The ghetto resistance movement had to pay 10,000 to 20,000 *zloties* for a pistol, 1,000 to 1,500 *zloties* for a hand grenade, 20,000 to 25,000 *zloties* for a rifle, and 40,000 *zloties* for a machine gun, while the highest prices then paid by the Home Army were 4,000 *zloties* for a pistol and 12,000 *zloties* for a machine gun. Obviously, high extortionist prices, in addition to the meager financial supplies of the ghetto whose means were nearly exhausted, made the possibilities for buying arms very limited.[22]

All these means—the acquisitions of arms from Polish organizations, the black market purchases, and secret productions—could not sufficiently arm the combat groups. According to existing sources, it is possible to estimate that the average person in the Jewish Fighting Organization had at most one pistol with ten to fifteen bullets, four or five grenades, and four or five Molotov cocktails. This means that, overall, the ZOB arms totaled a few hundred guns and a few thousand grenades and Molotov cocktails. It is also most probable that the Jewish Fighting Organization had about ten rifles, one submachine gun, and fifteen mines.

Careful attention must be paid to the makeup of arms. There was a relatively large number of pistols, a weapon whose usefulness in a regular city battle is not very great. Anielewicz's comment, written on the fifth day of the uprising, April 23, to his second-in-command Zuckerman on the Aryan side, is typical: "Remember, short-range arms are of no value to us today. We rarely use them. We urgently need grenades, rifles, machine guns, and explosives."[23]

The Jewish Fighting Organization had no submachine guns and no machine guns suitable for city fighting. The only effective arms found in relatively large quantities were grenades and Molotov cock-tails. Although the effective range of these arms is strictly limited (20 to 25 meters), the diameter they hit made them more effective than pistols.

The Jewish Military Union apparently was better equipped. According to Ber Mark, the ZZW group positioned on Muranowska Street had about 300 grenades, eight submachine guns, two machine guns (one light and one heavy), and a few thousand bullets. Mark also mentions that the day before the outbreak of the uprising, the Jewish Military Union gave up a certain quantity of arms to the Jewish Fighting Organization.[24]

The "wild groups" also had a certain quantity of arms available, but there is no data whatsoever which would enable us to estimate their number. Undoubtedly, these were short-range arms and cold arms having very little effect. There is also no doubt that in the first days of the uprising, when regular street battles took place, it was impossible to use these arms. These weapons could be used only in the next stage of the uprising, in night attacks and in the defense of certain bunkers.

If we generally accept the higher number mentioned, it is possible to assume that the arms held by the ghetto were as follows: a few thousand grenades and Molotov cocktails, a few hundred pistols, no more than twenty-five submachine guns, no more than ten machine guns, and twenty mines.

Training the Combat Units

The training of the combat units was a particularly difficult problem in the Warsaw Ghetto. The majority of the people in the Jewish Fighting Organization and the Jewish Military Union were too young to have served in the Polish army before the war. They were forced to learn both how to use arms and the tactics of city fighting while in the ghetto. Training was held under strict underground conditions, which made open-range practice impossible. Since there was no alternative, training was limited to theoretical instruction in underground hideouts.

The problem of training the command staff was more serious. The Jewish Fighting Organization had almost no officers or sergeants. The situation of the Jewish Military Union was better, but it also lacked trained officers. Both groups asked for the guidance of the Polish military organizations and some ZOB members took part in a course held in an underground hideout in Warsaw, on Marszal-kowska Street, No. 62, by a cell called the Bureau for Technical Research, under the command of the Home Army. This course was run by Major Zbigniew Lewandowski and Captain Leon Tarajkowicz, and dealt mainly with the problems of the production of explosives in underground conditions and in the tactics of street fighting.[25]

COMBAT ACTIONS PRECEDING THE APRIL UPRISING

The first armed clash with the Germans in the Warsaw Ghetto took place on January 18, 1943. The battles between the German forces and the Jewish Fighting Organization went on for four days.

On January 18, 1943, at 6:30 A.M., SS and German gendarmerie units entered the ghetto to renew the liquidation actions. The entrance of the Germans came as a surprise to the Jewish Fighting Organization, although the ZOB command knew that a new German gendarmerie unit numbering about 1,000 men had come to Warsaw. This unit had begun an intensive round-up on the Aryan side of the city on January 15. Thousands of Poles were seized and transferred to the Pawiak prison. Loaded trucks were seen moving day and night through Karmelicka Street in the direction of Pawiak. The Jewish Fighting Organization reached the mistaken conclusion that the Germans would not round up people on the Aryan side and carry out a liquidation action in the ghetto at one and the same time; therefore, they did not declare a military alert.

Contrary to what was expected, the Germans renewed the deportation from the ghetto on January 18. When the Germans entered the ghetto, the Jewish Fighting Organization was not ready for battle. The arms it had were too few, the training of the fighters was inadequate, and most of all, the organization's structure was faulty. In addition, they had not planned what action to take in the event of renewed deportation-extermination actions. A system of command for such an event had not been set up, and neither were communications or the transition of fighters to a state of military alert. The combat groups had no defined tasks.

We have no consistent data regarding the number of German forces that were to begin the liquidation action on January 18, 1943. According to Turkow, the German unit that was sent into the ghetto numbered about 1,000 men. On the other hand, the Polish Democratic Party's underground bulletin *Dzien (Today)* of January 19, 1943, reports that 600 gendarmes armed with two field guns entered the ghetto. It is also possible that the German unit received substantial reinforcement in the course of the battles. Ringelblum mentions that armored trucks, field guns and heavy machine guns were brought into the ghetto.[26]

Once the Germans entered the streets of the ghetto, communications between the ZOB command and all the combat groups could not be maintained. The command staff could not, therefore, enforce its authority over them. The great contribution of the commander, Mordechai Anielewicz, was that in spite of these grave circumstances, he decided on his own to battle against the Germans, since he had not been able to seek the advice of the Coordinating Committee. He succeeded in assembling only four groups of fighters. Surprised by the Germans, the remaining groups were cut off from the meager underground arms storehouses.

Therefore, on January 18, one combat group appeared in the central ghetto under the personal command of Anielewicz, and one combat group came to the area of the Toebbens and Schultz factories under the command of Yitzhak Zuckerman. The combat groups under Eliezer Geler and Ariyeh Wilner also turned up. All were very poorly armed,[27] as Zivia Lubetkin testifies: "We went out to the January uprising armed with only a few guns and a few grenades."[28] The arms held by the group that was under the direct command of Anielewicz totaled five pistols and five grenades. Zuckerman's group, which numbered forty people, had four pistols and six grenades. With these arms the battle began.[29]

The Jewish Fighting Organization operated in the following way: the combat groups mixed in with the masses of people who had been seized by the Germans and transported to *Umschlagplatz* (the loading area for the trains going to Treblinka). After a signal from the commander, the ZOB fighters attacked the Germans and then called out to the people to run. This tactic brought good immediate results. Surprised by the first strike, the Germans suffered losses. Yet the Jewish Fighting Organization did not have enough arms to continue the open street battle, and the members of the Jewish Fighting Organization suffered heavy losses from German machine-gun fire.

The group that was under the direct command of Mordechai Anielewicz attacked the Germans at the crossroads of Zamenhof and Niska streets. But the German fire was far too strong. Anielewicz's group was surrounded and destroyed. Jonas Turkow writes about this clash: "Mordechai Anielewicz was attacked on all sides by a large group of Germans. It came to a sharp battle between his group and the Germans. The Jewish fighters showed great courage. Mordechai Anielewicz grabbed a submachine gun from a German and killed him. All the other Jewish fighters died a hero's death in the battle."[30]

Other serious clashes took place on January 18, 1943, on Zamenhof, Muranowska, Mylna, and Franciszkanska streets, and on the crossroads of Nowolipki and Smocza streets. The Jewish Fighting Organization suffered heavy losses in these clashes, which Edelman describes: "It appears that we pay far too heavy a price in open street fighting. We are not prepared for it. We have no arms. We are going over to guerrilla warfare."[31]

After the experiences gained in the first day of battle, the Jewish Fighting Organization did go over to guerrilla warfare, using ambushes and attacks against groups of German gendarmes, with good results. Zuckerman's group inflicted many losses on the Germans— fifty Germans dead and wounded according to Turkow, a few score German dead and minimal losses for the Jewish organization according to Zivia Lubetkin.[32]

The commander of the German police in the district of Warsaw, SS Colonel Ferdinand von Sammern-Frankeneg, stopped the liquidation action on January 21 and took the German unit out of the ghetto. But in those four days of the action, the Germans had deported 6,500 people from the Warsaw Ghetto and had shot about one thousand people to death.[33]

It is hard to determine precisely the losses suffered by the Germans and by the Jewish Fighting Organization. In telegrams sent February 7 and March 11, 1943, by the Coordinating Committee to Shmuel Zygelboim, the Bund representative in London, there is mention of a few score German gendarmes dead.[34] These numbers are apparently exaggerated. In any case, losses for the Jewish fighters were much greater. According to Edelman, 80 percent of the members of the Jewish Fighting Organization were killed.[35] However, the number of ZOB members before the January battles is not known. Most likely their losses were much smaller than those mentioned by Edelman, otherwise it would be difficult to comprehend how they succeeded in renewing their combat activity so quickly.

The German sources known to us do not reveal why the deportations were discontinued. It is evident that the Germans had enough forces to liquidate the ghetto totally, suffering fewer losses than they did in April and May of 1943. It is quite possible that von Sammern-Frankeneg stopped the deportation-liquidation action for the purpose of renewing it after some time by "peaceful" methods, without having to resort to fighting out battles in the ghetto. From his later actions (which will be discussed later), it appears that von Sammern desperately wanted to prevent German losses and the loss of prestige. It can be assumed that his intention was to liquidate the ghetto by more devious means, by spreading illusion, terror, and fear, as had been done in the liquidation actions of the summer of 1942. And even more than wishing to prevent German losses, which, considering the arms situation in the ghetto, could not be great anyway, von Sammern seems to have feared that news of battles in the heartland of Poland, in a center as large and as strategic as Warsaw, would echo all over occupied Poland and even beyond.

The battles of January 18–21 were very important for the planning for the next ghetto battles: The young commanders and untrained soldiers gained valuable experience, and this had a direct effect on the uprising of April 1943. Zivia Lubetkin writes about this experience:

> The January uprising taught us, the Jewish Fighting Organization, how to prepare for the battle awaiting us. We learned that it was most important to put the people into a kind of military barracks, to plan the uprising so that all the groups would be ready in their positions, and to make sure that each company commander, each area commander, and each fighter would know what he was to do, so we would not be surprised when the Germans renewed the action.[36]

Another important outcome of the January battle was the general support the Jewish Fighting Organization gained in the ghetto and their recognition of the coming battle.

The period between January 22 and the start of the uprising was characterized, on the one hand, by the ceaseless attempts of the Germans to carry out "peaceful" deportations, and, on the other hand, by the increasing military preparations being made by the ghetto while effecting frequent small-scale combat actions.

In line with orders from the German authorities, German industrialists who owned factories in the area of the ghetto (Toebbens, Schultz, Stehmann, Schilling, and Hallmann) opened a propaganda campaign aimed at influencing the ghetto's population to leave of their own will for the "work camp" in Trawniki and Poniatowa. These industrialists promised the Jewish workers the opportunity of living out the war in these camps. Using the civilian industrialists instead of SS men was meant to create the impression that the Germans had changed their plans regarding the Jews and that they were now interested in a Jewish labor force. When this propaganda did not succeed, the Germans used terrorism, killing, and robbing the ghetto population and then returned to propaganda and persuasion.

The military organizations strongly resisted the propaganda, incitement, and terror of the enemy, carrying out a series of sabotage actions between January 24 and April 18, 1943: German factories were often set on fire and large quantities of raw materials and products meant for the *Wehrmacht* were destroyed. On March 6, ZZW fighters set an SS storehouse on Nalewki Street, No. 31, on fire, while at the same time, a ZOB group attacked the German industrial guard in the Schultz factories on Nowolipie Street, disarming and beating the German sentries and freeing over one hundred of the Jews imprisoned there. Another ZOB group burned a shipment of brush factory machines on the *Umschlagplatz*. On March 13, a reprisal action was held against the Germans who were terrorizing the ghetto. Battles were waged against groups of German and Ukrainian industrial guards and with an SS unit that was sent to the ghetto. At the end of March, another ZOB combat group, under the command of Zacharia Artstein, held a successful battle with a Polish Blue Police unit on Nalewki Street.[37]

In view of the failure of their methods, the Germans decided to send in a stronger unit, especially formed for the purpose of liquidating the Warsaw Ghetto. The ghetto replied with revolt.

THE GERMAN FORCE AND THE PROPORTION OF THE FORCES

For the coming battle, the Germans assembled a force which, according to their calculations, was sufficient for the immediate repression of the ghetto. Considering the many and varied forces available to them, they had no doubts whatsoever about the results of the expected clash. As was said, it was important for them to prevent an extended rebellion in a center as sensitive as Warsaw.[38]

The fact that the battles in the ghetto lasted several weeks proves that in spite of the decisive superiority of the German forces, they could not succeed in immediately repressing the uprising in the ghetto.

Two basic documents concerning the composition of the German combat force that was formed for the war with the ghetto have come down to us: (1) Reports of the Department of Internal Affairs of the Polish Government Delegacy, on the political situation in the country, compiled on the basis of intelligence reports of the Home Army, and (2) What is known as the Stroop Report, including an introduction and copies of daily reports which were set to Stroop's superior, SS General Krueger, who was stationed in Cracow.

Report No. 149 of the Department of Internal Affairs, dated April 20, 1943, stated:

On April 18, at 6 A.M., the German police, the SS, and the Blue Police were assembled at starting points. On the same day, at about 8 P.M., the ghetto was surrounded. On April 19, at 5:30 A.M., strong units numbering a total of 5,000 men entered the ghetto. These units were made up of two *Waffen* SS battalions, powerful gendarmerie units, Gestapo and SD units, Lithuanian Shaulis, Ukrainians, and Blue Police. . . .

The exchange of fire between the two sides went on until 10 A.M. Three Germans were killed, and twenty seriously wounded. At 10 o'clock, the operation was stopped and aid was requested from the army. Heavy arms and the cooperation of the air force were particularly demanded. At about 12 noon, the army turned down this request. It agreed only to send in engineering corps units, light mortars, and 12 armored vehicles. . . . A few antitank guns were also brought in.[39]

This report, which was compiled on the basis of AK intelligence information, was received from an informer active in the ranks of the Polish police and the source of other very reliable information. It is interesting that this source had already been given information on preparations being made for the liquidation of the ghetto on April 13: "The political authorities believe, and fear, that in the near future a rebellion will break out in Warsaw. Because of these fears, constant talks are being held between the political and the administrative authorities."[40] And on the day preceding the start of the operations in the ghetto, the same source reported: "Today, April 18, the Blue Police received an order to put 450 policemen and 13 officers on alert. The Blue Police were ordered to assemble in police buildings and await the order. The objective of the operation is not known. In any case, there has never been such a large concentration of police forces. The secret operation is to be carried out on April 19".[41]

Further details on the composition of the German force are found in the Stroop Report. Stroop details the makeup of the force under his command, formed for the battle with the ghetto, in the introduction to his report:[42]

The Stroop Report contains many discrepancies. What Stroop means by the expression "Average Number of Personnel Used Per Day," first of all, is not clear. In his daily reports, he generally gives much smaller numbers of forces being "used." Only in the report for April 20 does Stroop give a higher number—the number of 460 soldiers in Cavalry Battalion No. 1—74 more than the number given in the introduction. In any case, it is impossible to arrive at the average given in the introduction to the report from Stroop's daily reviews. Furthermore, there is no doubt that the "Average Number of Personnel Used Per Day" as reported by Stroop was smaller than the one

Units Used in the Action	Average Number of Personnel Used Per Day	
Command staff	Officers	Soldiers
Waffen SS	6	5
SS Panzer Grenadier Training and Reserve Battalion No. 3	4	440
SS Cavalry Training and Reserve Battalion No. 1	5	381
Ordnungspolizei		
SS Police Regiment No. 22, 1st Battalion	3	94
SS Police Regiment No. 22, 3rd Battalion	3	134
Engineering Emergency Service	1	6
Polish Police	4	363
Polish Fire Brigade		166
Security Police	3	32
Wehrmacht		
Light Anti-aircraft Battery No. 3, 8th Regiment	2	22
Engineers Detachment of Railway Armored Trains, Reserves Battalion	2	42
Reserves Engineers Detachment, 14th Battalion	1	34
Foreign Watchmen		
"Trawniki" Battalion	2	335
TOTAL	36	2,054

given after the event took place. According to Stroop, this number totaled 36 officers and 2,054 soldiers and noncommissioned officers, that is, 2,090 men, which, as we saw, is at least 3,000 less than the number stated by AK intelligence.

The Stroop Report contains other discrepancies. For example, in the information on the units given in the introduction to the report, Stroop does not mention field-gun units. In contrast, his survey of April 20 mentions the use of a 100-millimeter howitzer. If this is true, then a field-gun unit had to take part in the battles also, because a 100-millimeter howitzer is not an integral part of the equipment used by the units mentioned above. Nor does Stroop mention the use of the air force against the insurgents, although this fact is not doubted by many Polish and Jewish sources, including eye-witnesses, or of the third battalion of the 23rd Regiment of the *Ordnungspolizei* in his introduction. This unit is mentioned only in his report of May 15, where Stroop brings up the plan to leave this battalion in the ghetto to run the operation, after the majority of the force was taken out. Yet he does not say when this battalion began to take part in the ghetto battles. It is known that the 23rd Regiment of the SS police was stationed in Cracow. The third battalion of this regiment was probably sent to Warsaw as a reinforcement to Stroop's troops.

Stroop's adjutant, Captain Kaleske, confirmed in principle the use of the units mentioned by Stroop. However, he reports a much higher number of personnel in the units. In his opinion, the two *Waffen* SS units (the third battalion of the armored grenadiers and the first battalion of the cavalry) numbered about 1,000 soldiers each.[43]

On the other hand, it appears that, in general, the sources above do agree on the quality of the units, although opinion is divided regarding their numerical strength. The lowest number is the one stated by Stroop—2,090 men. According to Captain Kaleske, the two *Waffen* SS units alone totaled this number. Kaleske's numbers match those given by AK intelligence, which estimated that the force under Stroop's command totaled about 5,000 men.[44]

However, these documents throw little light on the armament of the German units. In his first communiqué, Stroop mentions the use of one 100-millimeter howitzer, one flame-thrower, three 22.7-millimeter antiaircraft guns, one armored truck, and two heavily armored trucks. But he does not mention other arms and does not report on the guns and machine guns being used by his forces. After the war, in answers written to the questions of Dr. Josef Kermish, Stroop, who was then imprisoned in Warsaw, declared: "The German units, like other forces that took part in the battles, were equipped and armed in the same way as combat units on the front. The grenadiers had armored vehicles and a number of light French armored trucks."[45] This is far too laconic a declaration to be relied on for any estimate of the fire power of the German force. However, it is possible to reach many conclusions on this by referring to the regulations concerning the German units in 1943. These regulations are presented in the American intelligence guide *Handbook on German Military Forces*, according to which the standard *Waffen* SS armored grenadier battalion, as determined by regulations, had: 868 soldiers, 548 rifles, 91 submachine guns, 60 light machine guns, 12 heavy machine guns, six 81-millimeter mortars, four 120-millimeter mortars, 6 antiaircraft guns, and about 20 armored tracks.[46]

The regulations for a *Waffen* SS cavalry battalion were very similar to those given above. In contrast with this, a reserve unit, for example, was organized very much like combat units on the front, although at times it had fewer heavy arms, according to the American guide. The two *Waffen* SS battalions that took part in the battles against the Warsaw Ghetto belonged to such units.[47]

The second foundation of the German combat force included the battalions of the 22nd Regiment of the SS police and a battalion of the 23rd Regiment of the same force. These two regiments belonged to the *Truppenpolizei* units, which were a part of the *Ordnungspolizei*. The operational battalions of the *Truppenpolizei* had previously belonged to the *Kasernierte Polizei*. So, for example, the first battalion of the 22nd Regiment had previously been the 301st Battalion stationed in Bochum, and the 3rd Battalion of that regiment had been the 307th Battalion stationed in Duisburg. According to the data given by the American intelligence handbook, the operational battalions of the *Ordnungspolizei*, which was formed from former *Kasernierte Polizei* battalions, were meant to serve in occupied territories. These battalions were organized and equipped according to the regulations governing military units, and differed from them only in that they had no heavy arms. A battalion numbered about 550 men and was composed of a command staff and four companies. It was armed with machine guns, antiaircraft guns, and armored vehicles. The regulations regarding *Ordnungspolizei* battalions were similar to those governing *Sicherungsbataillone*, which generally held 377 rifles, 100 pistols, 127 submachine guns, 31 light machine guns, and 6 heavy machine guns.[48]

We have no information concerning the armament of the Polish police and the Trawniki battalion at the start of the battles in the ghetto. From various reports it is known that these battalions were armed with rifles and machine guns, including heavy machine guns, but we do not know what the proportion of machine guns to rifles was in these battalions. We also know very little about the armament of the other units that made up the German force.

Anyway, it appears that the actual number of the German units, at least those of the *Waffen* SS battalions and the SS *Ordnungspolizei*, were much larger than those stated by Stroop. It is not possible that these units, which were stationed in an occupied country, would be as underequipped in relation to the regulations as Stroop reported. Careful calculations must be made to determine clearly the fire power of Stroop's force. For this purpose, we accept the "average number" as the armament of these units, and in proportion to these lower average numbers, reduce the number of arms available to the units. If we do not take into account the arms of the small units and the automatic arms and machine guns held by the Polish police and the "Trawniki" battalion, we arrive at the minimum average of arms held by Stroop's force, not including heavy arms:

Unit	Rifles	Submachine guns	Light machine guns	Heavy machine guns
Grenadiers 3rd Battalion	274	45	30	6
Cavalry 1st Battalion	246	40	27	5
1st and 3rd Battalion, 22nd Regiment of the Police	134	50	12	2
Polish Police	367			
"Trawniki" Battalion	337			
TOTAL	1358	135	69	13

To these numbers must be added the 15 armored vehicles probably held by the Germans (including 3 mentioned by Stroop in the first report on the battles of the morning of April 19 and the 12 mentioned by the *Wehrmacht*), a certain number of antiaircraft guns, field guns, and flame-throwers, a large quantity of explosives used by the engineering corps, and the air force planes which were also employed. In this way, we can get an idea of the arms used by the Germans in the Warsaw Ghetto.

Comparing the quantity of arms held by the Germans and that of the insurgents' units, it is possible to determine that the Germans' rifle and submachine gun superiority over the ghetto rebels' weaponry (not including pistols whose effectiveness in street battles was of little value), was already on the first day at a ratio of 27:1. Yet, in reality, this ratio was greater if we take into consideration the ammunition held by both sides.

We have no information regarding the ammunition held by the Jewish Fighting Organization and the Jewish Military Union. What is known to us is that the Jewish Fighting Organization barely had 10 to 15 bullets per pistol. The supply of ammunition for rifles and machine guns probably totaled a few score bullets per weapon. But we can reach a fair conclusion on the quantity of ammunition available to Stroop from the standards that were in effect during World War II for the German reserve units serving in the rear. This was as follows: 16 bullets per pistol; 20 bullets per rifle; 2,505 bullets per light machine gun; 4,750 bullets per heavy machine gun.[49]

After taking into account the difference in the ammunition supply, the ratio of 27:1 doubles or triples to reflect the real proportion of the fire power of the two sides. If we also consider the armored trucks, artillery, and air force employed by the Germans, we can speak without exaggeration of a 100:1 ratio of German fire power to that of the rebels.

In the calculations made above, the most common weapons held by the rebels—grenades and Molotov cocktails—are not taken into consideration because of their short range. Even so, this does not change the appearance of things, because the Germans had a far larger number of grenades and because the power of the explosives used by the Germans' engineering corps units was far greater than that of the Molotov cocktails held by the rebels.

The clearly superior combat training of the Germans must also be taken into account. As we have already explained, most of the members of the Jewish Fighting Organization and the Jewish Military Union were young people who received their combat training only in the clandestine conditions of the ghetto.

It is possible to state that in the history of mankind, no people ever went to battle with such disproportionate forces. No other event has aroused a struggle under such conditions. The people of the Warsaw Ghetto went to battle in spite of their total lack of chance for victory or survival, in order to actively protest against the greatest crime ever seen by mankind—the genocide, committed by Nazi Germany, of the Jewish people.

THE COMBAT ACTIONS

The First Day of the Uprising—April 19, 1943

The liquidation action which led to the uprising on April 19, 1943 was planned by the SS and police commander of the district of Warsaw, SS Colonel Dr. Ferdinand von Sammern-Frankeneg. He foresaw neither the uprising nor the battles in the ghetto that were to last for several weeks, despite the fact that he knew armed organizations existed in the ghetto, at least by January 18.[50] He also did not succeed in estimating the extent of the power of the resistance movement in the ghetto, or the scope of the preparations for the combat actions. Sammern's first steps and action on April 19 prove that he wanted at all costs to execute the plan for liquidating the ghetto without entering into battle. The force he prepared for the liquidation was much stronger than the one that was put together to carry out the deportation on January 18. Sammern apparently believed that this time, as in January, the Jewish combat groups would openly attack the German columns and instigate an open street battle. The armored vehicles were meant to secure the immediate repression of such action; the "pacification" of the ghetto, afterwards, by military and police forces numbering a few thousand men was not supposed to be difficult, in Sammern's opinion.

Apparently, either Sammern's superiors had a different opinion regarding the liquidation of the Warsaw Ghetto, or they did not trust his abilities; the liquidation of the ghetto was delegated to someone else. On April 17, 1943, SS Major-General Jurgen Stroop, police commander of the district of Galicia, was called in by the GG police commander, SS General Krueger. Krueger ordered him to leave immediately for Warsaw to take over from Sammern not only the command of the police in the district of Warsaw, but also the April 19 liquidation of the ghetto. Stroop was preferred for this role because of his very vast experience, first of all on the Soviet front (from July to October 1941), then in battle against the partisan movement as police commander of the district of Kirovgrad, (from March to June 1942), later as police commander of the district of Nikolayev (from June 1942 to February 1943), and finally as police commander of the district of Galicia.

Stroop arrived in Warsaw on the evening of April 17. Only the next day did Sammern receive the order from Cracow transferring his position to Stroop. That evening Sammern also received a communiqué suggesting that he would encounter armed resistance in the ghetto. Stroop wrote the following on this:

> The German command staff, and first and foremost SS and police commander Colonel von Sammern-Frankeneg, my predecessor who planned the final operation, did not expect any resistance whatsoever. Various partial deportations from the ghetto had been carried out previously. Dr. Sammern believed, therefore, that the course of the final operation would be similar. Only in the evening preceding the start of the action did he get a communiqué telling him that armed resistance could be expected. In spite of the fact that he did not believe in this possibility, he passed the communiqué on to General Krueger, so that he could take the necessary steps.[51]

Stroop was sceptical of Sammern's evaluation, and perhaps had even waited for his predecessor's failure. In spite of the instructions he had received from Krueger, Stroop ordered Sammern to begin the operation in the ghetto. He informed Krueger that, in his opinion, the operation must be initiated by the person who planned it. He was only to go to the area of the operation at nine o'clock.

As was called for in Sammern's plan for the first day of the action, the siege around the walls of the ghetto was to be reinforced by compactly stationed guard patrols, armed with rifles and machine guns. Afterwards, strong *Waffen* SS columns and armor were to break into the central streets of the ghetto, Nalewki and Zamenhof. This show of force was meant to serve as a preamble to the wide-scale round-up and the "pacification" of the ghetto.

At 2 A.M. on the dawn of April 19, the walls of the ghetto were surrounded by reinforced patrols of Germans, Ukrainians, and Latvians. At 2:30, Jewish scouts gave in their first report on the large concentration of German forces in the area of the ghetto. Military alert was declared. At 4 A.M. all the combat groups were in position.

According to the testimony of Simcha Ratheizer, a ZOB member, the first German columns marching in the direction of the ghetto were seen from an observation point at the crossroads of Nalewki and Gesia streets. The Germans were accompanied by an armored truck and troop vehicles. The column was flanked by a group of *Waffen* SS riding on bicycles. The movement of the armored trucks in the direction of the ghetto was also seen from the observation point on Muranowska Street.[52]

At 6 A.M., the dense German columns penetrated the ghetto through its two central streets—Zamenhof and Nalewki. The entrance of the units into the ghetto in dense columns confirms the assumption that Sammern did not expect attacks from positions that were prepared beforehand, but only took into account the possibility of a frontal clash, as was the case in January.

Counter to Sammern's expectations, the rebels' fire came from defense positions prepared on the crossroads of Nalewki and Gesia streets and Mila and Zamenhof streets. The Germans suffered some losses. The column marching along Zamenhof was especially hard hit. The position of the insurgents there was not near the walls of the ghetto, as it was on Nalewki Street, but 350 meters inside the ghetto. Here the rebels let the German column pass towards Muranowski Street. When the *Waffen* SS column came to the crossroads of Mila and Zamenhof, it stopped, not suspecting that an ambush awaited them. The column was meant to divide there in order to simultaneously comb a few streets in this area. The moment the column got ready to divide, four ZOB combat groups opened intense fire on it. At the same time, other combat groups blocked the Germans' escape.

In a report sent on April 20 to General Krueger, Stroop reported the following on this first battle:

> Closing of the ghetto commenced at 0300 hours. At 0600 there was a detailing of the *Waffen* SS (16 officers and 850 enlisted men) to comb out the remainder of the ghetto. The units had hardly begun when a strong

concerted fire attack was opened against them by the Jews and bandits. The tank used in this action and the two heavy armored cars were pelted with Molotov cocktails. The tank was twice set on fire. The enemy's fire attack at first caused a retreat of the acting forces. Losses in the first attack: 12 men (6 SS men and 6 "Trawniki" men).[53]

In this communiqué, as in Stroop's other reports, there are many inaccurate details. First of all, the numbers mentioned by Stroop regarding German losses are doubtful. Secondly, the first sentence of the report suggests that only two *Waffen* SS battalions (an armored Grenadiers' battalion and a cavalry battalion) took part in the first attack on the ghetto, although according to the losses he mentions, it must be assumed that the "Trawniki" battalion, or at least a section of it, also took part in this attack. The rest of the forces were probably employed in surrounding the ghetto.

After the retreat of the German units from the ghetto, Sammern tried to fire on the Jewish positions from a battery that was hastily built on the crossroads of Franciszkanska and Nalewki streets. However, the Germans' fire was not effective because they could not spot the rebels' positions. When the Jewish groups continued to shoot at the German battery, Sammern took his units out after a half-hour fire exchange. He then clearly recognized his mistaken estimate of the situation and saw that a carefully planned uprising was taking place, the very thing he wished to prevent at any cost. Following the failure of his plan, Sammern went to Stroop to inform him of the situation. Stroop himself reports of this:

> I cannot say what happened from the time Sammern entered the ghetto and until the moment he reached my house. The time was 7:30 in the morning when he appeared with his aide. He was nervous and said, "All is lost, we are not inside the ghetto, we cannot even reach the ghetto. There are wounded and dead." Sammern wanted to send a wire to Cracow to send in Stuka planes to destroy the ghetto with bombs. I explained to Sammern that in accordance with the order of Krueger, who was not in contact with the area, I must now intervene in this operation. I explained to him that a request for the aid of the air force was out of the question. I did not imagine that we would not be able to enter the ghetto, as we had the support of the *Waffen* SS, the police, and the security police.[54]

From Stroop's other reports it appears that Sammern was totally dismissed from his post and did not take any part whatsoever in the following operations. He did not join Stroop in the area of the battles.

Stroop arrived in the battle zone at 8 A.M. His first action was the reorganization of the forces and the formation of raid groups whose task was to expel the insurgents from their positions under the support of artillery fire and armored trucks.

At about noon the Nazi units, in their new formations, began a second attack on the positions of the Jewish Fighting Organization at the crossroads of Nalewki and Gesia streets. It is quite probable that Stroop requested the support of the air force that day, in spite of his earlier reservations. According to Edelman's testimony, the air force was already put into action on the first day of the battles, in the vicinity of Gesia Street. It can also be assumed that Stroop made sure his units were reinforced. According to report No. 14g of the Department for Internal Affairs of the Government Delegacy dated April 20, Stroop received twelve armored troop vehicles from the *Wehrmacht*, vehicles that are not mentioned in his reports to Krueger.[55]

After a six-hour battle, the Jewish groups that fought in the Gesia-Nalewki position retreated to Majzels Street. The retreating groups set the German factories and warehouses in the abandoned area on fire. The Germans took over the hospital building at Gesia Street, No. 6, and massacred the patients.[56]

At 4 P.M. the Germans attacked the Jewish Fighting Organization's positions on Muranowski Square. Edelman gives the following description of this battle: "At the same time, fierce battles were going on in Muranowski Square. The Germans were attacking from all sides. The surrounded fighters stubbornly defended themselves, and warded off the attack with superhuman efforts. Two machine guns and many other arms were captured. One German armored truck was burned, the second one that day."[57]

In view of the decisive superiority of the enemy fire, the rebels retreated from this position in the late afternoon. The same day, there were battles in a number of other points in the central ghetto, but none in the brushmakers' quarters or in the area of the Toebbens and Schultz factories.

Stroop reported the following to Krueger on the course of the battles after 8 A.M.:

At about 0800 hours, [there was a] second attack by the units, under the command of the undersigned. Although a small fire attack was reported, this operation succeeded in combing out the blocks of buildings according to plan. We caused the enemy to withdraw from prepared positions on the roofs and the upper stories into the cellars, bunkers, or sewers. While combing out the building, we caught only about 200 Jews.

Immediately afterwards, raiding parties were directed to bunkers known to us, with orders to pull out the Jews and destroy the dugouts. About 380 Jews were captured in this way. It has been stated that the Jews had taken to the sewers. The sewers were completely inundated to make staying there impossible. At about 1730 hours, we encountered very strong resistance from one block of buildings, including machine-gun fire. A special battle group defeated the enemy and invaded that block, but the enemy was not captured. The Jews and criminals resisted from base to base and escaped at the last moment by fleeing across lofts or through underground passages. At about 2030 hours the external cordon was reinforced. All units were withdrawn from the ghetto and dismissed to their quarters. Reinforcement of cordon by 250 *Waffen* SS men.[58]

In all cases like this, there are, of course, differences between the data given by German sources and that of various Jewish and Polish sources. In spite of these differences in the details, we can accurately survey the actions of the first day of the uprising.

The German attack that began at 6 A.M. was successfully warded off by the rebels. This success was made possible by the dense concentration of the German forces and their failure to locate the defense positions of the Jewish combat groups. The grenades and Molotov cocktails used by the rebels were highly effective in a short-range battle against the enemy, who were marching in compact columns.

After their realignment, the German units did not come near the rebels' positions, but shot at them with submachine guns, heavy guns, and perhaps even planes. Under these circumstances, the arms held by the rebels—grenades, Molotov cocktails, and a relatively substantial number of pistols—were not effective. The rebels, who were armed with a very small quantity of submachine guns and with little ammunition, were forced to retreat from the positions they had captured after a battle that had lasted a few hours.

The passive resistance of the residents of the ghetto that day was also effective. It explains the small number of Jews captured for "evacuation" (according to Stroop, a total of 580 people).

The Second Day of the Uprising—April 20, 1943

On the second day of the uprising, battles took place not only in the central ghetto, but also in the brushmakers' quarter, the area of the Toebbens and Schultz factories, and in the forbidden zone, known as "the area between the ghettos." The actions began at 7 A.M. with an attack by German raiding parties, each the strength of a reinforced platoon, on various resistance positions in the central ghetto. The fiercest attacks were directed against the ZZW positions on Muranowska Street. At the same time, from their positions in the area of the Toebbens and Schultz factories, groups of rebels attacked the German columns marching on Leszno and Smocza streets in the direction of the central ghetto. A battle, therefore, ensued for control of the area of the Toebbens factories. At 2 P.M., the Germans opened an attack in the brushmakers' quarter.

The greatest success the Germans had that day was on Muranowska Street. The ZZW groups fighting in this section were forced to retreat from the positions they had captured. One group numbering about twenty people passed through a tunnel it had dug to the "Aryan" side, after retreating from the position it captured while collaborating with a KB unit under the command of Captain Iwanski. This group reached the area of Jozefow near Warsaw, but after having been betrayed, was surrounded by the German gendarmerie and the Polish police. The few survivors who lived through the battle that followed later joined a partisan unit of the Polish People's Army (PAL), which was active in the region of Grojec.[59]

The same day, in the afternoon, the brushmakers' quarter was attacked. In the first of two communiqués concerning that day's battles that Stroop sent to Krueger, Stroop says:

At 0700 hours, raiding parties, each 1/36 strong and consisting of mixed units, were directed to comb out and search the remainder of the ghetto intensively. This search is still in progress; its first objective will be completed by 1100 hours. In the meantime, it has been ascertained that in the part of the ghetto that is no longer inhabited but not yet opened and that contains several armament factories and the like, there are several centers of resistance which hindered the moving of the tank stationed near by. Two raiding parties crushed these centers of resistance and opened the way for the tank's staff. We already have two wounded (*Waffen* SS) to register. The enemy is much more cautious than yesterday, since they have, of course, learned of the allotment of heavy arms.

My intention is to comb out completely the remainder of the ghetto, and then to clean out in the same manner the so-called uninhabited ghetto, which so far has not been opened. It has been ascertained in the meantime that the latter part of the ghetto contains at least 10 to 12 bunkers, some even in armament factories.[60]

In the second report sent that day Stroop states:

The resistance centers found within the uninhabited but unopened part of the ghetto were crushed by a combat group made up of *Wehrmacht* engineers with flame-throwers. The *Wehrmacht* had one wounded in this operation, shot through the lungs. Nine raiding units broke through as far as the northern limit of the ghetto. Nine dugouts were found. Their resisting inmates were crushed and the bunkers blown up. What losses the enemy suffered thereby cannot be ascertained with accuracy. Altogether, the nine raiding units caught 505 Jews today; those among them who were able-bodied were taken for transfer to Poniatowo. At about 1500 hours, I succeeded in bringing about the immediate evacuation of a block of buildings housing the Army Accomodation Office said to be occupied by 4,000 Jews. The German manager was asked to call to the Jewish workers to leave the block of their own will. Only twenty-eight Jews obeyed this request. Thereupon I resolved to evacuate the block by force or to blow it up. The staff of the AA Artillery, using three 2-centimeter-guns, had two men killed. The 10-centimeter Howitzer that also was used expelled the gangs from their strong fortifications and also inflicted losses on them, as far as we are able to ascertain. This action had to be broken off with the onset of night. . . . In one case the bandits had put down mines.[61]

In this communiqué, Stroop openly admits that he did not succeed in taking over the brushmakers' quarter. Actually, the rebels were still holding the whole of the brushmakers' quarter and most of the area around the Toebbens' factories that day, where they succeeded to a marked extent in preventing the Germans from carrying out the evacuation. The Germans, however, succeeded in forcing the rebels to leave all of the defense positions that were set up in the attics of buildings in the central ghetto. Yet they did not manage to crush the combat groups, which (except for the ZZW group that had left the ghetto) succeeded in evading the German raiding units that were combing the ghetto and in setting up new defense positions. The "wild groups" apparently also showed effective resistance.

In summary, the second day of the battles still did not bring the Germans serious results. The number of those captured for deportation was relatively small (505 people according to Stroop; meaning that, on the average, it took four Germans to capture one unarmed person), and the number of bunkers and hideouts destroyed was very small (nine out of the total 631 bunkers destroyed in the course of the entire uprising).

The discontinuation of the battles that evening took some of the pressure off the rebels. Fearing heavy losses in night battles, Stroop took his units out of the ghetto in the afternoon, while reinforcing the outer encirclement. This enabled the rebels to prepare for the next day of fighting.

The Third Day of the Uprising—April 21, 1943

A turning point in the course of the battles came on the third day. Stroop renewed the actions at 7 A.M., holding the main attack in the brushmakers' quarter. After a battle lasting several hours, he reached the conclusion that the operations, which until then had been based on the expulsion of rebels from their defense positions in the buildings, would not bring serious results. The rebels retreated in time from their positions, evaded the German force, and organized new defense points. The noncombatant population of the ghetto showed passive resistance. Under these circumstances, Stroop decided to try a new method—simultaneously burning whole blocks of buildings. This was first carried out in the brushmakers' quarter. This area, and later other sections of the ghetto, were flooded in a sea of flames. The rebels were in a grave situation; with the exception of the few who were well secured against fire, masses of people were forced to leave their hideouts and bunkers. Fire decided the outcome of the battles on that day. Stroop admitted this when he wrote the following in a report to Krueger:

> Start of operation: 0700 hours. The whole of the ghetto has continued to be cordoned off without changes since the start of the operation on April 19, 1943. Inasmuch as the special operation in the block of buildings housing the Army Accomodation Office in the eastern part of the ghetto had to be interrupted yesterday evening with the fall of darkness, one battle group, reinforced by engineers and heavy arms, was again put into action. After having combed out this gigantic block of buildings, which was ascertained to contain an enormous quantity of bunkers and underground passages, about sixty Jews were caught. In spite of all efforts, no more Jews could be caught from the 7,000 to 8,000 who stayed in this block. They retreated nonstop from refuge to refuge through underground passages, firing from time to time. I resolved, therefore, to blow up these passages as far as they were known, and subsequently to set the entire block on fire. Not until the extent of the fire became great did screaming Jews make their appearance. They were deported at once. We had no losses in this operation.
>
> The main body of the forces was detailed to cleanse the so-called uninhabited, but not yet opened part of the ghetto, by proceeding from south to north. Before this action started, we caught 5,200 Jews from the former armament factories and transported them under escort to the loading railway station provided for evacuation. Three search parties were formed, to which special raiding units were attached in order to attack or blow up the bunkers known to us. This operation had to be interrupted when darkness set in, after one-half of the area mentioned was combed out.

Apart from the Jews who were to be evacuated, 150 Jews or bandits were killed in battle, and about 80 bandits were killed by explosion in the bunkers.[62]

The next day Stroop sent a report on the events of the night of April 21 in the brushmakers' quarter:

Setting the block on fire achieved results in the course of the night. The Jews, who despite all search operations still stayed hidden under the roofs, in the cellars, and in other hideouts, ran outside the blocks trying to escape the flames in any way possible. Masses of them—entire families—already aflame, jumped from the windows, or tried to lower themselves down by means of sheets tied together or the like. Steps were taken so that these Jews, as well as the others, were liquidated at once.[63]

From then on, fire became a more serious problem for the fighters and the rest of the population than the actions of the military and police units. "We had to fight not against the Germans, but against the fire," Zivia Lubetkin stresses.[64] Edelman confirms this:

What the Germans could not accomplish, the all-encompassing fire did. Thousands of people are dying in the flames. The smell of burnt bodies is suffocating. Charred bodies are lying on the balconies of houses, window sills, and unburnt stone steps. The fire expels the people from the shelters, forces them to escape from prepared hideouts, from safe hiding places, attics, and cellars. Thousands are wandering around in the yards, awaiting seizure, imprisonment, or direct death at any moment at the hands of the Germans. . . . Hundreds of people are losing their lives by jumping from third or fourth floors. This is how mothers are saving their children from being burnt alive.[65]

Yet even under these circumstances, the rebels in the brushmakers' quarter were looking for additional ways to continue the struggle. Edelman writes on this also:

The fighters do not intend to die in the flames. We are putting all the bets on one stake and deciding to move to the central ghetto at any price. . . . The central ghetto can only be reached by breaching the walls that are surrounded on three sides by the gendarmerie, Ukrainians, and Blue Police. The two-meter-wide passage is guarded by twelve men. Five combat groups must break through here. One after the other, wearing shoes covered with rags to silence their steps, under intense fire and the highest tension, the groups under the command of Gutman, Berlinski, and Greenbaum are going in. They pass. The groups of Yurek

Blones is covering the rear. The moment the first fighters of this group
are out in the street, the Germans floodlight the place. Romanowicz puts
out the reflector with one shot. Before the Germans manage to find
themselves in this situation, we are all on the other side. After uniting
with the local combat groups, we are continuing to act. Great fires often
block whole streets.[66]

All through April 21, whole blocks of buildings in the central
ghettos were aflame. In this part of the ghetto, there was a series of
clashes between the rebels and the Germans on Mila, Niska, Szczes-
liwa, Wolynska, and Pokorna streets. The armed group operating out
of a bunker on Zamenhof Street, No. 20 resisted for several hours.
The fourth announcement issued by the Jewish Fighting Organization that day tells of warding off an attack of the enemy's armored
truck with the aid of Molotov cocktails and of the fire from the German artillery. It seems that the most organized resistance on the third
day of the uprising was that of the combat groups that fought in the
Toebbens area, which until then had not been combed by the Germans or set on fire by them. The above-mentioned ZOB announcement reports a grenade attack on SS columns on Leszno Street. A
ZZW group also attacked the Germans from a position at the crossroads of Nowolipie and Smocza and Nowolipki and Smocza streets.[67]

The Fourth Day of the Uprising—April 22, 1943

On April 22, the flames spread over almost the entire area of the
central ghetto, with the exception of a few blocks probably in the
western part. The conditions under which the rebels were forced to
fight were stated in the fifth announcement of the Jewish Fighting
Organization put out that day:

> The fourth day passed under the sign of the fires which gripped Swieto-
> jerska, Franciszkanska, Wolowa, and Nalewki streets, and in the
> afternoon—Zamenhof Street also. The fires were caused by flame-
> throwers and by the German artillery. The whole day, columns of smoke
> rising from the four streets towered over the entire ghetto. The fires in
> the houses bordering the ghetto walls near Franciszkanska and Swieto-
> jerska streets were burning with immense strength. The streets of the
> ghetto were filled with thick, heavy smoke. It was evident that the
> Germans used this horrifying system of burning the ghetto because they
> saw that by means of armed battles they would not break the resistance
> of the Jewish fighters. They decided to annihilate them with fire.
> Thousands of women and children are burning alive in the houses.
> Terrible cries and calls for help are heard out of the burning buildings.

Flame-enveloped people were seen in the windows of many houses, live torches. The fires did not break the spirit of the Jewish fighters. We are continuing the heroic resistance against the Germans.[68]

Hounded by flames and the artillery and machine-gun fire of the enemy, the combat groups in the central ghetto retreated through underground passages and tunnels in order to break through the combat formations of the German raiding units and to organize new defense positions in the rear, in buildings that were not yet burned. Sporadic battles also broke out in burned buildings in the brushmakers' quarter.

In a report sent to Krueger at 12 o'clock that day, Stroop announced:

> The main body of the units continued combing the buildings in the ghetto that had not been searched yet, progressing from the line we reached yesterday. This operation is still in progress. As on the preceding days, local resistance was broken and the bunkers discovered were blown up. Unfortunately, there is no way of preventing some of the bandits and Jews from staying in the sewers below the ghetto, and it is almost impossible to capture them, now that the flooding has been stopped. The city administration is not in a position to overcome this nuisance. Neither did the use of smoke candles and the introduction of creosote into the water have the desired effect. Cooperation with the *Wehrmacht* is splendid.[69]

In the course of this day, the Germans did not carry out serious attacks in the Toebbens and Schultz area. Because of this, the combat groups in this area tried to attack the Germans, in order to ease the burden of the central ghetto. Edelman writes the following about the battles in this area: "The fighters are in their positions everywhere. In the Toebbens and Schultz area, they are trying first and foremost to disrupt the orderly movement of the German army to the central ghetto. They are throwing grenades from balconies, windows, and roofs and shooting at the vehicles of the SS men."[70]

The rebels' greatest achievement was that most of the fighters survived the four days of fierce battle. Under these bitter circumstances, they still managed to stay in contact with Zuckerman, the representative of the Jewish Fighting Organization on the "Aryan" side. On April 22, instructions were sent to him to send in immediately grenades, bullets, and rifles. The ineffectiveness of the pistols was stressed.

The Fifth Day of the Uprising—April 23, 1943

On the fifth day of the battles, Stroop changed the method of operation in the ghetto. He reached the conclusion that he would not be able to wipe out the rebels by having raiding units move through section by section to comb out the ghetto. Even burning the ghetto did not bring the Germans the desired results.

Stroop's new plan called for the division of the central ghetto into twenty-four sectors. Search parties were assigned to each one of these for the purpose of carefully combing the sector, destroying the defense positions found in it, seizing the people found in hiding, and blowing up the shelters that were discovered. Stroop hoped that this simultaneous operation, covering the entire area of the central ghetto, would enable him to put down the uprising in one day. In a report to Krueger, he stated that all the units under his command received notice of his intention to complete the liquidation of the ghetto that day.[71]

The rebel groups in the central ghetto also changed their tactics that day. In an April 23 letter written by ZOB commander Mordechai Anielewicz to Zuckerman, who was on the Aryan side, we read:

> As of this evening, we are going over to guerrilla warfare. Two of our battle units are going out tonight. They have two tasks: patrol and the acquisition of arms. And know, pistols have no value at all; we hardly used them at all. We need grenades, rifles, machine guns, and explosives. I cannot describe the conditions that Jews are living under to you. Only very exceptional individuals will survive. All the rest will die sooner or later. Our fate has been decided. In all of the bunkers where our fighters are hiding, it is impossible to light a candle at night for lack of air.[72]

Edelman also writes on the change in the rebels' tactics:

> In view of the very different circumstances, the Jewish Fighting Organization is changing its tactics. The battles and clashes are now taking place mostly at night. During the day the ghetto is completely dead. The ZOB patrols meet the German patrols only in very dark streets. The ones who fire first are the winners. Our patrols traverse the entire ghetto. Many die each night on both sides. The German and Ukrainian patrols are made up of large groups; they often set up ambushes.[73]

In spite of the switch, in principle, to night attacks, battles took place during the day also. In his report to Krueger that day, Stroop wrote:

Shots were fired even against the cordoning units from one of the blocks. An attack by a special battle group was ordered, and every building was set on fire in order to smoke the bandits out. The Jews and the bandits held on until the last moment, and then fired on the units. They even shot with carbines. A number of bandits who were shooting from balconies were hit by our men and crashed down.[74]

In the same report, Stroop also mentions an incident in which Molotov cocktails were thrown at a German truck, wounding two policemen who were riding in it. On April 23, the Germans began an intensive attack on the Toebbens and Schultz area. Here again they used the method of setting each building on fire. In response, the Jewish combat groups burned the German warehouses on Pawia and Smocza streets. By the end of that day, the Germans still had not succeeded in crushing all of the defense positions in the buildings in that area.

A ZZW combat group, under the command of Nathan Szulc, that day attempted to blow up the Gestapo building at Zelazna Street, No. 103. The attack did not succeed. The group got into a skirmish with a German unit it encountered, and most of its members were killed.[75]

The Sixth Day of the Uprising—April 24, 1943

Although the focus of the battles was now on night operations, a series of battles at various resistance points in the ghetto took place on the morning of the sixth day of the uprising. Describing the situation in the ghetto, the report written by the Jewish National Committee on April 24 states:

1. Today, the sixth day of a fierce struggle, the ghetto has not yet been taken. The cleansing of the areas captured by the enemy is continuing. In spite of this, the fighters are carrying out a courageous guerrilla battle against the enemy even in these areas, and in several resistance points in the streets, particularly in blocks of houses. The Germans are blowing up these buildings with mines.

2. The consolidated ZOB units which are in contact with each other are assembling in the remaining areas, which are still quite large. The enemy has not yet held a general assault on these areas, which are close to Okopowa and Powazki streets. These sections of the ghetto have remained relatively quiet, except for some small and ineffective clashes between the German units and the fighters. Only in the evening were some incendiary bombs dropped from planes. These set fire to various points in the ghetto (particularly in the area of Muranowska, Gesia, Nalewki, Okopowa). The ghetto is burning. The

fighters, on their part, are setting fire to the German factories and warehouses. Among those burned were the large uniform factories. There were few explosions during the day. The noise of machine guns and artillery is stronger and more frequent between 9 and 11 in the evening.[76]

The night battles which took place on April 24, around blocks of buildings, are also mentioned in Stroop's report. In the report for that day he writes:

Today towards evening, the raiding parties having returned, we attacked a certain block of buildings, situated in the northeastern part of the former ghetto. At 1815 hours, a search and battle group entered the premises, the building having been cordoned off, and found that a great number of Jews were inside the building. Since some of these Jews resisted, I ordered the building set on fire. Not until the street and all the courtyards on either side were aflame did the Jews, some of them on fire, emerge from these blocks. Some tried to save their lives by jumping into the street from windows and balconies, after having thrown down beds, blankets, and the like. Over and over again the Jews kept on firing almost until the end of the action; thus the engineers' group, under machine-gun protection, had to invade the exceedingly strong concrete building towards nightfall. Termination of today's operation, April 25, 1943, at 0145 hours.[77]

All day April 24, fierce battles continued in the Toebbens and Schultz area. Armed rebel groups resisted from positions in buildings on Leszno Street, Nos. 74, 76, and 78; Nowolipie Street, Nos. 23, 67, and 68; and Nowolipki Street, Nos. 21 and 41. In an attempt to repress the resistance, Stroop ordered the entire area set on fire. It soon became a sea of flames, as the brushmakers' quarter and the central ghetto had previously been.

On the sixth day of the uprising, the insurgents tried, as they had tried during the first days of the uprising, to save the noncombatant population from the fire and from being captured by the Germans. On this day, the combat groups under the command of Bryskin and Rotblat, successfully evacuated groups of people from the endangered bunker at Mila No. 19 to a bunker on Mila Street, No. 9.

However, that day brought additional painful losses and suffering to the ghetto residents. On that day Stroop informed Krueger: "1,660 Jews were seized for evacuation. 1,814 were removed from the bunkers. About 300 were shot. A countless number of Jews burned or died in the bunkers. Twenty-six bunkers were blown up.[78]

This kind of progress in the murderous operation led Stroop to believe that he would succeed in completing his operation against the ghetto by April 27. In a report sent to Krueger he wrote: "As far as can be foreseen, the great continuous operation will last until the second day of Easter (April 27)."[79]

The Seventh Day of the Uprising—April 25, 1943

In hope of quickly ending the continuing battles, Stroop again changed his tactics in the ghetto. The main task, this time, was delegated to seven raiding groups numbering seventy men each. Each group was directed to a specific block of buildings which it was to comb again, and in case of resistance, to burn. At the same time, Stroop called in the air force again to drop incendiary bombs on the ghetto. The ghetto soon became a huge sea of flames. In the announcement of the Jewish National Committee on the situation that day, it is said: "Incendiary bombs were again dropped from planes this afternoon. Between ten and twenty fires were seen. Tremendous flames rose above the ghetto in the evening. The Germans are again not letting the firemen do their work. The shooting of heavy howitzers and the blasts of grenades the Germans scatter underneath houses they captured disrupt the threatening silence that prevails on this side."[80]

Stroop also informed Krueger of the "sea of flames seen over the ghetto."[81] In spite of this, the resistance did not stop. In his report to Krueger, Stroop wrote: "Today we again encountered repeated armed resistance. In one bunker we captured three pistols and explosives."[82]

The rebels made desperate attempts to bring in arms and ammunition from the outside, after their ammunition, grenades, and explosives had almost run out. A ZOB group of scouts whose task it was to organize the contacts with the "Aryan" side through the sewer network, encountered the enemy. All the members of this group fell in battle.[83]

The Second Week of the Uprising—April 26 to May 2, 1943

By the end of the first week of battles, the Germans had succeeded in destroying the last defense positions of the rebels, which had been set up in buildings in the ghetto. All the buildings, with the exception of several German factories prepared for evacuation, were set on fire. When the ZOB and ZZW combat groups could no longer hold on above ground, they moved down to underground bunkers, from which they organized attacks against the German forces. Some "wild groups" also continued resisting. Thousands of noncombatant residents tried to continue to hide in bunkers and various shelters still in existence.

During the entire second week of the revolt, battles went on for control of the bunkers. German raiding groups combed the ghetto, day and night, to discover and blow up the bunkers and to capture and kill those living in them. The rebels, on their part, organized attacks in order to disrupt the Germans' actions and inflict losses on the enemy. Desperate resistance with the poorest of means was carried out in bunkers that were discovered.

This fierce, continuous resistance is mentioned in all of Stroop's daily reports. For example, on April 26 he wrote: "Almost all the search parties report resistance, which, however, was broken completely by the fires, or by blowing up the bunkers. 1,330 Jews were taken out of the bunkers and liquidated immediately. 362 Jews were killed in battle."[84] And on April 27, Stroop stated:

> The search parties pulled 780 Jews out of the bunkers and shot 115 Jews who resisted. . . . At 1600 hours a special battle group, made up of 320 officers and men, started cleansing a large block of buildings situated on both sides of Niska Street, in the northeastern part of the former Jewish residential area. After the search, the entire block was set on fire, having been completely cordoned off. In this section, a considerable number of Jews were caught. As always, they remained in the bunkers, which were either below the ground or in the lofts of the buildings, until the end. They fired their arms until the last moment and then jumped down into the street, sometimes from as far up as the fourth floor, but not until the flames made any other escape impossible.[85]

In the report of April 28, he wrote: "We attacked a nest of the Jewish military organization on the border of the ghetto. . . . Today we again encountered strong resistance in many places. We crushed it."[86] And on April 29: "We captured 2,359 Jews from the burning buildings. We killed 106 of them in battle."[87] In the report of April 30, he stated: "We were forced to use artillery in a battle for one of the buildings."[88] And on May 1, he said: "In the operations planned for today, 1,026 Jews were captured, 245 of them were killed in battle or while resisting. The Jews we captured today were all removed from the bunkers by force."[89] In the report of May 2, Stroop wrote: "Seven men were lost when shots were fired on the external cordon, and in the attack of some Jews who broke out from a sewer entrance outside the former ghetto. The scouting parties of the *Waffen* SS which operated during the night sometimes encountered armed resistance from Jews who ventured to emerge from their holes and bunkers under the protection of darkness."[90]

On April 28, the tenth day of the revolt, two telegrams were sent. One was sent by the Coordinating Committee to Zygelboim and Schwarzbart, the second to the Polish government-in-exile in London by the Government Delegacy in Warsaw. In its wire, the Coordinating Committee says:

> This is the tenth day the Warsaw Ghetto is fighting with great courage. The SS and the *Wehrmacht* are closing in on it. The bombardment continues nonstop. Forty thousand Jews are being opposed by artillery, flame-throwers, and incendiary bombs dropped by planes. Resisting blocks of buildings are blown up with mines. Clouds of smoke envelop the city. Women and children are burning alive. The enemy is killing on a massive scale. German guard patrols are stationed near the entrances to the sewers. The fighters are struggling stubbornly. They are inflicting heavy losses on the enemy.[91]

And the Polish Government Delegacy reported: "The ghetto has been courageously fighting since April 19. In spite of the use of artillery and tanks, the ghetto has not been overcome. This new front is disturbing the Germans very much."[92]

The ZOB and ZZW combat groups suffered heavy losses in the battles of the second week of the revolt. The losses of the "wild groups" that resisted were undoubtedly much more serious. The conditions of the struggle in the ghetto grew substantially worse. The rebels' combat groups were forced to carry out isolated attacks. The report of the Jewish National Committee of April 28 speaks of the battle conditions at that time: "The past few days, the battles have acquired a clearly partisan and fragmented character."[93] This report also stresses that aside from the superiority of the enemy's forces, two other factors weakened the power of the rebels: the lack of ammunition and the fires. Under these circumstances, the idea of breaking out of the ghetto and continuing the battle in the partisan movement was brought up. The continuation of the operations in the area of the ghetto was by now almost impossible.

Some of the ZZW combat groups that fought in the central ghetto made an attempt to leave the ghetto on April 27 in collaboration with a Security Corps group under the command of Captain Henryk Iwanski. After a battle lasting several hours, both groups succeeded in escaping the ghetto. However, they were besieged in a block of buildings outside the border of the ghetto, and most of the members of these groups were killed in the battle. In the report he sent to

Krueger on April 27, Stroop writes about a battle outside the ghetto with a group of Jewish insurgents numbering 120 people, who were well armed with guns, rifles, light machine guns, and grenades. According to Stroop, the Germans succeeded in killing twenty-four members of this group and in capturing fifty-two others.[94]

In contrast with this, a Jewish Fighting Organization group's attempt to leave the ghetto on April 29 through the sewer canals, with the aid of the People's Guard, did succeed. The next day the ZOB group was transferred by the People's Guard to the forest of Lomianki near Warsaw.[95]

Independent of the attempts to take groups of fighters out of the ghetto, actions in the area of the ghetto were intensified at the end of the week. On the evening of May 1, ZOB combat groups held a series of attacks against the Germans. That day, the Germans again brought in artillery for the battles with the insurgents, and a large-scale battle was staged between the Nazis and five ZOB combat groups, under the command of Berlinski, Blones, Edelman, Greenshpan, and Gutman, which operated from a bunker on Franciszkanska Street, No. 30. The battle began after the Germans discovered the bunker and lasted for three days, until May 3. Half the members of these groups fell in this battle. The survivors succeeded in escaping and moved their base of attack to a bunker on Franciszkanska Street, No. 22. A few moved to the bunker housing the ZOB headquarters on Mila Street, No. 18.

On May 2, Police and SS commander of the *General Gouvernement* General Krueger, Stroop's direct superior, came from Cracow and visited the area of the Warsaw Ghetto battles.

The Third Week of the Uprising—May 3 to 9, 1943

The battles of the third week of the revolt were different from those of the preceding week. Battles continued over certain bunkers which served as bases for the rebels and as hideouts for the population from the threat of deportation and liquidation. The command of the uprising, ZOB headquarters, existed almost until the end of the week, May 8. The battles were still coordinated to a certain extent and discipline on the whole still prevailed.

In all of his daily reports to Krueger, Stroop writes of the continuing resistance of the rebels in the ghetto. In the report of May 3, we read: "In most cases, the Jews resisted with arms before leaving the bunkers. . . . The Jews and the bandits sometimes fired pistols with both hands. The Jews cannot be induced to leave their bunkers until several smoke candles have been thrown in. . . . Some of the scouting parties operating in the ghetto were shot at last night. . . . These scouting parties reported that groups of armed bandits were marching through the ghetto."[96] In the report of May 4, Stroop writes: "In order to enable the scouting parties to take the Jews by surprise, the scouting parties tie rags and other things around their shoes at night. In skirmishes between the scouting parties and the Jews, thirty Jews were shot."[97] On May 5, he states: "In several places, the Jews again resisted until they were captured."[98] And on May 6: "356 Jews were shot while resisting, and during a skirmish. In this skirmish, the Jews fired from 8-millimeter pistols and other calibers and threw Polish grenades."[99] In the report of May 7, Stroop writes: "A large but unknown number of Jews who refused to leave the bunkers and resisted with arms died in the bunkers when they were blown up."[100] And on May 8:

> The first six days of fighting against the Jews and bandits were hard, but now we must state that we are catching those Jews and Jewesses who were ringleaders in those days. Every time a bunker is opened, the Jews in it offer resistance with the arms at their disposal—light machine guns, pistols, and hand grenades. Today we again caught quite a number of Jewesses who carried loaded pistols in their undergarments.
>
> A total of 1,091 Jews were caught in the bunkers today. About 280 Jews were shot in battle. A countless number of Jews were killed in the forty-three bunkers that were blown up.[101]

Finally, in the report of May 9, Stroop wrote: "319 bandits and Jews were shot in battle."[102]

The continuing battles in the ghetto were also mentioned in the daily reports of the Polish police.[103] The following, for example, was written in the report of May 6: "At the last moment, the Germans ordered the intensification of the guard patrols around the ghetto, and the watch increased to war proportions, because the Jews hiding in the bunkers carry out many guerrilla attacks in the ghetto and outside of it." And in the report of May 7, the police say: "The ghetto seems to have come back to life. Jewish ghosts have come out of the bunkers and dugouts and opened fire again. There is a great number of victims on both sides." In the report of May 8, the following is stated: "In the area of the ghetto and its borders, there is heavy shooting and the noise of explosions. Light antitank artillery is used against cellars, various underground hideouts and bunkers. Victims die on both sides."

The rebels suffered very heavy losses in these battles. Attempts to take combat groups to the partisan movement continued all week. Yet attempts to take combat groups out of the ghetto, which was surrounded by a strong chain of army and police forces, met with great difficulties. Only on May 9 did they succeed. This, however, was one day too late, as it was no longer possible to rescue the ZOB command staff. About 100 Jewish Fighting Organization members, along with the commander, Mordecai Anielewicz, were discovered in the organization's central bunker on Mila Street, No. 18. This was the place from which the fighters carried out attacks against the Germans, and here they awaited the return of emissaries who organized the escape of the ZOB combat groups through the sewers to the partisan movement.

On May 7, the Germans discovered the bunker, and Stroop informed Krueger of this on that day. A battle took place, at the end of which the Germans used smoke candles to force the rebels out. Most of the fighters, along with the commander, Anielewicz, died. Only a few were rescued. This took place on May 8, the twentieth day of the uprising.

The next day, on May 9, a group of ZOB fighters numbering fifty people began a thirty-hour march through the sewers in the direction of Prosta Street. On May 10, at 8 o'clock in the morning, thirty-four fighters came crawling out onto Prosta Street, on the "Aryan" side of the city. Members of the People's Guard and a truck awaited them there. The ZOB fighters were taken to the forest of Lomianki, where they joined the group that had been taken out of the ghetto earlier. The rest of the ZOB fighters in this group did not leave the sewers in time and were killed in battle with the enemy.

Other rebel groups also tried to get out of the ghetto at the end of the third week of the uprising. Some of these succeeded in breaching the encirclement of the ghetto. Because they lacked the proper contacts on the "Aryan" side, however, almost all of the members of these groups fell in clashes with the Germans a short time after leaving the ghetto. Zivia Lubetkin writes on this:

> A few armed groups attacked the German guard near the gate of the ghetto. These groups defeated the German guard units and went through the gate. Most of the groups left the ghetto this way. However, all of our people, with the exception of a few, were killed in the streets on the "Aryan" side because they did not know where to go and had no addresses whatsoever. They were forced to go through streets where the enemy awaited them at every step. All of them were killed in clashes with the Germans.[104]

The ZOB combat groups under the command of Artstein, Gutman, Farber, and Mellon, and a number of "wild groups" remained in the ghetto and continued the battle.

The Last Stage of the Uprising

The combat groups that remained in the area of the ghetto continued to fight even after Anielewicz's death. The Coordinating Committee reports on these battles in a telegram sent to London on May 11, 1943:

> There are still some pockets of resistance left in the heroic struggle of the Warsaw Ghetto. The Jewish Fighting Organization displayed the highest devotion and the spirit of courage. The engineer, Klepfisz, one of the pillars of the armed resistance, died a hero's death. The cruelty of the Germans is terrifying. Many Jews were burned alive. Thousands were shot or transferred to camps. The leaders of the Judenrat were shot: Lichtenbaum, Wielikowski, Stulman, and Stanislaw Szereszewski. Thousands still remain underground and in the workshops of the ghetto. The shops, and particularly the shelters, are being liquidated in the midst of passive and active resistance. The Germans are setting fire to blocks of buildings, one after the other, and blowing them up with mines and bombs. There are echoes of explosions, and fires. The ghetto continues to be surrounded by the gendarmerie, as are the entrances to the sewers. Those escaping from the hell of the ghetto are captured and shot on the spot. The Jewish Fighting Organization continues to exist in the ghetto. Its heroism is coming to its end. . . .[105]

In his reports to Krueger, Stroop also writes about this period. On May 10, he reports: "The resistance offered by the Jews has not been weakened today. In contrast with the previous days, it seems that those members of the main Jewish combat group, who are still alive and have not been liquidated, have returned to the ruins still within their reach with the intention of shooting the acting detachments and inflicting casualties on them."[106] On May 13, Stroop writes: "When we captured one bunker, a real skirmish took place, in which the Jews not only fired from 8-millimeter pistols and Polish Vis pistols, but also threw Polish "pineapple" hand grenades at the *Waffen* SS men."[107] On May 14, he reports: "The night patrols clashed with armed bandits several times. These bandits fired a machine gun and small arms. . . . A total of 398 Jews were caught today, and 154 Jews and bandits were shot in battle."[108] In the same report, Stroop tells of his visit in the afternoon to the area of operations of *Waffen* SS General von Herff.

On May 15, Stroop determined that the mission of liquidating the

THE RESULTS OF THE UPRISING

The Germans had losses both in personnel and in certain materials in the Warsaw Ghetto uprising. However, it is difficult to reach an accurate estimate of those losses. In a report to Krueger, Stroop mentions sixteen dead and ninety wounded. Polish and Jewish sources give other numbers. For example, an AK intelligence report from the end of April 1943 states: "In the first two days of battle the following losses were caused: The German units—about 60 dead and wounded, the Polish police—12 wounded."[115] According to a PPR intelligence report from April: "The German losses in the first two days totaled 150 dead, and by the Friday before the holiday [April 23], they had 700 dead and wounded."[116]

These numbers are closer to the ones mentioned by the Jewish National Committee and the Bund in a telegram and a letter sent to New York and London. In a telegram to the Joint Distribution Committee in New York, dated May 15, 1943, the Jewish National Committee said: "The Jewish fighters killed over 300 Germans, and wounded about 1,000."[117] And in a letter from the Bund representative in London dated June 22, 1943, it is said: "The German losses total over 1,000 dead and wounded. Great material damages were caused to the factories serving the German war industry, which were destroyed and burnt by the Jewish Fighting Organization."[118]

On the basis of this information, the Polish historian Waclaw Pateranski estimates that in the first ten days of fighting, the Germans had 400 dead and over 1,000 wounded.[119] There is no doubt that these numbers are exaggerated. It is impossible to believe that the rebels could have caused such great losses with the poor and meager arms they held. It is also impossible to believe that the units under Stroop's command could have continued the battle in the ghetto had their losses really been this heavy. The real losses caused to the German force were probably only somewhat greater than those mentioned by Stroop.

But in any case, German losses should not be viewed as the main result of the uprising. The fact that the Germans were forced to carry out extended battles in a center as large and important as Warsaw is much more decisive. The resistance of the Jewish units—as described by AK commander General Stefan Rowecki—was "unexpectedly strong and surprised the Germans."[120] Rowecki said this in a report for the period of April 24 to May 7, which was sent to the Polish government-in-exile in London. In a later report for the period of May 8 to May 14, General Rowecki said: "The continuation of the resistance for such a long time is viewed as a disgrace by certain German circles."[121]

The duration of the battle in the Warsaw Ghetto is the main reason that there was a wide response to the uprising throughout Poland and also beyond. This response was intensified by the very fact that the revolt broke out in a ghetto, which in reality was a concentration camp. Because of this, the Warsaw Ghetto uprising had a very real influence not only in stimulating the resistance in other ghettos and camps, but also in encouraging the activity of the Polish underground. This more tangible result of the Warsaw Ghetto uprising was best described by the Polish military historian, General Jerzy Kirchmayer:

> The defense of the Warsaw Ghetto ended, but the idea of an armed struggle, in whose name this battle was held, broke through the walls of the ghetto, continued to exist, and remained so until the victory. It was brought to the forests by those who escaped from the ghetto and joined various partisan units. Since the April revolt, we have met Jews in almost all of the units in the forest, and they are very daring and ready for an armed battle. On the other hand, the idea of an armed struggle penetrated the hearts of many Poles who witnessed it in the in the area of Zamosc or in the Warsaw Ghetto. The military significance of the Warsaw Ghetto Uprising lies first of all in the response it received from the Polish public.[122]

Another important result of the Warsaw Ghetto uprising was pointed out by the Polish underground journal *Gwardia Ludowa (Freedom-Equality-Independence)*, the paper of the Socialist organization. In issue number 4 of May 1943, an article titled "The Struggle of the Warsaw Ghetto" said: "The Jews of Warsaw revealed to us what may possibly be the most important truth about the weakness of the Germans. Because of this, we will learn from the experience of Warsaw's Jews in our next armed struggle in Poland."

This uprising was significant to the development of the resistance in Poland. It must be remembered that the Warsaw Ghetto uprising was the first large armed revolt in Central Europe. The Warsaw Ghetto was also the first quarter of a large city in the occupied countries from which the Germans were expelled, even for a short time, the first to wave the banner of revolt, and the first into which the Germans could not enter. This very real fact was emphasized by the PPR bulletin *Gwardzista* of May 20, 1943, in an article titled "The Fighting Ghetto": "The heroic resistance of the Warsaw Ghetto has been going on for a month. This is the largest and longest act of armed resistance in the occupied lands (not including Yugoslavia, where the battles have the character of a revolt)."

Another direct result of the uprising was the escape of a number of rebels from the ghetto. They continued the struggle in the partisan movement, first and foremost as part of the Anielewicz unit in the forests of Wyszkow.

The results of the uprising exceeded by far the expectations of the commanders of the resistance movements in the Warsaw Ghetto. The revolt lasted longer than could have been foreseen. The fear of Mordecai Anielewicz, that no one would know where the fighters were buried, did not come true. This tragic and unique revolt sent waves throughout the whole world, and the name of the young commander has entered history and will still be remembered when the names of many other distinguished division, corps, and even army commanders of World War II probably will be forgotten.

And yet, the uprising did not diminish the scope of the annihilation of the Jews of Warsaw. There were too few survivors among the last Jews of the ghetto to make it possible to conclude that the uprising increased the chances for survival. What the Warsaw Ghetto uprising did offer was the chance for death in battle instead of the inevitable death in the gas chambers. This possibility would not have been available without the supreme efforts made to organize and equip the resistance forces under conditions of isolation, hatred, and cruel persecution—under ghetto conditions.

The results of the Warsaw Ghetto uprising would never have been achieved if it had not been for the possibility of arming the ghetto with weapons, which, although few, were enough to force battle on the Germans. The lack of weapons was the main reason an armed resistance was not offered during the deportation from the Warsaw Ghetto in the summer of 1942. Had larger quantities of arms been supplied to the Jewish military organizations in the ghetto, the results of the uprising might have been even more serious.

CHAPTER 11
ARMED RESISTANCE IN OTHER GHETTOS

CONDITIONS FOR PLANNING ARMED UPRISINGS IN THE smaller ghettos were very different from those in the Warsaw Ghetto. Only in Warsaw was it possible to prepare an extensive underground network of passages and bunkers, without which it would have been impossible to consider resistance for a period of several weeks to an enemy with such vast military superiority. Nowhere else could a few hundred fighters in concealed hideouts maintain a state of military alert, rendering any surprise operation by the Germans impossible.

Efforts made by the Jewish Fighting Organization in Czestochowa, the second largest ghetto in the *General Gouvernement*, had the same objectives as in Warsaw. Similar political and propagandist preparations were made here and the structure of the Jewish Fighting Organization in the Czestochowa Ghetto was similar to that in Warsaw. The attempts to acquire and produce arms and to establish contacts with the Polish underground were also the same. But the small size of the Czestochowa Ghetto was the major factor preventing large-scale building of secret bunkers and underground passages. It was also impossible to keep armed groups in a state of military alert, ready to act at any moment, without the Germans' knowledge, and this, apparently, was the reason that, despite serious preparations, there was no revolt, but only sporadic resistance in one bunker.

The Jewish Fighting Organization in the Cracow Ghetto dismissed from the start the idea of armed resistance in the ghetto; it moved its operations outside to the Aryan side of the city, and later out of Cracow altogether.

In the other small ghettos, the active underground movements worked in two basic directions: first, toward consolidation, in most cases around one point of resistance, and second, toward transferring organization members to the partisan movement. In several cases, the two strategies were combined.

Armed resistance movements in several ghettos developed—to a large extent—under the influence and even the leadership of the resistance movements in the Warsaw Ghetto. Activity was carried out by the Jewish Fighting Organization. Despite extreme difficulties, some ties existed with the leadership of the Jewish Fighting Organization in Warsaw. At the same time, independent fighting organizations, not necessarily affiliated with specific political groups, were formed in several ghettos.

Following is a brief survey of the armed resistance organizations in the ghettos outside of Warsaw.

THE JEWISH FIGHTING ORGANIZATION IN CZESTOCHOWA

As in the Warsaw Ghetto, the underground political organizations in the Czestochowa Ghetto tried to form a unified fighting body as early as 1941. Here also, objective conditions made it possible to establish this kind of organization only after the deportation of the summer of 1942, when the ghetto shrank to a great extent and actually turned into a forced labor camp.

Representatives of several underground organizations first met to discuss the formation of a fighting force as early as August 1941, but the session had no tangible results. Meetings continued through the winter of 1941–1942, but a consensus on armed resistance as a basis for a common plan of action did not reach the practical stage because of the mass arrests of underground activists on April 30, 1942. Nevertheless, the contacts continued between several political organizations (Left Poalei Zion, the General Zionists, the Bund, and the communists).[1]

Besides their participation in attempts to form a unified fighting organization in the Czestochowa Ghetto, the communists tried to transfer their members to the partisan movement affiliated with the Polish Workers Party (PPR). In May 1942, five people were chosen to leave the ghetto and join the first unit of the People's Guard (GL), which had been established then and which planned to initiate partisan activity in the area of Tomaszow Mazowiecki. The communist group from the ghetto was to meet the Polish emissaries near the Jewish cemetery in the Zawodzie neighborhood. But the Poles did not appear because the above-mentioned GL unit (under the command of Franciszek Zubrzycki), had meanwhile been defeated, soon after its first attempted partisan action. The Jews, waiting in vain for the emissaries from Zubrzycki's unit, were surprised by a German *Schutzpolizei* unit. All of them died in the short skirmish that followed, along with a German policeman.[2]

The liquidation action which began on September 23, 1942, continued until October 5. The Germans deported about 39,000 people to the extermination camp in Treblinka and killed about 2,000 others on the spot, mainly for offering passive resistance. Most of the leaders and the members of the underground organizations were killed in the ghetto or in Treblinka. The ghetto shrank into a forced labor camp of about 6,500 people, including 1,000 "illegals," Jews who had no German work certificates and, therefore, no right to live.

Underground members who survived renewed the efforts to establish a fighting organization, and at the end of November 1942, after a series of meetings, the Jewish Fighting Organization in Czestochowa was established. Mordechai Zylberberg ("Mojtek") was appointed commander and Sumek Abramowicz second-in-command. The basic cell numbered five people. At first, the fighting organization in Czestochowa included 70 people, but in the following few months it grew to number 300 members.[3]

One of the new organization's first tasks was to collect money for arms acquisition. Heniek Wojdyslawski, a member of the group stationed at Nadrzeczna Street, No. 66, known as "Group 66," recalls: "The group's efforts were first of all directed at purchasing arms, which no organization outside the ghetto could supply. Any valuables each person still had from home and all the profits from the sale of food were directed towards this objective. . . . "Group 66" lived in great poverty, eating only dry black bread, and often little of that. Yet the group acquired two guns."[4]

Money for arms was acquired in two ways: by taxation of the few ghetto residents who still had some means at their disposal and by the secret sale of goods taken out of warehouses on Garibaldi Street, where the Germans stored the belongings of the Jews they deported.

Efforts to obtain arms on the "Aryan" side involved sacrifices. Mietek Ferleger, commander of "Group 66," was the first to leave the ghetto for this purpose. At the end of December 1942, he was arrested by a *Bahnschutz* policeman (from the railroad service) close to the place where he was supposed to receive the arms that had been bought. Ferleger knocked over the policeman and ran away. But he was chased and captured by the Germans, who shot him to death after twenty-four hours of torture. Following his death, Yaakov Ripstein commanded "Group 66."[5]

Some time later the organization's emissary "Zoska" (last name unknown), who transferred arms from Warsaw to Czestochowa, was killed. Returning to Czestochowa, she noticed that a detective had been following her from Warsaw and knew that he would probably turn her over to the Germans. Zoska attacked him, but was surrounded by German police who were called in; she was killed in the fight with them. Three more of the organization's members (Silberberg, Kantor, and Renia Lenczner) were surprised by the Gestapo near Czestochowa in the Kamionka Quarter the moment they were to receive arms that had been bought. They wounded several Germans, and Silberberg and Kantor managed to break out and return to the ghetto. Renia Lenczner, who was seriously wounded, fell into the hands of the Germans. She was killed after being tortured by the Gestapo.[6]

Efforts were made to produce arms by the primitive means that were available. Chemicals were obtained from the Judenrat's pharmacy and used to produce Molotov cocktails. This was done by the amateur chemist Kaufman and by Heniek Wiernik.

Earthworks were also begun. Two underground passages were dug, by groups numbering a hundred people, working in three shifts. Laborers included youths who did not belong to the Jewish Fighting Organization, but willingly followed all instructions of its command staff.

The Czestochowa Ghetto organization had fairly close ties with the Jewish Fighting Organization in Warsaw. Its emissaries and particularly Itzhak Windman ("Lala") went to Warsaw several times and brought back arms acquired with the aid of the ZOB leadership in Warsaw.

A turning point in the history of the Czestochowa organization came during January 1943, with the first, unsuccessful, attempt at armed resistance. All Jews in the ghetto were ordered to Ryneczek Square, where it was understood that a new selection for deportation was to be made. Only one of the organization's command staff, Mendel Fiszlewicz, was in the ghetto along with a small group of members. All the others were at work outside the ghetto.

Fiszlewicz and his comrades were faced with the dilemma of whether to hide or to go to Ryneczek Square and resist the deportation as was expected. They had no arms except Fiszlewicz's one pistol and Itzhak Feiner's knife. The few other arms the organization had at the time were taken by members who had tasks outside the ghetto. Nevertheless, Fiszlewicz decided to go to the square.

When the members of the organization came to the square, the selection process was already under way. German gendarmes immediately surrounded the group and forced its members to stand in the row of Jews selected for deportation. Fiszlewicz attacked the commander of the action, Lieutenant Rohn, wounding him in the hand with his pistol. But after the first shot, Fiszlewicz's pistol stopped working. At that moment, Feiner attacked Rohn's deputy, Lieutenant Soport, with his knife. The gendarmes opened fire. Fiszlewicz was killed, and Feiner was seriously wounded. The Germans then took twenty-five men out of the lines and shot them on the spot. Afterwards, they took 300 people under heavy guard to the police station, among them all the fighters who went to the square with Fiszelwicz. The next day, this group was moved to Radomsko, where the final deportation of the remaining Jews was then being carried out.

The members of the organization's command, who had been working outside the ghetto and returned only in the evening, decided to rescue the people in Radomsko. Windman and Lustiger were sent, but succeeded in rescuing only a few women, who returned to Czestochowa. Most of the deported members of the organization were shot while jumping off the train, or captured and killed on their way back to Czestochowa.[7]

There are parallels between the action in Czestochowa on January 4, 1943, and the events in the Warsaw Ghetto during January 18–21. In both cases, part of the population was deported to the extermination camp in Treblinka. And in both Czestochowa and Warsaw, the fighting organizations were faced with the immediate decision of whether to resist. In Czestochowa, more than in Warsaw, the events betrayed the weakness of the fighting organization and the lack of preparation. In both cities, the commanders of the fighters reached the necessary conclusions. In Warsaw the experience acquired in the January battles led to the concentration of the combat groups and the maintenance of a constant state of alert. Thus, the battle which broke out on the morning of April 19, 1943, was a surprise to the Germans and not to the Jewish fighters.

Such a development was out of the question in the Czestochowa Ghetto. Its small area made it impossible to maintain large underground groups of fighters ready for the renewal of the deportations. In spite of this, the commanders of the organization in Czestochowa did not give up plans for active resistance to the deportations. They understood how slim the chances were to organize a battle, let alone survive it. Therefore, they also made plans for a transition to partisan activities in the surrounding area, or to sabotage actions outside the ghetto, on the "Aryan" side of the city, without abandoning the idea of resistance in case of another deportation. Efforts made by the Czestochowa organization to establish partisan units were discussed in the chapter dealing with the Jewish partisan movement in the area of Kielce.

Of the sabotage acts carried out by the Czestochowa organization outside the ghetto, the best known is the one of April 22, when a group of Jewish fighters sabotaged a railway track near the city.

On June 25, 1943, the Germans unexpectedly began the final liquidation of the ghetto. The population and even the organization were completely taken by surprise. The Germans transported the labor groups to various points outside the ghetto. Some members of the fighting organization went with the workers, but most remained in the ghetto. At about 12 o'clock, it became known that the deportations would probably be renewed. The organization's command staff immmediately ordered an "alert." The few arms were distributed, and all the fighters went down to their positions in the bunkers.

At 3 o'clock, they learned that the workers had returned to the ghetto. If a deportation was planned, the Germans would most likely have seized them at once. Since no one was seized, confidence that there would not be a deportation that day took hold, the alert was canceled, and the fighters left their positions. In Bunker No. 1 only the organization's commander Mordechai Zylberberg, who was ill then, and Lutek Glickstein, who was guarding the arms storehouse, remained.

At about 4 o'clock, a rather unusual hour, the Germans suddenly began rounding up people. The houses on Nadrzeczna Street, Nos. 66, 86, and 90, the main positions of the Jewish Fighters Organization—were cut off under heavy fire. The surprised members of the organization, who had just left their positions, tried in vain to return to the bunkers and seize their arms. Only twenty succeeded in reaching the arms storehouse and firing at the last moment. Most were killed by German bullets, when the entrance to the underground passage housing the arms storehouse was assaulted.

The resistance offered by the few fighters who did manage to reach the bunkers was broken by the strong German fire. Thirty grenades, eighteen pistols, and two rifles were captured. Of the defenders only Lutek Glickstein succeeded in escaping the bunker. Another group, which defended the entrance to the underground passage on Garnacarska Street, No. 40, also survived the first battle. They went through the passage and barricaded themselves in a nearby house, intending to escape the next day to the surrounding forests and establish a partisan unit. Only a few succeeded. Six fighters under the command of Rivka Glanc, who had only two pistols and one grenade, were cut off by the German police. All of its people fell in the uneven clash. This was the last battle of the Jewish fighters in the Czestochowa Ghetto.[8]

THE JEWISH FIGHTING ORGANIZATION IN CRACOW

The founders and activists of the resistance movement in Cracow saw no possibility whatsoever of planning a serious resistance within the ghetto. Therefore, the Cracow organization shifted its armed operations almost from the very beginning to the "Aryan" side of the city and to the surrounding forests. After mass arrests and the fall of most fighters, the remaining ZOB members continued their activity in the Plaszow concentration camp. Thus the activities of this organization continued, in various contexts—in the ghetto, in the "Aryan" part of the city, in the forest, and in a concentration camp.

The main element of the Cracow resistance movement was made up of members of the Akiba youth movement headed by Shimon Drenger, Gusta Drenger, and Abraham Leibowicz. Before World War II, Shimon Drenger had been the editor of the *Divrei Akiba* journal, published in Cracow. Together with his wife, Gusta, he came to Wisnicz at the end of 1941. In December 1941, at the nearby Kopaliny farm, they founded a training farm where members of "Akiba" worked. This training group became the core of the fighting organization.[9]

A second underground group in the Cracow Ghetto was made up of members of other organizations, particularly Hashomer Hatzair, the communists, and a socialist group that for some time had been in contact with the Polish Socialist Party.[10]

In October 1942, after a period of negotiations, a unified Jewish fighting organization was founded, which at the end of the year numbered 100 members. The chosen command staff included Hesiek Bauminger, Aharon (Adolf) Libeskind, Gola Mira, Leibowicz, Binyamin Halbereich, and Shimon Drenger. The organization was divided into three combat groups headed by Libeskind, Adek Lipszyc, and Yosef Lewinger.

Countless efforts were devoted to making contact with Jewish resistance organizations in other places. Regular ties existed for a long time with Tomaszow Mazowiecki, Tarnow, Rzeszow, Przemysl, and Bochnia, the commanders of the Jewish underground in Warsaw.

Efforts were also made to form ties with the Polish underground. A joint meeting of the Polish and Jewish socialists took place at the end of 1941. However, in this meeting, the representatives of the Polish socialists spoke against aid to the ghetto, because of the dangers involved. The Jewish socialists walked out in protest.[11]

In 1942, Jewish communists who were active in the ghetto made contact with the Polish communists, accepted the command of the Polish Workers Party, and were even officially called the 14th Unit of the PPR, Krakow-Podgorze. When the Jewish communists later joined the Jewish Fighting Organization, they passed their contacts with the Polish communists on to its command staff.[12]

As in Warsaw and Czestochowa, the most pressing task in Cracow was the acquisition of arms. The first two pistols were bought with great difficulty, and it was decided to employ them in combat without delay. At the end of October 1942, a group of six ZOB members were sent from the Cracow Ghetto to the partisan movement in the region of Rzeszow. The group was armed with only two pistols and one knife. The group had neither bases nor contacts in the area. Gusta Drenger writes about the group's first action:

> When our group of five [this is a mistake, the group numbered six people] came to the village, a rumor spread in the surrounding area that a unit numbering 300 armed rebels was in the forests. It is not known who spread these rumors; it was as if they spread by themselves. Fear fell upon the area, and because of this, we were soon betrayed. The peasants wanted to prevent acts of terror and hurried to inform on us. The hunt lasted two days. The forest was heavily surrounded, but no one dared to penetrate it deeply. They shot from rifles in all directions. The noise of the shooting continued nonstop, until the gendarmes grew tired, and admitted they had enough and that they were on the enemy's track. The hunt ended.[13]

Although the first ZOB partisan group survived this hunt without losses, it was apparent that it was impossible to continue the actions in that area because of the hostile stand of the local population. Some time later there was an unexpected clash with the Germans. All the members of the group, with the exception of Zygmunt Maller, fell. Two German gendarmes were also killed in this skirmish.

During the same period, the fall of 1942, many partisan groups arose spontaneously from among the Jewish population who had escaped in mass to the forests during deportations to the extermination camps and went to the forests of the district of Cracow. There is almost no information on the fate of these groups, but they were undoubtedly all wiped out in the large-scale hunts undertaken by the Germans.

After the tragedy that struck the first Cracow ZOB partisan group and the large-scale hunts against the independent Jewish groups in the surrounding forests, the leadership of the Cracow organization concluded that it must temporarily give up partisan activity from bases in the forests. A new type of struggle evolved—striking at German targets on the "Aryan" side of the city, after which the Jewish fighters returned to the ghetto. The fighters returned to the ghetto because it was proved that the "Aryan" side could not serve as a permanent base for the Jewish underground fighters; only the ghetto was a "natural" base for the Jewish fighters, for there they could hide between operations.[14]

On the basis of documents we have, it is possible to list the combat actions of the Cracow organization, carried out outside the ghetto between November and December 1942:

1. Sabotage of the Cracow-Bochnia railway line, which caused a train to run off the track
2. A raid on the Optima clothing storehouse, from which a certain amount of German uniforms and shoes were taken
3. An attack on a railway warehouse on Wroclawska Street
4. The killing of a German gendarmerie corporal on Starowisnia Street
5. The killing of an SS man on the esplanade near Karmelicka Street
6. The killing of a German soldier on the esplanade near Sebastian Street
7. The killing of a German pilot in the Blonie quarter
8. The killing of two Gestapo detectives in a beer hall on Golenbia Street
9. The killing of a senior clerk of the German administration
10. The burning of the military barracks of the "Todt" organization in the Grzegorska quarter[15]

In the course of these operations, the organization acquired additional firearms, and could now plan serious attacks. The most important of these took place on December 22. Grenades were thrown at the Cyganeria coffee house in the center of the city, which was a regular meeting place for German officers. According to Polish data, eleven Germans were killed in this action, and thirteen were wounded.

Soon after the Cyganeria operation, the Germans succeeded in tracking down the Jewish organization. At the end of December, about twenty people were arrested in Cracow. Some time later, another ten were arrested in Bochania, and still later another six or seven Hashomer Hatzair members were caught in Cracow.[16] On December 15, 1942, a communiqué concerning the first arrests was sent to SS *Obergruppenfuehrer* Wolf in Hitler's command staff. This communiqué says:

> During the searches for the well-known terrorist Abraham Leibowicz, a couple of Jews were found in a hideout: Adolf Libeskind, born on 3.10.1912 in Zabieszow, the county of Cracow, now residing in the Cracow Ghetto, Limanowski Street, 18/19; and Yehuda Tennenbaum, born on 16.8.1920 in Cracow, now living in the Cracow Ghetto, on Krakusa Street, 17/20. After an intense exchange of fire, both were shot. The hideout was found in the cellar of a building housing only German clerks. The Jews were disguised as Poles and held false identity cards *(Kennkarten)*. The Polish housekeeper allowed them to enter the building in exchange for a large sum of money. The following were found in their hideout:
>
> A Mauser pistol, no. 182890, 7.65 caliber
> A Mauser pistol, no. 201999, 7.65 caliber
> A Polish Vis pistol, no. 19063, 9 mm. caliber
> 54 bullets for a 7.65 caliber gun
> A radio receiver
> One typewriter . . .[17]

Hannah Spitzer, Hannah Sternlicht, and Springer were killed in other places while offering resistance during arrest. Other members of the organization were taken to prison in Montelupich. The wave of arrests brought a temporary halt to the activity of the organization in Cracow.

In April 1943, the Montelupich prisoners were transferred to the Plaszow concentration camp. On the way, the prisoners attacked their German escort in an attempt to escape. A few, including Leibowicz, were killed in the skirmish, and others were taken to Plaszow. A few of the fighters, among them Shimon Drenger, Gusta Drenger, and Gola Mira, succeeded in escaping. The first two fled while wounded.[18]

The escapees tried immediately to renew their activities. Margot Drenger, who was hiding in Bochnia, explains that on May 1, she met Shimon and Gusta Drenger in the street. The two still had wounds (they had been shot in the legs) from their escape from the transport. Margot Drenger brought them to one of the bunkers that had been prepared in the vicinity of Wisnicz. In addition, Margot Drenger testifies:

It is quite likely that they would have survived the war. However, a short time afterwards, they began again with partisan activity. They put out a bulletin, organized actions, and mainly transferred arms from Cracow to Warsaw. They fell while carrying out one of these missions. It is not known when or under what circumstances they were captured and killed.[19]

Shimon and Gusta Drenger gathered around them all the survivors who fled the Cracow Ghetto during its liquidation in March 1943. Under exceedingly difficult circumstances, they initiated partisan actions in the area of Bochnia-Wisnicz, aided by Maria Pazda, a Polish woman who lived not far from Plaszow.[20]

The renewal of partisan activity by the Cracow Jewish organization aroused a negative reaction among the local Polish population. Aside from the Polish Workers Party, which was weak and lacked influence in this area, there was no Polish underground organization there that sought armed actions against the Germans. Conflict between the Jewish partisans and the Home Army soon broke out. A serious incident took place in September 1943 on Yom Kippur eve. As a result of betrayal by one of the peasants, a Jewish hideout was discovered in the village of Tymow. A group of partisans belonging to the Cracow ZOB unit went to the village to punish the informer. The group included Shimon Drenger, Yechiel (Chilek) Wojdyslawski, his brother Yochanan, and the two Kaufer brothers. The operation was not successful. Chilek Wojdyslawski was seriously wounded and died two days later.

Local AK groups under the command of Mikulski began murdering Jews in hiding. This led to reprisals by Jewish "wild groups" still in the area, and by the Cracow ZOB partisans.

Remnants of the Cracow Jewish Fighting Organization held on until the summer of 1944, although they carried out very limited combat actions. On September 7, a unit went out to burn the house of a priest who had preached to his congregation that Jews still hiding in the forests must be exterminated. This triggered a very sharp reaction by the local AK groups. Surviving members of the Jewish organization had built a new base in a bunker in the Kamionna hills. The local forest watchman, Kaczmarczyk, discovered the partisans' hideout and called in a German hunt. In the battle that followed, Mina Najgurt and Lewkowicz were killed.

Some time later the surviving partisans of the Cracow ZOB were surprised by an unexpected assault from local AK groups, in which eight or ten Jewish partisans were killed. The survivors, who saw no way to continue their activity, decided to make the dangerous attempt to cross the border to Slovakia, and from there to Hungary. The attempt succeeded, and the fighters of the Cracow Jewish Organization continued their underground activity in Budapest within the framework of the "Hanoar Hazioni," after merging with the survivors of Bedzin's organization.[21]

THE FIGHTING UNDERGROUND IN THE RADOM GHETTO

Attempts made in the Radom Ghetto to establish a united Jewish fighting organization did not succeed. Instead of a united fighting organization, based on affiliation with a specific political organization, the underground groups formed in Radom were based on the personal ties and mutual trust among schoolmates, neighbors, and relatives. One of such groups, headed by the Bornstein brothers (Zalman, Leib, and Yona), was formed immediately after the first large deportation from the Radom Ghetto in August 1942, when more than 30,000 people were sent for extermination. Only 4,000 Jews were left.

The first steps taken by the group were aimed at finding contacts with representatives of the Polish underground, whose aid was expected for arms acquisition and finding a base for partisan actions in the area. The group did not intend to engage in armed resistance within the ghetto.

Their first contact was a Pole who worked in an armament factory in Radom, who promised to supply four pistols, at 4,000 *zloties* each. But Bronowski betrayed the group. Instead of delivering pistols to the ghetto, he put a box containing rocks in the appointed place on Walowa Street. After this, contact was made with Abelski, a Polish communist and a former prisoner of the Bereza-Kartuzka camp (a concentration camp for political prisoners in prewar Poland). Abelski promised to help the Radom group obtain arms and establish ties with the Polish partisan movement. The Bornstein brothers also reached a Polish socialist party activist, Maciejszczyk, from whom they received underground newspapers and the promise of help in making more connections. The organization acquired some weapons through these two contacts and also succeeded in stealing four pistols from the SS arms storehouse.

Having established ties with Abelski, part of the Bornstein group left the Radom Ghetto, which was by then, the end of October 1942, a forced labor camp, for the Swietokrzyskie mountains where they planned to begin partisan actions. However, they found no Polish partisans there, in spite of Abelski's information. Furthermore, the Germans conducted a large hunt in the Swietokrzyskie mountains in which a large number of local people took part, and in which several of the organization's members were killed. Nevertheless, the survivors still tried to establish a partisan base here. Suddenly they were attacked by unidentified armed Polish groups, and another five Jewish fighters were killed. Discouraged by the hostile attitude of the local population, the survivors decided to return to the ghetto. It appears that after the failure of this attempt, no important actions were carried out by the survivors of the Bornstein group.

In addition to this group, there were loose underground youth groups in the Radom Ghetto, which tried to find ways to carry out an active armed struggle. One of them, under the command of Noah Szlaperman, was mentioned in the testimony of Dr. Weinapel, a former prisoner in the Radom Ghetto, but we have no further information on the activity of this or the other small youth groups in Radom.[22]

ARMED UNDERGROUND IN THE SMALL GHETTOS

What typified the underground in small ghettos such as Wlodawa, Zelechow, Radzyn, Markuszow, Kamionka, Dzialoszyce, Iwaniska, and Rzeszow was preparation for the formation of partisan units in the surrounding areas. This was due to the proximity of the forests and to the clear understanding that it was totally impossible to carry out armed resistance in the ghettos themselves. Since almost all the activity of these organizations centered on preparations for partisan actions, the basic facts of which have been discussed in previous chapters, we shall limit ourselves here to a brief description of the organization of resistance in these ghettos.

Wlodawa

The first group in Wlodawa was organized by Moshe Lichtenberg, apparently as early as September 1942. This group succeeded in acquiring and smuggling a quantity of arms into the ghetto and preparing a base for partisan actions in the Parczew forests. Lichtenberg's group left for these forests and undertook partisan actions before the deportation of most of the Jews of Wlodawa to the Sobibor extermination camp on October 24, 1942.

After this deportation, a ghetto in Wlodawa was formed for the remaining Jews and those of the surrounding area. It was then that Leon Lemberger (Lukowski) organized an underground group in the ghetto, and, in the beginning of 1943, after smuggling a few arms into the ghetto and making the necessary preparations, left the ghetto with this group and joined Lichtenberg's partisans.[23]

Zelechow

In the summer of 1942, an underground organization was established in Zelechow headed by Josef Mlynowski. It formed ties with and aided the Soviet partisan unit, which under Alekseyev's command was active in the area. On September 30, 1942, when the Germans began to liquidate the ghetto, this group fled to the forests. There they operated as a partisan unit under Mlynowski's command, collaborating closely with Alekseyev's Soviet unit.[24]

Radzyn

The first underground organization here, aiming to develop partisan activity in the area, formed as early as the spring of 1942. It appears that at the beginning of the year, a five-member group left the ghetto to establish a base for partisan activities in the area of Suchawola. The group's arms included two pistols and a rifle. A short while after reaching the forest, the group met with a unit of Soviet soldiers who had fled a prisoner-of-war camp. Unfortunately, one night these Soviet soldiers turned against the Jews and stole their arms, shoes, and clothing. Following this incident, the members of the group returned to the ghetto and did not attempt to enter the forest again. Some time later, another resistance organization formed in Radzyn under the leadership of Yitzhak Kleinman. In January 1943, its members left the Radzyn Ghetto, which by then was much smaller, and formed a partisan unit that was active in the surrounding forests.[25]

Markuszow

In this ghetto, there was an underground youth organization of about fifty people. Mordechai Kirshenbaum and the Gothelf brothers (Yerucham and Yaakov) played leading roles in it. The group succeeded in smuggling a few arms into the ghetto, and afterwards left for the nearby forests where it initiated partisan actions.[26]

Kamionka

A youth group committed to armed resistance was organized here by Ephraim Bleichman. As in nearby Markuszow, some arms were brought into the ghetto, but later the group left for the forests, where they eventually joined Shmuel Jegier's Jewish partisan group.[27]

Tomaszow Lubelski

The underground organization formed here was headed by Mendel Heler. Contacts were made with Poles who promised to acquire arms for it. In return, the Poles (whose affiliation is not known) betrayed the group and executed a few of its members. Despite this, the organization's activities continued, and in September 1942, after acquiring some arms, a combat group left for the forest, where it carried out local partisan actions.[28]

Iwaniska

The youth organization that was formed here devised a plan to escape the well-guarded ghetto. Small quantities of arms were bought from Poles and secretly smuggled into the ghetto. However, because there were too few arms for a larger, consolidated partisan unit, they decided to divide the people into small groups, which could be situated in different areas of the forest after their escape from the ghetto. Each group was to build a bunker for itself, hide until conditions improved, and engage the Germans in battle only in self-defense. In accordance with this approach, the group did not choose an overall leader and did not organize regular communication between the various groups. But the approach proved to be fundamentally wrong. The Germans, in collaboration with the local peasant population, quickly discovered most of the people, few of whom were armed. Those who survived eventually joined the GL units which came into the area.[29]

Dzialoszyce

The Jews of Dzialoszyce established an underground organization under the leadership of Moshe Skoczylas, a former member of the Polish Communist Party. Skoczylas succeeded in making contact with the Polish communists Jan Zareba, from the nearby town of Pinczow, and Zachariasz, from the village of Korkow, which was also close by. Through them, contact was later made with the top PPR activists in the area, Wladyslaw Jaworski and Franciszek Szwaja. It was largely thanks to these ties that the members of this organization succeeded in escaping from the ghetto and in establishing a partisan unit known by the name "Zygmunt."[30]

Rzeszow

Members of Hashomer Hatzair, headed by Sala Mol and Hinda Grol, established an underground fighting organization here, which had ties with the Jewish underground in the ghettos of Cracow, Tarnow, and Jaslo. None of its members survived. Two of them—Moshe Traum and Avraham Ojgarten—were caught during an unsuccessful attack on a local Polish police station. They were executed. This group probably had contact with the Polish underground. The Pole Tadeusz Wiatr gave testimony on the ties between the Polish underground and a secret organization in the Rzeszow Ghetto headed by a man called "Kuba." According to Wiatr, members of the organization bought some arms through Poles and later escaped to the nearby forests where they carried out partisan actions.[31]

In a few ghettos—Opatow, Miedzyrzec Podlaski, Sandomierz, Tarnow, and Pilica—attempts to begin partisan actions in the surrounding areas did not succeed. However, there was armed resistance in the ghettos when the Germans held deportations to the extermination camps. Following are the principal facts about such resistance.

Opatow

The agricultural training farm near the city Opatow served as the base for its fighting organization. As in Kopaliny, the farm served only as a cover for underground activity, in which Kalman Czernikowski played a leading role. In time, the Opatow groups succeeded in forming ties with the leadership of the Jewish underground in Warsaw and under its influence began accumulating arms and preparing for armed resistance in case of deportations by the Germans. These preparations were severely limited when most of the youths, along with Czernikowski, were taken away to a forced labor camp in the Lublin area, and later to Skarzysko. From then on, young women made up the majority of the organization.

The plan for action was very simple. The arms bought from Poles were hidden in the attic of the synagogue. When the Germans began the liquidation of the ghetto, the organization's members planned to go to the storehouse and resist, using the synagogue as their base. The storehouse, however, was discovered by the Gestapo, apparently as a result of betrayal by one of the arms suppliers. The synagogue was suddenly surrounded by Germans, and a number of women who were there at the time were shot on the spot. To intimidate the ghetto, the Germans then took people away to an unknown destination. A while later, when the Germans actually began to liquidate the ghetto several hundred Jews fled to the surrounding forests.[32]

Miedzyrzec Podlaski

A unified underground was established in the Miedzyrzec Podlaski Ghetto, with help from members of Hashomer Hatzair, Left Poalei Zion, and the communists. The organization's committee also had ties with the leadership of the Jewish resistance in Warsaw, and succeeded in accumulating a certain quantity of arms. However, we have no reliable information on the organization's activities, other than reports from German sources of several small clashes. The report of the *Ordnungspolizei* in the district of Lublin dated July 18, 1943, speaks, for instance, of an assault carried out some time before against a group of *Wehrmacht* soldiers in Miedzyrzec: one German was killed and three others were wounded, while two members of the assault group were killed. Another *Ordnungspolizei* report dated September 10, 1943, speaks of a clash between the police and the gendarmerie and a group of Jews who were entrenched in one of the buildings in Miedzyrzec. The *Hauptwachmeister* Johan Renischek was killed, and five Jews were shot in this attack; among them were two women.[33]

Sandomierz

The underground organization here strove from the very start for the establishment of a base for partisan activities in the nearby forests. Ties were formed with the local AK group, but ended in tragedy: The Jewish emissaries who left the ghetto for a meeting were killed by the AK men. The organization then ceased its attempts to transfer youths for partisan activities. Jewish youths resisted with the few arms they had during the liquidation of the ghetto, but apparently none of them survived. The resistance here is known to us only from Polish sources.[34]

Tarnow

After the first deportation to the Belzec extermination camp between June 11 and June 13, 1942, a fighting organization was established here under the leadership of the Hashomer Hatzair members Josef Bruder, Rivka Schusler, and Shmuel Springer and Communist Party member Melech Bienstock. Contact was made with the Polish underground, and four pistols were purchased from it. During the transfer of additional arms to the ghetto, Shmuel Springer was caught and executed. On September 10, the Germans held another deportation to the extermination camp. Considering the ill-fated chances of any action in the ghetto, this group decided to escape to the forest to carry out partisan actions. Some of the organization's members, under the command of Josef Bruder, did reach a forest in the area of Tuchow (20 kilometers from Tarnow), but they were soon surrounded by a large SS unit. All but three of the Jewish fighters fell in the battle. The remaining three returned to the ghetto and continued with underground activities there.

On September 1, 1943, when the Germans began their final liquidation of the ghetto, the Jews resisted with arms. The battles went on through September 2. Unfortunately, there is no information on the battles or on the preparations that were made for the resistance, for no one who took part in the organization's activities and in the resistance survived. As in Sandomierz, reports of the armed resistance offered by the Jews in the Tarnow Ghetto come only from Polish sources.[35]

Pilica

The members of the local Gordonia, Hashomer Hatzair, Paolei Zion, Akiva, and Freiheit movements established a unified organization of about sixty people in Pilica. The group had ties with the local Socialist Fighting Organization cell, under the command of First Lieutenant Rudolf, which helped them bring a certain quantity of arms into the ghetto. Collaboration between the two organizations also extended to a few combat actions in the surrounding area, and three bunkers were prepared outside the ghetto to serve as a base for the planned partisan actions. However, soon after the liquidation of the ghetto in Pilica on September 5, 1943, the Jewish bunkers were discovered and destroyed after a short battle. All the Jews apparently fell in battle.[36]

CHAPTER 12
ARMED RESISTANCE IN THE CAMPS

THE CAMPS ESTABLISHED BY THE GERMANS AND DISTRIB-uted densely throughout the *General Gouvernement* comprised a unique battle arena for the Jewish resistance movement. The conditions for preparing resistance and the chances for any combat action's success were much more complex than those in the ghetto. The residents of the ghetto had some freedom of movement inside the closed Jewish quarter. In contrast, opportunities for movement and contact between the prisoners in the German camps were limited to the barracks or the place of work, and even there the prisoners were under almost constant supervision by the camp's staff.

The conditions for resistance also varied widely in different kinds of Nazi camps: mass extermination camps, concentration camps, forced labor camps, and prisoner-of-war camps. Limited by the scope of this study, we will not discuss these differences extensively, but rather confine ourselves to describing the general characteristics of these camps and the conditions for organizing resistance in a number of camps in the *General Gouvernement*.

GENERAL CAMP CONDITIONS

The unimaginable extent of the terror that prisoners in German camps were subjected to presented an extreme obstacle to the organization of resistance actions. The prisoners had no legal rights and no means of defense whatsoever. Their fate was completely in the hands of the camp's command staff, guards, and clerks, whose harshness towards the prisoners knew no limit. Any prisoner was liable to suffer the cruelest of tortures, or the worst possible death for any offense and for any inoffense, for that matter. The chronic hunger and the living conditions, which led to the complete exhaustion and physical degeneration of masses of prisoners, limited the possibilities for resistance much more than the circumstances in the ghettos.

Another factor which curbed the initiation of resistance was the principle of the prisoner's collective responsibility. Any unsuccessful attempt was paid for not only with the lives of those who took part in it, but also with the lives of other prisoners. In addition, the success of one group of prisoners (an escape, for example) usually led to the death of others left behind. The civilian population outside the camps was also subject to the death sentence, usually without trial, for any help given to a fugitive or a prisoner planning an act of resistance, particularly if he or she was a Jew. This obviously made it extremely difficult to form ties with or get help from the local civilian population.

Furthermore, although methods of fencing off and supervising the camps were not the same everywhere, the common system—a ring of fences and barriers that not only isolated the camp from the outside world, but also separated the various sections within the camp—also impeded resistance. Similarly, the watch towers, which were built close to one another, and the strong lighting ensured a good view of the camp and its surroundings in order to prevent the escape of individuals and to defend the entire camp with machine-gun fire in case of a mass revolt.

The typical system of barriers is exemplified by Plaszow camp near Cracow. This camp was isolated from the outside world by a triple barrier—an electric fence, a special barbed-wire fence, and a regular barbed-wire fence. There were fifteeen additional barriers made of iron wire inside the camp, separating its various parts, while the main section of prisoner barracks was separated from the rest of the camp by an additional electric fence. There were three kinds of watch towers in and around the camp: towers two meters high were placed every twenty meters, for supervising the various parts of the camp and guarding the internal barriers which prevented the movement of prisoners from one section to another; towers five to eight meters high were stationed around the outside fence of the camp and equipped with installations for heavy machine guns, telephones, and alarm systems, and towers fifteen meters high overlooked the entire camp. Furthermore, outside the camp there were field units (*Feldwachen*), overlooking the outside barriers and the area around the fences. Each one of these posts had electrical panels which could transfer electric current to various parts of the iron-wire barriers.[1]

All of these factors—unlimited terror, inhuman living conditions, the principle of collective responsibility, the death sentence for civilian accomplices, and the complicated system of barriers and watches—almost nullified any chance of organizing resistance, particularly armed action. Even the formation of an organizational framework for a camp underground had to overcome incredible hardships, and smuggling any arms into the camp was an extremely complicated procedure. Because the escape of a group of prisoners greatly endangered the remaining prisoners, initiative in this direction was effectively checked, and attempts to escape in groups from the camp rarely succeeded. Any attempt to resist involved the danger of the physical liquidation of all the prisoners, regardless of the success or failure of the rebellion.

The extent of this study does not make it possible to discuss in detail the situation in the various camps or the differences between them regarding the conditions for organizing resistance. We will, therefore, limit ourselves to a brief description of this situation in a number of camps in the GG

THE UPRISING IN THE TREBLINKA EXTERMINATION CAMP

The extermination camp in Treblinka was established in July 1942, not far from the penal forced labor camp for Jews and Poles, which had existed in this area since 1941. Hence, the name of the extermination camp was Treblinka II, as opposed to the labor camp, which was called Treblinka I. This was the largest extermination camp after Auschwitz; historians estimate the number of this camp's victims to have been between 700,000 and 900,000.

The extermination camp was built in a flat area of swamplands, where the population was sparse. Zdzislaw Lukasiewicz, the Polish judge and investigator who oversaw the investigation of Nazi crimes in Treblinka after World War II, describes the camp's surroundings as follows:

> The region is convenient for killers. It is impossible to see the surroundings of the camp from either the road or the path, which are only several hundred meters away from its borders. A pine forest growing on the hills along the borders of the camp serves as an excellent barrier from curious eyes. The area on the west is completely desolated. No settlement exists as far as the eye can see. Only on the south is there a road to

the camp and a side path to a stone quarry, both of which pass near the camp's border. Neither the path nor the road is open to regular traffic. And anyway, no one goes on the road of his own free will, and the side path is used only for the transportation of stone. The area to the east and the south is low. From the watch tower, it is easy, therefore, to scare away or kill a bothersome passer-by."[2]

The extermination camp was divided into two parts: the administrative section and the extermination camp itself. In the first part there were barracks for the guards, an arms storehouse, and in a special section, workshops where the prisoners labored and barracks housing the inmates. The gas chambers, trenches and ovens, and a barrack for the prisoners forced to work there were in the second section of the camp. In the camp's jargon, the administrative section was called Camp No. 1, or the Lower Camp, and the extermination camp was called Camp No. 2, or the Upper Camp. The largest group of prisoners was forced to sort the clothing and the possessions of the Jews who had been exterminated. There were also various groups of skilled workers who performed such tasks as reinforcing and camouflaging the fence, groups employed in services for the SS men, groups that worked in a barrack unpacking the belongings of the deportees, and a special group called the "Gold-Juden," who sorted jewelry and money found in clothing and other belongings.[3]

The two parts of the camp were separated by a tall dirt wall which prevented an overall view of the camp from the inside. The entire camp (a rectangle measuring 400 meters by 600 meters) was surrounded by a tall barbed-wire fence 3 meters high. Outside the fence, an anti-tank barrier acted as a security belt, and on the four sides of the camp there were five watch towers. The camp's guards included Germans, SS men who held key positions, and a battalion of Ukrainian guards.[4] In the summer of 1943, during the last stage of the preparation for the uprising, there were 500 prisioners in the lower camp and in the upper camp, 200 people.

The whole time the camp existed, the Jewish prisoners resisted in various ways. Intensive passive resistance and mutual aid predominated. There were very frequent escapes and many acts of spontaneous resistance by individuals and groups. Although this study deals only with organized armed resistance, the special significance of the escapes from the camp must be mentioned. In spite of the strict supervision, prisoners managed to flee Treblinka and to give the world reliable, detailed information on this extermination camp. Some, like Rabinowicz, Nowodworski, Salbe, Krygier, Jerzy Rajgorodzki, and Abraham Krzepicki, overcame incredible hardships and succeeded in reaching the Warsaw Ghetto in order to give the Jewish underground organization information on Treblinka. Between December 1942 and January 1943, Abraham Krzepicki wrote out a very detailed testimony on Treblinka for Dr. Emanuel Ringelblum's underground archive. It was not the only testimony by a Treblinka refugee recorded by Ringelblum. As early as the fall of 1942, immediately after the end of the first large deportation from the Warsaw Ghetto (September 13, 1942), the first reports by fugitives from Treblinka were handed in. The Jewish underground transferred detailed information on Treblinka based on these reports to London through the Polish Home Army.[5]

As was said above, the Germans handed down cruel collective punishment any time some form of resistance was offered. For example, in August 1942, when one of the prisoners wounded Max Biala, an SS guard, who died on the way to the hospital in Ostrow, the Ukrainian guards showered heavy fire on the prisoners, who had been ordered to assemble, killing 150 of them. And when the Jewish prisoner Berliner wounded the SS *Scharfuehrer* Buehler with a knife on September 11, 1942, in retaliation the Ukrainian guards first bludgeoned Berliner and two other Jews to death with their spades and then shot and killed at least ten others. A large-scale massacre was led by the Ukrainians in November 1942, after a transport of deportees from the Siedlce Ghetto revolted. And at the end of 1942, the same was done following the armed resistance of deportees from the Grodno Ghetto, in which a few SS men had been killed.

It is not possible to determine when the underground organization that led the uprising of August 2, 1943, began its activity. According to the testimony of Shmuel Reizman, there were some seeds of an underground organization as early as September 1942; by the end of that year, a disciplined, consolidated, and structured organization already existed.

The commander of the underground in Treblinka was Dr. Julian Chorazycki, who worked in the SS infirmary. His closest aides were Galewski, an engineer; Rakowski, who succeeded Galewski as camp elder, or *Lageraelteste;* Ziela, apparently a former officer in the Czechoslovakian army; Sudowicz, another engineer; Kurland; Dr. Lechert; and Dr. Tyras.[6]

The underground was organized into five-man units, headed by someone who was appointed by and responsible to the organization's leadership. At the time, only the unit leaders knew who the head of the underground was. These five-man units were placed in all of the work groups on both sides of the camp. And, although we do know that a few groups included two or more combat units, we do not know the overall number of units active in the camp.

The organization's main aim was an armed revolt that would destroy the camp and allow the prisoners to escape. According to this plan, the organization first of all prepared to acquire arms. This was to be done in two ways: by buying arms from the Ukrainian guards, and by stealing them from the guards' storehouses. In spite of the strict supervision of the SS, the prisoners who sorted the clothing of those who had been killed managed to hide some of the money and jewels they found, which, it was believed, could be used to buy arms from some Ukrainian guards at very high prices. The plan to smuggle arms out of the storehouses seemed to have a chance because one of the members of the underground, Eugeniusz Turowski, a technician who worked in various parts of the camp, succeeded in making himself copies of keys to the storehouses.[7]

The money and valuables were given to the underground's commander, Dr. Chorazycki, who tried to make contact with the Ukrainians. His efforts, however, came to nothing and ended in tragedy. Kalman Feigman tells of this:

> One day Kurt Franz [the deputy camp commander] entered the infirmary and searched Dr. Chorazycki. He found money on him, something absolutely forbidden in the camp. Chorazycki knew that death awaited him. He attacked Franz, but the latter broke away from him. The doctor jumped through the window. After walking a few steps, he stumbled and fell. Apparently he managed to swallow some kind of poison.
>
> They lifted Chorazycki up. He still showed some signs of life. All the prisoners were assembled in the camp's courtyard. They lined us up in rows and ordered us to watch how they could wash out the doctor's stomach. The cruelest of them all, the Ukrainian Rogoza, opened the doctor's mouth, pulled his tongue with some kind of sharp instrument and poured water in. After this Franz jumped on Chorazycki's stomach, and with his shoes on started to skip on his stomach. Two Jews were forced to pick the doctor up feet first, and so the water came out. They repeated this a few times. However, Chorazycki did not move. They put him nude on a bench and beat him. The doctor showed no signs of life. He was apparently dead. They did not manage to revive him for new tortures.[8]

On May 3, 1943, the camp elder Rakowski was shot, also for the crime of holding money. He had been one of the underground's commanders. The money found on him was also intended for arms acquisition.

After the tragic deaths of these two men, attempts to buy arms from the Ukrainians ceased. But when the Germans ordered the prisoners to clean and flatten an area near the arms storehouse, the organization did get a chance to take arms out of the usually well-guarded storehouses. This was the time to use the keys made by Turowski. The attempt succeeded, and the few arms that were taken were hidden in the potato storehouse.

Now it was imperative to hasten the start of the uprising, before the Germans discovered the arms hidden in the camp. A plan was drawn up to penetrate the arms storehouse again, the day the revolt was to start. The arms taken were to be hidden in a number of places prepared earlier, to which the underground's people had easy access. According to the plan for revolt, the members of the organization were to grab the arms and take predesignated combat positions, from which they were to fire simultaneously against all five watch towers. At the same time, other groups of prisoners were to set the camp on fire with materials prepared beforehand. A special platoon was to cut the telephone wires to prevent the camp's command from calling in reinforcements. Immediately after overcoming the guards in the watch towers, the prisoners, armed with firearms or knives, were to attack the guards' barracks where the Ukrainian guards usually stayed between their watches in the lookout towers. Following the liquidation of these guards, the prisoners were to break out of the camp in any way possible. It was expected that all the fugitive prisoners would manage to get quite a distance away from the camp before the search parties caught up with them. The main tactician of this plan was Kurland, a member of the underground's command staff.[9]

Communication between the five-man units of the organization was a very complicated process considering the conditions in the camp. It was particularly difficult to pass information and coordinate actions with the people of Camp No. 2. Despite the difficulties, this was accomplished without arousing the suspicion of the camp's staff.

The uprising was fixed for August 2, 1943, at 4:30 P.M., a day the prisoners knew that half of the German staff and some of the Ukrainians were to go bathing in the Bug River and were to be outside of the camp.

On the morning of the appointed day, Turowski opened the guards' storehouse with his secret keys. The prisoners in the construction commando working nearby began their task. Alfred Boehm and a few others took out the arms, placed them in wagons, and covered them with bricks and boards. Yaakov Domb, who drove the garbage wagon, took these arms and brought them to the designated

places. While going around the camp he whispered the agreed password to the prisoners, first in Hebrew: "Today is Judgment Day";
then in Polish: "We will get four and a half portions of bread." This
meant that the uprising was set for that day at 4:30 in the afternoon.
Arms and grenades were taken out, but it turned out that most of the
grenades were not usable because they had no detonators.

Other plans for the revolt had also been made. Axes and knives
had been prepared in the workshops, which were to be used in the
assault on the barracks of the Ukrainian guards. Yaakov Domb prepared tools for cutting the barbed-wire fences. Sonia Grabinska, who
worked in the laundry, was ordered to take out linens and bring them
to the prisoners barracks so that the rebels could take them before
their flight. The rebels also took money to buy food and possibly
arms.

In summary, all the preparations were completed during the
morning and afternoon of August 2 according to plan. During those
eight hours, nothing had aroused the suspicion that extensive preparations were being made for an uprising. It looked, therefore, as if the
rebels had succeeded in overcoming the problem of keeping their
plans completely secret, an accomplishment that depended on the
right combination of many factors: At any moment one of the nearby
Germans might come close to the arms storehouse, see the prisoners
sneaking into it, go to one of the places where the arms were stored,
or encounter someone hiding a knife or an axe. Yet the successful
combination of circumstances did not last forever. According to Tan-
chum Greenberg's testimony, at about 4 o'clock, half an hour before
time fixed for the revolt, an SS man called Kiwe stopped a young
prisoner whose pocket looked suspiciously swollen. When the prisoner was searched and a substantial amount of money was found, the
youth was taken to Barrack No. 2 and cruelly tortured. It was feared
that he would not stand up to the torture and that the Germans
would receive information that would give them time to plan a
counter-operation. Members of the organization who were close by
saw the head of Barrack No. 2 speaking with Kiwe. It looked as if the
latter was giving the Germans some kind of information. The underground leaders who were hastily called for a discussion accepted
Salzberg's suggestion to immediately kill Kiwe. In retrospect, this
undoubtedly was a mistake. The underground member Strawczynski, who was present at the time, testifies that while leaving the
barracks, Kiwe had shown no signs of nervousness and had not even
taken his gun out of its holster. It can be concluded, therefore, that
neither the youth nor the head of the barrack said anything, and that

the incident had not aroused any special suspicion. In spite of this, the decision to kill Kiwe was not rescinded. According to the instructions of the underground, Wolowejczyk shot him with a pistol he had just received. A second SS man, Sochomil, riding by on a bicycle, was also shot and killed.[10]

These two seemingly insignificant shots alarmed the Ukrainian guards in the posts and in the watch towers. They opened heavy machine-gun fire, and the uprising was forced to start before the appointed time.

Members of the underground tried to reach the arms hideouts despite the fire of the Ukrainian guards. Only a few managed to take out the arms and fire at the watch towers. The camp was immediately set on fire, earlier than planned. A few moments later huge flames enveloped the entire area. The telephone lines were disconnected. A few of the rebels called out to the Ukrainians to stop firing, telling them that a revolt had broken out in Berlin and that the war had come to an end. The Ukrainians who complied with these calls came down from the towers and were killed; their arms were taken to be used in the remainder of the battle. But the rebels did not succeed in coordinating the assault on the barracks of the guards. A few groups of rebels shot at them on their own, without planning or coordinating their actions. Despite this, great confusion prevailed among the guards because of the unexpected turn of events. A number of guards were killed, and a substantial number of the prisoners could now break out of the camp.

Not all the Jews succeeded in escaping from the camp, however. A small number of prisoners, particularly those from Camp No. 2, remained behind. Some of them were later deported to Sobibor, where they formed with others the so-called *Restkommando*. These people were killed in the beginning of September 1943.

The prisoners who succeeded in escaping the Germans who came after them immediately were forced to divide up into small groups and to try to find hideouts in the surrounding forests. Their fate and chances for survival depended totally on the attitude of the local Polish peasant population. The fear of German penalties, among other factors, usually determined whether help would be given to Jewish fugitives. Kalman Feigman testifies to this:

> It was necessary to divide up into several groups because it was hard for a large number of people to hide. Our group numbered fifty people. . . .
> We dug a trench in the forest near Treblinka and covered it with plants and leaves. We remained in this trench during the day. At night, armed

with a rifle and two pistols, we went to the peasants to find food. "Get out of here. We don't want to die because of you," the peasants said. However, we had no alternative, we had to eat. . . . We met no Germans at that time. They did not penetrate the forests. Yet we did meet AK people. There were exchanges of fire with them, but none of us were wounded. We remained in these forests until the liberation.[11]

A great deal of help was given to one group of fugitives by the forest watchman Serafinowicz, from the village of Mostowka in the area of Wyszkow. This man helped the rebels reach the forest of Sterdyn and hide there. Seventeen of the people who took part in the uprising in Treblinka reached the forest of Sterdyn, largely because of Serafinowicz's help. This group hid there for an entire year before the liberation of the area on August 8, 1944.

Four of the people who took part in the uprising—Yaakov Wiernik, Shmuel Reizman, Sonia Grabinska, and Friedman—reached Warsaw, where they came into contact with the commanders of the Jewish underground. Thus news of the camp and of the uprising was transferred to London. These people later took part in the Polish Warsaw Uprising in the summer of 1944.

Another Treblinka fugitive, Oscar Strawczynski, met a Jewish partisan group belonging to the Anielewicz unit. He joined this group and continued the struggle against the Germans with its people. Other rebels, among them Feigman, joined the Polish army immediately after the liberation of Treblinka and took part in the regular battles against the Germans. One of the youngest participants in the uprising, Henryk Sperling, fourteen years old, was captured during an attempt to reach Czestochowa. He was transferred to Auschwitz and from there to Dachau.

Of the whole, about twenty of the participants in the uprising in Treblinka survived until the end of World War II.[12]

THE UPRISING IN THE SOBIBOR EXTERMINATION CAMP

The Sobibor extermination camp was established in May 1942 and lasted until October 1943. During this period about 250,000 Jews were killed here, most of whom came from the ghettos in the district of Lublin. Others came from other areas of Poland, and from Holland, Czechoslovakia, Germany, France, Austria, and Minsk, the capital of Byelo-Russia. The structure of the camp, its methods of operation, and its system of supervision were similar to those of Treblinka.

Sobibor was south of Wlodawa and situated near a railway track not far from the Chelm-Brest road. The forests of Parczew, which were one of the main areas of partisan activities in occupied Poland, were 20 kilometers northeast of the camp. However, the partisans had no access to the surroundings of Sobibor. This area was under the strict watch of German army and police units, and its proximity to the railroad track and the road made it easy to transfer victims for extermination, while efficiently guarding the surroundings.

The camp was divided into several smaller camps separated and isolated from each other by a barbed-wire fence. The entire camp was surrounded by both an iron-wire fence and a mine field 15 meters wide. The camp's guards included SS men and Ukrainian watchmen. In nearby Chelm, Brest, and Biala Podlaska, there were fortified posts of the German army and the SS police.

As in Treblinka, there were quite a few attempts at resistance in Sobibor by individuals and groups, both spontaneous and organized. Only fragmentary information exists on these, because almost all of those who took part were killed. An exception is the well-planned resistance carried out on October 14, 1943. A group of twenty people who escaped the camp and survived provide accurate information on this uprising as well as on a few other resistance attempts.

For instance, these people tell of incidents of spontaneous resistance before the gas chambers. One such incident, on which we have detailed information, took place on April 30, 1943, when a group of Jews who had arrived in a transport saw what awaited them and attacked the SS men, wounding a few of them. Another incident occurred in September of that year, when Jews who were brought from the Minsk Ghetto attacked the SS guards. This attack was quickly suppressed with machine-gun fire. Resistance was also offered by a group of prisoners who were among the last forced laborers in the Belzec extermination camp, and who after its final liquidation, were brought to Sobibor. These people, who knew the ways and mechanisms of the extermination camps, rebelled. They were all killed during their revolt by automatic machine-gun fire.[13]

We also have information on escapes in which force was used. From the testimony of Eda Lichtman, we know of the escape of five prisoners, among them two women, on Christmas Eve 1942, in which one of the fugitives, Pesia Liberman, was killed during a clash with the Germans. In July 1943, there was an escape by a group of forty *Waldkommando* prisoners who had been cutting wood in the forest. A few prisoners belonging to this group, accompanied by a guard, went to get water. They killed him with a knife they had hidden and fled. When they did not return to their place of work, the rest of the guards began searching for them. In the confusion that ensued, all the other

Waldkommando prisoners also escaped. All those captured in the chase were brought back to the camp and shot in front of the other prisoners. Only a few succeeded in escaping: Adam Wang, Podchlebnik, Yehezkel Mencha, and Jozef Kopp survived until the liberation of Lublin. After the liberation, Jozef Kopp was killed by local anti-Semites when he went to visit his birthplace in the district of Lublin.

In September 1943, another escape was attempted by the prisoners of Auxiliary Camp No. 3, who worked near the gas chambers. They dug an underground passage from their barracks to the other side of the fence surrounding the camp. But in the last stage of the digging, the passage was discovered. The guards in the watch tower opened machine-gun fire and killed all the prisoners in the auxiliary camp.[14]

The prisoners also made several attempts to plan an uprising in Sobibor. There are a few bits of information on an attempt made in the summer of 1943, apparently under the leadership of a former Dutch naval officer, which in some of the testimonies is called the "Dutch Rebellion." According to this plan, the prisoners were to equip themselves by breaking into the guards' arms storehouse, escape, and look for ways into the partisan movement, a plan similar to the Treblinka uprising. Because of undetermined circumstances, however, the Germans noticed the prisoners preparing for the rebellion. Seventy-two prisoners, mostly Dutch Jews, were accused of planning a revolt and executed. But a few of these rebels survived and took part in a later, successful uprising.[15]

The group that carried out the uprising on October 14, 1943, was apparently formed immediately after the liquidation of the so-called "Dutch Group." Two things made this possible. The survivors of the former underground group, and particularly Leib Felhendler and Itzhak Lichtman, immediately began planning another revolt. They were aided by a group of former Red Army soldiers who were brought from the Minsk Ghetto in September 1943. By the end of September, an underground organization already existed including many long-term prisoners and also the newcomers from Minsk. The commanders of this organization were Alexander Pechorski, a Red Army officer from Minsk, and Leib Felhendler, from the Dutch group.

In addition to this underground organization, there were secret groups in Sobibor numbering a few people, sometimes even ten or more, which planned and organized escapes from the camp, occasionally in collaboration with the Ukrainian guards. These small groups were an obstacle and a danger to Pechorski's and Felhendler's central organization and made it imperative to organize all the underground activities in the camp into one disciplined organization.

The organization's leadership considered several kinds of revolts, among them one calling for setting the camp on fire and a mass escape through an underground passage. Then, at the end of September or the beginning of October, they drew up a plan. According to this plan, several SS men were to be called into the workshops in the area of the camp with the alibi that they were to try on uniforms or shoes that had been made for them. These SS men were to be killed with knives and their arms taken to be used against guards in the watch towers.[16]

The uprising demanded strict coordination not only of the actions of every group, but also the actions of individual underground members. It was therefore necessary to hold consultations with at least some of the members of the organization to discuss the plans for the uprising and to decide on what tasks had to be performed. Yaakov Biskupicz, who took part in the uprising, describes this meeting: "When Yom Kippur came, we asked the Germans to allow us to hold prayers. They, of course, refused. But in their wickedness they allowed us to hold a party with music that day. . . . The entire barrack assembled, about 300 young men and women. While the youths near the door sang, a meeting of the underground was held inside."[17]

During this meeting, all the details regarding the uprising were planned: first, the problem of asking the SS men into the workshops—to which workshops and at what time and when the rebels would be supplied with the knives and axes prepared by Spengler—was decided; and then the questions of who would kill the SS men and how the arms were to be transferred by members of the organization were settled. In addition, a plan was drawn up for the attack on the posts and the guards' arms storehouse, and specific tasks were delegated to the prisoners who worked in the Germans' apartments.

According to plan, the SS men were called into the workshops between 2:00 and 4:00 P.M., hours chosen so that the SS men would be liquidated and most of the arms acquired by 4:15 P.M., the time of the daily roll call in the camp. The members of the organization were to utilize the assembling of all of the prisoners, (which usually took place before the official roll call when the Germans came), to tell every one of this decision and divide the prisoners into groups for the attack on the watch posts.

The first stage of the uprising went as planned. The Germans came to the workshops suspecting nothing and were killed with knives or axes. Within two hours, ten Germans were secretly killed and their pistols taken. It was now important to seize as many arms as possible before the roll call without arousing the guards' suspicion. According to plan, Lerner and Manche broke into the camp's headquarters and killed the SS guards Baeckman and Klatte. At the same time Schwartz disconnected the electricity, and Duniec cut the telephone wires.

Then, there was suddenly a turn for the worse. A car carrying two SS men, Bauer and Frenzel, suddenly entered the camp. They encountered a group of prisoners who were on their way to the hiding place for two rifles and a sub-machine gun. Frenzel understood the situation and opened fire, killing two members of the underground, Dr. Bresler and his son. The other members of the group returned the fire. This alerted guards earlier than expected, a few minutes before the roll call and the appointed signal for the attacks on the guard posts.[18]

The Germans with Frenzel at their head opened heavy fire from a machine gun on the prisoners who were already assembled in the courtyard. Pechorski's greatness as a commander was displayed when he succeeded in overcoming the confusion and calling on all the prisoners to attack the guard posts by quickly telling the various groups in which direction to fire. Pechorski's move surprised the Germans. The rebels succeeded in overcoming some of the guard posts and getting outside the fence. And although many were killed in the mine field surrounding the camp, some managed to pass the mine barrier and reach the area outside the camp. It is difficult to determine how many fell under the fire of the guards and in the mine field, or how many died on the German side during the battle with the rebels.

A few hours later, a German chase, including many forces who were called in from the surrounding area, went out after the rebels. The force that took part in this chase included a battalion of the 23rd Regiment of the *Ordnungspolizei* under the command of Captain Wulbrant, the 4th Company of the 689th Battalion of the *Siecherungsbattalion* under the command of Major Hans Wagner, and a few *Wehrmacht* units from the Lublin area.[19]

Both the number of those who died in the clash with the pursuing German forces and that of the prisoners who escaped unarmed from Sobibor and were later killed is not known. Because of the magnitude of the German forces, the Sobibor fugitives were compelled to divide up into very small groups and to try to get as far away as possible from the camp in hope of meeting partisans.

The fate of several fugitives is known. Some, headed by Pechorski, reached the eastern shore of the Bug. On October 22, after eight desperate days of running, they met the partisans of the Soviet Voroshilov unit. Four of the Sobibor rebels, among them two Jewish women from Holland, reached Yechiel Greenshpan's Jewish partisan unit. Six rebels who tried to reach Greenshpan's unit were killed near the village of Hola by an armed Polish group under the command of the Piatek brothers. Leib Felhendler joined a Soviet unit which he met in the area of Krasnik. This unit was under the command of Radecki. Shimon Rozenfeld, who was wounded in one leg, hid with a Polish peasant in the village of Janow near Chelm Lubelski until the liberation of this area. After the Russians entered Chelm, he joined the Red Army, took part in a few battles on the front, and went into Berlin. On the walls of the defeated *Reichstag* he wrote the words "Sobibor-Berlin." Yaakov Biskupicz reached a Soviet unit under the command of Kaplun in Polesie. Moshe Bahir (Szklarek), Plaszkowski, and the Sobelmans (a father and son) reached Kovpak's partisan group. Plaszkowski and the elder Sobelman fell in the last partisan battles, a short time before the unification of the partisans and the advancing Red Army. Zelda Metz was hidden by a Polish farmer for several months and received Aryan documents, which later enabled her to stay in Lvov until the liberation of the city.[20]

On the whole, the names of twenty Sobibor rebels who lived to see the fall of Hitler are known. Two died after the liberation. In June 1945, Leib Felhendler was killed by a Polish anti-Semitic gang in his apartment on Kowalska Street, No. 4 in Lublin. The youngest participant in the uprising, Zvi Sobelman, fell in battle near Latrun in Israel's war of independence.[21]

THE JEWISH FIGHTING ORGANIZATION IN THE PLASZOW CONCENTRATION CAMP

The Plaszow concentration camp was one of the largest in the *General Gouvernement*. Established in December 1942 as a *Julag* (from *Judenlager*, a camp for Jews), its name was later changed to *Zwangsarbeitslager des SS und Polizeifuhrers im Distrikt Krakau* (the SS and Cracow District Police Forced Labor Camp). In January 1944 it was turned into a concentration camp and subordinated to the central SS authorities. A total of 150,000 prisoners passed through this camp, and 80,000 of them were killed there. The majority of the inmates and victims of Plaszow were Jews, but about 20,000 Poles also passed through Plaszow, mainly those suspected of belonging to underground organizations.[22]

As in Treblinka, Sobibor, and most other forced labor camps, there were ceaseless attempts at escape, sabotage, and armed resistance in Plaszow. And as in the other camps, all or almost all who took part in these attempts were killed. The bits of information that have been preserved do not make it possible to determine accurately the circumstances and other matters regarding all these actions. But the report of the Department for Internal Affairs of the Polish Government Delegacy for the period of August 15 to September 15, 1943, among other sources, reveals that there were frequent escapes from Plaszow. This report reads: "From time to time, there are encounters with groups of fugitives numbering dozens or even scores of Jews who escaped from the camp itself (Plaszow) or from their places of work."[23]

The same source also reports of a serious act of armed rebellion that took place at the end of August 1943:

> On August 18, late in the evening, sixteen Ukrainian guards and over 300 Jews escaped in two trucks belonging to the camp's command. According to the police, the fugitives took enough arms and ammunition with them for 100 men. Since this escape, no one has been allowed outside the camp and an investigation is being held. In retaliation for this, the German and Ukrainian police shot 200 Jews. On August 31, it was determined that three trucks loaded with the corpses of the dead left the camp.

The number of the prisoners who escaped and, even more so, the quantity of arms taken appear exaggerated. Yet, there is no doubt that an armed resistance movement organized by the Jewish prisoners in collaboration with the Ukrainian guards did exist. The fate of its members is not known, just as the fate of those who escaped from Plaszow in 1943 is unclear. It is impossible to find even one testimony about them in the archives from people connected with the active underground resistance during the summer of 1943; it is, therefore, possible to conclude that none of these people survived. We have fairly accurate information on an underground group which was organized in October 1943, however. This group adopted the name Jewish Fighting Organization, emphasizing their continuation of the tradition of the Cracow Jewish Fighting Organization in Plaszow.[24]

The ZOB group here was mostly made up of prisoners who had a special status in the camp. Only these prisoners had some freedom of movement in the camp, without which no underground activity could be possible. For example, five members of this organization held the title of *"Kapo"*: Moshe Hecht, *Kapo* of the baths; Victor Traubman, *Kapo* of the metal workshop; Moshe Sternlicht, *Kapo* of the carpentry workshop; Wilek Machauf, *Kapo* of the electricians; and Langer, *Kapo* of the blanket storehouse. Four others, because they worked for SS men, also had relative freedom of movement. These were Helena Sternlicht, who worked as a servant for the camp's commander, Amon Goeth; Josef Fuglewicz, who worked as a servant for an SS man called Schedt; Adam Stab, who served the *Untersturm-fuehrer* Rabel; and Shmuel Kepler, who taught Goeth and his mistress, Maniola, horseback riding. Kepler enjoyed special privileges and great freedom of movement in the camp; he even succeeded in leaving the camp several times.[25]

Adam Stab, Victor Traubman, and David Herz stood at the head of the organization, which was divided into three combat units, commanded by Moshe Sternlicht, Weinreb, and Immerglueck.

The main task of the underground was arms acquisition. In January 1944, members of the organization managed to steal two 6.5-millimeter pistols from sleeping guards. Two additional pistols were brought from the arms storehouse by smiths working at plating its roof. A member of the organization named Sperling made copies of the keys to the storehouse and took more weapons, bringing the total of the organization's weaponry to six pistols and one rifle.

Secret arms production was also developed in this camp. Ignacy Loker, Ber Fisher, and Victor Reif invented a way to produce grenades from pump pipes, using very primitive methods. According to the testimony of Yaakov Sternberg, two physics teachers from the Hebrew Gymnasium in Cracow—Yeshayahu Driblat and Zvi Mereminski—also took part in the production of the grenades.

Attempts were also made to establish contact with the Polish underground. Shmuel Kepler made contact with a PPR member called Laptas. The camp's doctor, Stencel, another member of the organization, managed to contact a representative of the Polish Socialist Party. These contacts, however, did not bring the aid that was expected.[26]

A well-concealed bunker for hiding the arms was built near the metal workshop. According to the dictates of the organization, an uprising was to take place in the event of the liquidation of the camp, which would mean the death of its inmates or their transferral to another location for extermination. The plan called for the electricians to disconnect the current to the barbed-wire fence. At the same time, armed underground members were to attack several guard posts. The destruction of these posts was to ease the escape of a certain number of prisoners from the camp, who might then reach the nearby forests and join the partisans.

The death of the underground leader, Adam Stab, in the middle of 1944 was a heavy blow to the organization. Stab was to meet with a Ukrainian guard to buy arms, but the latter betrayed him. In his interrogation, Stab managed to convince the camp's command that his attempt to acquire arms was an individual personal matter, intended only for his own escape. Stab was publicly tortured and beaten to death in front of the other prisoners by Goeth with a hammer weighing 5 kilograms. Stab's courage prevented the SS from discovering the existence of the organization, which continued its activities.

The deportation of the inmates of Plaszow began in September 1944. Most of the prisoners were taken to the Gross-Rosen camp. The organization was forced to decide whether or not to carry out a revolt. At the time, it had information that for now, anyway, most of the prisoners were to be taken to another camp and not to be killed. Despite this, Weinreb's group wanted to carry out the attack on the guard posts in order to reach the forest. The majority turned this down for three reasons: (1) the deportation did not imply the liquidation of the prisoners and, therefore, there was no need for a desperate act of resistance; (2) the organization in the camp could not rely on any help whatsoever from the outside; and (3) because of the small number of arms held by the organization, the chance for a successful attack on the guard posts was very slim. The majority's opinion was that, at best, the attack would make it possible for only a very few people to reach the forest. Their escape, if it really did succeed, would be paid for by the lives of hundreds of other prisoners who would be shot to death. In view of this, the organization decided not to carry out the attack. So the members of the organization, along with the other prisoners, were transferred to other camps, mainly to Gross-Rosen.[27]

Plaszow was the only place where it was decided, after deliberations, to cancel plans for an uprising after careful, months-long preparations had been made for it, under the worst possible conditions.

ARMED RESISTANCE IN SMALLER CAMPS

Ostrowiec Swietokrzyski

The underground organization in Ostrowiec Swietokrzyski, which was led by the Kopel brothers and Moshe Stein, was mentioned in chapter five. This organization was established at the end of 1942 or the beginning of 1943. Contact was soon made with a Polish group called *"Zwiazek Odwetu"* (The Revenge Group), which numbered twenty people and operated in Ostrowiec under the banner of the Home Army. With this tie, it was possible to buy twelve pistols, smuggle them into the camp, and some time later, help a group of seventeen prisoners escape from the camp. The escapees were to organize a partisan group in the surrounding area under the command of the Home Army. This attempt, however, ended in tragedy. The fugitive prisoners were killed by the *Zwiazek Odwetu.* The details of this murder were revealed in Sandomierz in September 1949, at the trial of the Ostrowiec group's leaders—Jozef Mularski, Edward Perzynski, and Leon Nowak.

For a long time this tragedy held back other attempts by members of the Stein brothers' organization to escape. Only in the summer of 1944 did the organization renew the escape efforts for prisoners and initiate partisan activity in the area.

At the end of 1943 a second underground group formed in the camp, with no connection to the Stein brothers' organization. This group succeeded in making contact with a local AK unit under the command of Marian Swiderski ("Dzik") from the Nurt battalion, which was under the influence of the Polish Socialist Party. A number of weapons were smuggled into the camp with the help of the AK group, and on January 16, 1944, a group of thirty partially armed prisoners escaped. Most of them apparently were caught very soon by the German police; only a few succeeded in reaching Swiderski's group, which was then in the Opatow area. It seems that only one member of this group, Nechemia Wurman, survived the partisan battles.[28]

Budzyn

The existence of an underground group in the forced labor camp in Budzyn is known to us mainly from the memoirs of the Polish partisan, Tadeusz Szymanski.[29] The commander of this group was Josef Michel. Members of the organization were able to form ties with two Polish workers who were employed in the building of stoves, Feliks Lukasik and Piotr Dryka, both members of the Polish Workers Party. The German engineer, Angenent, who was the work foreman in the frame department, helped make this contact.

The Budzyn organization acquired certain sums of money to be used for the purchase of arms. They planned to escape to the partisans after they had a certain quantity of arms. The money was transferred to Grochulski, a resident of the village of Urzedow and a member of the Polish Workers Party. Because this man was known to have been a Polish Communist Party activist since before the war, the Jewish prisoners trusted him. Grochulski promised to purchase the arms and to let the prisoners who succeeded in escaping from the camp use as a base his house, where they could await an emissary from the Polish partisans.

Szymanski does not give the date of the first escape attempt. He states only that this attempt ended in failure and that the head of the organization, Josef Michel, was killed. Apparently this happened at the end of 1943 or the beginning of 1944. After some time, there was a successful escape by a second group of thirteen people. There is no information on the fate of these people and it is almost certain that none of them survived. It is also known that other escape attempts did not succeed. Szymanski does not write extensively on the reason for the failures, and only mentions Grochulski's betrayal: "Sokol (as Grochulski was known) helped the Jews escape from the camp in Budzyn, and found places for them in the villages near Urzedow, particularly with our supporters [the Polish Workers Party]. However, the money paid to Sokol by the fugitives for arms was not given to the organization, but kept by Sokol. There were rumors that the house he built for himself was paid for by this money."[30]

Later on in his memoirs, Szymanski writes that Grochulski was sentenced to death by a court of the People's Army and executed.

Wolanow

The work camp in Wolanow, west of Radom, was one of the first in the region of Kielce. The Jewish prisoners worked in a local mine, and the camp was situated in barracks in a nearby estate. In the fall of 1942, an underground group was established with the aim of organizing escapes to the partisan groups in the surrounding area. At the end of 1942, contact was made with the Jewish partisan group under the command of Julian Eisenman, which was active nearby. Preparations were made for an organized escape by the prisoners who were to join Eisenman's partisans. In the interim, however, Eisenman's unit was crushed.

A few months later, contact was made with a Polish civilian named Kozlowski, who worked near the mine. With his help, a few pistols were bought and smuggled into the camp. Some time later, contact was made with the local AK cell. After taking the arms from the Jewish prisoners, the AK men cut off the tie, thereby breaking their promise to help the Jewish prisoners escape and to accept Jews into the AK partisan unit. Following this, the attempts to escape from the camp were halted.[31]

Jastkow

A small forced labor camp for Jews was established in Jastkow, 11 kilometers west of Lublin, in the middle of 1942. The men worked in a stable belonging to a SS cavalry unit, and the women cooked, cleaned, and washed clothes in the Germans' apartments. After some time, the prisoners initiated underground activity, at the head of which stood Eli Zang, officially serving as the camp elder.

Although a few arms and some ammunition were stolen from the SS post, there were not enough for an armed breakout from the camp. The proximity of an SS unit also rendered a group escape impossible. Because of this, it was decided to aid the escape of individuals who were to join the local partisans. The first to escape was Moshe Pelc, who succeeded in reaching the Jewish partisan unit under the command of Shmuel Jegier; others escaped and joined Jegier's unit later.

Another form of underground activity in Jastkow was sheltering Jews who had escaped transports to the death camps but could not find hideouts in the area. Evidently, the hideout in the camp was only temporary and very unsafe. On January 8, 1943, for instance, when a prisoner who escaped from Jastkow and headed for Jegier's unit was captured and shot to death, the German command held an inspection in the camp. Although they found no arms, they did find the fugitives. Two days later Eli Zang, head of the camp's underground, was shot to death. Some time later all of the prisoners of Jastkow were transferred to the camp in Drohucza near Trawniki.[32]

Minsk Mazowiecki

After liquidating the ghetto in Minsk Mazowiecki on August 21, 1942, the Germans left behind four hundred Jews. They were imprisoned in a forced labor camp established in the Mikolaj Kopernik school, known, therefore, as the Kopernik Camp. When, on January 10, 1943, an SS and Polish police unit began to liquidate the camp, the prisoners barricaded themselves in the building and resisted with the simplest of means—sticks, stones, and bricks. Three Germans were wounded in the first clash, whereupon they gave up the idea of forcing the rebels out of the building, and first shelled it with machine guns and later set it on fire. All of the prisoners died in the flames.

According to the testimony of the Polish doctor, Stanislaw

Eugeniusz Wisniewski, a resident of Minsk Mazowiecki, this rebellion was headed by a tailor named Greenberg, whose entire family had died during the liquidation of the ghetto.[33]

Skarzysko-Kamienna

A large forced labor camp for Jews was established in Skarzysko-Kamienna in August 1942. The inmates were employed in the local Hasag armament factories (*Hugo Schneider Aktiongesellschaft*). The living and working conditions in this camp were very harsh, and the terror was among the worst of all the German concentration camps. On the whole about 15,000 Jews had passed through this camp; 10,000 of them died here.

There is only very fragmentary information on the underground in this camp. However, the existing sources do testify to fairly strong underground activity there. It is almost certain that a few clandestine groups were active at the same time, with no connection among them. There were a few cases when arms were found on prisoners who planned to escape, and a few of those caught, among them Lola Mendelewicz, were hanged before the entire camp. A few acts of sabotage against the industrial production are also known.

The Polish underground journal *Informacja Biezaca (Current News)*, issue no. 12 of March 26, 1943, reported that twenty prisoners from the camp in Skarzysko-Kamienna escaped on February 7, 1943, after disarming the German gendarme. According to the data of the Polish underground, the rate of escapes from the camp grew at the end of 1943, but the fate of the escapees is unknown. The report of the Department of Internal Affairs dated December 31, 1943, states that Jews who escaped from Skarzysko started many fires in the surrounding area.[34]

Kielce

After liquidating the ghetto between August 20 and August 24, 1943, the Germans left 2,000 Jews from among the former 23,000 residents of Kielce. Those left behind were concentrated in the new Ludwikow forced labor camp. An underground was soon formed under the command of David Buchwiner, Gershon Lewkowicz, and Chmielnicki, who succeeded in establishing ties with the Polish underground. A few pistols were purchased and smuggled into the camp, and clandestine grenade production was developed, mainly by Kalman Gertler and David Buchwiner. According to Shlomo Reis's report, the underground succeeded in accumulating ten pistols and sixty grenades. The organization planned an armed rebellion with these arms, which was to enable a mass escape of the prisoners, who were to join partisan activities in the area.

The preparations, however, were noticed by the camp-elder Johan Spiegel, who betrayed his friends hoping to buy his own life. On May 29, 1943, following this betrayal, the camp was unexpectedly surrounded by strong police units, and the organization members were caught and executed. The camp was liquidated, and the thousand prisoners who had been held here were transferred to forced labor camps in Skarzysko-Kamienna, Blizyn, and Pionki.[35]

Pionki

One underground group from Kielce was transferred to the camp in Pionki and tried to continue its activity. This camp's prisoners worked in an armament factory along with paid Polish laborers. According to one of the survivors, Shlomo Reis, contact was made with Home Army member Stefan Zdunek and joint sabotage actions were carried out. The Jewish group devoted itself particularly to organizing escapes in order to initiate partisan actions in the surrounding area, and on May 10, 1944, there was a successful escape by a group of twenty people.

While fleeing the German chase, these escapees divided up into two groups. One of them met a Polish Socialist partisan unit under the command of "Huragan" near the village of Suchowola. Some time later, the incident (which was discussed in chapter 5) almost brought about the deaths of all these Jewish partisans. Following this, the Pionki refugees moved to the Russian "Svoboda" partisan group, which was under the command of Pioter Don.

The second group of escapees was attacked in June 1944 by an NSZ unit, and four Jews were killed. Then on November 5, in another NSZ attack, a fifth member of the group, Bomkowicz, was killed. The surviving fugitives hid in the surrounding forests, continually persecuted by the German hunts and by NSZ groups, until the Red Army arrived in January 1945.[36]

Krasnik

An underground organization in the forced labor camp at Krasnik in the district of Lublin was established in the fall of 1943. They made contact with the members of the Polish Workers Party in the village of

Rzeczyca, which was then the center of activities of the Polish communist partisans in the area south of Lublin, and with the aid of these PPR members, succeeded in smuggling some pistols into the camp.

In November 1943, after the liquidation of a number of camps in the district of Lublin, preparations began for the escape of seventeen organization members. It succeeded, and the fugitives immediately divided up into two groups in order to lessen the danger and hardships on the way to the partisans in the forests. One group was killed on its way by local peasants, apparently members of an anti-Semitic underground. The second group reached the village of Rzeczyca and was accepted into the ranks of the People's Army. Members of this group took part in the partisan battles in the Janow forests, where most of the fighters were killed.[37]

Kruszyna

A small forced labor camp for Jews existed during the second half of 1942 in an army training area in Kruszyna, in the region of Kielce, where the prisoners did construction work. On December 17 and 18, 1942, there was a hastily planned resistance action here. It appears that none of the 557 people who took part in this action survived. The only known document describing the course of events is the report of the local gendarmerie guard commander, Lieutenant Eggen. According to his report, the Germans decided to liquidate the camp in the middle of December 1942, after construction work in the training area was finished. The prisoners were told of the evacuation plans. Suspecting that they were to be sent to an extermination camp, the prisoners decided to resist with knives or even with bare fists.

According to Eggen, unrest among the prisoners influenced the decision to hasten the liquidation of the camp. When the prisoners were ordered to assemble on the morning of December 17, the prisoners attacked the German gendarmes and a group of French policemen annexed to them. Eggen himself was wounded in the neck during the clash. The Germans and the French opened fire, killing six prisoners. Four prisoners managed to escape. Only after an additional squad of French policemen was brought in did the camp's command manage to force the prisoners back into the barracks. Lieutenant Eggen writes in his report:

> Because of the aggressive stand of the Jews, I was forced to ask for reinforcement from French policemen to prevent escapes by Jews during the night. Major Schad immediately ordered the guard reinforcement

and supplied us with four machine guns and acetylene torches to light the camp's fence.

I reported these events to the gendarmerie in Radom, and they promised me that on the morning of December 25 they would immediately send twenty-five Ukrainians and fifteen gendarmes to Kruszyna from Jedlinsk, where the gendarmerie from Bialobrzegi was evacuating the Jews.

Despite the fact that, following the order of Major Ruschansky, two trucks were given to us for the 60-kilometer trip, the attempts to escape were renewed on December 18, 1942, when the Jews were being put on the trucks and in spite of the presence of a large number of French policemen and twenty-five Ukrainians. They were forced to use their arms and to shoot at almost all of the Jewish groups being brought to the trucks. The French, whose main task was to supervise the Jews, enthusiastically participated in finishing off the Jews who were wounded. Together with those killed the day before, 113 Jews were shot during the action in Kruszyna and around the camp for offering resistance or attempting to escape.[38]

Krychow

As in Kruszyna, there was spontaneous active resistance here during the deportation of the prisoners from the forced labor camp in Krychow in the district of Lublin. The course of events here is known from the memoirs of one of the few surviving prisoners, the engineer Arnold Hindels. According to him, when the Germans held a selection in the camp on August 14, 1943, eighty prisoners were taken and sent to the Sobibor extermination camp. The following day the remaining prisoners were ordered to march all day to the Hansk agricultural farm. This aroused the suspicion of the prisoners and they decided to fight the accompanying guards if it appeared that they were really being taken to Sobibor. They were taken to the Hansk farm, however, and at the end of the work day, the German foreman, the engineer Holzheimer, said that the Krychow prisoners would be moved the next day, August 16, to Annopol. Meanwhile, it became known that the camp was surrounded by a new SS unit. There was no longer any doubt that the camp was to be liquidated. A plan to resist was drawn up during the night, and primitive weapons such as knives, rocks, and sticks were gathered. This resistance was organized in large part by the Oberlaender family (the brothers Aniel, Benno, and Menasse and their sister Luisa).

When the appointed signal was given at dawn, the prisoners broke the gates of the barracks and opened an attack on the German guard posts. The SS fired with machine guns from the watch towers and killed almost all the prisoners. Only a few managed to flee the camp and the German pursuit.[39]

Trawniki and Poniatowa

After the suppression of the Warsaw Ghetto uprising, about 25,000 Jews were deported to the forced labor camps in Trawniki and Poniatowa (15,000 went to Poniatowa and 10,000 to Trawniki). Among them were some ZOB members who, immediately after arriving in the camps, began to carry out any underground activity possible. Their extensive activity demands a separate study. We will only stress here that the underground members managed, in spite of great hardships, to smuggle some arms into the camps and to begin preparations for an armed rebellion. The central problem for the rebellion was one of timing. It was impossible to plan an armed mass escape from the camp like the ones in Treblinka or Sobibor. Even in the event of a total success, there was no way to hide thousands of fugitives. On the other hand, it was difficult to decide on the escape of only the few underground members, because this would immediately endanger the lives of all the other inmates.

The sudden liquidation of the camp came as a surprise to both the underground members and the other prisoners. They, of course, did not know that after the success of the uprising in Sobibor, Himmler had immediately ordered the liquidation of a number of camps in the *General Gouvernement*, among them Trawniki and Poniatowa. But apparently the Germans knew something of the preparations for resistance in these places. According to Polish sources, the two camps were surrounded by strong SS units on November 3, 1943, and the Jews resisted with arms throughout the liquidation. All the fighters, to the last man, fell in the battle while surrounded by large forces. The others were killed or burned to death in the camp's barracks, while the remaining prisoners were brought to the nearby forest and shot. The death of all of the underground members makes it impossible, of course, to determine the details of the preparation for this uprising and the course of the actual struggle.[40]

ARMED RESISTANCE IN THE LUBLIN PRISONER-OF-WAR CAMP

The camp in Lublin, at Lipowa Street, No. 7, which held Jewish prisoners-of-war, both privates and sergeants, who took part in the war of September 1939, was a unique place. Although the organizational structure of the camp and its living conditions were basically similar to those in other forced labor camps and some concentration camps, this camp eventually became a special arena for underground fighting.

The first group of war prisoners, about one thousand men, was brought here in December 1939. These Jewish prisoners-of-war came from the eastern part of Poland, the area which the Red Army had entered during the second half of September 1939 and which was annexed later to the Soviet Union. It can be assumed that the issue of war prisoners from these areas was a subject discussed by both the German and Soviet authorities, for the prisoners were told that they would be returned to the Russians in exchange for prisoners from the western part of Poland. It is possible that this is why the Jewish prisoners-of-war were concentrated in the Lublin camp, which was then considered a transit camp *(Durchgangslager).* But even though it held prisoners-of-war from the start, this camp was subordinated to the SS rather than to the *Wehrmacht* and later officially bore the name "Camp of the SS and Police Command in the District of Lublin" *(Lager des SS und Polizeifuehrers fuer Distrikt Lublin).*

At the end of December the prisoners were taken out of the camp and forced to march toward the new German-Soviet border. Only a few, including Dr. Shindler, remained behind. Most of the prisoners were killed near Parczew and Miedzyrzec Podlaski by the SS unit which accompanied them, headed by *Sturmbannfuehrer* Dolf. Only a few survived thanks to the efforts made by the Jews of Parczew.[41]

During the first half of 1940, 3,200 Jews from area occupied by the Germans were brought to the camp. They were held for some time and then sent home. On December 10 and December 16, 1940, 518 more Jewish war prisoners from camps in Eastern Prussia were brought to this camp. On January 28, 1942, another group of 2,000 prisoners-of-war came. These two groups, along with the original 2,500 prisoners, remained in the camp in Lublin for almost two years.[42]

The conditions in the camp on Lipowa Street were totally different from those of other prisoner-of-war camps under the Reich. Although the situation of the Jewish prisoners-of-war in the other places was also very harsh, the rights of prisoners, even Jews, were respected to a certain extent in the camps that were subordinated to the *Wehrmacht.* The SS, on the other hand, enforced a system of torture, beatings, and physical penalties from the very beginning. The prisoners suffered starvation and slept on boards without blankets or straw. They were told that when they arrived in Lublin, they lost their rights as prisoners-of-war and were now under the supervision of the SS, who would treat them as regular Jewish prisoners. Because of this, they decided to begin a struggle for their rights as war prisoners. This struggle, which was particularly effective in its first stage, set the stage for an armed resistance movement.

The prisoners immediately elected a committee and demanded that it be officially recognized. Dr. Krojt, a sergeant in the Polish army, was chosen head of the committee. Although the SS sanctioned the prisoners' committee, it immediately began to pressure its leaders to agree to rescind their rights as prisoners-of-war. To add terror to fear, Dr. Krojt was taken away from Lublin and sent to a concentration camp. Brandel was chosen head of the committee in his place. When the Germans pressured him also, Brandel understood the danger awaiting him; a few days later he escaped from the camp with some fellow prisoners.

The camp's command reacted with great cruelty to the escape of Brandel and his friends. On the dawn of February 4, 1941, in the freezing cold, the prisoners were expelled barefoot from their barracks. They were harshly beaten for several hours, and dogs were set against them for several more. Nine died on the spot, and about sixty others, frostbitten and wounded, had to be taken to the hospital.[43]

This incident—called the "Black Night" by the prisoners—did not break the spirit of resistance. Roman Fisher was chosen as the new head of the prisoners' committee, and with the help of all the prisoners and their stand of solidarity, he managed to get the SS command to agree to introduce a more moderate regime in the camp and to improve living conditions. Fisher displayed great talent for organizing and strong spirit in his dealing with the camp's SS command. According to Josef Reznik, one of the camp's survivors, Fisher did a great deal for the camp's underground:

> First Fisher organized us from the inside, and this was an important step in the struggle with the Germans for the prisoners' rights. We did not accept the claims of the Germans that we were only Jews and not war prisoners. We fought to be recognized as Polish soldiers, prisoners-of-war from a country that had been defeated and now no longer existed. Because of this, we did not take off our uniforms. When one of us went to work, he always wore clean clothes and his shoes shone like the shoes of a soldier.[44]

The entire camp was divided by the prisoners' committee into three battalions, thirteen companies, and several platoons. Commanders were appointed in accordance with this division, whom the committee managed to get the SS to let assign the prisoners their places of work; before, this was done by the SS men, who ruthlessly seized the prisoners for work. For this purpose, the committee received the camp's file (the list of prisoners), which later proved to be an important key to organizing escapes. An aid fund was set up in which the prisoners deposited the money they had brought from Germany or the pay they received when they worked outside the camp. These funds were later used to purchase arms.

The committee was soon put to a serious test in its struggle to defend the prisoners' rights. The camp's command issued an order that the prisoners were to wear a mark on their sleeves like all the Jews in the *General Gouvernement,* to symbolize their not having the special prisoner-of-war status of other Lipowa Street inmates. In compliance with the committee's decision, no one followed the order; as a result of this show of solidarity, the camp's command rescinded the order. There was also sudden improvement in the living conditions of the camp. The food portions were increased, and the sleeping boards were enlarged and covered with fodder and blankets. Consent was even given to open a theater in the camp. All these improvements helped to strengthen the authority of the prisoners' committee.

The work places outside the camp set up by the Germans were very valuable to the camp's underground, because they allowed the 600 prisoners who worked there a certain freedom of movement in the city. The underground movement particularly benefited from the cells in the Bobulan Hospital on Warszawska Street, the hospital near the military barracks of the former 8th Regiment, the armament storehouse, and the patient reception area *(Krankensammelstelle)* near the military hospital. The prisoners who worked there acquired the trust of the German guard and, therefore, were given even more freedom. This was particularly true of those who worked delivering uniforms, clothing, and linens between the minicipal laundry and the hospital, for along with their uniforms, the wounded German soldiers who entered the hospital also gave in their personal arms. A few of the prisoners working here managed to gain access to the storehouses and in this way acquired some weapons for the underground movement, particularly from soldiers who died, because the fact that their arms were missing was less likely to be discovered.

When the Germans established a row of workshops in the camp which belonged to the SS factories *(Deutsche Ausruestungs-Werke,* DAW), most of the prisoners were employed there. The production manager was a German civilian named Rolph, who had a humanitarian attitude towards the Jews and, on several occasions, informed members of the prisoners' committee of the camp command's plans.

But things took a turn for the worse following the outbreak of the German-Soviet war. Acts of terror in the camp increased, and on some occasions, prisoners caught outside the camp were hanged.[45]

In October 1941, about 500 prisoners were moved to a new camp in the Majdan Tatarski quarter of Lublin. They worked installing barbed-wire fences around the camp and building barracks for several months. The SS officers in charge of the construction work, Dorenberger and Dolf, were extreme sadists. Prisoners feared being transferred to this camp known as Majdanek, which until February 1943 was officially a prisoner-of-war camp (Kriegsgefangenenlager). In the beginning, Soviet prisoners-of-war were sent there, and it was seriously believed that the Jewish prisoners-of-war from the camp of Lipowa Street would also be put here.[46]

In December, about 300 Soviet prisoners came to the camp in Lipowa Street. After a short stay in the camp, they were given Nazi uniforms and incorporated into the guard units (Wachtbattaillionen). They took part in the liquidation of the ghettos in the Lublin area and of Lublin itself. It was from them that the Jewish prisoners found out that 100,000 Soviet prisoners-of-war had been killed near Chelm Lubelski, where they had been kept out in the open in a field surrounded by a high voltage fence. The prisoners were given no food for several weeks, and many starved to death. The extreme hunger led to cases of cannibalism. Only a few hundred of the very strong survived, and they were given the option of serving the Germans.[47]

This kind of information served as a warning to the Jews to intensify preparations for resistance. A rescue committee headed by Fisher and including Szelupski, Przysucki, Jegier, Goldberg, and Zajf was established. Since it was clear that an armed uprising carried out in the camp would be destined to decisive failure from the start, the possibility of organizing group escapes to the forests and conducting partisan activities from prepared bases were considered. For this purpose, contacts were sought in the surrounding area, but this met with great hardships. The Jews who had been imprisoned in the Lublin Ghetto since March 1941 could not give any support to the resistance movement in the camp, and making contacts with Polish underground organizations was most difficult. Since the prisoners in the Lipowa camp came from the eastern part of Poland, they did not know the area of Lublin and did not have past ties with the local Polish population. In addition, there were no active partisan groups in the Lublin area at the time, and the Polish underground organizations did not show much interest in the fate of Jewish prisoners-of-war. Only at the end of 1942, when they began to establish partisan units, did PPR representatives come there to make contact with the prisoners-of-war and to give them some help with partisan activities. Special initiative was shown by the Polish Socialist Party (PPS) who tried to interest Polish and British government authorities in the fate of the Jewish prisoners.[48]

Yet time was pressing. The great deportation from Lublin was carried out between March 17 and April 29, 1942. About 30,000 Jews had been sent to the extermination camp in Belzec or killed in the surrounding area. There was need for immediate action. By this time, a certain number of arms had been acquired and hidden in the camp's laundry, and contact had been made with a group of Poles who said they were members of the underground. The prisoners had no way to investigate people who offered support. The contacts with them were made mainly by the commanders of the prisoners' battalions, Walach and Seufert. The Poles were given money to purchase arms and prepare a partisan base in the Janow forests.[49]

The decision to liquidate the camp in Lipowa Street and transfer the prisoners to the Majdanek camp was apparently made in the summer of 1942. On August 17, the Germans ordered the transfer of the initial group, a few hundred prisoners, and this triggered the first spontaneous act of armed resistance. When the prisoners realized that they were being taken to Majdanek, they attacked the SS guards accompanying them. The guards responded with a shower of fire and grenades. These events are described by Joseph Cynowiec, one of the survivors:

> In August 1942, there was resistance action by the prisoners. When the group was moved down Zamojska Street and had reached the Bystrzyca bridge, we understood that we were being taken to Majdanek. There they would take away our uniforms and turn us into extermination camp inmates. A spontaneous escape started. The German and Ukrainian guards began to shoot and about eighty prisoners were killed. However, the Germans paid a heavy price then. There was a group of shoemakers with us who were taken straight out of the workshops, and they had taken the knives they worked with along with them. This group attacked the Germans and began to cut them. A few Germans were killed. A number of prisoners escaped. However, some of them returned to the camp later, because they had no place to hide.[50]

A communiqué describing this incident, and fully confirming the course of events described by Cynowiec, was passed on to London as part of the report of the Information Department of the Government Delegacy, dated October 5, 1942.[51]

The Germans refrained for some time from renewing the transfer of Jewish prisoners-of-war to Majdanek. Yet it was clear that this was only temporary. Pressure, therefore, was put on the Poles who had promised to help prepare bases for partisan activities in the Janow forests. In the middle of October, they reported that all was ready for receiving fugitives from the camp.

A group of forty prisoners, under the command of Ressler, was chosen and given arms and money. They were to be the first to leave the camp and were given the task of preparing the groundwork for future escapes. The escape succeeded, and the group reached the Janow forests and hid in the bunker prepared by the Poles. This was done without arousing the Germans' suspicion for two reasons. First, the list of prisoners was in the hands of the committee. Second, a number of fugitives from various forced labor camps had come at this time to hide in the Lipowa camp because it had much better conditions than regular Jewish labor camps. The "guests" from the other camps were secretly given Polish army uniforms worn by the prisoners-of-war. They would appear at roll calls and be sent to workplaces outside the camp in place of the escaped prisoners-of-war. As long as the number of prisoners present at roll call was the same, the command was not suspicious.[52] But soon two members of Ressler's group unexpectedly returned to the camp and gave news of the tragedy that had befallen its people. Gruber tells of this in his testimony:

> The members of the group of forty who had fled to the Janow forests through the contacts with the Polish Military Organization were killed at the hands of members of that group. This became known after some time. The POW men dug a bunker and ordered the group to hide in it. Afterwards, they murdered them in the bunker with grenades and machine guns. Only two survived.[53]

This outright killing greatly depressed the prisoners and shook their trust in the rescue committee. The prisoners accused their commanders of recklessness in forming ties with people they knew almost nothing about. Various groups of prisoners-of-war who worked outside the camp now tried to make contact with the Polish underground on their own.

The group of prisoners who worked in the *Krankensammelstelle* made contact in October 1942 with the Polish communist activist Pawel Dabek, who was sent by the PPR leadership to organize People's Guard groups in the area of Lublin. Because of this, he took an interest in the prisoners-of-war whom he saw as excellent material for the partisan movement. The Jewish commanders at this workplace were Kaganowicz, Jegier, and Gruber. Dabek promised them help in organizing escapes of groups of twenty prisoners, who were to be sent to the Kozlow forests. PPR cells were organized at this time in two villages in the area of these forests, Wola and Przypisowka, and these were to help the fugitives initiate partisan actions under the auspices of the Polish Workers Party. Kaganowicz and his group agreed to Dabek's plan and gave him money to purchase arms. After this they began making preparations to escape from the camp.

The escape of the thirty-five-man group organized by Kaganowicz took place on October 28, 1942. Although the group's members did not manage as planned to get to the camp's laundry that day to take the guns, submachine gun, and ammunition hidden there, it was impossible to change the date of the escape set by Dabek. They decided to escaped unarmed, hoping to receive weapons from the Polish Workers Party.

As in the case of Ressler's group, the camp's command did not notice the escape of Kaganowicz and his friends. The rescue committee, however, concluded that the uncoordinated, "wild" escapes would not remain hidden from the Germans for long, and that escape would soon be impossible for the remaining prisoners. Because of this, they drew up a plan for the escape of all the prisoners in the camp. The physician, Dr. Shindler, convinced the Germans that there was danger of a lice epidemic in the camp and that all the prisoners must at once be sent together to the baths and the whole camp disinfected. The plan was that while the prisoners were assembled in the bathhouse courtyard, they would rebel, attack the accompanying guards, who most likely would include only part of the camp's watchmen, and later escape to the surrounding forests. Efforts were made to strengthen the ties with the Polish underground whose help was expected after the escape.

The plan to gather all the prisoners near the bathhouse began to work. The Germans agreed to take all the prisoners to the baths and decided on Saturday, November 14, as the date for the disinfection.

Meanwhile, Kaganowicz's group reached the forest. But they did not find the emissaries that Dabek had promised would be there. With no arms the fugitives could neither act nor defend themselves during hunts. Running from place to place in an unknown area, they quickly realized that without arms or contacts they could not survive in the forest even for a short time. The only way was to try to take the arms hidden in the camp. Kaganowicz and his men knew that it was relatively easy to reach the arms held by the prisoners who worked in the hospital. Sent to Lublin to get help and arms, Stefan Finkel managed to reach the hospital near the barracks where Dov (Ber)

Berezin worked, and from which he managed to take a certain quantity of arms and hide them.

Berezin did not know of the plan for the mass escape of the prisoners. Therefore, he seriously began to carry out Kaganowicz's plan with the aid of eleven other prisoners who worked there. They removed twelve rifles, a few pistols, ammunition, uniforms, and blankets and packed them together with the linen that was to be taken to the laundry. It was evident that when the Germans discovered the escape from one place of work, they would punish others in different workplaces. Because of this, they told the prisoners working in the Bobulan hospital and in the ammunition storehouse of the escape plans and suggested that they run away that day also. They did not manage to say anything to the prisoners working in other places.

The twelve prisoners who worked in the Bobulan hospital also had managed to hide a certain quantity of arms, shoes, linens, and blankets. Like the equipment at the hospital near the barracks, these were also made to look like a bundle supposedly prepared for delivery by truck to the laundry. Trucks were ordered to come to both hospitals on November 11. The twenty-two prisoners who worked in the armament storehouse also planned to escape that day.

The situation was complicated: Szrunk, who worked in the Bobulan Hospital, knew of the plans for the mass escape on November 14 and tried to oppose the hastily planned escape from the two hospitals, but his arguments convinced no one. Nobody believed it was really possible for all the prisoners to escape. Furthermore, because he could not dissuade the small groups of prisoners and because he was under pressure from his friends, Szrunk decided to join them. In his testimony, Berezin said that Szrunk felt great remorse and "cried because he felt he betrayed his friends."

The escape was a total success. The unaccompanied German drivers suspected nothing and began to drive the prisoners and their bundles to the laundry. When they got a certain distance away from the hospital, the prisoners forced the drivers to leave Lublin and to go to the Kozlow forests, where they unloaded the vehicles, freed the drivers, and went to meet Kaganowicz.

The simultaneous escapes from three places of work by armed prisoners who overcame German army drivers alerted the Germans, who immediately tightened their watch over the remaining prisoners. In view of this, the mass escape planned for November 14 was canceled. The Germans stopped the prisoners' work outside the camp, and the 200 prisoners who had formerly been housed in their work places in the military storehouses were ordered to return to the camp. The prisoners' bitter experience, however, led them to believe that this meant that they were being sent to Majdanek, and they offered resistance. During this, the second incident of active resistance by the prisoners, the majority escaped. But most were recaptured by the Germans very soon or turned themselves in and were killed. Only a few members of this group survived.

Some time later, there was an unsuccessful escape by fifteen prisoners. They were caught on December 14 in the area of Krasnik and shot.[54]

In the beginning of 1943, the Lipowa camp was removed from the direct authority of the SS commander in the area of Lublin, Odilo Globocnik, and subordinated to the Majdanek camp command, under *Standartenfuehrer* Karl Otto Koch. This led to conflicts between Globocnik and Koch, and to rumors received by the rescue committee that the Lipowa camp might be liquidated because Koch wanted the whole camp to move to Majdanek.

In view of this situation, the rescue committee ordered an alert, and the prisoners decided to resist with the few arms they had managed to smuggle into the camp. At the same time, the Germans increased the watch around the camp, bringing in a new unit made up of groups of SS, Ukrainians, and Lithuanians. However, the conflict between Koch and Globocnik suddenly ended with Globocnik's victory. The Majdanek guard was brought back from Lipowa, and after a six-week break, the camp returned to the command of Globocnik. The danger that the prisoners would be transferred to Majdanek passed for the time being.

A short time later, the camp was again put on alert for an uprising. In the beginning of March, Roman Fisher and other members of the rescue committee were taken away and interrogated under torture. This was interpreted in the camp to mean the renewal of the preparations to send the prisoners to Majdanek, and an order to prepare for an armed uprising was given. The prisoners remained awake all night without removing their uniforms and shoes. The unrest among the prisoners and the alert, however, did not go by unnoticed by the Germans. That night Fisher and his friends were returned to the camp, because in Fisher's opinion, the guard unit was not very strong at this time and the camp's command did not want to take the risk of a prisoners' rebellion.

Still, the tension did not cease, and on March 30, another group of thirty men escaped. Only half succeeded in reaching the partisans. Fisher was among them. With the help of Colonel Kowalski, he reached Warsaw where his wife was hiding. Fisher hoped to make contact there with representatives of the Home Army and organize help for additional escapes from the camp. Following his efforts, two AK representatives came to the camp where they made contact with Liberman and gave him Fisher's orders. But escapes with the help of the Home Army never materialized.

The existence of the rescue committee ceased with Fisher's escape, and for some time the prisoners remained without leadership. Later, though, another attempt to organize was made by Zysman, Friedman, and Tepman, who had ties with Lipowski, a Pole who supplied thirty pistols, three grenades, and 300 bullets.

In the beginning of October, an unexpected inspection was held in the camp, and some of the arms hidden in the barracks were found. When a group of ten underground members who worked in the tannery workshop and had some pistols hidden in their workshop learned of this, they got the German guard completely drunk and escaped. In the area of Belzyce, they met a group of armed Poles who said they were AK members but suddenly opened fire on the Jewish group, killing six. The four survivors found their way to the Jewish partisans after wandering for a long time.

In the meanwhile, changes took place which decided the fate of the camp. The new SS and police commander in the district of Lublin, *Grupenfuehrer* Sporrenberg, received orders from Krueger to liquidate the Jewish work camps in the area of Lublin as part of the *Erntefest* campaign. The camp on Lipowa Street was to be liquidated along with other camps. The date set for this was November 3, 1943. That day, 18,400 Jews were shot in trenches near the Majdanek crematory, among them the prisoners from the camp in Lublin.[55]

The report of the Government Delegacy sent on December 8, 1943, describes the strict watch under which the Jewish prisoners were taken to Majdanek: "In the first week of November the last of the Jews from the camp in Lipowa Street (prisoners-of-war who were former Polish soldiers, and a group of tradesmen) were deported to Majdanek under heavy SS guard. They were taken away early in the morning, with a long gap between groups. There was one SS man for every two Jews."[56]

On the way, a password was given by the former Hebrew teacher, Szosznik, and the prisoners rebelled. According to the above-mentioned report, "the Jews broke through the encirclement and began running, shouting 'Long live freedom'." The SS guard opened heavy fire and only ten prisoners managed to escape. The number of those who fell in this last attempt at resistance is not known. The remaining prisoners were shot in Majdanek, refusing to the last minute to remove their army uniforms.[57]

THE BORKI CAMP

The events in the Borki camp are a tragic epilogue to the history of the Lublin prisoner camp. They ended in one of the most dramatic escapes in the annals of World War II.

On November 3, the Germans held a selection in Majdanek whose aim turned out to be the execution of the prisoners. Sixty-one Jewish prisoners-of-war from Lipowa were taken away after this selection and brought to the Borki camp in Chelm Lubelski. They were annexed to Unit 1005 *Enterdungsaktion-Sonderkommando*, which was ordered to burn the bodies of 30,000 people whom the Germans had shot and buried there in mass graves. These were mostly Soviet prisoners-of-war, as was evident from the buttons and bits of uniforms found. Eight trenches filled with the bodies of these soldiers were opened, one of which also contained bodies of soldiers in Italian uniforms and those of a few hundred Jews, among them children from Hrubieszow, as documents found later testified. The bodies were put into stacks of one thousand and burned. Every day the Germans removed about thirty sacks containing ashes of bones, trying to completely erase every trace of the massacre there. The watch was very tight. The number of German guards was greater than that of Jewish prisoners, and a group of Gestapo clerks also did special service. The German commander of the camp was Rohfing.

Oscar Berger was chosen as the representative of the prisoners and was also the central organizer of the resistance committee. He began his activity on almost the first day he got there. It was evident that the Germans were erasing all traces of their crimes and would, therefore, make sure no Jewish witness lived.

Escape during work hours was out of the question in view of the very heavy German watch. A plan was made to build an underground passage from the barrack to the outside of the fence of the camp. It was completed after six strenuous weeks of work under extremely harsh conditions. The prisoners had had to dig without tools in frozen ground. Their gravest problems were removing the excavated dirt and camouflaging the entrance to the passage from the frequent rounds of inspections held by the Germans. Unfortunately, because they had no way to measure while digging, the outside opening of the passage was far from its appointed place.[58]

The escape was planned for the dawn of December 24, 1943. The first to enter the passage was the principal organizer of the escape, Berger, who took upon himself the responsibility of guiding the group through the passage and beyond. Ten volunteers followed him, their order having been decided by lot. Another lot was drawn later among the remaining fifty prisoners. The escape through the passage is described by Josef Sterdyner, who was number seven in the first group of ten volunteers:

> When I came out of the underground passage, I saw I was about a meter in front of the trench and not in it as planned. There was a mistake in the calculation of the slope of the area. Jumping into the trench from the distance of one meter was not difficult. However, when I reached the trench, I saw no one even though we had agreed that everyone would wait here. I moved all along the trench, jumped the barrier and ran to the forest. . . . There I already heard shooting and sirens and saw flares. When I reached the road I found Szechter and Josef Reznik.[59]

The cause for the early siren is explained in Reznik's testimony:

> We were to sabotage the city's telephone lines, cut the barbed-wire around the camp, and come around to the guardhouse where the Germans were asleep to take grenades, throw them, and in this way, secure our escape. . . . Rolicki from Wilna, a very big man, was with us. The passage opening was too narrow for him. We had to push him up. There was noise and this alerted the Germans. It was impossible to wait for everyone.[60]

It is not known how many prisoners managed to escape, under what circumstances they died afterwards, or how many fell during the escape through the passage itself. But we do know that, on the whole, only three of the Borki camp prisoners survived and that the fate of each of them is interesting.

Josef Reznik hid for several months and later reached Yechiel Greenshpan's partisan unit in the Parczew forests. Lipman Aronowicz and Singer reached the forest, and with the help of the forest watchman managed to make contact with Soviet partisans. Both were accepted into the Soviet *Krasni Partisan*, commanded by a Soviet Jew called Abramowich. Singer fell in one of the battles. When the partisan unit joined the regular Red Army, Aronowicz continued to fight as a Red Army soldier until he was wounded during a battle in the Carpathian mountains. After a stay in a hospital in Crimea, he was sent to General Batow's army and reached the city of Bart on the

Baltic Sea. Sterdyner tells of his experience after the escape from Borki in his own testimony: "After a long period of wandering, I reached the village of Siedliszcze. I went to the smith and asked his help. I found out from him that the partisans were to come here. He also promised to help. . . . The partisans from across the Bug came and agreed to accept me into their ranks. I remained with them until July 25, 1944. I came to Lublin with the first Soviet tanks."[61]

All three survivors of Borki testified in the 1962 trial held against the Borki war criminals in Heilbronn, Germany.

CHAPTER 13
JEWS IN THE POLISH WARSAW UPRISING

IT IS IMPOSSIBLE TO DETERMINE EXACTLY HOW MANY JEWS were in Warsaw on August 1, 1944, the day that the Polish revolt broke out. Dr. Emmanuel Ringelblum set the number of Jews who hid in the city after the ghetto uprising at approximately 15,000. Adolf Avraham Berman, one of the chief activists in the Jewish National Committee, determined that there were about 12,000 Jews hiding in Warsaw and the surrounding areas. Both estimates seem high. According to the report of the Jewish National Committee written in 1944, there were only 5,000 Jews under its protection in Warsaw. And although there were several thousand more Jews in Warsaw who did not benefit from the help of the committee or who were not in need of it, it is doubtful that the total number of Jews in Warsaw in the summer of 1944 reached 10,000.[1]

The Jews in Warsaw during the first half of 1944 can be divided into three groups. The first group included those who lived on Aryan papers, and who, because most of them worked, could move about the city using false papers. The second group consisted of Jews who hid in various places, and because of their appearance or lack of suitable documents, could not venture forth from their place of refuge. The third group was made up of Jews who were in the concentration camp on Gesia Street or in the Pawiak prison. Hundreds of these Jews, especially those in the first group, were active in the Polish underground organization.

The Polish revolt which was prepared by the Home Army initially encompassed most of the quarters in the western part of the city. The AK command did not manage to stir up a revolt in the eastern part of the city (the quarters of Praga, Grochow, and Saska Kepa) and in some of the western suburbs (Okecie and Marymont). In the quarters of Ochota and Wola the revolt ceased after a few days.

Polish historiography has devoted much time to this revolt, to its causes, and to its political and military manifestations. Most historians believe that this revolt was the result of faulty political calculation. It led to the sacrifice of many lives, and caused much suffering among the civilian population of Warsaw; it brought about great destruction in the city and great losses to the people without attaining even one of the political or military goals set by the AK command. According to the historian Pobog-Malinowski, the decision to fight in Warsaw was an immature political act on the part of the Polish government-in-exile and its subordinates, the underground leadership in Poland.[2] But the revolt in Warsaw in 1944 was not merely the result of a faulty political calculation. From the military point of view, the preparation of this operation was insufficient and its execution faulty, yet, with all that, the rebels and the whole population of Warsaw demonstrated great dedication and courage during the battles.

Many Jews who remained in Warsaw joined the revolt. A small number who were previously connected with the Home Army units were mobilized; others who were not connected with the Polish underground, or those who belonged to the People's Army, which was not included in the secret decision to carry out the revolt, reported willingly for battle and were accepted into fighting units or assigned to assist in building fortifications or in various services for the rebels. A group of Jews from the Jewish Fighting Organization formed a separate fighting unit within the ranks of the People's Army. Another group that participated in the revolt were prisoners who had been freed from the concentration camp on Gesia Street.

The commander of the Home Army, General Bor-Komorowski, set the total number of Jews who participated in the revolt at approximately 1,000.[3] It is possible that the number of participants was much higher.

The participation of the prisoners from the Gesia Street concentration camp is worthy of special consideration. This camp, which was called "Gesiowka," was established in 1943 as a branch of the Majdanek concentration camp. In the second half of July 1944, 4,000 prisoners were still held there. The Germans began to evacuate the camp at the advance of the Red Army, which was moving towards Warsaw, but at the outbreak of the revolt in Warsaw, the camp was not yet completely evacuated. There were about 400 prisoners in the camp itself, while dozens more were in workplaces outside the camp.

Several of the camp's fugitives and Jews who had fled the Pawiak prison hid in the ruins of the former ghetto.[4]

About a half hour after the outbreak of the revolt, the first group of prisoners who were working outside the camp in what was once *Umschlagplatz* were freed. (Two years previously, hundreds of thousands of Jews had passed through there on their way to their death in Treblinka.) Although made up mainly of Jews from Greece and Hungary, this group of prisoners also included a few Jews from Belgium and France, and Yisrael Chaim Goldstein, a Polish Jew who recounted the actual history of these prisoners in his book *Seven in a Bunker*.[5] During the first days of the revolt, the freed prisoners worked constructing barricades for the rebels. They carried out this task under heavy German fire. Afterwards, most of them joined the AK fighting units. The first of them to fall in battle was David Edelman from France.

On August 5, when the Zoska and Wigry battalions retreated under the pressure of the German attacks from the Wola quarter after unsuccessful battles in this part of the city, they were given the task of breaking through the old city. The path they took passed through the Gesia concentration camp. After this clash with the Germans, 348 Jews including Greek, French, Polish, Rumanian, and Hungarian citizens and twenty-four women were freed. All of the liberated prisoners immediately reported of their own will to the ranks of the Home Army. Some joined fighting units, mainly the Zoska, Parasol, and Wigry battalions. Others, who were technicians, formed a platoon for the repair of tanks. (There were three captured tanks in the hands of the rebels in this sector.) Others served in the weapon repair factories that were set up in the building of the Swieta Kinga School on Okopowa Street.

The former prisoners fought with great courage and dedication. Second Lieutenant Tadeusz Zuchowicz, a Pole who took part in the liberation of the camp, recalls one such incident of bravery in the battle that took place on the ninth day of the revolt:

> I remember that on approximately August 9, three German tanks came forth from Powazkowska Street. As they crossed the junction of Okopowa, one of the tanks was hit by the shots from our "Fiat" (English mortar for tank warfare and the destruction of bunkers). The SS crew jumped from the tank and fell as they were wounded by our bullets. The other two tanks retreated up Powazkowska Street and fired their machine guns. The commander of the sector shouted: "Who will succeed in entering the immobilized tank and turn the gun and hit the two retreating tanks?" One of the Jews jumped up like a cat and darted in the

direction of the "Panther" which was no longer a danger for us. Already he was at the entrance to the turret. We watched holding our breath as he slowly turned the cannon. The two retreating tanks were already 200 to 300 meters away. Suddenly the air shook with a loud noise and a streak of fire shot out of the barrel of the gun. As we looked on, the tank already turned into a burning heap of metal. The second tank escaped. Our victorious Jew emerged with a glowing face while his lips were set in a stern rebellious expression. The commander of the sector, the major, ran towards him and kissed both of his cheeks and pinned the cross of "Virtuti Militari" on the chest of the Jew. We all clapped for him and blessed him.[6]

The freed prisoners were received with special enthusiasm by the quartermaster of the Wigry Battalion, Captain Feliks Cywinski. Cywinski provided the freed prisoners with food from the unit's storehouse and even supplied some of them with clothes. This man, to whom Yad Vashem granted the decoration of "The Righteous Among Nations," on his own initiative, without the help of any known organization, offered refuge to twenty-six Jews until the start of the revolt. At the outbreak of the revolt, when Cywinski, an AK officer, was mobilized by his own regiment, he mobilized into action all of those Jews and placed them into various rebel units. Only one elderly couple was left behind. After the liberation of the camp at Gesia Street, Cywinski established a special unit which was composed of former prisoners and several of the Jews who had hidden under his protection. This was to be a platoon of the Wigry Battalion. Shmuel (Stanislaw) Kenigswein was appointed commander. He too had hidden under the protection of Cywinski. He had been a boxer in Maccabi Warsaw and a sergeant in the Polish army. According to the testimony of a soldier of his unit, Erno Hermonovics, over forty former concentration camp prisoners joined the platoon, although losses incurred during the battles gradually diminished its ranks.[7]

The Jewish platoon of the Wigry Battalion defended the positions near St. Johan Church and suffered heavy losses. Afterwards the platoon fought to the bitter end, which came with their surrender in the Czerniakow quarter.[8]

Many of the former prisoners who were taken into the auxiliary units worked in the construction of fortifications. At the end of their work, they were left to suffer their fate: they had neither food nor shelter. Their repeated requests to join the fighting units of the Home Army or to be placed in other auxiliary works remained unanswered. It was only when the units of the People's Army appeared in the city that the former prisoners turned to their commander and offered their continuing services to the revolt. Jan Fotek, the Pole who was given the task of dealing with the former prisoners from Gesia camp by the AL command in the old city, testifies to this:

> There were large groups of Jews in the old city, mainly from Czechoslo-vakia and Hungary, who had been freed by the rebels in the area of the former ghetto. Many times they approached us with the request that we provide them with weapons and that we allow them to join the rebel ranks. This was not possible then because of the difficulties resulting from an insufficient arms supply. However, we had to find some way to grant these people who were being chased by the Nazis the satisfaction of participating in battle and the opportunity to retaliate after all the crimes their people had suffered from. After continuous debates the idea was suggested to establish a unit made up of these people who, despite the lack of weapons, could still contribute something in battle; more-over, every day the tasks of the unarmed population were increased. In this way a unit made up entirely of Jews was established and took part in the Warsaw revolt. The command named the unit the "AL Auxiliary International Jewish Brigade." I was responsible for assembling this unit. This was no easy task for me. I did not know anyone from the group, and was the only Pole in the unit. I began by finding suitable living quarters in military barracks which would house all the groups. I then chose several men who seemed to be especially energetic and in-vited them for consultation. I was told that one of the men I had chosen, Dr. Stern from Bratislava, was considered the leader of these men. I thus appointed Dr. Stern head of the headquarters of the brigade and in-structed him to give other suggestions. In this way the brigade was organized within several hours, so that I could begin carrying out vari-ous duties. There were several construction workers in the brigade. I gave them the task of strengthening and expanding the construction of the position of the 3rd Battalion of the People's Army. As a result of the work of the brigade, three or four barricade lines, fortifications, and posts were built that could be defended with little manpower. As we dug trenches in front of the bunkers we had the feeling that our posi-tions could not be captured by the enemy. Indeed, after the war the builders of Warsaw encountered difficulties in dismantling these fortifications.[9]

According to the data of the Polish historian Antoni Przygonski, there were approximately 150 soldiers in the Jewish brigade.[10] In time as the battles continued, the brigade was equipped with arms, and in the end, took on the task of defending the positions it had built. On September 23, the Germans opened a full-scale attack on these posi-tions. As Fotek writes: "The concentrated attack of the Germans pushed back the defenders to the area of Prosta and Dluga streets.

Enemy pressure increased day by day. The International Jewish Brigade suffered such heavy losses that in effect it ceased to exist. The few remaining soldiers sought refuge in the center of the city."[11]

The third Jewish unit in the Warsaw revolt was the Jewish Fighting Organization platoon under the command of Yitzhak Zuckerman. At the outbreak of the revolt, Zuckerman contacted the AK command and suggested that a Jewish unit be formed within the framework of the Home Army. He was refused. It was only after a few days, when the few AL units in Warsaw began to mobilize intensively, that Zuckerman succeeded in contacting the AL command, which gladly accepted the offer of a Jewish unit within its framework. However, not many of the ZOB survivors managed to contact Zuckerman in the turbulence of the battle. Thus, many of them looked for their own way to various Polish units, mainly AK units.

The ZOB platoon established by Zuckerman was annexed to the 3rd Battalion of the People's Army and took upon itself the defense of the position near Mostowa Street in the old city. With the suppression of the revolt in this quarter, the platoon crossed over into the Zoliborz quarter, where known fighters from the Jewish underground in Warsaw fell, among them Pola Elster, Hirsch Berlinski, and Eliyahu Erlich.[12]

The commander of the Jewish Fighting Organization published an appeal to those Jews who remained alive in Warsaw asking them to take an active part in the revolt.

In addition to those in the ZOB unit and the Jewish Brigade, several dozen more Jews fought in the various Polish units of the People's Army. Some of them were among the central organizers and commanders of the People's Army in the revolt. The Jewess Helena Kozlowska and two men shared the leadership of the Polish Workers Party, which served as the political headquarters of the AL units; and among the Warsaw command of the People's Army were the following officers: Captain Menashe Anastazy Matywiecki, Captain Stanislaw Kurland, and Captain Edward Lanota. All three fell on August 26, 1944, when the AL headquarters in Warsaw was bombed in the course of the battles around the old city.

Among the AL unit commanders were such Jews as Lieutenant Jan Szelubski (a member of the resistance leadership in the prisoner-of-war camp in Lublin and a partisan in the Janow Forests), who commanded a company of the People's Army in the Powisle sector; Lieutenant Edwin Rozlubirski, second-in-command of the Czwartacy unit; Lieutenant Michal Jaworski; and the Second Lieutenants Reich (a former ghetto fighter), Ludwik Herszberg, and Hirsh (Ryszard)

Zelwianski. The commander of the Home Army, General Komorowski, personally bestowed the highest decoration, "Virtuti Militari," upon Lieutenants Szelubski and Rozlubirski. They were the only officers of the People's Army who were awarded this decoration.[13]

Jews also filled important roles in the ranks of the Socialist Fighting Organization (SOB). One of its company commanders was Second Lieutenant Marian Merenholc, ("Victor"), who fell in battle on the first day of the revolt. Another of the organizers, Shimon Jaffe, also fought in its ranks and fell at the beginning of the revolt. Aleksander Marcus (Markowski) also fell in these ranks; according to the testimony of the Polish fighter Zygmunt Rytel, "Marcus was the best of snipers and can be credited with the slaying of more than one German."[14] Another who fell in the revolt within the ranks of the Socialist Fighting Organization was the well-known doctor, Stefan Alperin.[15]

And yet, most of the Jews who participated in the Warsaw revolt fought in the ranks of the Home Army from the beginning of the revolt. During the course of battle, some of them attained officers' ranks and filled various positions of command. Many Jews among the rebels had had much experience in battle with the Germans, while several dozen others had fought in the Warsaw Ghetto Uprising. Among them, in addition to the ZOB members mentioned above, was a group of ten to twenty fighters of the Jewish Military Union who, after the suppression of the revolt in the Warsaw Ghetto, hid in the Aryan sector. They did not establish a separate Jewish unit, but at the outbreak of the revolt joined various Home Army units, mainly the Baszta unit.[16]

At least several dozen other Jews came from various partisan units. Among them were Jewish partisans from the Anielewicz unit, who had come back to Warsaw after the disintegration of their units, and several men who had taken part in the uprising in Treblinka.

All of the Jews who participated in the Warsaw revolt had been through many bitter experiences—fearful escapes after their actions in the Warsaw Ghetto, disguised lives in the Aryan sector, the losses of entire families, and so forth. Many, like the fugitives from Radom who had reached Warsaw and had hidden in the Aryan sector, had escaped from other towns.

In the testimonies of both Poles and Jews, special emphasis is placed on the guides who, because of their experience in the battles of the Warsaw Ghetto Uprising, had helped to maintain contact between various areas of the revolting city that had been cut off by the

Germans. They accomplished this by transporting the rebel units through the sewer system. As the AK officer Piotr Stachewicz explains:

> The part played by the guides experienced in the sewer system was most valuable. Corporal Henryk Poznanski, a member of the Jewish Fighting Organization, especially excelled in this task: he had been liberated from the concentration camp on Gesia Street and was called "Bystry." During the ghetto revolt, he transported food and arms to the Jewish fighters. Several days before the breakthrough of the Parasol unit, he transferred the general command of the Home Army along with General Bor. Furthermore, he guided the command of the Northern Group with Lieutenant Colonel Wachnowski. Finally, he guided the command of Parasol from the rearguard units of the Northern Group. This was his schedule on August 31.[17]

Later on in his testimony, Stachewicz tells of "Bystry's" death in the battle in Czerniakow.

The Jewish National Committee's emissary, Shoshana (Emilka) Kosower, led the AK units under the command of Colonel Seweryn and Major Olgierd Rudnicki-Sienkiewicz through the sewer system. She was awarded the Cross of Honor and given the rank of second lieutenant. At the height of the revolt, the Jewish emissary Sophia Friedental ("Stasia") led the Home Army units from the center of the city to Czerniakow, where she fell in battle. The emissaries "Maria," "Janka," "Stefa," and "Emilia" (known only by their nicknames) fell in battle and were buried in mass graves on Wspolna, Marszalkowska, and Mokotowska streets.[18]

Most of the Jews in Polish units appeared as Poles and concealed their Jewish identity. When they fell in battle they were buried under the Polish Catholic names they had adopted. These Jews hid their Jewishness because of the deep-rooted anti-Semitism of a considerable portion of the Polish population of Warsaw and of the Polish soldiers in the revolt. We learn of the manifestations of this anti-Semitism through the testimonies of Jews and Poles alike. Mieczyslaw Fuks who participated in the revolt describes the reaction of the Polish population to Jews who ventured forth from their hiding places at the outbreak of the revolt: "The population pointed their fingers at them. They did not sympathize with them at all. They were in fact apathetic towards them. They were amazed that they managed to stay alive but mocked them nevertheless. The poison Germans penetrated them with was recognized. Because of the population's negative attitude to the Jews, many Jews lost their lives."[19] Irena

Palenkier, who also participated in the revolt, testifies to similar phenomena: "Despite the fact that the Zoliborz quarter was in the hands of the rebels and not under German rule, here too the Jews had to be certain that they would not be discovered because the reaction of the Polish population could have been tragic for the hiding Jews."[20]

The Polish noblewoman Helena Krukowiecka hid Jews in her house on Mokotowska Street. At the outbreak of the revolt they left their hiding places thinking that the danger had passed. Krukowiecka testifies to the reaction of the surrounding population:

> The first to react was the janitor. He spat and exclaimed, "Tfoo, I thought that she was a decent woman and here she is hiding Jews in her house." A group of rebels from Wola moved into our area. They soon learned of how disloyal a Pole I was. Two of them burst into my apartment and began to plunder it. They stole the food supply that was prepared for the time of the revolt. They took all of the sheets and blankets and kitchen utensils. One of them even threatened to kill me when night came because I had hidden Jews in my house.[21]

The anti-Semitism of a large part of the Polish population influenced the atmosphere in the fighting units. This anti-Semitism penetrated even those units which had leftist tendencies and was the cause of more than one serious incident. Waclaw Zagorski ("Lech Grzybowski"), the commander of the 2nd Battalion in the Chrobry II group of the Home Army, writes about such an incident in his *Diary of a Rebel*, written during the revolt and published afterwards. Zagorski describes an incident with a Jewish sergeant called Igra in one of the battalion's companies. At the beginning of his diary Zagorski writes about the circumstances of Igra's joining the revolt:

> From among the several young men who yesterday were saved from being shot to death at Hala Targowa, two reported this morning and asked to be accepted into the unit which had saved their lives. It seems that one of them has an university education; he appears as a sergeant and adopts the name "Igra." He knowingly pointed out on the map the new German shooting bunkers which had been built by citizens in three days after their expulsion from Bendarska and Mariensztat streets. He supplied concrete information about the number of Germans, their locations, weapons, and finally the crimes which he had witnessed.[22]

A few days later Zagorski wrote in his diary: "Yesterday, after the fall of Sergeant Blyskawica, the command of his squad was given to Sergeant Igra. Within two weeks he gained the trust of his comrades in arms and was recognized in battle."[23] Some time later, Zagorski writes, the conflict broke out:

> Another unpleasant incident awaits me this morning. Sergeant "Igra" asks to be released from service and will not discuss the reason for this. With no difficulty I clarified what this was all about. "Igra" is a Jew. Not only did I not know this, but I would never have thought it. In his appearance, behavior and accent it is impossible to distinguish any traits which were considered Semitic. No one asked his name. I have no idea how his secret was revealed to the boys who recently had joined the unit. They may have asked him directly, without hesitation. From that day on "Igra" never had a moment of peace. In his presence, they would recount the most degrading anecdotes about the Jews. They would carry on scheming conversations about him as if they did not know he was there. "Igra" suffered and they played the game of cat and mouse with him. I knew who those who initiated this game were. I called them to my office and told them that whether they like or do not like Jews is a private matter. But I would not tolerate either anti-Semitism or racism in my battalion. I told them of Jews who had not only been fighting in our ranks from the first day of the revolt, but who long before the revolt were affiliated with us in a common underground struggle. I told them how "Igra," who was saved by our patrol from among a group of citizen prisoners who were shot on Hala Mirowska, reported for battle immediately and how he contributed so greatly by keeping Grzybowska Street in our hands during the most difficult weeks. The boys listened and recognized the truth in my words. They claimed that they had nothing against other Jews, that they respected Heniek. They also claimed that they liked Stasiek, respected Sergeant Lolek, but wondered why "Igra" did not want to say he was a Jew. I tried to find reasons which would explain "Igra's" request and to prove their behavior was unjustified. Aleksander, Basia, and Wislanski joined the discussion. The youths agreed with everything, but still supported the one who repeated over and over again with the stubbornness of a lunatic: "I do not want my commander to be a Jew." I decided to send him to a reserve company, but "Igra" stubbornly insisted on his request to be released from the army entirely. He was convinced that this would be better for him and his company. He wanted to devote his energy to the assistance organization for the surviving Jewish population of free Warsaw. I am sorry about "Igra." He was a brave soldier and an exemplary sergeant. However, according to the existing principle I release him from service as he himself demanded.[24]

Captain Zagorski, who was strongly opposed to anti-Semitism, like many liberal, tolerant men had to turn back in the face of the fanaticism that was widespread among the rebel units. Zagorski's battalion was made up mainly of socialists. However, a large group from the National Armed Forces was also accepted into this unit, and the extreme chauvinism of the neighboring battalion of the Chrobry II group influenced even a unit like Zagorski's, where the members and supporters of Polish Socialist Party dominated. But the situation of the Jews in other rebel units was much worse.

Tzadok Zvi Florman who commanded a company in the uprising, passing as a Pole under the name of Tadeusz Kaniowski, testifies to anti-Semitism in these rebel units. He tells the story of three fighters from the Jewish Fighting Organization who were in hiding (Ya'akob Putermilch, Baruch Spiegel, and the engineer Bronislaw Topaz) and then were transferred to his unit. As they could not contact the ZOB command at the outbreak of the revolt, they approached the command of the Home Army and asked to be attached to a combat unit. According to the testimony of Florman, the soldiers in his company opposed the acceptance of the Jews. Their reason was very simple—the Jews were superfluous, and as they said, "It is entirely possible to liberate Poland without the Jews." Moreover, two soldiers turned to Florman without hesitation and said: "Lieutenant, why do we need Jews? We will take them to a dark corner and beat them on the back with an iron pole." However, in this case, the three ZOB fighters were accepted into the AK unit and were saved from death only by the stand of the company commander whose soldiers did not know that he himself was a Jew.[25]

At the beginning of the revolt, extreme anti-Semitic groups who belonged to the National Armed Forces murdered many Jews who ventured from their hiding places and from the underground. Afterwards, the situation was somewhat improved, and articles condemning the crimes committed against the Jews began to appear in the rebels' press. But again the situation worsened with the suppression of the revolt as the discipline in the rebels' units became slacker. Many Jews were killed, both civilians and fighters in the ranks with the rebels. In his book *Seven in a Bunker*, Haim Goldstein writes: "A decisive majority of the Poles who fought were loyal to the Jews and even exhibited a friendly attitude. The number of killers was small."[26] Goldstein may be right, but the tragedy was that the majority who were loyal to the Jews and even encouraged them in their bitter situation did not make the expected efforts to oppose the extreme nationalist elements who were responsible for murdering Jews. In his memoirs, Goldstein described one case where there was positive interference. This was during the construction of a barricade on Mostowa Street by a group of prisoners who had just been liberated from the concentration camp on Gesia Street. They were still wearing the typical dress of the German concentration camp inmates. Suddenly screams were heard: "Death to the Jews!" After the screams there were shots. Two Jews in concentration camp dress were killed. The aggressors shouted: "We do not need Jews. Shoot every one!" However, several Poles interfered and by a miracle managed to save the other prisoners, who were working for the uprising, from the hands of the anti-Semitic hoodlums.

There is another case described in his book. When his company was resting outside the line of fire near Mlawska Street, Goldstein entered a discussion with his commander, an officer holding the rank of first lieutenant. Suddenly a volley of submachine-gun fire was heard. Everyone looked around. On the road lay a dying man. At his side there was a second man who at that moment was shouldering a submachine gun. This was the gun with which he had treacherously killed his comrade in arms, a rebel. He saluted the lieutenant and said: "To hell with it, he was a Jew." The lieutenant looked at Goldstein and began to apologize. "What can I do? He does not belong to our unit. I cannot do anything."[27]

Wladka Miedzyrzecka describes a murder which was carried out on the fifth day of the revolt in the railroad workers' house on the corner of Zelazna and Chmielna streets. Several Jews tried to find shelter from the shelling of the German artillery. Three of them had a Jewish appearance and were arrested by an AK patrol. They were told that in liberated Poland there was no place for Jews. The patrol opened fire. Yehoshua Salomon was killed. The other two managed to escape, although one of them, Lutek Friedman, was wounded.[28]

The fighter Alina Grelewska, who joined the Home Army before the outbreak of the revolt, describes an incident which took place during the last weeks of the revolt:

> Following an explosion next to the Paladium cinema, an underground wall of the theater collapsed. Our unit was situated there. Suddenly there appeared before us a group of Jews who had hidden in this area. There were more than ten of them, mostly men. They were all in a terrible state, unshaven and completely exhausted. It was difficult to know how they got there. It seemed that someone had locked them in. It also appeared that someone was supplying them with food, for even then (the second half of September—the seventh week of the revolt) we found several tins of food. Confusion prevailed in the unit. A known hoodlum, a retarded and illiterate man nicknamed Ryszard who was a soldier in the AK unit that found the group of Jews, shouted: "Shoot them." Other voices saying the same could be heard. But Ryszard's shouts were the loudest.[29]

It was only due to the continual interference of Grelewska, whose comrades in arms did not suspect that she herself was Jewish, that this group was saved.

Waclaw Zagorski describes the murder of seven Jewish women by the initiative of Captain Stryjkowski ("Hal"), the commander of the 1st Battalion of the Chrobry II group.[30] This was not the only instance of the murdering of Jews by Captain Stryjkowski's soldiers. With the permission and under the direct command of Lieutenant Okrzeja, on September 10, 1944, a group of eight soldiers from the 1st Battalion also killed fourteen Jews who were in a house on Prosta Street.[31]

The Jewish officer Dr. Roman Born-Bornstein, who served as the head of the health services in the center of the city during the rebellion, describes the circumstances surrounding the murder of approximately thirty Jews in a house on 30 Twarda Street. He also reports the murder of a Jewish engineer leaving a hospital after visiting his wounded brother, an AK soldier. The killing of approximately thirty Jews on 25 Dluga Street, at the hands of the National Armed Forces in the Old City, and a murder in the military hospital at 22 Zlota Street by the AK military police are also recorded.[32]

It is as impossible to determine the exact number of those murdered as it is to establish the exact number of Jews who fell in battles with the Germans, or as a result of the German bombing and shellings. The Warsaw revolt, which was a tragedy for the population of Poland's capital, was an additional catastrophe to the surviving Jews who were hiding in the city.

The total failure of the revolt was evident immediately. It had already been suppressed by September, and on October 2, 1944, the Home Army surrendered. In keeping with the demands of the victors, it was necessary to evacuate the western part of Warsaw, which had again been conquered by the German army. The fate of the population of Warsaw was placed in the hands of the Germans with no guarantees as to their outcome—whether the population would be sent to transit camps, prison camps, work camps, concentration camps, or extermination camps. The mood of those evacuated and the general situation and atmosphere in the capital was reminiscent of the tragedy of the Warsaw Ghetto during the deportation to Treblinka in the summer of 1942. Guta Wilner testifies on the course of the evacuation and mood of the population:

> The cars were made to carry cattle, open and very high. They were quickly filled with people who were crowded as they stood next to each other because there was no room to sit. One could hear screams and

shouts. After the train was hermetically shut, it began to move. Where it was moving and to what end remained a huge puzzle. Someone began to scream: "They are taking us to make soap out of us. They are leading us—like the Jews—to the ovens, to be slaughtered." When the train stopped at various stations, someone would mercifully throw us some tomatoes or potatoes. People would pounce upon this food like wild animals. They were ready to gouge out their neighbors' eyes.[33]

Sometimes one of the rebels would resist when he saw the cruel process of evacuation but this would most often end in tragedy. Leslaw Bartelski, the Polish historian, writes about such a case: "Most of those who returned to Dworkowa were shot. One of the rebels, it is impossible to determine which one, shouted: 'Boys, do not let them slaughter us like the Jews,' and empty-handed they attacked the German gendarmes. This was probably First Lieutenant Goral, the commander of a cavalry unit. The Germans began to kill. One hundred fifty rebels from the B1 and B2 companies and cavalry soldiers paid with their lives for this attempt to rebel."[34]

Thus, the rebellion of the Home Army failed, after it had prepared itself for this struggle for nearly four years and although its means were far greater than those of the Warsaw Ghetto. During the revolt, the Home Army in Warsaw had received large quantities of arms from Soviet, British, and American air drops. According to the Polish historian Przygonski, it had received a total of 40 tons of arms and 120 tons of food from the Soviets and 52 tons of arms from the British and the Americans. The objective conditions for the preparation for the struggle by the AK units were also totally different from those of the Jewish Fighting Organization which operated in the enclosed and besieged ghetto. And although the military situation in Europe at the time of the ghetto revolt was entirely different from that during the time of the Polish revolt, it is also clear that their helplessness in the face of German superiority in numbers and weaponry was the same.[35]

Contrary to the suspicion of a considerable portion of the Polish public in Warsaw, the Germans did not intend to carry out the slaughter of the Polish population. The Germans rescinded the plan (formulated in August 1944) to evacuate the population of Warsaw to concentration camps.[36] Only a portion of this population were in fact sent to the concentration camp in Auschwitz. A large number (according to several sources, about 40,000 people) were killed during the first days of the revolt on August 5 and 6, during the huge massacre at Wola and Zoliborz, carried out by Reinefart's and Kaminski's German units. After the suppression of the revolt, the fighters were considered prisoners-of-war and were sent to prisoner-of-war camps.[37]

The fate of the Jews was quite different. Those who were noticed or informed on by others were shot immediately. On the day of surrender, October 2, in Krasinski Square, the Germans shot several dozen Jews who had been prisoners of the Gesia camp and who had participated in the revolt. The Jews, whether they were fighters or unarmed civilians, sought various escape routes. Most of them left Warsaw and tried either to mingle with the Polish civilian population or to reach prisoner-of-war camps as long as they could hide the fact that they were Jews.

Several Jews tried to cross to the eastern bank of the Vistula, which only a few weeks before had been conquered by the Soviet and Polish armies. Among the first to cross the river on September 26 were four participants in the revolt who had been prisoners in the Gesia camp. One of them was the lawyer Bela Harap from Transylvania. These four were the first eyewitnesses of the Jewish epic in the days of the Polish revolt in Warsaw; they also met with Jewish organizations which had begun activity in the liberated areas of Poland on the eastern bank of the Vistula. Among the few who succeeded in crossing to the east bank of the Vistula was Edward Kupferberg-Halski, an officer in the Polish army in September 1939. Afterwards, he escaped from a prisoner-of-war camp and took part in the battles against the Germans in the Red Army in the beginning of the German-Soviet war. Once again he was taken prisoner and once again he fled and joined the AK underground. Among other activities, he had a hand in smuggling arms into the Warsaw Ghetto. He fought in the Polish revolt, and after the defeat he succeeded as only a few others did, in crossing the Vistula. He reported for duty in the regular Polish army and did his military service on the front, holding the rank of major.[38]

Several Jews managed to reach the Puszcza Kampinowska forest and joined the AK unit which operated there. Shmuel Wilenberg, among others, was in this group. He had been a fighter in the Treblinka revolt. All of the Jews who were at Puszcza Kampinowska had to pass as Poles.

About 500 Jews, among them many of those who had taken part in the revolt, decided to remain in the destroyed city and hide in the bunkers which had been constructed in haste in the ruins of the city. For many of them, leaving the city together with Polish population would have meant certain death because of their external appearance. Hiding in the bunkers gave them the hope of remaining alive until the renewal of the Russian offensive. The Jews in the bunkers were the only residents of Warsaw after the entire population was taken out of the city during the first days of October 1944. Bernard Goldstein, an activist in the Jewish resistance, writes about this: "Warsaw became an empty city. Aside from the Jews who remained in the underground bunkers, there were no other residents there. During those months the capital of Poland became a Jewish city."[39]

A group of the Jewish Fighting Organization, which included Yitzhak Zuckerman and Zivia Lubetkin, hid for some time in a bunker on Promyka Street and, with the help of the Polish underground, managed to leave from there and to reach Lesna Podkowa, where they remained until the liberation of those territories in January 1945. After they managed to contact Adolf Berman who had also managed to escape Warsaw, they renewed the activity of the Jewish National Committee. The ZOB emissary Lodzia Hamerstein-Bukowska played a valuable role in communication between the Jewish National Committee activists and in the renewal of their activities.[40]

Another group of former ZOB members hid in a bunker on the corner of Sosnowa and Sienna streets, and in a bunker at 26 Wspolna Street twenty-nine more Jews hid. Among them were the Jewish public figures David Guzik and Bernard Goldstein, who were mentioned above; Spiegelman and Wiernik, participants in the Treblinka revolt who had escaped to Warsaw; a Greek Jew who was a former prisoner in Gesiowka; and several others from among the fighters of the Warsaw revolt. A few of the former partisans from the Anielewicz unit had also moved to the bunkers. In another bunker there were forty-one rebels, among them Roman Fisher, the organizer of the resistance movement in the prison camp in Lublin, and the Pole, Colonel Wladyslaw Kowalski, who after hiding and helping in the Aryan sector decided to share the fate of the Jews at the outbreak of the revolt. A group of fighters from Shmuel Kenigswein's Jewish platoon hid with their commander in the ruins of the old city on the corner of Kilinski and Krzywe Kolo streets. Another group of forty Jewish fighters from the revolt hid in the ruins of the block houses on Zlota and Sienna streets.[41]

Chaim Goldstein, in *Seven in a Bunker*, describes life in the bunker at 8 Franciszkanska Street, where six Jews, including several who had taken part in the Warsaw rebellion, and a Polish priest who had also fought in the revolt hid. Goldstein also describes meeting ten more people who had fought in the revolt as part of the People's Army and moved to the bunker on Kozla Street after the defeat. This group was discovered by German soldiers, and all its members fell after a short battle.[42]

The Germans unearthed about half of the existing bunkers. In Bernard Goldstein's opinion, only 200 of the 500 Jews who were in hiding lived to the day of liberation on January 17, 1945.[43] In those days, the ruined city of Warsaw was a front-line position. The consequent flow of great numbers of German soldiers led to a drastic deterioration of the situation for the Jews in hiding. The first of the bunkers to be discovered was unearthed and destroyed on October 27. Seven Jews (including three Hungarians) died after an armed struggle.[44]

Details pertaining to the circumstances of the discovery of other bunkers and the death of the majority of Jews in hiding are not available. On January 17, 1945, the ruined city of Warsaw was liberated by units of the First Polish Army. The many Jewish soldiers in these units met the Jews who survived in the bunkers and who had fought in the Warsaw uprising. A Jewish officer Lieutenant Colonel Maksmilian Kasztelanski described one of these meetings:

> As a result of the January offensive, I found myself in Warsaw. My first steps were toward the area of the former ghetto. As I walked along a street a man approached me and asked: *"Amchu?"* I did not understand what he meant. He then asked me directly if I was a Jew. This man led me to one of the totally demolished streets and along paths twisting through the ruins. He led me into a bunker which had served as a hideout from the Germans. My chance acquaintance described how he had been saved from extermination. Eighteen people hid in the bunker, which was very well organized. The Jews in hiding had homemade grenades. They had been in hiding there for four months.[45]

SUMMARY AND CONCLUSIONS

IN OUR STUDY WE HAVE DISCUSSED A RANGE OF PROBLEMS related to the Jewish armed resistance and traced its development in the four districts of the *General Gouvernement*—Lublin, Warsaw, Cracow, and Radom. We have looked at three separate battle areas, the partisan units, the ghettos, and the camps, and we have also dealt with the part played by Jews in the Polish revolt in Warsaw in the summer of 1944. We have demonstrated that the isolation of the Jews during a period of the most extreme terror (much more extreme than the terror imposed on other conquered peoples) and afterwards, during the genocide made a distinct impression on the Jewish resistance movement and led it to develop a unique character and a unique range of possibilities and functions.

The armed resistance movement in the ghettos and in the camps had several common characteristics. In both, the underground resistance consisted of an enslaved population, enclosed in an isolated and limited area, utterly exhausted by constant hunger, and denied even minimal essential sanitary conditions. These factors were not the same in the various ghettos and camps. Usually conditions were worse in forced labor camps than in ghettos, and most extreme in concentration and extermination camps.

The major objective of resistance efforts in the ghettos—and especially in the Warsaw Ghetto—was the expression of armed protest against the German murderers' actions, a protest under conditions which absolutely precluded any hope of saving the trapped ghetto inhabitants, with the exception of the rare miracle of an individual escape or rescue.

The objectives of armed resistance operations in the extermination camps was the destruction of the mass murder installations (gas chambers) and the creation of the opportunities to rescue prisoners by breaking out of the camps and escaping to the partisans. Breaking out and escaping in order to continue the armed struggle in the forests was also the goal of resistance in the smaller forced labor camps. In the Plaszow concentration camp as well as in larger forced labor camps, the aim of the fighting underground was to create conditions for escape from camps for prisoners who would continue the struggle in the forest. The conditions in the camp closed off all hope of saving the majority or even many of the prisoners.

In the Jewish prisoner-of-war camp in Lublin, the unrealistic idea of a mass escape was abandoned. Efforts were concentrated on making it possible for a few necessarily carefully chosen groups to escape for the purpose of continuing the struggle within the partisan movement.

Even the character and function of the Jewish partisan movement were different from those of the Polish partisans, although they struggled in the same areas. In both cases, the fighting was carried out from bases in the forests. However, in the Polish partisan movement most of the groups were equipped and trained before leaving for the forest base, which in most cases had been prepared in advance. After a series of unsuccessful skirmishes, the Polish partisan units usually would disperse and their members would be sent either back home or told to prepare hiding places in order to reorganize, when the situation was appropriate. These units were established not only for military purposes (for war with the occupying forces), but to a greater extent for internal political purposes. In almost every case they represented the armed forces of a particular political body, in order to assure it of control or partial control of the government of Poland after the expulsion of the Germans.

On the other hand, Jewish fighting groups in the forests were made up of fugitives from the ghettos and the camps who had not had the opportunity of preparing in advance for the struggle. Their major task was to fight for survival, both for the groups themselves and for the unarmed Jews hiding under their protection. Immediately upon their arrival in the forests, the Jewish groups were compelled to fight endless defensive battles with the occupying forces who relentlessly combed the forest in search of Jews in hiding. These clashes were decisive during the first stage of the fighting when the Jewish partisans operated purely for self-defense. In time (as early as 1943), the Jewish units began to take the offensive, attacking the enemy's military and economic targets.

In spite of its special character, however, the Jewish fighting movement was to a certain extent a part of the armed Polish underground. Many Jewish partisan units collaborated with the Polish partisan movement and a number of Jewish units belonged to the People's Army and had combat roles in the planning or in the framework of the organization itself. Within the People's Army there were also multinational partisan units where the part of the Jewish members was substantial. Jews fought against the occupying forces in many units of the People's Army, the Socialist Fighting Organization, and even the Home Army. And a large number of Jews were active in the Polish revolt in Warsaw in the summer of 1944.

The Jewish fighting movement in the *General Gouvernement*, therefore, was composed of two elements: the isolated element (made up of the underground resistance in the ghettos and camps and the Jewish partisan units), and the element which was an integral part of the Polish fighting underground (including the Polish partisan movement and the Polish Warsaw Revolt). The first was the more significant of these two, both from a quantitative point of view and in terms of the ramifications of its operations. The number of Jews who took part in the fighting in the ghettos and camps and in Jewish partisan units was much greater than the number of Jews in the Polish underground. Moreover, the Jewish underground fighting activities had a far greater impact and a greater moral significance than the struggle of Jews in the Polish organizations.

There were also two streams in the armed Jewish resistance in the *General Gouvernement:* the political and the spontaneous. In the large ghettos—Warsaw, Czestochowa, and Cracow—as well as in several smaller ghettos, the youth organizations (for the most part Zionist, but also including the Communist and Bundist youth) established the unified Jewish Fighting Organization. The leadership of the Jewish Fighting Organization in the Warsaw Ghetto made all possible efforts to influence centers in outlying towns, to maintain contact with them, to ensure some degree of coordination in leadership and in planning, and to offer them assistance in the form of advice and money. Because of the extreme isolation of the Jewish population in the closed ghettos and camps and despite the great efforts made, these attempts were only partially successful. Under the given circumstances, the ZOB emissaries were able to reach only a small number of Jewish concentrations. In the small ghettos, cut off from Warsaw, underground organizations were established mostly by political youth organizations. These, however, were not a continuation or branches of the larger organizations. In these ghettos underground groups assembled on the basis of the mutual trust of their members, without considering former political and organizational ties. In addition to the Jewish Fighting Organization, the Jewish Military Union was established in the Warsaw Ghetto. But it made few efforts to operate in outlying towns.

The Jewish partisan units operated in the majority of cases outside any political organization, and in this way they differed considerably from Polish partisan units, which were always affiliated with a certain political organization. Exceptions to this rule were the ZOB units and certain unaffiliated units which eventually joined the People's Army.

A dry description of events can in no way teach us about the activities of the Jewish population. One must remember the differences in the situations of Jews and non-Jews, in this case the Poles, during the Nazi conquest. The Jewish population was imprisoned in the ghettos and camps, where, because of hunger and terrible sanitary conditions, many lives were lost even before the "Final Solution." The circumstances surrounding the preparation for the struggle and its actual beginning were extremely more difficult than those of the Polish population, which although also persecuted and suppressed by terror, did not lose their freedom of movement and did not face total extermination. We did not discuss in detail the armed resistance movement of the free population as opposed to the organization of a population imprisoned in ghettos and camps, but concrete differences between the situations of the two populations did not account for all the factors that contributed to the polarization of conditions for preparing an armed revolt by the two population groups—Polish and Jewish. Let us then briefly examine some additional factors:

Timing was clearly a factor. The timing of the Jewish population's armed actions was dictated by the dates of the deportations. Thus, the armed activity of the Jews preceded that of the Polish underground. Most of the Jewish partisan units were established during the second half of 1942, when the Polish partisan movement did not in effect yet exist. The Warsaw Ghetto uprising and the armed activities in the other ghettos and camps preceded the Polish revolt in Warsaw and the major battles of the Polish partisans, which began in the summer of 1944.

The timing of the armed activities of the Jews, which was dictated by the acts of extermination of the Germans, forced the Jews to enter into battle when the political and military situation in Europe was far from ripe. Because of this, the resistance movement between 1942 and 1943 encountered much greater difficulties than the resistance in 1944, when the collapse of the Third Reich was imminent and the Red Army had already penetrated Poland.

A basic condition for the success of any resistance movement in occupied Europe was support from the outside by at least one of the Allies. The underground organizations of all the occupied nations in Europe were able to enjoy this support, except for the Jews. Also, some of the underground organizations were a kind of continuation of the standing army which had been defeated by the German army, and as such they could take advantage of the equipment which had been hidden and the manpower of this army. In addition the government-in-exile and the military units of an occupied country which was established abroad often fulfilled a primary role in the maintenance of an underground organization in that country.

For a real understanding of the problem, let us review the actual military and monetary support that was given to the Polish resistance movement. At the end of September 1939, before the final surrender of the Polish army to the Germans, the command instructed a group of officers of the General Staff to take out the following supplies from the military storehouses and hide them for use by the Polish underground: 566 heavy machine guns, 1,097 light machine guns, 31,391 rifles, 6,493 pistols, 40,000 grenades, 28 light antitank guns, 25 guns, and over 5,000,000 bullets.[1]

Beginning in February 15, 1941, the British and American air forces and the Polish air force that was established in exile carried out flying missions and drops for the Polish underground. Up until the end of 1944, 853 flights to Poland were organized, of which 484 planes reached their destinations and carried out operations for the Home Army (241 of these were planes with Polish crews, 135 had British crews, and 107 had American crews). In the parachuting operations 63 planes and 59 crew members, among them 24 Poles, 34 British, and 1 American were lost.[2]

These parachutings supplied the Home Army with several thousand weapons. These drops were the AK's only source of fuses and electric igniters, which allowed for the development of the production of explosives and grenades. Due to the raw materials which were supplied by the parachutings, 250,000 grenades were produced in underground factories. The parachutings also supplied a considerable quantity of antitank guns of the "Fiat" type. According to General Komorowski, this source furnished about one-third of the supply of weapons and ammunition held by the Home Army. In addition, 345 parachutists were dropped into Poland to strengthen the Polish underground.[3]

Monetary assistance was also provided in this way—

approximately 35,850,000 dollars in currency and gold, 19,900 German marks, and 90,500,000 *zloties*. The amount of money received allowed the Polish underground organizations to build its forces with salary payments to workers. Thus, for example, an officer in a senior position of the Home Army received a salary of 2,400 *zloties* a month and an administrative worker (a typist) 2,000 *zloties* a month. The Polish historian Czeslaw Madajczyk thus states: "For the members of the resistance, the underground was a place of work where there was much danger involved in terms of personal safety, but which nevertheless offered reasonable conditions for existence."[4]

The money received also made it possible to supply and equip the partisan units before they were sent to battle from their bases in the forest. Thus, for example, in 1943, the Home Army gave a one-time payment of approximately 5,000 *zloties* in order to complete the winter supplies of each partisan. The cost of upkeep for a partisan unit of fifty people for one month was fixed by the AK command at 60,000 to 70,000 *zloties*.[5]

The People's Army received similar help from the Soviet Union. This assistance, which was very modest in 1942, was increased in the second half of 1943 and reached its peak in the spring and summer of 1944 with the establishment of the Polish partisan command.

Until now the data regarding the total number of flying missions carried out to assist the People's Army has not been published. The first parachutists from the Soviet Union who came to organize the armed communist underground arrived in December 1941. In 1942 several other groups arrived, and from the middle of 1943, the Soviet air force carried out regular flight missions to aid the People's Army.

In conclusion, the arms and money for the organization of the armed struggle against the occupation reached the Polish underground from the hidden supply of the Polish army, from outside help (drops from England and the Soviet Union), from purchases on the black market (which were possible as a result of the money received from the outside), and from underground production (which was possible thanks to the raw materials dropped in by the flight missions). Quantities of arms acquired through attacks on Germans or purchased with money collected from the general public accounted for a very small portion of the available resources.

The sources of supply mentioned above were decisively, almost entirely, outside of the reach of the Jews. The Home Army, which was subordinated to the Polish government-in-exile and which was the primary force of the Polish underground, did not at all consider the needs of the Jewish population or of the Jewish resistance movement. The strategic assumptions of this organization were directed towards general armed activity, which was meant to break out when the German occupation of Poland collapsed. Until that time—so they calculated—they should limit themselves to preparation only, without entering the struggle with the German armed forces. The possibility of armed resistance was taken into account only in case of need to defend the ethnic Polish population.

These calculations were clearly defined in Order No. 71, dated November 1, 1942, from the national AK commander, General Rowecki. Among other items, it lists:

1. Concerning the extermination of the Jews being carried out by the conqueror, a certain uneasiness has been aroused in the Polish population that after the conclusion of this operation, the Germans will begin to destroy the Poles in the same way; I order to maintain a reserved position and take steps to calm the public. Although the main goal of the Germans is to suppress our people, it is possible that they will attempt to destroy those who resist, using the methods of extermination used against the Jews.
2. If the Germans attempt this, they will encounter resistance activity on our side. Without hesitation, even if the time of our revolt has not yet come, the units which are subordinated to me will go out to battle to defend the people. In this case we shall go over from resistance to attack, and we will cut off the main lines of the enemy on the eastern front.
3. In order to avoid possible provocation from the enemy, I reserve for myself the right of decision as to the time and area in which we shall open the struggle.
4. I order the commanders of the cells and districts to inform me without delay of cases when the Germans use against our people the same methods of mass liquidation which were used against the Jews.[7]

Assistance to Jewish citizens or to the Jewish armed movement was not taken into account in the plans of the Home Army command.

In the ghettos and camps the resistance movement managed to make contact with the Home Army. However, despite these many attempts, the Home Army did not supply any arms from its stores either to the resistance movements in the ghettos and camps or to the Jewish partisan units. An exception is the Jewish Fighting Organization in the Warsaw Ghetto which received the following from the Home Army: 90 pistols, 500 defensive hand-grenades, 100 hand-grenades for attacks, 15 kilograms of plastic with ignition fuses, a light submachine gun and materials to prepare Molotov cocktails.

It should be noted that the quantities noted above were a minute part of resources owned by the Home Army at that time. In the warehouses in the area of Warsaw alone, the Home Army stored 135 heavy machine guns, 190 light machine guns, 6,045 rifles, 1,070 pistols, 7 antitank guns, and large quantities of bullets.[8]

Besides these arms, the Jewish underground received monetary help from the Polish Government Delegacy totaling 37,000,000 *zloties* and 50,000 dollars, which, according to the average rate of the dollar then (200 *zloties* to the dollar), came to a total of less than a quarter of a million dollars, that is less than 1 percent of the total sum which the Delegacy received from abroad for the needs of the underground. Moreover, all this money was destined for the assistance of Jews who were hiding in the Aryan sector after the liquidation of the ghettos (mostly for the Jews of Warsaw and partially for the Jews of Cracow, Lvov, and other places). Not even one cent was budgeted for the Jewish armed underground.

The Jewish fighting underground in the ghettos and camps made contacts with the People's Army and attempted to acquire certain quantities of arms from it. However, we do not know of any cases in which weapons that were supplied by the People's Army reached the Jewish underground organizations which operated in the ghettos and camps. An exception is again the Jewish Fighting Organization in the Warsaw Ghetto, which received small quantities of arms.

In contrast with this, the Jewish partisan units that officially belonged to the People's Army received relatively large quantities of arms. Up to the middle of 1943, these quantities were modest, because of the meager supply held by the People's Army. From the middle of 1943 the People's Army began to receive considerable amounts of arms from Soviet drops. The Jewish partisan units that belonged to the People's Army received arms from these drops in the same ways as the other partisan units belonging to this organization. The first Jewish units to be equipped with arms from the Soviet drops from the middle of 1943 were the units of Greenshpan, Jegier, Gruber, and Braun, which operated in the area of Lublin.

In sum, the difference in the situation of the Jewish resistance movement in the *General Gouvernement* and the resistance movements of every other people in occupied Europe resulted from the following factors:

1. The special situation of the Jewish population during the German occupation
2. The lack of support from any power in the anti-Hitler alliance or of any political power with influence in the free world

3. The discriminatory stand of the Polish government-in-exile and the majority of the Polish underground

Despite insurmountable difficulties, which no other people in occupied Europe encountered, the armed Jewish resistance movement in the *General Gouvernement* was an undeniable fact from the middle of 1942 to the end of 1944 and contributed to the armed struggle against the German forces in occupied Poland. Let us attempt to summarize its role:

1. The rebels of the Warsaw Ghetto forced a struggle on the Germans for several weeks in the heart of occupied Europe, in a large and strategic center such as Warsaw, while the front line was at a distance of 1,200 kilometers; hence, the special impact, moral significance, and propaganda value of this revolt, and its influence on the revival of the armed struggle in occupied Poland. The armed activities in other ghettos and camps had an influence, although to a lesser degree.
2. The Jewish partisan units took part in some of the largest and most serious partisan battles in the area of the *General Gouvernement* (for example, near Kolkow on October 12, 1943, near Rablow on May 14 and 15, 1944, near Wola Wereszczynska on June 18, 1944, in the Janow forests in June 1944). The takeover of several small towns by Jewish units had great influence on morale, even if this lasted only for a short time. Examples of this were Klwow, December 22, 1942; Markuszew and Garbow, in May and June 1943, and Ostrow Lubelski on May 17, 1944. Greenshpan's Jewish unit took part in the assault and takeover of the city of Parczew on April 16, 1944. Jewish partisan units carried out over thirty train sabotage actions (derailing trains and destroying stations), destroyed forty of the enemy's economic installations (mainly mills and dairies), destroyed over ten police posts and several *Wehrmacht* positions (for example, in Widlanki and Kolacze).
3. Aside from the contribution in the general fighting against the German occupation, we should take into account a special aspect of the Jewish armed resistance—the struggle for survival. Under the auspices of the Jewish partisan units, family camps were set up in the forest for Jews in hiding. At least 3,000 defenseless people, refugees from ghettos and concentration camps, sought shelter under the protection of the Jewish partisans. To these must be added the hundreds of Jews who hid in the villages and enjoyed the protection and support of the Jewish partisans. And finally, armed activities in some of the camps allowed a number of the prisoners to es-

cape to the forests where there were means and chances for survival.

There is great significance in the fact that the rebellion in the extermination camps of Treblinka and Sobibor (and also outside of the area of the *General Gouvernement* in Auschwitz) destroyed the installations which were used in mass murder, the gas chambers, and ovens. This was not done by the air forces or by sabotage groups or by partisans of any country in the anti-Nazi alliance.

The duration of the German occupation of the *General Gouvernement* was responsible for the fact that only a few of those who sought shelter under the protection of the Jewish partisan units were rescued. Among the family camps, only the one in the Parczew forests continued to exist until the liberation. Most of the Jews who hid under the protection of the partisans in the villages were killed.

We will not analyze here whether the Jewish resistance movement could have had a greater success in the framework of the overall armed struggle in Poland. A more intensive activity by the Jewish movement would have been possible only with the good will and support of the Home Army, which was the main force in the Polish underground. The fact is that neither the AK command nor the Government Delegacy (of the Polish government-in-exile in London) wanted this kind of operation. However, aside from the strategic considerations of the Home Army, it is very doubtful whether Poland had the conditions needed for an intensive partisan struggle against the German forces at the end of 1942 and the beginning of 1943, during the height of the development of the Jewish resistance movement. Nevertheless, there were certainly conditions for an intensive rescue operation, yet this depended totally on the attitude of the Polish underground and the public. Initiative was shown in this realm by the head of the department for Jewish affairs of the AK command, Colonel Henryk Wolinski, who in a report to his superiors dated February 12, 1943, stated the following: "The only realistic possibility for saving a substantial number of people lies in the creation of a backbone for them in the forests in the form of partisan units."[9] Wolinski's initiative was blocked by the Home Army command. All the efforts made by him and the Jewish underground leaders did not bring the expected results.

Under the existing conditions, although the Jewish armed resistance movement could contribute to the general armed struggle against the German occupation forces in Poland, it could not really have had influenced the fate of the Jews sentenced to extermination. The results achieved were scanty and, at the most, modest. However, the efforts made to achieve even these results demanded the greatest efforts and sacrifices, unparalleled in the armed underground of any other people in occupied Europe. No other resistance movement faced the need to solve a problem as complicated as planning an armed struggle in places that were as isolated and closed as the ghettos and the camps. No other partisan movement in Europe organized and operated under the conditions the Jewish movement worked under. And no other resistance movement of any people in Europe suffered losses and hardships similar to those suffered by the armed Jewish movement in the *General Gouvernement*. After rebellions in the ghettos, the Jews continued the struggle in the partisan movement and in the Polish Warsaw Revolt, after which only a few dozens of the Warsaw Ghetto fighters survived. The proportion of those in the armed Jewish partisan groups who fell in battle can be estimated at 80 percent. The number of those among the Jewish fighters who fell in the camps reached 90 percent. These proportions are a few times larger than the losses suffered by the non-Jewish armed underground organizations.

In summary, the Jewish armed resistance movement in the *General Gouvernement* was established, developed, and operated under the worst possible conditions, unparalleled anywhere else. Participation in this movement demanded the greatest sacrifice and the greatest ability to overcome exceptional obstacles. The dedication demonstrated and the fact that unimaginable obstacles were overcome testify to the quality and greatness of this movement.

ABBREVIATIONS

AK — *Armia Krajowa* (Home Army)

AL — *Armia Ludowa* (People's Army)

AMSW — *Archiwum Ministerstwa Spraw Wewnetrznych* (Archives of the Ministry for Internal Affairs in Warsaw)

AZHP — *Archiwum Zakładu Historii Partii* (Archives of the Institute for Communist Party History in Warsaw)

AZIH — *Archiwum Zydowskiego Instytutu Historycznego* (Archives of the Jewish Historical Institute in Warsaw)

BGKBZH — *Biuletyn Głównej Komisji Badania Zbrodni Hitlerowskich w Polsce* (Bulletin of the Main Commission for Investigation of Nazi Crimes in Poland) published in Warsaw

BZIH — *Biuletyn Zydowskiego Instytutu Historycznego* (Bulletin of the Jewish Historical Institute in Warsaw)

GG — *General Gouvernement*

GL — *Gwardia Ludowa* (People's Guard)

KB — *Korpus Bezpieczenstwa* (Security Corps)

NSZ — *Narodowe Sily Zbrojne* (National Armed Forces)

PLAN — *Polska Ludowa Akcja Niepodleglosci* (Polish People's Independence Action)

POW — *Polska Organizacja Wojskowa* (Polish Military Organization)

PPR — *Polska Partia Robotnicza* (Polish Workers Party)

PPS — *Polska Partia Socjalistyczna* (Polish Socialist Party)

WPH — *Wojskowy Przeglad Historyczny* (Military Historical Review) published by the Military Historical Institute in Warsaw

YVA — Yad Vashem Archives, in Jerusalem

ZOB — *Zydowska Organizacja Bojowa* (Jewish Fighting Organization)

ZZW — *Zydowski Zwiazek Wojskowy* (Jewish Military Union)

NOTES

CHAPTER 1
The Specific Problems of the Jewish Partisan Movement

1. Władysław Pobóg-Malinowski, *Najnowsza historia polityczna Polski, 1939–1945* (Modern political history of Poland, 1939–1945) vol. III (London: 1960), p. 381.

2. Ibid., p. 379.

3. Lev N. Bychkov, *Partizanskoye Dvizheniye v gody vielikoy otiechestviennoy voyny, 1941–1945* (The partisan movement during the years of the great fatherland war, 1941–1945) (Moscow: Mysl, 1965), p. 375.

4. *Publicystyka konspiracyjna PPR, 1942–1945* (Underground press of the Polish Workers' Party, 1942–1945) vol. I (Warsaw: Ksiazka i Wiedza, 1962), p. 5.

5. Ibid., p. 31.

6. Ibid., p. 45.

7. Józef Niecko, ed., *Zelazne kompanie Batalionów Chłopskich* (The iron companies of the Peasants' Battalions) (Warsaw: 1954), p. 80.

8. Jerzy Kirchmayer, *Powstanie warszawskie* (The Warsaw rising) (Warsaw: Ksiazka i Wiedza, 1959), p. 27.

9. Ibid. Also see Tadeusz Rawski, Zdzisław Stapor, Jan Zamojski, *Wojna wyzwolencza Narodu Polskiego w łatach 1939–1945* (The independence war of the Polish nation, 1939–1945) (Warsaw: MON, 1963), p. 401.

10. Tadeusz Bór-Komorowski, *Armia Podziemna* (The secret army) (London: Veritas, 1949), p. 66–67.

11. *20 lat Ludowego Wojska Polskiego, druga sesja naukowa poświecona wojnie wyzwolenczej narodu polskiego* (Twenty years of the Polish People's Army— Second scientific conference on the independence war of the Polish Nation) (Warsaw: MON, 1967), p. 140.

12. Bogdan Hillebrandt, *Partyzantka na Kielecczyźnie, 1939–1945*, (The partisan movement in the Kielce region, 1939–1945) (Warsaw: MON, 1967), p. 475.

13. Zbigniew Załuski, *Czterdziesty czwarty—wydarzenia, obserwacje, refleksje*

(The year forty four—events, observations, after-thoughts) (Warsaw: Czyteinik, 1968), p. 185.

14. Hillebrandt, *Partyzantka*, p. 506.

15. YVA, Nuremberg document, NOKW 2931.

16. AZHP, file 202/II-2, p. 231.

17. Kazimierz Leszczynski, "Opracowanie materiałów ankiety z roku 1945 na temat: Eksterminacja ludności na ziemiach polskich w latach, 1939–1945" (Paper based on the inquiries from 1945 on the extermination of population on Polish territories, 1939–1945) BGKBZH, vols. 8–11.

18. Kazimierz Sidor, *Trzeci front* (The third front) (Warsaw: MON, 1955), p. 197.

19. Hillebrandt, *Partyzantka*, p. 65–66.

20. AZHP, file 202/II-11, p. 226.

21. YVA, file 0-51/DN-31/3520.

22. AZHP, file 202/III-51, p. 11.

23. *"Katowskie pachołki"* (Servants of the hangmen), published in the underground paper *Agencja Prasowa*, 30 December 1942; also in AZHP, file 203/III-128, p. 68.

24. Zygmunt Klukowski, *Dziennik z lat okupacji Zamojszczyzny* (Diary from the occupation years in the Zamosc region) (Lublin: LSW, 1959), p. 290.

25. Kazimierz Radziwonczyk, "Udział Wehrmachtu w walce z ruchem partyzanckim" (Participation of the German Army in operations against the partisan movement), *WPH*, no. 4 (1964), pp. 168–169.

26. Kazimierz Radziwonczyk, "Niemieckie siły zbrojne w okupowanej Polsce" (German armed forces in occupied Poland), *WPH*, no. 4 (1962), pp. 60–61.

27. Hillebrandt, *Partyzantka*, pp. 220–221.

28. *Polskie siły zbrojne w drugiej wojnie światowej, tom trzeci: Armia Krajowa* (Polish armed forces in World War II. Vol. 3: The Home Army) (London: Sikorski Institute, 1951), p. 431.

29. Pobog-Malinowski, *Najnowsza historia*, p. 412.

30. Jerzy Zbigniew Hirsz, *Lubelska prasa konspiracyjna, 1939–1944* (Underground press in the Lublin region, 1939–1944) (Lublin: LSW, 1968), pp. 473–474.

31. AZHP, file 202/I-6, p. 24.

32. AZHP, file 202/II-22, p. 132.

33. AZHP, file 202/II-24, p. 22.

34. AZHP, file 202/III-22, p. 132.

35. AZHP, file 202/III-28, p. 48.

36. Klukowski, *Dziennik*, p. 299.

37. AZHP, file 202/XV-2, p. 31.

38. *Polskie siły zbrojne*, p. 431. Also see Radziwonczyk, *Niemieckie siły zbrojne*, p. 71.

39. *Polskie siły zbrojne*, pp. 324–325, 339.

40. *20 lat Ludowego Wojska Polskiego*, pp. 136, 470.

CHAPTER 2
The forests of Parczew and Wlodawa

1. Tatiana Berenstein, "Martyrologia, opór i zagłada ludności zydowskiej w dystrykcie lubelskim" (Martyrology, resistance and destruction of the Jewish population in the Lublin district), *BZIH*, 21 (1957).

2. Edward Gronczewski, *Kalendarium walk Gwardii Ludowej i Armii Ludowej na Lubelszczyźnie* (Calendar of armed action of the People's Guard and the People's Army in the Lublin region) (Warsaw: MON, 1966), pp. 226–227. Also see YVA, file M-1/E-1249.

3. Józef Garas, "Oddziały Gwardii i Armii Ludowej w Obwodzie Lubelskim" (Units of the People's Guard and Army in the Lublin region), *WPH*, no. 3 (1959), pp. 134–136.

4. Zygmunt Mankowski and Jan Naumiuk, *Gwardia Ludowa i Armia Ludowa na Lubelszczyznie (1942–1944), Zrodla* (The People's Guard and People's Army in the Lublin region, [1942–1944], Documents) (Lublin: LSW, 1960), p. 62. Also see YVA, file 0-3/2085.

5. YVA, file 0-3/2019.

6. AZIH, Testimony no. 2426; YVA, files 0-3/1787, 0-33/24.

7. YVA, file 0-3/1787.

8. Gronczewski, *Kalendarium*, p. 31.

9. Mankowski and Naumiuk, *Gwardia Ludowa*, p. 32.

10. YVA, file 0-3/2019.

11. Mankowski and Naumiuk, *Gwardia Ludowa*, p. 32. Also see Wojciech Sulewski, *Na partyzanckich ścieżkach* (Warsaw, 1968), p. 40.

12. Mankowski and Naumiuk, *Gwardia Ludowa*, pp. 35–36. Also see Wojciech Sulewski, *Lasy Parczewskie* (The Parczew forests) (Warsaw: Wiedza Powszechna, 1970), p. 91; YVA, file 0-3/2019.

13. *Dos Naye Lebn* (Yiddish daily, Lodz), 18 November 1946.

14. *Ja syn ludu polskiego, Wspomnienia i relacje dzielaczy PPR, GL i AL*, (I the son of the polish people: Memoirs and testimonies of leading members of the Polish Workers' Party, the People's Guard and People's Army) (Lublin: LSW), p. 130. Also see YVA, file 0-3/1824.

15. YVA, file 0-3/2019.

16. Ibid.

17. YVA, file 1824.

18. AZIH, Testimony no. 2766; Mankowski and Naumiuk, *Gwardia Ludowa*, p. 62; YVA, file 0-33/24.

19. YVA, file 0-3/1787.

20. YVA, file 0-33/24.

21. AZIH, Testimony no. 514; YVA, file 0-3/1787.

22. AZIH, Testimony no. 2766; YVA, file 0-33/24.

23. Radziwonczyk, *Niemieckie siły zbrojne*, pp. 56–57.

24. YVA, files 0-3/2080, 0-3/2019.

25. Ibid.

26. Mankowski and Naumiuk, *Gwardia Ludowa*, p. 62.

27. Sidor, *Trzeci front*, p. 197.

28. Ibid.

29. Garas, *Oddziały Gwardii*, p. 197; YVA, files 0-3/2212, 0-3/1824.

30. Sidor, *Trzeci front*, p. 197.

31. Mankowski and Naumiuk, *Gwardia Ludowa*, p. 71.

32. AMSW, Gendarmerie Lublin, file 170, p. 51.

33. AZHP, file 202/III-21, p. 14.

34. Mankowski and Naumiuk, *Gwardia Ludowa*, pp. 71–72.

35. YVA, file 0-3/1824.

36. Sulewski, *Lasy Parczewskie*, pp. 155, 268; Mankowski and Naumiuk, *Gwardia Ludowa*, p. 130; Gronczewski, *Kalendarium*, p. 245.

37. Gustaw Alef-Bolkowiak, *"Folks-Sztyme,"* (Yiddish daily, Warsaw), no. 110 (16 July, 1964).

38. Sulewski, *Lasy Parczewskie*, p. 132.

39. Mankowski and Naumiuk, *Gwardia Ludowa*, p. 117; Garas, *Oddziały Gwardii*, p. 114; Gronczewski, *Kalendarium*, pp. 92–93.

40. YVA, file 0-3/2212.

41. Leon Bielski, *Spotkanie z ziemia*, (Meeting with the land) (Warsaw: Ksiazka i Wiedza, 1965). Also see YVA, files 0-3/707, 0-3/1824, 0-3/2212, 0-16/458.

42. Tadeusz Szymanski, *My ze spalonych wsi* (We from the burned villages) (Warsaw: MON, 1965), p. 298. Also see Garas, *Oddziały Gwardii*, p. 144; Gronczewski, *Kalendarium*, p. 228.

43. YVA, files 0-3/3009, 0-3/2858.

44. Mankowski and Naumiuk, *Gwardia Ludowa*, p. 141.

45. Gustaw Alef-Bolkowiak, *Gorace dni* (Hot days) (Warsaw: MON, 1962), p. 153.

46. YVA, file 0-3/2937.

47. Mankowski and Naumiuk, *Gwardia Ludowa*, p. 154.

48. Sulewski, *Lasy Parczewskie*, p. 179.

49. *Ja syn ludu polskiego*, pp. 152–153.

50. Bychkov, *Partizanskoye Dvizheniye*, p. 379.

51. Gronczewski, *Kalendarium*, p. 219.

52. YVA, file 0-16/5.

53. Radziwonczyk, *Niemieckie siły zbrojne*, p. 78.

54. AMSW, *Gendarmerie Lublin*, file 34, p. 19.

55. Mankowski Naumiuk, *Gwardia Ludowa*, p. 229.

56. Radziwonczyk, *Niemieckie siły zbrojne*, p. 78.

57. Archives of the Military Historical Institute in Warsaw, file III/19/200.

58. Waldemar Tuszynski, "Lipcowe walki Armii Ludowej w lasach Parc-zewskich w czasie wielkiej akcji przeciwpartyzanskiej 'Cyklon' (The July battles of the People's Army in the Parczew forests during the great antiparti-san operation "Zyklon"), *WPH*, no. 2 (1964), p. 124.

59. Garas, *Oddziały Gwardii*, p. 146; Mankowski and Naumiuk, *Gwardia Ludowa*, p. 292; YVA, file 0-3/2858.

60. YVA, file 0-16/5.

61. YVA, file 0-3/2080.

62. YVA, files 0-3/2080, 0-16/5.

63. Fryderyk Zbiniewicz, "Działania zgrupowania Czornego," (Activities of the Czorny group) *WPH*, no. 3 (1959), p. 70; YVA, file 0-16/5.

64. Mankowski and Naumiuk, *Gwardia Ludowa*, p. 271.

65. Gara, *Oddzialy Gwardii*, p. 147.

66. Waclaw Poteranski, Maria Turlejska, Waldemar Tuszynski, Maria Wil-usz, *Dowodztwo Glowne GL i AL. Zbior dokumentow z lat 1942–1944* (Main Com-mand of the People's Guard and People's Army. Selected documents, 1942–1944) (Warsaw: MON, 1967), p. 322. Also see Mankowski and Naumiuk, *Gwardia Ludowa*, pp. 291–292, 358.

67. Radziwonczyk, *Niemieckie siły zbrojne*, p. 79.

68. YVA, file 0-16/5.

69. *Ja syn ludu polskiego*, p. 125; YVA, file M-1/E–924.

70. Tuszynski, *Lipcowe walki*, p. 124.

71. YVA, file 0-3/2080.

72. AZIH, files of the Organization of Jewish Partisans, which include a list of the names of 102 partisans in the Jewish company of Yechiel Greenshpan.

73. Gustaw Alef-Bolkowiak, *Folks-Sztyme*, no. 110 (16 July 1964). Also see YVA, file M-1/E-828.

CHAPTER 3
Between Pulawy and Lubartow

1. *WPH*, no. 4 (1962), p. 36.

2. David Shtokfish, ed., *Hurbana ugevurata shel haayara Markuszów* (The destruction and heroism of the town of Markuszów) Tel Aviv, 1955).

3. *BZIH*, no. 21 (1957), p. 47. Also see, YVA, file 0-3/3104.

4. Shtokfish, *Hurbana ugevurata*, pp. 195–226.

5. Shtokfish, *Hurbana ugevurata*, pp. 159–194, 350–387.

6. AZIH, Testimony no. 4368.

7. YVA, file 0-16/5.

8. Shtokfish, *Hurbana ugevurata*, pp. 283–299.

9. *Ja syn ludu polskiego*, pp. 30–31, 54, 166.

10. M. Litvin and M. Lerman, eds., *Dos buch fun Lublin* (The book of Lublin) (Paris, 1952), pp. 555–556.

11. YVA, file 0-3/3104.

12. Shtokfish, *Hurbana ugevurata*, pp. 159–194; YVA, file 0-16/5.

13. *Ja syn ludu polskiego*, p. 18.

14. Shtokfish, *Hurbana ugevurata*, p. 376. Also see Gronczewski, *Kalendarium*, p. 44

15. Garas, *Oddziały Gwardii*, p. 113; Gronczewski, *Kalendarium*, pp. 46–50.

16. YVA, file 0-16/5.

17. Mankowski and Naumiuk, *Gwardia Ludowa*, p. 13.

18. Radziwonczyk, *Niemieckie siły zbrojne*, p. 76.

19. Shtokfish, *Hurbana ugevurata*, pp. 159–194.

20. Mankowski and Naumiuk, *Gwardia Ludowa*, pp. 74, 81.

21. Garas, *Oddziały Gwardii*, p. 113; YVA, file 0-3/3104.

22. Alef-Bolkowiak, *Gorace dni*.

23. AMSW, *Gendarmerie Lublin*, file 72, p. 77; file 109, p. 23.

24. Jan Wójtowicz, *Na północ od Lublina* (On the north from Lublin) (Warsaw: MON, 1966), p. 163; YVA, microfilm JM/2846.

25. AMSW, *Gendarmerie Lublin*, file 109, p. 41. Also see Gronczewski, *Kalendarium*, p. 81.

26. M. Grosman, ed. *Yizkor buch: A mazeyve unzer shtetl Kurow* (Memorial book to our town Kurow) (Tel Aviv, 1955), pp. 215–218; AZIH, Testimony no. 2521.

27. Mankowski and Naumiuk, *Gwardia Ludowa*, p. 197; Gronczewski, *Kalendarium*, p. 99.

28. Radziwonczyk, *Niemieckie siły zbrojne*, p. 76.

29. YVA, file 0-16/5.

30. Mankowski and Naumiuk, *Gwardia Ludowa*, p. 165.

31. Shtokfish, *Hurbana ugevurata*, pp. 272–282.

CHAPTER 4
South of Lublin

1. T. Berenstein-Brustin, "Gerushim vi an etap fun der daytsher farnichtunspolitik legabey der yidisher bafelkerung" (Deportations as a stage in the German policy of the destruction of the Jewish population), *Bleter far geshichte* (January–June 1950), tables 1–11.

2. David Shtokfish, ed., *Sefer Frampol* (The Frampol book) (Tel Aviv, 1966), p. 59.

3. Berenstein-Brustin, "Gerushim."

4. Klukowski, *Dziennik z lat okupacji*, p. 277.

5. Ibid., p. 289.

6. Ibid., p. 290.

7. Ibid., p. 291.

8. Ibid., pp. 291–292.

9. AMSW, *Gendarmerie Lublin*, file 107, p. 162.

10. Ibid., p. 83.

11. *Okupacja i ruch oporu w dzienniku Hansa Franka* (Occupation and resistance in the diary of Hans Frank) (Warsaw: Ksiazka i Wiedza, 1972), vol. II: p. 119.

12. *Tomashover yizkor book*, (The memorial book for the town Tomaszow Lubelski) (New York, 1965), p. 773.

13. Shtokfish, *Sefer Frampol*, pp. 98–99.

14. Ibid., p. 100.

15. YVA, file 0-3/3630; Zdzisław Rosinski, "Powstanie i poczatkowa działnośc oddziału partyzanckiego imienia Tadeusza Kościuszki" (The creation and initial activities of the partisan unit Tadeusz Kosciuszki), *Biuletyn Wojskowej Akademii Politycznej, Seria Historyczna*, no. 3 (1959), p. 14.

16. Idem.

17. AZIH, Testimony no. 1474.

18. Rosinski, *Powstanie i poczatkowa działalnośc*, p. 36.

19. Shtokfish, *Sefer Frampol*, pp. 103–104.

20. Rosinski, *Powstanie i poczatkowa działalnośc*, p. 41.

21. YVA, file M-1/E-711.

22. Rosinski, *Powstanie i poczatkowa działalnośc*, pp. 23–24.

23. Ibid., p. 42.

24. Ibid., p. 25.

25. YVA, files 0-3/2557, M-1/E-714.

26. Mankowski and Naumiuk, *Gwardia Ludowa*, pp. 44–45.

27. Radziwonczyk, *Niemieckie siły zbrojne*, p. 76.

28. Gronczewski, *Kalendarium*, pp. 219–239.

29. Shtokfish, *Sefer Frampol*, pp. 104–109.

30. Szymanski, *My ze spalonych wsi*, pp. 242–243. Also see: *Ja syn ludu polskiego*, p. 229.

31. YVA, file 0-3/2932.

32. Gronczewski, *Kalendarium*, p. 231.

33. Szymanski, *My ze spalonych wsi*, p. 236.

34. Ibid., p. 243.

35. *Ja syn ludu polskiego*, p. 229.

36. Idem.

37. YVA, file 0-3/2932.

38. Mankowski and Naumiuk, *Gwardia Ludowa*, pp. 44–45.

39. Szymanski, *My ze spalonych wsi*, p. 260.

40. YVA, file 0-16/348; *Ja syn ludu polskiego*, p. 229.

41. Archives of the Military Historical Institute in Warsaw, file III 19/221.

42. Szymanski, *My ze spalonych wsi*, p. 99.

43. Klukowski, *Dziennik z lat okupacji*, p. 391; *Ja syn ludu polskiego*, p. 79.

44. Mankowski and Naumiuk, *Gwardia Ludowa*, p. 188.

45. Jerzy Markiewicz, *Paprocie zakwitɫy krwia partyzantów* (Fern flowers grew on partisan blood) (Warsaw: Ludowa Spoldzielnia Wydawnicza, 1962), p. 37.

46. Waldemar *Tuszynski, Lasy Janowskie i Puszcza Solska* (In the Janow and Solska forests) (Warsaw: Ksiazka i Wiedza, 1970), p. 95.

47. Klukowski, *Dziennik z lat okupacji*, p. 444.

48. Tuszynski, *Lasy*, p. 149; Markiewicz, *Paprocie*, pp. 108–111, 260–280.

49. AZIH, Testimony no. 275; YVA, file 0-3/2932.

50. *BZIH*, no. 21 (1957), p. 49; AMSW, *Gendarmerie Lublin*, file no. 170, p. 134.

51. Litvin and Lerman, *Dos buch fun Lublin*, pp. 549–552.

52. Yaakov Adini, ed., *Bychawa sefer zikaron* (Bychawa memorial book) (Tel Aviv, 1969), pp. 312–313.

53. AMSW, *Gendarmerie Lublin*, file 39.

CHAPTER 5
The district of Radom

1. YVA, files 0-3/1252, 0-3/2343; AZIH, Testimony no. 520; Adam Rutkowski, "Martyrologia, walka i zagɫada ludności żydowskiej w dystrykcie radomskim podczas okupacji hitlerowskiej" (Martyrology, struggle and destruction of the Jewish population in the Radom district during the Nazi occupation), *BZIH*, nos. 15–16 (1955), p. 182.

2. Bogdan Hillebrandt, *Partyzantka na Kielecczyźnie*, p. 496.

3. Ibid., p. 228.

4. Ibid., p. 471.

5. Archives of the Military Historical Institute in Warsaw, files III/19/115 and III/19/253.

6. Ibid.

7. Józef Garas, *Oddziaɫy Gwardii Ludowej i Armii Ludowej 1942–1945* (Units of the People's Guard and People's Army 1942–1945) (Warsaw: MON, 1963), pp. 285, 295; Zygmunt Bieszczanin, "Ze wspomnien dowódcy Gwardii Ludowej i Armii Ludowej w Krakowskiem" (Memoir of a commander of the People's Guard and People's Army in the Cracow region), *WPH*, no. 3 (1963), p. 435.

8. Bieszczanin, *Ze wspomnien*, pp. 285, 295.

9. Archives of the Military Historical Institute in Warsaw, file III/19/181.

10. Ibid., file III/19/253; AZIH, Testimony no. 6226.

11. Garas, *Oddzialy Gwardii Ludowej*, p. 287.

12. Bolkowiak, *Gorace dni*, p. 38; Hillebrandt, *Partyzantka na Kielecczyźnie*, p. 83.

13. *Warszaɓa, Lewa Podmiejska 1942–1945. Z walk PPR, GL, AL* (Book on the activities of the Polish Worker's Party, People's Guard and People's Army in

the western suburbs of Warsaw, 1942–1945) (Warsaw: MON, 1971), p. 249.

14. Józef Jarosz, *Ze wspomnien dowódcy okregu GL i AL* (Memoir of a regional commander of the People's Guard and People's Army) (Warsaw: MON, 1967), pp. 29–33.

15. AZHP, file 191/III-2, p. 11; AZIH, Testimonies nos. 4428, 4451.

16. Jerzy Piwowarek, "Działalność oddziału imienia Ziemi Kieleckiej" (Operations of the Kielce Land partisan unit), *WPH*, no. 2 (1962), p. 319.

17. Piwowarek, *Działalność*, pp. 232–324.

18. Hillebrandt, *Partyzantka na Kieleccźynie*, pp. 511–556.

19. Ibid., p. 236.

20. Piwowarek, *Działalność*, p. 334.

21. AZHP, file 203/III-135, p. 198.

22. Piwowarek, *Działalność*, p. 335.

23. M. Shucman, ed., *Sefer Chenstochov* (Czestochowa Book) (Jerusalem: Enciklopediya shel galuyot, 1968), pp. 237–278.

24. Shucman, *Sefer Chenstochov*, pp. 183, 259; Ryszard Nazarewicz, *Nad gorna Warta i Pilica* (On the Wartha and Pilica rivers) (Warsaw: MON, 1964), pp. 178–179.

25. Bernard Mark, *Powstanie w getcie warszawskim. Zbiór dokumentów* (The Warsaw Ghetto uprising. Collection of documents) (Warsaw: Yiddish Buch, 1963), pp. 348–349.

26. Liber Brener, "Ruch podziemny czestochowskiego getta" (The underground movement in the Czestochowa Ghetto), *BZIH*, nos. 45–46 (1963), p. 173. Also see Shucman, *Sefer Chenstochow*.

27. AZIH, Testimonies nos. 945, 3056, 4953.

28. Jarosz, *Ze wspomnien*, p. 132.

29. A. S. Stein, ed., *Radom*, (Tel Aviv, 1961), p. 287.

30. AZHP, file 202/I-8; Rutkowski, *Martyrologia*, pp. 131–132.

31. YVA, file 0-3/1252.

32. YVA, file 0-3/2306.

CHAPTER 6
Mazovia and Podlasie

1. T. Berenstein-Brustin, "Di gerushim un di farnichtung fun di yidishe yeshuvim in varshever distrikt" (The deportations and the destruction of the Jewish settlements in the Warsaw district), *(Bleter far geshichte* (April–June, 1951).

2. Underground newspaper *Prawda*, October 1942, copy in YVA, file 0-25/38.

3. Berenstein-Brustin, "Di gerushim." Also see *BGKBZH*, vol. X, pp. 239–248; vol. IX, pp. 209–214.

4. Serafin Aleksiejew, "Zgineli bez wieści" (Lost for ever), *BZIH*, nos. 65–66 (1968), pp. 235–248.

5. Wolf Jasny, ed., *Yizkor buch fun der zelechover yidishe kehile* (Memorial book for the Jewish Community in Zelechow) (Chicago, 1953); AZIH, Testimony no. 44.

6. YVA, file 0-3/2078.

7. Idem.

8. Alef-Bolkowiak, *Gorace dni*, p. 61.

9. Eliahu Porat, ed., *Sefer Kock* (The book of the town Kock) (Tel Aviv, 1961), pp. 225–290; Yitzhak Zygielman, ed., *Sefer Radzyn* (The book of the town Radzyn) (Tel Aviv, 1957), pp. 306–308.

10. Józef Sek-Malecki, *Armia Ludowa w Powstaniu Warszawskim: Wspomnienia* (The People's Army in the Warsaw Rising: Memoir) (Warsaw: Iskry, 1962), p. 13; Jonas Turkow, *In kamf farn lebn* (The fight for life) (Buenos Aires: Farband fun poylishe yidn, 1949), p. 314; Władka Peltel-Miedzyrzecka, *Mishney everey hahoma* (From both sides of the wall) (Beit Lohamey Hagetaot, 1962), p. 181; YVA, file 0-3/2726; AZIH, Testimony 5016.

11. Stanisław Wronski and Maria Zwolakowa, *Polacy-Żydzi, 1939–1945* (Poles and Jews, 1939–1945) (Warsaw: Ksiazka i Wiedza, 1971), p. 141.

12. AZHP, file 202/XV-2, p. 87.

13. *Bleter far geshichte*, vol. 17, pp. 35, 122.

14. AZHP, file 202/II-23, p. 22.

15. *Bleter far geshichte*, vol. 17, p. 124.

16. AMSW, *Gendarmerie Lublin*, file 107, p. 47.

17. Ibid., p. 43.

18. *Bleter far geshichte*, vol. 17, p. 41.

CHAPTER 7
The District of Cracow

1. Garas, *Oddziały Gwardii*, pp. 339–342.

2. E. Podhorizer-Sandel, "O zagładzie Żydòw w dystrykcie krakowskim" (About the destruction of Jews in the district of Cracow), *BZIH*, no. 30 (1959), pp. 87–110.

3. Kazimierz Leszczynski, "Eksterminacja ludności na ziemiach polskich w latach 1939–1945. Województwo Krakowskie" (The extermination of population in Poland, 1939–1945. District of Cracow), *BGKBZH*, vol. IX, pp. 113–169.

4. Hilel Har-Shoshanim and Yitzhak Turkow, eds., *Radomysl rabati vehasviva. Sefer Yizkor* (Memorial book of the town Radomysl and region) (Tel Aviv, 1971); YVA, file 0-33/894; AZIH, Testimony no. 3215.

5. AZIH, Testimony no. 3215.

6. YVA, 0-33/894.

7. Józef Garas, "Oddziały Gwardii Ludowej i Armii Ludowej w Obwodzie Krakowskim" (Units of the People's Guard and People's Army in the Cracow region), *WPH*, no. 4 (1960), p. 188.

8. AZHP, file 202/III-28, p. 308.

9. Wanda Chodorowska, ed., *Wspomnienia chłopów z lat 1938–1948*

(Memoirs of peasants, 1938–1948) vol. III (Warsaw: Ksiazka i Wiedza, 1969), pp. 474–475.

10. Józef Boleslaw Garas, *Oddziały Gwardii Ludowej i Armii Ludowej, 1942–1945* (Units of the People's Guard and People's Army, 1942–1945) (Warsaw: MON, 1971), p. 299.

11. YVA, Nuremberg document no. NO-2044.

12. Wronski and Zwolakowa, *Polacy-Zydzi.*

13. YVA, file 0-53/43-29.

14. YVA, files 0-53/43-23, 0-53/43-39, 0-53/42-374.

15. YVA, file 0-53/42-53.

16. AZHP, file 202/III-21, p. 17; Maria Rychlik, *Smierć daje życie; Wspomnienia więźniarki Oswiecimia,* (Death gives life: Memoir of an Auschwitz camp prisoner), Cracow: Wydawnictwo Literackie, 1967, p. 26.

CHAPTER 8
Jews in Polish Partisan Units

1. Marian Malinowski and Jerzy Pawłowicz, *Polski ruch robotniczy w okresie wojny i okupacji hitlerowskiej* (Polish worker's movement during the war and Nazi occupation) (Warsaw: Ksiazka i Wiedza, 1964), p. 405.

2. Helena Balicka-Kozłowska, *Hanka—Wspomnienia o Hance Szapiro-Sawickiej* (Hanka: Memoir about Hanka Szapiro-Sawicka) (Warsaw: Iskry, 1962).

3. Poteranski and Turlejska, *Dowództwo Główne,* p. 398.

4. Malinowski and Pawlowicz, *Polski ruch robotniczy,* pp. 155, 202, 314, 484.

5. Waldemar Tuszynski, "Ze zrodel ludowej partyzantki. Pierwszy oddział GL imienia Stefana Czarneckiego" (The beginnings of the people's partisan movement. The first partisan unit of the People's Guard named Stefan Czarnecki), *WPH,* no. 3 (1968), pp. 82–84.

6. YVA, files 0-3/3405, 0-3/3586; Irena Perkowska-Szczypiorska, *Pamiętnik łączniczki* (Memoir of an underground liaison officer) (Warsaw: Czytelnik, 1967), pp. 95–96; Jerzy Duracz, *Odwet* (Reprisal) (Warsaw: MON, 1962), pp. 119–120.

7. Jerzy Janusz Terej, *Rzeczywistość i polityka* (Reality and politics) (Warsaw: Ksiazka i Wiedza, 1971).

8. Szymanski, *My ze spalonych wsi,* p. 141.

9. YVA, files 0-3/581, 0-3/3156.

10. YVA, file 0-16/590.

11. Terej, *Rzeczywistość,* p. 277; *Warszawa lat wojny i okupacji 1939–1949,* Zeszyt 2 (Warsaw during the years of war and occupation, Book 2) (Warsaw: PAN, 1972), p. 196.

12. YVA, file 0-3/822.

13. Jan Nowak, ed., *Materiały źródłowe do historii polskiego ruchu ludowego* (Sources of the history of the Polish peasants' movement) vol. IV, (Warsaw: Ludowa Spoldzielnia Wydawnicza, 1966), p. 134.

14. YVA, file 0-3/1570.

15. YVA, file 0-16/348.

CHAPTER 9
Jews in Commando Units

1. Nikołaj Prokopiuk, "Z działalności radzieckich oddziałów rozpoz-nawczo-dywersyjnych na terenie Polski w latach, 1944–1945" (The operations of the Soviet reconnaissance and sabotage units on Polish territory, 1944–1945), *WPH*, no. 1 (1970).

2. Idem.

3. Idem.

4. Idem.

5. Ibid., p. 187

6. YVA, files 0-3/2950, 0-3/3270.

7. YVA, file 0-3/2950.

8. "Narada byłych partyzantow zabuzanskich w Zakładzie Historii Partii" (Conference of former partisans from the territories East of the Bug River, in the Institute for Party History), *WPH*, no. 4 (1960), p. 438.

9. Shlomo Straus-Marko, "In der partizaner optaylung oyfn nomen fun Wanda Wasilewska", in the *Yiddishe Shriften*, (Yiddish monthly), April 1965, p. 23.

10. Hirsz, *Lubelska prasa*, pp. 548–551.

11. *WPH*, 1 (1966), pp. 397–398.

12. Jerzy Tarnowski, *Z Tucholskich borów. Wspomnienia* (In the Tucholskie forests. Memoirs) (Gdynia: Wydawnictwo Morskie, 1963), p. 17.

13. Adam Heistein, "Walczacy Zydzi polscy" (The fighting Polish Jews), in the *"Nasz Glos"* (Jewish, Polish language weekly), 22 July 1966.

14. *WPH*, no. 3 (1963), pp. 447–449.

CHAPTER 10
The Warsaw Ghetto Uprising

1. Jan Karski, *Story of a Secret State* (Boston: Houghton Mifflin Co., 1944), p. 323.

2. Mark, *Powstanie*, pp. 342–351.

3. Zivia Lubetkin, *Aharonim al hahoma* (The last on the wall) (Eyn Harod, 1946), p. 25.

4. Emanuel Ringelblum, "Stosunki polsko-zydowskie w czasie drugiej wojny światowej" (Polish-Jewish relations during the Second World War), *BZIH*, no. 30 (1959), pp. 56–60.

5. Emanuel Ringelblum, *Ktovim fun geto. Band 2. Notizn un ophandlungen, 1939–1944* (Writings from the ghetto. Volume 2. Notes and transactions, 1939–1944) (Warsaw: Yiddish Buch, 1963), p. 109–110.

6. Jonas Turkow, *Ozoy iz es geven: Hurban Varshe* (This is how it was: The destruction of Warsaw) (Buenos Aires: Farband fun poylishe yidn, 1949),

p. 404; Philip Friedman, *Martyrs and Fighters: The Epic of the Warsaw Ghetto* (New York: Praeger, 1954), p. 202.

7. Bernard Mark, *Walka i zagłada warszawskiego getta* (The fight and destruction of the Warsaw Ghetto) (Warsaw: MON, 1959), p. 149.

8. Marek Edelman, *Getto walczy. Udzial Bundu w obronie getta warszawskiego,* (The ghetto fights: The participation of the Bund in the defense of the Warsaw Ghetto) (Warsaw: KC Bundu, 1945), p. 48.

9. Helena Balicka-Kozłowska, *Mur miał dwie strony* (The wall had two sides) (Warsaw: MON, 1958), p. 83

10. Edelman, *Getto walczy,* p. 49.

11. Friedman, *Martyrs and Fighters,* pp. 202–203; Józef Kermisz, *Powstanie w getcie warszawskim* (The Warsaw Ghetto uprising) (Lodz: CZKH, 1949), pp. 17–18.

12. Turkow, *Ozoy iz es geven,* p. 408.

13. Edelman, *Getto walczy,* p. 48.

14. Ringelblum, *Stosunki,* p. 57.

15. YVA, file 0-3/3068; Chaim Lazar-Litai, *Masada shel Varsha. Hayirgun Hazevai Haleumi bamered geto varsha,* (Masada of Warsaw: The Jewish Military Union in the Warsaw Ghetto uprising) (Tel Aviv: Mahon Zabotynski, 1963), pp. 239–241.

16. Ringelblum, *Stosunki,* p. 57.

17. Turkow, *Ozoy iz es geven,* p. 464.

18. AZHP, file 76/3.

19. Lubetkin, *Aharonim al hahoma,* p. 31, Edelman, *Getto walczy,* p. 47.

20. Mark, *Walka i zaglada,* p. 249.

21. Turkow, *Ozoy iz es geven,* p. 465; Edelman, *Getto walczy,* p. 50.

22. *Polskie siły zbrojne,* pp. 326–327.

23. Mark, *Powstanie,* p. 262

24. Idem.

25. *Przegląd techniczny. Numer specjalny. Polska technika w walce z okupantem* (Technical review. Special number. The Polish technology in fight against the conqueror) (Warsaw, 1966) p. 16.

26. Turkow, *Ozoy iz es geven,* p. 458; Ringelblum, *Stosunki,* p. 58.

27. Turkow, *Ozoy iz es geven,* p. 460.

28. Lubetkin, *Aharonim al hahoma,* p. 25.

29. Ibid. p. 26

30. Turkow, *Ozoy iz es geven,* p. 461.

31. Edelman, *Getto walczy,* p. 47.

32. Lubetkin, *Aharonim al hahoma,* p. 26.

33. Ringelblum, *Stosunki,* p. 58.

34. AZHP, file 202/I-7, pp. 10–12.

35. Edelman, *Getto walczy* p. 47.

36. Lubetkin, *Aharonim al hahoma,* p. 30.

37. Turkow, *Ozoy iz es geven,* pp. 406–407; Mark, *Powstanie,* pp. 215–220.

38. AZHP, file 78/III-332, p. 61.

39. AZHP, file 202/II-21, p. 34.

40. AZHP, file 202/II-21, p. 29.

41. Idem.

42. *The Report of Juergen Stroop Concerning the Uprising in the Ghetto of Warsaw and the Liquidation of the Jewish Residential Area,* (Warsaw: Jewish Historical Institute, 1958).

43. Josef Wulf, *Das Dritte Reich und seine Vollstrecker. Die Liquidation von 500.000 Juden in Ghetto Warschau* (The Third Reich and its performers: The liquidation of 500,000 Jews in the Warsaw Ghetto) (Berlin: Arani, 1961), p. 73.

44. *The Report of Juergen Stroop.*

45. AZHP, file 76/III-332.

46. *Handbook on German Military Forces. War Department Technical Manual, TM-E 30-451,* (Washington, D.C.: U.S. Department of War, 1945), p. II-52.

47. Ibid., p. II-31.

48. Georg Tessin, *Zur Geschichte der Ordningspolizei, 1936–1943. Teil II. Die Stzebe und Truppeneinheiten,* (History of the Order Police. Part II. Staffs and Units), p. 29.

49. *Handbook on German Military Forces,* pp. II-57, VI-21.

50. Wulf, *Das Dritte Reich,* p. 184.

51. Idem.

52. Tuvia Bożykowski, *Cvishn falendike vent* (Among falling walls) (Warsaw, 1949), p. 11

53. *The Report of Juergen Stroop,* p. 33

54. AZHP, file 76/III-332, p. 61.

55. AZHP, file 202/III-21.

56. Mark, *Powstanie,* p. 54.

57. Edelman, *Getto wałczy,* p. 55.

58. *The Report of Juergen Stroop,* pp. 33–34.

59. Turkow, *Ozoy iz es geven,* p. 311.

60. *The Report of Juergen Stroop,* p. 34–35.

61. Ibid., pp. 36–37.

62. Ibid. pp. 38–39.

63. Ibid., p. 40.

64. Lubetkin, *Aharonim al hahoma,* p. 35.

65. Edelman, *Getto wałczy,* p. 59.

66. Ibid., pp. 57–58.

67. AZHP, file 202/XV-2, p. 310.

68. Idem.

69. *The Report of Juergen Stroop,* pp. 41–42.

70. Edelman, *Getto wałczy,* pp. 59–60.

71. *The Report of Juergen Stroop,* p. 45.

72. Nachman Blumental and Josef Kermish, eds., *Hameri vehamered bageto*

varsha. Sefer mismahim (Resistance and uprising in the Warsaw Ghetto. Document Book) Jerusalem: Yad Vashem, 1965), p. 220.

73. Edelman, *Getto waɫczy* p 61.
74. *The Report of Juergen Stroop*, pp. 45–46.
75. Mark, *Powstanie*, p. 83.
76. Idem.
77. *The Report of Juergen Stroop*, pp. 48–49.
78. Ibid. p. 49.
79. Ibid. p. 50.
80. AZHP, file 202/XV-2, p. 317.
81. *The Report of Juergen Stroop*, p. 52.
82. Idem.
83. Mark, *Powstanie*, pp. 97–98.
84. *The Report of Juergen Stroop*, pp. 55–56.
85. Ibid. p. 57.
86. Ibid., p. 60–61.
87. Ibid., p. 62.
88. Ibid., p. 64–65.
89. Ibid., p. 66–67.
90. Ibid. p. 70.
91. AZHP, file 202/I-7, p. 20.
92. Idem.
93. AZHP, file 202/XV-2, p. 320.
94. *The Report of Juergen Stroop*, p. 58.
95. Bernard Goldstein, *Stars Bear Witness* (London: Gollancz, 1950), p. 288.
96. *The Report of Juergen Stroop*, pp. 72–73.
97. Ibid., p. 75.
98. Ibid., p. 77.
99. Ibid., p. 79.
100. Ibid., p. 82.
101. Ibid., p. 85.
102. Idem.
103. Mark, *Powstanie*, p. 295.
104. Lubetkin, *Aharonim al hahoma*, p. 35.
105. AZHP, file 202/I-7, p. 23.
106. *The Report of Juergen Stroop*, p. 89.
107. Ibid., p. 96.
108. Ibid., pp. 99–101.
109. Ibid., p. 103.
110. Ibid., p. 105.
111. Mark, *Powstanie*, pp. 300–301.
112. YVA, microfilm JM/2847.
113. Mark, *Powstanie*, p. 155.

114. Balicka-Kozłowska, *Mur mial dwie strony*, p. 53.

115. Mark, *Powstanie*, pp. 335–337.

116. Ibid., p. 269.

117. AZHP, file 202/I-7, p. 93.

118. AZHP, file 202/I-35, p. 183.

119. Wacław Poteranski, "Walka warszawskiego getta" (The struggle of the Warsaw Ghetto), in the Polish weekly *"Kultura"*, 21 April, 1963.

120. Mark, *Powstanie*, pp. 335–337.

121. Ibid.

122. AZHP, file 76/III-335. *Wojskowe znaczenie powstania kwietniowego* (The military significance of the April rising), by Jerzy Kirchmayer, p. 78.

CHAPTER 11
Armed Resistance in Other Ghettos

1. Brener, *Ruch podziemny*, pp. 160–161.

2. M. Borkiewicz, ed. *Czas wielkiej próby* (The time of great experience) (Warsaw: Ksiazka i Wiedza), 1970, p. 379.

3. YVA, file 0-3/3514.

4. Idem.

5. Idem.

6. Brener, *Ruch podziemny*, p. 164.

7. Idem.

8. Nazarewicz, *Nad górną Wartą* p. 124.

9. YVA, file 0-3/1687; Moreshet Archives in Givat Haviva, file A.316.

10. A Nirensztein, "Ruch oporu Żydów w Krakowie pod okupacją hitlerowska," (Jewish resistance in Cracow under Nazi occupation), *BZIH*, no. 3 (1952), p. 145; YVA, file 0-16/320.

11. Moreshet Archives file A.316.

12. Józef Zając, *Toczyły sie boje* (Battles were going on) (Warsaw: Czytelnik, 1965).

13. Gusta Dawidsohn-Draenger, *Pamiętnik Justyny* (Justyna's Memoirs) (Cracow: CZKH, 1946), p. 56.

14. Nirensztein, *Ruch oporu*, p. 142.

15. Dawidsohn-Draenger, *Pamiętnik Justyny*, p. 14.

16. YVA, file 0-3/1686.

17. YVA, file 0-51/DN-31/348-350.

18. Moreshet Archives file A.26.

19. YVA, file 0-3/1686.

20. YVA, file 0-3/1391, 0-3/3284.

21. Arie Bauminger, Meir Bosak and Michael Gelber, *Sefer Kraka, Ir vaem beIsrael* (Book of the Jewish Cracow) (Jerusalem, 1959), pp. 425–428.

22. Stein, *Radom*, pp. 287–289.

23. YVA, file 0-33/24.

24. Jasny, *Yizkor buch*, pp. 262–266.

25. Zygelman, *Sefer Radzyn*, p. 306.

26. Shtokfish, *Hurbana ugevurata*, pp. 195–226.

27. Idem.

28. *Tomashover yizkor buch*, p. 773.

29. YVA, file 0-3/1252.

30. Archives of the Military Historical Institute in Warsaw, file III/19/253.

31. YVA, file 0-3/2981.

32. YVA, file 0-3/2343.

33. AMSW, *Gendarmerie Lublin*, file 107, pp. 47, 136. Also see Edwarda Mark and Bernard Mark, "PPR a kwestia żydowska w okresie okupacji" (The Polish Worker's Party and the Jewish question during the Nazi occupation), *Z pola walki*, no. 1 (1962), p. 60.

34. YVA, microfilm JM/2845.

35. Józef Birken, "Udział szomrów tarnowskich w ruchu oporu," (The participation of members of the Hashomer Hatzair in the resistance movement in the town of Tarnow), *Mosty* (Jewish, Polish-language weekly, Lodz), 6 May, 1947.

36. YVA, file 0-16/33.

CHAPTER 12
Armed Resistance in the Camps

1. Yaakov Shtendig, *Plaszów—hatahana haaharona shel yahadut Krakow* (Plaszow: the last station of Cracow Jewry) (Tel Aviv: Menora, 1970), pp. 70–73.

2. Zdzisław Łukasiewicz, *Obóz stracen w Treblince* (Death camp in Treblinka) (Warsaw: PIW, 1946), p. 7.

3. Idem.

4. YVA, file TR-10/709, pp. 81–91.

5. AZIH, files Ring II/297, Ring II/299.

6. YVA, files 0-3/1586, 0-3/2267, TR-10/709, pp. 119–120.

7. Abraham Krzepicki, "Treblinka," *Bleter far geshichte*, January–June 1956, pp. 126–128.

8. YVA, file 0-3/1586.

9. YVA, file 0-3/3131.

10. YVA, file 0-3/568.

11. YVA, file 0-3/1586.

12. YVA, file 0-3/568.

13. YVA, file 0-3/2353; Adam Rutkowski, "Ruch oporu w Sobiborze" (Resistance in Sobibor), *BZIH*, nos. 65–66 (1968), p. 7.

14. YVA, files 0-3/1291, 0-3/2353, 0-16/458.

15. Rutkowski, *Ruch oporu*.

16. AZIH, Testimony no. 6397.

17. YVA, file 0-3/2353.

18. Rutkowski, *Ruch oporu*, p. 35.

19. Radziwonczyk, *Niemieckie siły zbrojne*, p. 73.

20. Aleksander Peczorski, "Powstanie w Sobiborze" (The Uprising in Sobibor), *BZIH*, no. 3 (1952), p. 43; YVA, files 0-3/1900, 0-3/707, 0-3/2212, 0-16/458.

21. YVA, file 0-3/707.

22. *Proces ludobójcy Leopolda Goetha przed Najwyższym Trybunałem Narodowym* (The trial of the mass murderer Leopold Goeth before the Highest National Tribune) (Warsaw: CZKH, 1947).

23. AZHP, file 202/II-21.

24. Shtendig, *Plaszów*.

25. YVA, file 0-3/692.

26. *Proces ludobójcy*.

27. Shtendig, *Plaszów*.

28. YVA, file 0-3/2107; AZHP, file 202/III-21, p. 2.

29. Szymanski, *My ze spalonych wsi*, pp. 139–142.

30. Ibid., p. 122.

31. Stein, *Radom*, p. 287.

32. YVA, file 0-3/3380.

33. AZIH, Testimony no. 6204.

34. YVA, file 0-3/1316; AZHP, files 202/II-8, 202/II-12, p. 192.

35. YVA, file 0-3/2985; AZIH, Testimonies nos. 1791, 3012.

36. AZIH, Testimony no. 64.

37. David Shtokfish, ed., *Sefer Krasnik. Sefer zikaron lekehilat Krasnik* (Memorial book for the Jewish community of the town of Krasnik) (Tel Aviv, 1973), pp. 434–441.

38. *Bleter far geshichte*, vol. 17, pp. 138–140.

39. Arnold Hindls, *Einer kehrte zuruek: Bericht eines Deportierten* (A man comes back: The report of a man who was deported) (Stuttgart: Deutsche Verlags-Anstalt, 1965), pp. 96–97, 125.

40. Artur Eisenbach, *Hitlerowska pollityka zagłady Żydów* (Nazi policy of the extermination of Jews) (Warsaw: Ksiazka i Wiedza, 1961), pp. 549–550; AZHP, file 202/II-8.

41. Hebrew University of Jerusalem, Institute for Contemporary History, Oral History Division, Testimony no. 1573.

42. Tatiana Berenstein, "Obozy pracy przymusowej dla Żydów w dystrykcie lubelskim," (Forced labor camps for Jews in the Lublin district), *BZIH*, no. 24 (1957), p. 10.

43. YVA, file M-21/12-289.

44. YVA, file 0-3/2292.

45. AZIH, Testimony no. 4368.

46. Tatiana Berenstein and Adam Rutkowski, "Żydzi w obozie koncentracyjnym-Majdanek" (Jews in the Malaenek concentration camp) *BZIH*, no. 58 (1966), p. 32.

47. AZHP, file 202/III-28.

48. AZHP, file 202/I-54, p. 258.

49. YVA, file 0-16/5.

50. YVA, file 0-3/3009.

51. AZHP, file 202/III-7, p. 146.

52. YVA, file 0-16/5.

53. Idem.

54. YVA, file M-1/E-925.

55. AZIH, Testimony no. 2521; Berenstein and Rutkowski, *Zydzi w obozie*, p. 40.

56. AZHP, file 202/II-12, p. 107.

57. Idem.

58. YVA, files 0-3/2292, 0-3/2346, 0-3/2775.

59. YVA, file 0-3/2346.

60. YVA, file 0-3/2292.

61. YVA, file 0-3/2346.

CHAPTER 13
Jews in the Polish Warsaw Uprising

1. YVA, file 0-6/31 and microfilm JM/1537, frame 124; Adolf Abraham Berman *Beyimey hamahteret* (The days of the underground) (Tel Aviv: Menora, 1971), p. 181.

2. Pobóg-Malinowski, *Najnowsza historia Polski*, vol. II pp. 627–628.

3. YVA, file M-2/133.

4. Tatiana Berenstein and Adam Rutkowski, "Obóz koncentracyjny dla Zydów w Warszawie, 1943–1944, *BZIH*, no. 62 (1967).

5. Chaim Yitzhak Goldstein, *Zibn in a bunker* (Seven in a Bunker) (Warsaw: Yiddish Buch, 1962), pp. 119–126.

6. AZIH, Testimony no. 5678.

7. Labor Archives in Tel Aviv, file 123/VII-3; AZIH, Testimony no. 6297.

8. AZIH, Testimony no. 6297.

9. Borkiewicz, *Czas wielkiej próby*, pp. 233–234.

10. Antoni Przygonski, *Udział PPR i AL w Powstaniu Warszawskim* (The participation of the Polish Worker's Party and the People's Army in the Warsaw Uprising) (Warsaw: Ksiazka i Wiedza, 1970), p. 73.

11. Borkiewicz, *Czas wielkiej próby*, p. 233–234.

12. Berman, *Beyimey hamahteret*, pp. 185–186.

13. Ibid., p. 184.

14. Borkiewicz, *Czas wielkiej próby*, p. 178–179. Also see YVA, file 0-3/3156.

15. Wronski and Zwolakowa, *Polacy—Zydzi*, p. 264.

16. Lazar-Litai, *Masada shel Varsha*, p. 321.

17. Piotr Stachewicz, "Parasol" (Fighting unit—Umbrella), *WPH*, no. 4 (1969), p. 349.

18. Michael Borwicz, *Arishe papirn*, vol. II (Aryan Papers) (Buenos Aires: Farband fun poylishe yidn, 1955), pp. 222–223.

19. YVA, file 0-16/450.

20. YVA, file 0-3/1285.

21. YVA, file 0-3/2518.

22. Wacław Zagórski, *Wicher wolności—Dziennik powstanca* (Freedom storm: Diary of an insurgent) (London, 1957), p. 81.

23. Ibid., p. 95.

24. Ibid., p. 213.

25. YVA, file 0-3/2993.

26. Goldstein, *Zibn in a bunker*, p. 118.

27. Ibid., p. 125–128.

28. Peltel-Miedzyrzecka, *Meshney everey hahoma.*

29. YVA, file 0-3/1617.

30. Zagórski, *Wicher wolności*, pp. 287–289.

31. Ber Mark, "Der varshever oyfshtand fun oygust–september 1944 un di tragedie fun di varshever yidn" (The Warsaw uprising of August–September 1944 and the tragedy of the Warsaw Jews) *Folks-Sztyme*, 10 August 1954.

32. YVA, file 0-33/1157.

33. YVA, file 0-3/395.

34. Lesław Bartelski, *Powstanie warszawskie* (The Warsaw rising) (Warsaw: Iskry, 1965), p. 320.

35. Antoni Przygonski, *Z problematyki powstania warszawskiego* (Problems of the Warsaw uprising) (Warsaw: MON, 1964), p. 53.

36. Nuremberg Document PS-1166.

37. Przygonski, *Udzial PPR i AL*, p. 119.

38. "Udział Zydów w Powstaniu Warszawskim" (The participation of Jews in the Warsaw uprising) in the *Głos Ludu* (Polish daily, Lublin), 6 January 1945.

39. Bernard Goldstein, *Stars Bear Witness* (London, 1950), pp. 202–216.

40. Berman, *Beyimey hamahteret*, p. 187.

41. Bernard Goldstein, *Stars Bear Witness*, p. 269.

42. Chaim Goldstein, *Zibn in a bunker*, p. 128.

43. Bernard Goldstein, *Stars Bear Witness*, p. 276.

44. Nuremberg Document NOKW-2636.

45. YVA, file 0-3/1793.

SUMMARY AND CONCLUSIONS

1. *Polskie siły zbrojne* vol. III pp. 324–325.

2. Bór-Komorowski, *Armia Podziemna*, p. 74.

3. *Polskie siły zbrojne*, pp. 338–340.

4. Czesław Madajczyk, *Polityka Trzeciej Rzeszy w okupowanej Polsce* (The Policy of the Third Reich in occupied Poland) vol. II (Warsaw: PWN, 1970), p. 26.

5. *20 lat Ludowego Wojska Polskiego*, p. 136.

6. Radziwończyk, *Niemieckie siły zbrojne*, p. 7.

7. Ireneusz Caban and Zygmunt Mańkowski, *Związek Walki Zbrojnej i Armia Krajowa w okręgu lubelskim, cześć druga—Dokumenty* (Union for Armed Struggle and Home Army in the Lublin region, Part Two. Documents) Lublin: LSW, 1971), p. 60.

8. *Polskie siły zbrojne*, pp. 324–326.

9. AZHP, file 202/XV-2, p. 207.

BIBLIOGRAPHY

Ainsztein, Reuben. *Jewish Resistance in Nazi-Occupied Eastern Europe*. New York: Barnes and Noble, 1974.

Arad, Yitzhak. *The Partisan: From the Valley of Death to Mount Zion*. New York: Holocaust Library, 1979.

Arad, Yitzhak; Gutman, Yisrael; and Margaliot, Abraham, editors. *Documents on the Holocaust*. Jerusalem: Yad Vashem, 1981.

Bauer, Yehuda. *The Holocaust in Historical Perspective*. Seattle: University of Washington Press, 1978.

Bauer, Yehuda. *The Jewish Emergence from Powerlessness*. Toronto: University of Toronto Press, 1979.

Bauer, Yehuda, and Rotenstreich, Nathan, editors. *The Holocaust as Historical Experience: Essays and a Discussion*. New York, Holmes & Meier, 1981.

Borzykowski, Tuvia. *Between Tumbling Walls*. Beit Lohamei Hagetaot, 1972.

Dawidowicz, Lucy. *The War Against the Jews: 1939–1945*. New York: Bantam Books, 1976.

Gilbert, Martin. *Atlas of the Holocaust*. Jerusalem: Steimatsky, 1982.

Goldstein, Bernard. *The Stars Bear Witness*. New York: Viking, 1949.

Gutman, Ysrael. *The Jews of Warsaw, 1939–1943: Ghetto, Underground, Revolt*. Indianapolis: Indiana University Press, 1982.

Gutman, Yisrael and Rothkirschen, Livia, editors. *Catastrophe of European Jewry: Antecedents, History, Reflections*. Jerusalem: Yad Vashem, 1976.

Hausner, Gideon. *Justice in Jerusalem*, New York: Schocken, 1968.

Levin, Nora. *The Holocaust: The Destruction of European Jewry, 1933–1945*. New York: Schocken, 1972.

Mark, Ber. *Uprising in the Warsaw Ghetto*. New York: Schocken, 1975.

Meed, Vladka. *On Both Sides of the Wall: Memoirs from the Warsaw Ghetto*. New York: Jewish Labor Committee, 1972.

Novitch, Miriam. *Sobibor: Martyrdom and Revolt*, New York: Holocaust Library, 1980.

Ringelblum, Emmanuel. *Polish-Jewish Relations During the Second World War.* Jerusalem: Yad Vashem, 1974.

Suhl, Yuri, editor. *They Fought Back: The Story of Jewish Resistance in Nazi Europe.* New York: Schocken, 1967.

Yad Vashem. *Jewish Resistance During the Holocaust: Proceeding of the Conference on Manifestations of Jewish Resistance. Jerusalem, April 7–11, 1968.* Jerusalem: Yad Vashem, 1971.

Ziemian, Joseph. *The Cigarette Sellers of the Three Crosses Square.* New York: Avon, 1977.

Zuckerman, Isaac, editor. *The Fighting Ghettos.* New York: Belmont-Tower, 1971.

INDEX